Computers in Our World

Applications and Challenges

Fourth EDITION

Richard Vedder | Deborah Morley | Beverly Amer

CENGAGE Learning

Australia • Brazil • Japan • Korea • Mexico • Singapore • Spain • United Kingdom • United States

CENGAGE Learning

Computers in Our World: Applications and Challenges, Fourth Edition

Computers in Our World, 2nd Edition
Beverly Amer

Understanding Computers in a Changing Society,6th Edition
Deborah Morley

Own Material, 4th Edition
Richard Vedder

For product information and technology assistance, contact us at
Cengage Learning Customer & Sales Support, 1-800-354-9706
For permission to use material from this text or product,
submit all requests online at **cengage.com/permissions**
Further permissions questions can be emailed to
permissionrequest@cengage.com

This book contains select works from existing Cengage Learning resources and was produced by Cengage Learning Custom Solutions for collegiate use. As such, those adopting and/or contributing to this work are responsible for editorial content accuracy, continuity and completeness.

ISBN: 978-1-337-70463-2

Cengage Learning
20 Channel Center Street
Boston, MA 02210
USA

Cengage Learning is a leading provider of customized learning solutions with office locations around the globe, including Singapore, the United Kingdom, Australia, Mexico, Brazil, and Japan. Locate your local office at:
www.international.cengage.com/region.

Cengage Learning products are represented in Canada by Nelson Education, Ltd.

For your lifelong learning solutions, visit **www.cengage.com/custom.**

Visit our corporate website at **www.cengage.com.**

Brief Contents

Computers in Business and Industry 1

While computers have had a major impact on a wide range of fields and disciplines, none has been more affected by the computer than business and industry. Almost every day you complete a business transaction that involves computer technology — whether it is the automatic teller machine at the bank, the bar code scanner at the supermarket, or the personalized text message you received this morning.

Today, businesses of all sizes use computers and technology in every aspect of commerce — from product design and manufacturing to sales, billing, and the final delivery of goods to customers. In this chapter, you will learn more about the use of computers in the factory, in retail sales and marketing, in banking, and in the office. The chapter also looks at how technology in the workplace affects your health, as well as the quality of your work life. Finally, the chapter looks ahead to review how technology will change the economy and employment in the future.

THE GREAT SOCIO-ECONOMIC REVOLUTIONS

The world in which we live – full of computers that define and shape our everyday lives and business activities – often is referred to as the Information Age. The phrase, **Information Age**, along with the related idea of an **information economy** or the **new economy**, refers to the concept that instead of only producing tangible goods like shampoo, tires, and running shoes, businesses and industries are using information to help provide core services or are producing, processing, and distributing information as their main product.

The introduction of such new technologies as the transistor and the microprocessor powered the changes that define the Information Age. This shift, however, is not the first time new technologies have fundamentally transformed the world of work. Before the 20th century, humanity experienced two major socio-economic revolutions directly relating to the world of work: the Agricultural Revolution and the Industrial Revolution.

Thousands of years ago, humans fed themselves by hunting and gathering and were largely migratory. Over time, however, agriculture took hold as a practice. Farmers found they could produce the same amount of food from one acre that a hunter-gatherer could obtain from 100 acres. The invention of a new technology – a plow drawn by animals – made farming even more efficient, allowing communities to produce a surplus of food, introduce new crops, and free up people for other types of work. Over time, farms were organized into businesses, and farmers began using new fertilizers, artificial feed for animals, and new drainage systems. Technological improvements, such as the seed drill and threshing machine, continued to drive the agricultural economy (Table 1-1).

At the end of the eighteenth century, the Industrial Revolution unleashed the second radical change in the world of work. The shops of artisans and craftsmen were changed by new technologies that automated their work efforts. In the textile industry, the introduction of the flying shuttle and the spinning jenny accelerated the weaving process and began the mechanization of the textile industry. The introduction of the steam engine in 1763 changed the face of transportation, while other key innovations such as the telegraph, the sewing machine, the cotton gin, and electricity changed communications, manufacturing, and agriculture. With these technologies came an exponential increase in productivity, as each laborer could create many more products in the same time.

TABLE 1-1 Major Societal Shifts

AGRICULTURAL REVOLUTION **Inventions and Innovations**	*INDUSTRIAL REVOLUTION* **Inventions and Innovations**	*INFORMATION REVOLUTION* **Inventions and Innovations**
■ Domestication of wild plants; selective breeding of plants; plow	■ Steam engine	■ Television
■ Domestication of wild animals; selective breeding of livestock	■ Cotton gin	■ Transistor; microprocessor
■ Concept of land as private property	■ Telegraph	■ Computers
■ Villages, towns, cities	■ Transatlantic cable; telephone	■ Satellites
■ Literacy	■ Incandescent light bulb	■ Lasers
■ Organized religions	■ Induction electric motor	■ Fiber-optic technologies
■ Empires; nation states	■ Diesel engine; automobile	■ The Internet
	■ Airplane; rockets	■ Smartphones
	■ Radio; motion pictures	■ The Internet of Things
	■ Assembly line	■ Genetic engineering
	■ Vaccination; antibiotics	■ Robotics

Humanity has experienced three major shifts relating to the world of work. In each era, new technological inventions and innovations were at the heart of the social and economic changes. Will biotechnology or nanotechnology fuel the next great socio-economic revolution?

The newest revolution in the work world is the Information Age, whose origins started in the 1950s with the emergence of the transistor. Following in the footsteps of movies, radio, and television came such inventions as the microprocessor, computers, satellites, lasers, fiber optics, networks, cellular phones, and more. Like the plow and the cotton gin, these technologies allow workers to work more efficiently and be more productive. By the 1990s, these technologies created a whole new way to work, allowing office workers to work from home while communicating via cellular phones, e-mail, and instant messaging. In manufacturing, computer systems on the factory floor began providing up-to-the minute information to help firms make decisions on product design, inventory management, and shipping. Today, computer technologies are used in almost every business or industry. The following selections explore the use of computers in the factory, in retail sales and marketing, in banking, and the office.

COMPUTERS IN THE FACTORY

Factories are where most of the products of everyday life are made, from the smallest microprocessor in your cellular phone to the jumbo passenger airplane. Computer technology has changed – and continues to change – the factory dramatically. While fewer individuals than ever work in factories, factories produce a wider range of products than ever before for a global customer base. Computer technology and automation are behind this, allowing factories to reduce design time, maximize the use of machines manufacturing the products, and track the shipping of products from order to final shipment.

CAD, CAE, CAM

Computer-aided design (CAD) is the use of a computer and special software to assist in product design (Figure 1-1). With CAD software, designers can use graphics and models to represent a product on screen, which allows them to produce more accurate drawings than those sketched on paper. CAD software also allows designers to modify a design, dynamically change product features, and perform calculations to optimize the design for production.

Using computer-aided design lets companies reduce the product design cycle, which can help companies get better products to market faster. For example, the product development team at Adidas, the second-largest sporting goods provider in the world, must design up to 60 new shoe styles each year. For every new shoe, the time from idea to shipping product – referred to as the *cycle time* – is from 12 to 18 months. Most of that time is needed for manufacturing, which means the design team has only four to six weeks to design and create a prototype of a new shoe. Using CAD, designers can take a certain shape or a particular design requested by a customer and quickly determine if it can be manufactured. The CAD system also allows designers to rework designs quickly, creating three-dimensional models that are sent to show sales and marketing departments exactly how the shoe should look to appeal to customers.

Computer-aided engineering (CAE) uses computers and special software to test product designs. Using CAE, engineers can evaluate the design of a car or a bridge before it is built. CAE programs simulate the effects of wind, temperatures, weight, and stress on product shapes and materials. They give designers and engineers the ability to analyze and verify their designs in the early stages of the product development process - when design alterations still are relatively easy and inexpensive. For example, BMW realizes considerable time savings in the development and testing of a vehicle using CAE. Actual physical prototypes are built only after each

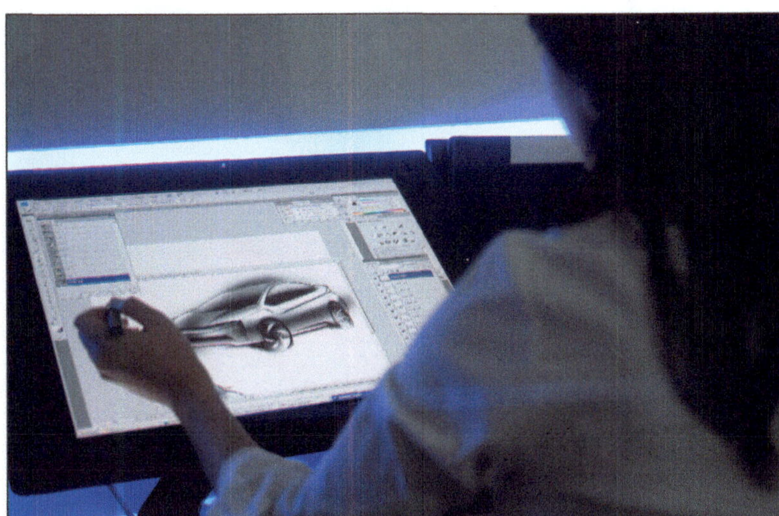

Figure 1-1 Using CAD software and digitizing tablet, designers from companies like BMW can use graphics and models to represent a product on screen, which allows them to produce accurate drawings and fine-tune them before actually producing models.

individual component is checked and analyzed by BMW engineers with the help of CAE.

Computer-aided manufacturing (CAM) is the use of computers to direct the machines that produce and assemble a product. CAM production equipment includes software-controlled drills, welding, and tooling machines, as well as specialized robots. Once a design is complete, computer-aided manufacturing helps speed the process of creating the actual product – even a product as simple as a chocolate. Yorkshire Moulds, for example, uses computer-aided manufacturing to reduce the time required to manufacture highly detailed chocolate molds. The traditional time-consuming method of hand carving the models took almost two weeks. With the new digital process using CAD and CAM, the chocolate molds are created in just three days. Instead of sending physical models back and forth, Yorkshire Moulds now shares its digital models via e-mail, so that companies such as Hershey's and Cadbury can approve the size, shape, or specific placement of their logos on each mold. Once the designs are approved, Yorkshire Moulds uses computer-aided manufacturing tools and exports them directly to the machines that cut each molds – thus eliminating errors introduced by hand carving and reducing production time by 75 percent.

These software solutions – CAD, CAE, and CAM – can be combined into a **computer-integrated manufacturing (CIM)** system that incorporates the many different operations of the product design and manufacturing processes.

3D Printing

A new addition to the world of manufacturing is the computer technology known as 3D printing. **3D printing** is a manufacturing process which uses a three-dimensional computer model to make a corresponding real object. Typically, the computer builds the object one layer at a time using a printer spraying heated plastic, a technique very similar to ink-jet printing (Figure 1-2). But some 3D printers use a laser to carve the object from a plastic medium. Manufacturers use 3D printing for making models, as well as plastic parts. However, the basic technology has a great many other applications. General Electric has adapted 3D printing to create metal parts for jet engines. Medical researchers have printed replacement bone structures, as well as skin and kidney tissues. Some futurists believe that, like a phone or TV, there will be a 3D printer in every home, creating a host of different products using downloaded instructions purchased by the customer.

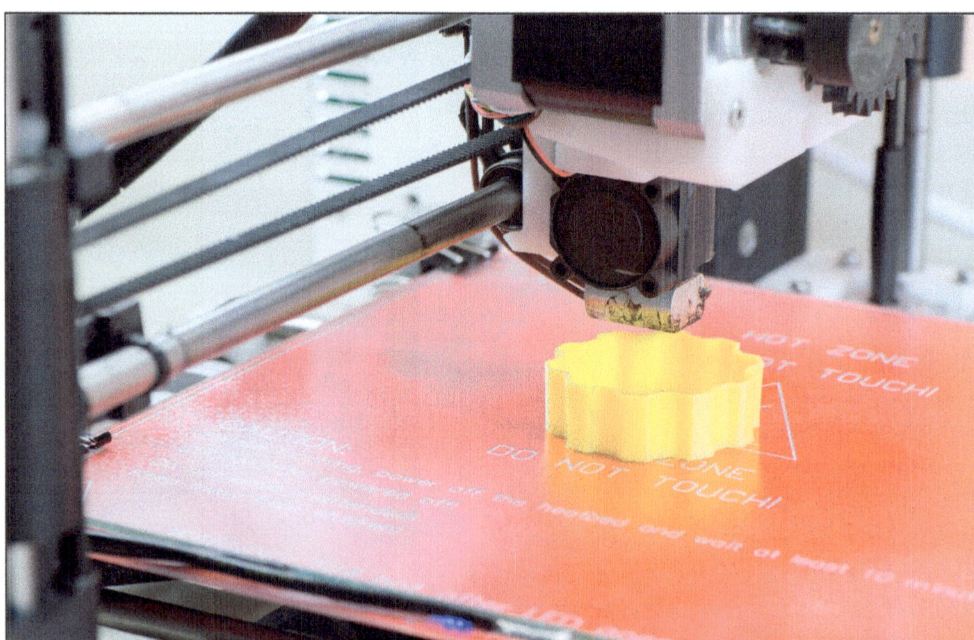

Figure 1-2 3D printing.

Manufacturing Resource Planning

A wide range of software and computer technologies helps make factories more efficient in the scheduling, planning, and manufacturing process. Many of these tools come under the category of **manufacturing resource planning (MRP)** systems, which integrate various production and process control systems into a single computerized system. The components of an MRP system include: job scheduling, inventory control, shipping management, distribution, and warehouse management.

JOB SCHEDULING A **job-scheduling system** or **production-scheduling system** helps factory managers decide when to initiate production based on the supplies on hand and customer demand. During the winter holiday season, for example, a factory might receive a sudden increase in orders for the hottest new snowboard. The factory must respond rapidly in order to meet the demand, rescheduling production of other products for different times or other machines, while quickly moving the raw materials for the snowboard into place. Many production scheduling systems deliver real-time customer order information right to the factory floor, so that the snowboards – and other in-demand products – are immediately scheduled for production and hit the shelves before the snow melts. Another example is Dell Computer, a company that has a build-to-order process in which they customize and manufacture each computer according to the customer's order. Using this build-to-order process, Dell allows you to order a computer that exactly matches your required specifications via their Web site. Once Dell receives the order, the production scheduling system sends input to the inventory control system to pull the parts needed to build your new computer. The parts then are delivered to the assembly line, where the computer is manufactured and sent to the warehouse for shipping.

INVENTORY CONTROL, SHIPPING, AND WAREHOUSE MANAGMENT A key challenge for a factory and its warehouse is to manage inventory, so enough parts are available to continue production, without overstocking parts and having inventory that is obsolete or unused. Usually part of the organization's supply chain, an **inventory control system** tracks the current supplies of inventory and matches this against anticipated future orders to ensure that enough component parts, such as tires and brake pads, are available to manufacture the shipment of new trucks. Another approach to inventory management involves **just-in-time manufacturing**, which lets manufacturers purchase and receive components just before they are needed on the assembly line. For example, Dell's build-to-order process – which is an example of just-in-time manufacturing – helps prevent the company from being stuck with inventory that may become obsolete. Instead of having entire computers gather dust in a warehouse, Dell can place orders for or manufacture specific parts in direct response to an order, thus ensuring each part gets used and little inventory is wasted.

For those items in the warehouse, a **warehouse management system (WMS)** is used to track items received, generate pick lists to pack customer orders, label a package for shipping, and track its receipt by the customer. When you place an order for books over the Web, that order data is sent to a warehouse management system, which matches available stock to the order, enabling personnel to determine if your order can be filled immediately. Staff members with radio frequency-based handheld computers then pick each book for your order, scanning each bar code as they go, to confirm that the right title was selected (Figure 1-3). This information is transmitted back to the WMS, which deducts the inventory count for that item in real time. Based on the order size, the WMS references a database of boxes to determine which box size is appropriate for the order, and then automatically generates the shipping label. Once the box is shipped, the WMS might send a shipping confirmation back to the Web site, which e-mails this information to you to let you know the order is on its way. The end result is that you receive the order on time, with exactly the books you requested.

Industrial Robots

Many factories also use industrial robots – computer-controlled machines designed to perform work that would be hazardous to people. To date, the greatest success in using robotics in the factory is in executing limited and repetitive actions, such as assembling

Figure 1-3 Order data from customers is sent to a warehouse management system, which matches available stock to the order, enabling the personnel to determine if an order can be filled immediately. Staff with radio frequency-based handheld computers then scan each item's bar code as they pick it for shipping.

simple industrial parts and performing jobs such as welding (Figure 1-4). Robotic arms, for example, are used to move heavy parts into and out of machines, while other robots are used to manipulate devices such as paint sprayers. Robots also are used in the warehouse to move heavy items from stacks of items and automatically pack boxes.

Figure 1-4 In today's factory, computer-controlled robots are used to move heavy parts into and out of machines and to control devices, such as welding tools and paint sprayers.

COMPUTERS IN RETAIL SALES AND MARKETING

Computer technology has also changed the face of retail sales and marketing. The next time you head to the bookstore to browse for the latest bestseller and have a cup of coffee, notice all of the computers around you. Today, most retail sales locations – whether the department store, drugstore, toy store, or bookstore – are filled with computers and systems used to streamline the browsing and buying experience.

Point-of-Sale (POS) Systems

When you have finished shopping, you head to the checkout lane, where a cashier uses a point-of-sale system to complete your transaction and accept your method of payment. A **point-of-sale (POS) system** is a special kind of order-processing system that records purchases, processes credit or debit cards, and updates inventory.

In a grocery store, for example, the POS system is a combination of electronic cash register, bar code scanner, and printer. A **bar code scanner** is an input device that uses laser beams to read the **bar code** on a product (Figure 1-5). A bar code is an identification code that consists of vertical lines and spaces of different widths. The bar code represents data that identifies the manufacturer and the item. A bar code scanner reads data by scanning the width and spacing of the bars in the code. The bar code does not, however, contain price data. This is stored separately in the system. When the bar code is scanned, the data is matched to a file containing the price for that code, which then displays it on the POS terminal.

Figure 1-5 A bar code scanner reads a bar code by using a laser that detects the width and spacing of the bars. The bar code does not contain the item's price.

Different products use different types of bar codes. Retail and grocery stores use the **UPC (Universal Product Code)** bar code, while libraries use the Codabar bar code, and the United States Postal Service uses the POSTNET bar code. Books use the International Standard Book Numbering (IBSN) bar code, not only to identify book titles but also their various publication formats (hardcover, paperback, ebook, and so on).

When the cashier scans the bar code on a product, a computer uses the manufacturer and item numbers to look up the price information and complete product name in the database. Then, the price of the item in the database shows in the display device, the name of the item prints on the receipt, and the item being sold is recorded so the inventory can be updated.

All sales are recorded in the central database as soon as they are finalized at the cash register, so that store managers can run reports to evaluate special promotions and spot fast-moving items. In larger store chains, the POS systems are connected over a network to allow managers to review the chain-wide sales. The output from the POS serves as inputs to other systems, including payment-processing systems, inventory control systems, and accounting systems.

Payment Processing and Credit Authorization

If you use a credit or debit card to pay for your order, your payment request must be checked by a **credit-authorization system** before the transaction is approved (Figure 1-6). Today, most merchants use POS terminals to read your credit data either from a computer chip embedded within the card or from the magnetic stripe on the back of the card. When using a debit card, you must enter a personal identification number (PIN) using a keypad on the terminal. Some terminals also accept payment submitted wirelessly by a service app (ex., Apple Pay™) installed on the customer's smartphone. The POS terminal then uses a network connection to a payment-processing service, which then sends the request on to your credit company or an **acquirer**, which is an organization that collects credit-authentication requests and provides retailers with a payment guarantee. When the acquirer gets the credit authentication request, it checks to see that the card number, expiration date, and PIN are valid; that the credit card is not over the limit; and that the card usage is not outside normal limits (a stolen card, for example, might have numerous transactions in a very short span of time). The PIN is compared against the database in the bank's computers. If everything is authenticated, the sale is approved and the acquirer sends back an approval code. If not, the sale is denied for that card and you must provide a different form of payment.

Inventory Control Systems

Information from the POS also feeds directly into the company's inventory control system, so the warehouse is aware that replacement products need to be put on the shelves. The inventory control system provides a real-time look at the total count of products in the store and warehouse and provides alerts when designated reorder points set by the user are reached. When replacement items are being stocked on shelves, hand scanners are used to record the bar codes to update the inventory database and show that items are again available.

As stores get larger and the numbers of items stocked increases daily, more and more stores are allowing customers to access inventory databases over the Web to see what is in stock and at which area stores. Your local electronics store, for example, may provide a computer that allows you to search the inventory

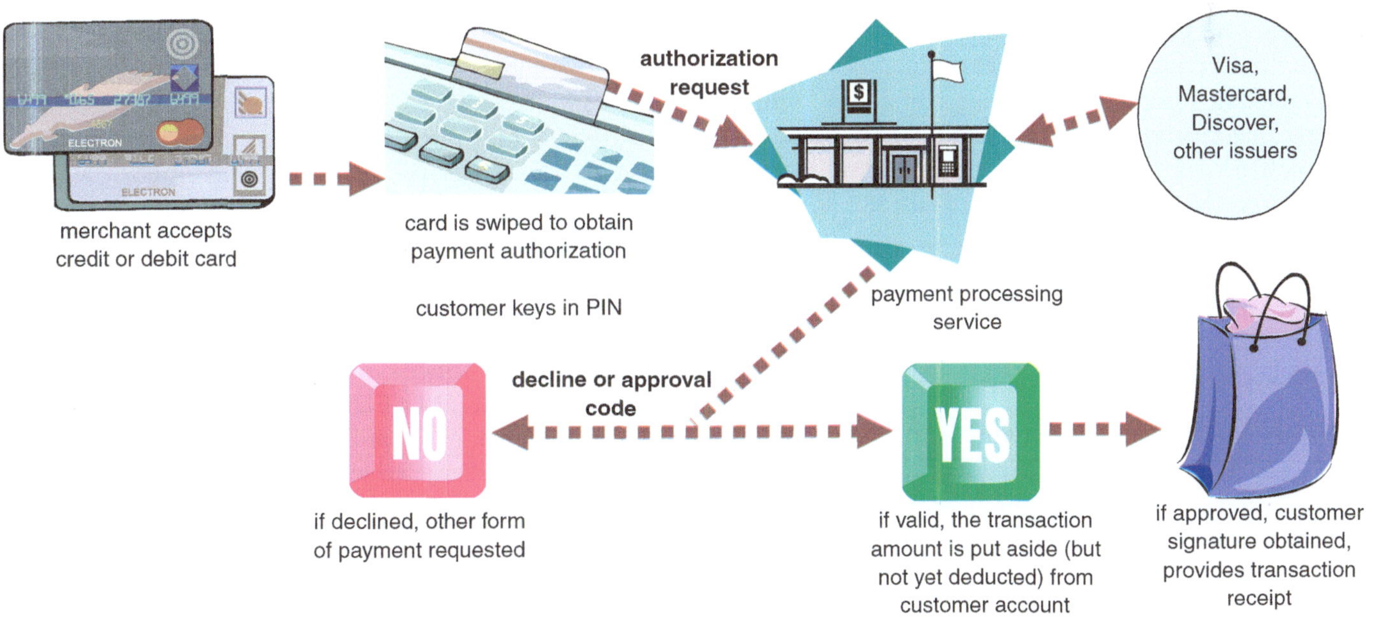

Figure 1-6 If you use a credit or debit card to pay for your order, your payment request must be checked by a credit-authorization system before the transaction is completed.

database for that store to see if a specific product is available and where it is. The retailer might even allow you to search for an item online and then reserve it for pickup at a local store (Figure 1-7). When you reserve the item, the inventory system decrements the count of available items by one, so the next customer has an accurate view of available inventory.

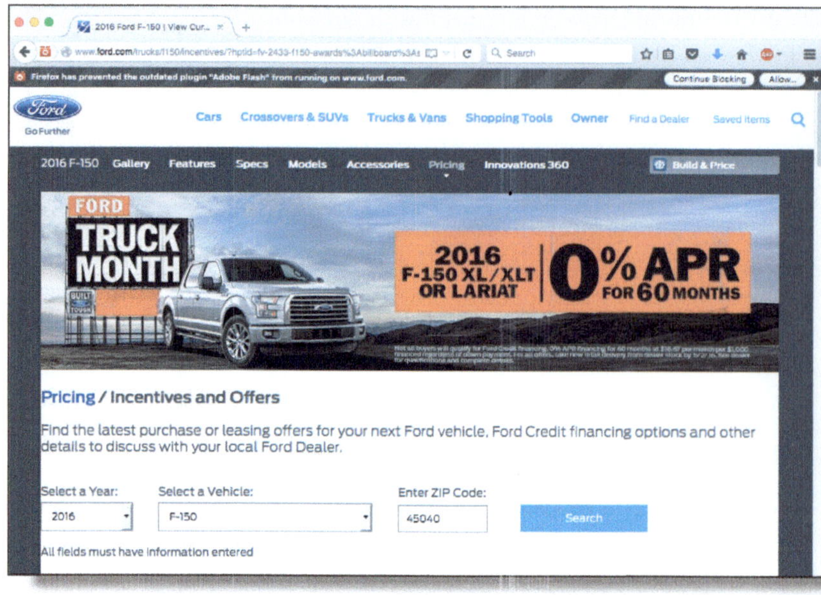

Figure 1-7 Websites, such as ford.com, allow customers to search the inventory database to see if a specific product is available. Customers then can reserve the product for pickup at a local dealer.

Accounting and Finance Systems

A company's financial and accounting computer systems also receive information from the POS, so that the company can track sales, returns, and other transactions. Accounting departments track, analyze, and prepare reports covering every financial transaction that occurs within the company, while the finance department manages the company's money as efficiently as possible. Accounting software makes it easier to track and manage everyday transactions, such as sales and payments to suppliers. Financial software helps managers budget, forecast, and analyze the financial health of the business.

Marketing and Sales

A good salesperson will tell you that the key to sales and marketing success is identifying, locating, and contacting a potential customer, along with understanding that customer's desires and needs. Computers have made it easier than ever for companies to market and sell products to a wider range of customers, while offering specific promotions tailored to individuals. The goal of creating a marketing database is to stay close to customers by keeping an electronic record of customer contacts in an effort to improve all future communications.

DATABASE MARKETING Each time you complete a purchase in a store or online using a credit or debit card, information about your purchase probably is stored in a large marketing database that later will be used to market additional products to you. This practice, called **database marketing,** allows companies to mine customer databases and create marketing lists to mail you catalogs or send you advertising e-mails and text messages. For businesses, having the ability to query databases and target their marketing efforts is a huge asset.

For example, rather than offering the same incentives to all customers, Ford Motor Company uses database marketing to determine which cars might benefit from a promotion and which will continue to be hot, even with a price increase. To do this, Ford collects daily sales data from dealerships and uses it as input for computer models that predict which incentives will be most tempting to customers. The output also shows what cars need a boost in a regional market – and what cars do not. Knowing this, Ford can focus their marketing dollars where it will matter, possibly offering a $3,000 rebate on a full-size truck in New England, but only a $500 rebate on that same truck in the Midwest. The net result is that Ford can spend a lot less on rebates than their competitors, which helps lead to higher profits.

CONSUMER PREFERENCES Marketing databases not only help companies identify what you might like, they also give you a chance to tell a company your interests. Today, many retail Web sites have preference centers that allow customers to sign up for e-mail newsletters, promotions, or specific catalogs. Other sites give you the option to set up reminders for special occasions such as a friend's birthday. The Web site sends an e-mail to you a few days in advance of the occasion with possible gift ideas from their available products. Companies also can determine your preferences based on your past buying behavior. Amazon, for example, displays a recommendations page for you each time you visit the site, promoting specific products based on your past purchase (Figure 1-8).

Modern database marketing means you lose some control over information about yourself – information such as what books you read, what food you buy, and what types of music you like. It is important to read a firm's privacy policy to find out how they use the personal information you provide them. Companies, marketers, and government agencies simply may use your information to process your order or they may use it to market products, services, or promotions to you. They might, however, share your information with others, so that your e-mail is filled with **spam** – unsolicited, junk e-mail sent as part of an electronic mass mailing.

Some organizations offer you choices about how your personal information is used. For example, some marketers let you **opt in** to receiving marketing messages, which means you will not receive e-mails and other types of marketing messages unless you sign up and specifically request they be sent to you (many companies allow you to opt in via the Web site). You also can opt in to allow companies to share your personal information. More frequently, firms allow you to **opt out** – that is, instruct them not to share your information with others or use it for promotional purposes. Marketing e-mails often include an opt-out link at the bottom that you can click to be removed from the mailing list; businesses also make opt-in and opt-out services available to customers online or over the phone.

SOCIAL MEDIA **Social media** is the collection of websites and computer applications that allows people, organizations, and companies to share information and develop professional or personal contacts. You can use social media to connect with family and friends (ex., Facebook), blog your opinions (ex., Twitter), or build professional contacts (ex., LinkedIn). Over the past few decades, social media

Figure 1-8 Amazon uses your past purchases to identify other products you might be inclined to purchase.

has become enormously popular: Facebook has over a billion monthly, active, unique users; Twitter has over 300 million and LinkedIn over 250 million. Mostly free to use, social media tools are easy to use, encourage personal expression, and help users find like-minded people.

Social media marketing is use of social media by companies to attract new customers, nurture present customers, and in general grow their businesses by promoting products and services. One of the ways to do this is for businesses to post content at Twitter, YouTube, and other sites which point readers back to the company's Facebook page or website. Also, companies can use the communication strengths of social media to improve their customer service and thereby gain attention by "electronic word-of-mouth."

COMPUTERS IN BANKING

Modern banking illustrates the growing trend to provide products and services to customers electronically, without the need for a "brick and mortar" (i.e., physical) store. For many, the face most customers associate with their bank is not the teller at a local branch. It is the keypad on an ATM or the home page of the bank's online banking Web site. Computers and technology have changed the banking industry in numerous ways – most noticeably, in a bank's use of computers to handle everyday transactions once managed by people.

Electronic Funds Transfer

At the core of the changes in the banking industry is a technology called **electronic funds transfer (EFT)**. EFT allows users connected to a network to transfer money from one bank account to another. Both businesses and consumers use EFT for a wide range of financial transactions. Businesses use EFT to purchase and pay for goods from vendors. Both businesses and consumers pay bills online by instructing their banks to use EFT to pay creditors. Other EFT transactions include withdrawing cash from an ATM, depositing a paycheck directly in an employee's account, or making a purchase in a store using a debit card.

AUTOMATED TELLER MACHINES (ATMs) An **ATM**, or **automated teller machine**, is a self-service banking machine that connects to a host computer through a network, which in turn ultimately connects to a bank's computer databases. For many people, the ATM is the only place they interact with their bank, and that interaction occurs outside bank branches, grocery stores, convenience stores, movie theaters, shopping malls, and gas stations – wherever banks place ATMs so customers can conveniently access their accounts.

While an ATM allows you to complete a variety of banking transactions – withdraw cash, deposit money, transfer funds, or inquire about an account balance – the ATM really is just a terminal with input and output devices (Figure 1-9). To access a bank account, you insert your credit/debit card or bankcard into the ATM's card reader, which reads account data on the bankcard's magnetic strip or embedded data chip. Alternatively, some banks allow customers to establish their identity to the ATM machine via smartphone. The host processor uses this information to route the transaction to the cardholder's bank. The ATM also asks you to enter a personal identification number (PIN), which verifies that you are the correct holder of the card. Your PIN is **encrypted**, or encoded into an unreadable form, so that unauthorized individuals cannot read it. When your transaction is complete, the ATM prints a receipt for your records.

If you have requested a cash withdrawal, the host processor uses electronic funds transfer to move the correct amount from your bank account to the host processor's account. The host processor then sends a message to the ATM over the network, authorizing the machine to dispense the cash.

DIRECT DEPOSIT When you first take a new job, the human resources person may ask if you would like to receive your paychecks via direct deposit. **Direct deposit** is a means by which an organization can transfer funds electronically to a specified bank, which then makes payments to accounts of individuals or companies. Many businesses use direct deposit to eliminate the need for paper paychecks. Instead, you receive a pay stub showing how much money was deposited in your account. The process of completing the direct deposit, as shown in Figure 1-10, is completely transparent to you; the paycheck simply shows up in your account at the end of each pay period. The government also uses direct deposit to distribute Social Security and Veterans benefits, and even tax refunds (Figure 1-11). Direct deposit has benefits for payer and payee: companies and government agencies save hundreds of millions of dollars in costs and productivity gains, and you save time and trips to the bank or ATM.

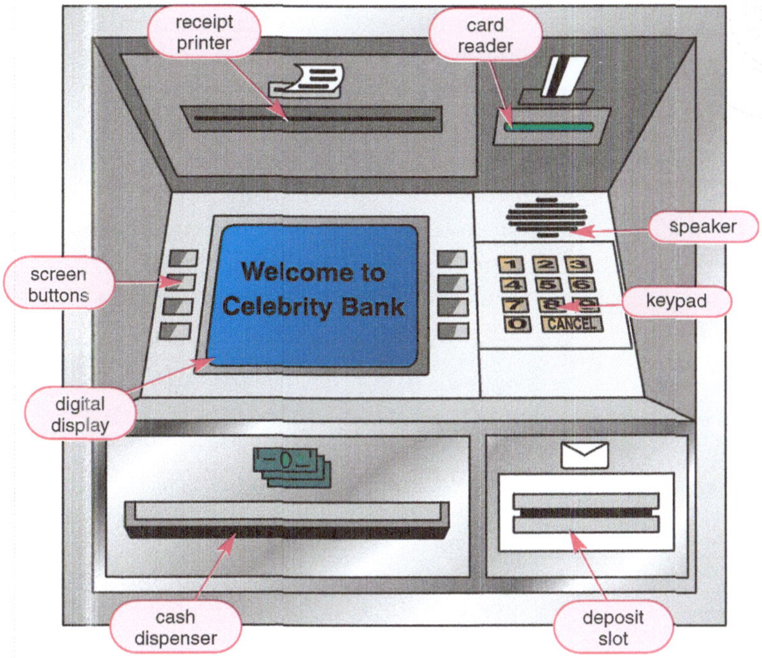

INPUT DEVICES	OUTPUT DEVICES
Card reader — Captures the account information stored on the magnetic stripe or embedded data chip for input to host processor	**Speaker** — Emits sounds when key or area on touch screen is pressed
Keypad — Captures the personal identification number (PIN) and other customer-input data to complete transaction	**Display screen** — Shows messages to step the cardholder through the transaction process
Touch screen — Captures customer selections instead of, or in addition to, using a keypad	**Receipt printer** — Generates outputs a paper receipt as a record of the transaction
Deposit slot — Allows customer to input physical items for deposit, such as cash or a check	**Cash dispenser** — Dispenses cash in the amount of the transaction

Figure 1-9 An ATM has several input and output devices to allow you to complete a range of banking transactions.

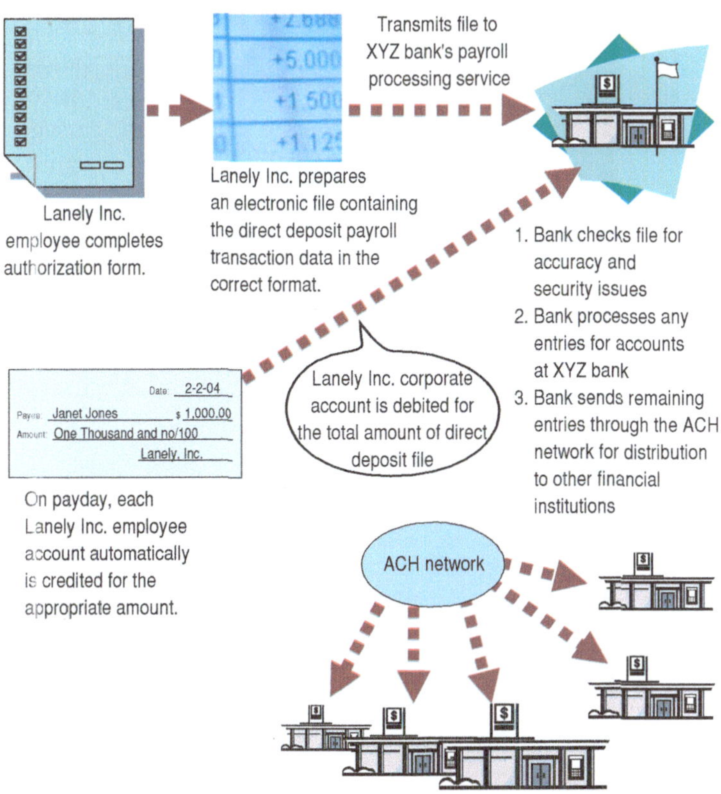

Figure 1-10 Many businesses use direct deposit to deposit employee paychecks in their personal accounts electronically.

AUTOMATED CLEARING HOUSE (ACH) Each time you use your ATM card to pay for a purchase, electronic funds transfer also is used to move the funds from your account back to your bank's account. That transaction takes place using an **automated clearing house (ACH)**, which is a company or group responsible for sorting automated payment instructions to allow the transfer of funds electronically. ACH is used any time a person or business authorizes another person or business to draw funds from your checking or credit card account. For example, your fitness center may use ACH to deduct your monthly membership fee from your account, or a retailer may use ACH when you make a purchase via their Web site. The ACH network acts as the central clearing facility for all EFT transactions.

You may have noticed that there is a slight delay between the time you make a purchase and the time the funds actually are removed from your account. During that time, the payments are held in computers on the ACH network, awaiting clearance to be sent to the appropriate bank.

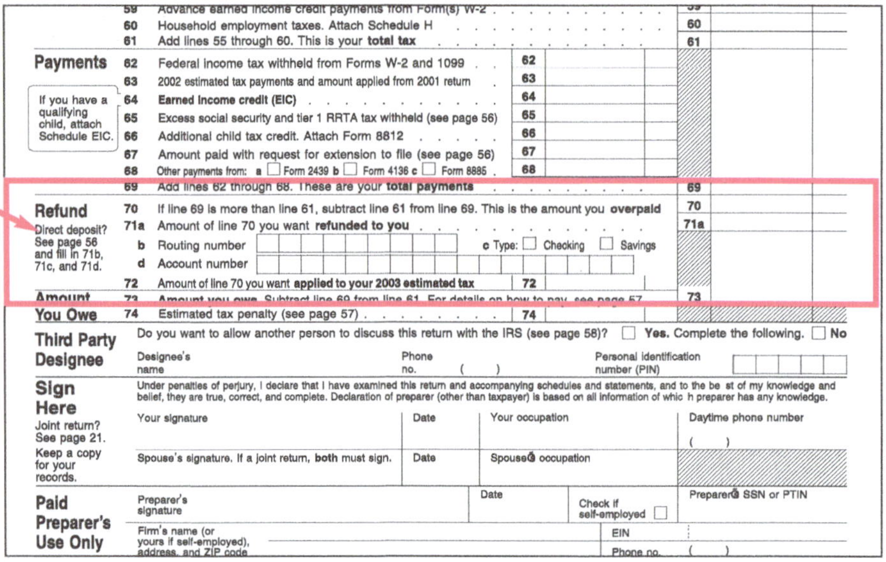

59 Advance earned income credit payments from Form(s) W-2 . . . 59
60 Household employment taxes. Attach Schedule H . . . 60
61 Add lines 55 through 60. This is your **total tax** . . . 61

Payments
62 Federal income tax withheld from Forms W-2 and 1099 . . 62
63 2002 estimated tax payments and amount applied from 2001 return . 63
If you have a qualifying child, attach Schedule EIC.
64 **Earned income credit (EIC)** . . . 64
65 Excess social security and tier 1 RRTA tax withheld (see page 56) 65
66 Additional child tax credit. Attach Form 8812 . . . 66
67 Amount paid with request for extension to file (see page 56) 67
68 Other payments from: a ☐ Form 2439 b ☐ Form 4136 c ☐ Form 8885 . 68
69 Add lines 62 through 68. These are your **total payments** . . . 69

Refund
Direct deposit? See page 56 and fill in 71b, 71c, and 71d.
70 If line 69 is more than line 61, subtract line 61 from line 69. This is the amount you **overpaid** 70
71a Amount of line 70 you want **refunded to you** . . . 71a
b Routing number c Type: ☐ Checking ☐ Savings
d Account number
72 Amount of line 70 you want **applied to your 2003 estimated tax** 72

Amount You Owe
73 Amount you owe. Subtract line 69 from line 61. For details on how to pay, see page 57 73
74 Estimated tax penalty (see page 57) . . . 74

Third Party Designee
Do you want to allow another person to discuss this return with the IRS (see page 58)? ☐ **Yes.** Complete the following. ☐ No
Designee's name Phone no. ( ) Personal identification number (PIN)

Sign Here
Joint return? See page 21. Keep a copy for your records.
Under penalties of perjury, I declare that I have examined this return and accompanying schedules and statements, and to the be st of my knowledge and belief, they are true, correct, and complete. Declaration of preparer (other than taxpayer) is based on all information of whic h preparer has any knowledge.
Your signature Date Your occupation Daytime phone number ( )
Spouse's signature. If a joint return, **both** must sign. Date Spouse's occupation

Paid Preparer's Use Only
Preparer's signature Date Check if self-employed ☐ Preparer's SSN or PTIN
Firm's name (or yours if self-employed), address, and ZIP code EIN Phone no. ( )

Figure 1-11 If you provide your account information, the Internal Revenue Service (IRS) can deposit your tax refund directly into your checking or savings account.

Smart Credit Cards

A **smart card**, which is comparable in size to an ATM card or credit card, stores data on a thin microprocessor embedded in the card (Figure 1-12). Unlike the typical credit card, which has a magnetic stripe that stores data that cannot be changed, the data stored on a smart card can be updated instantaneously.

For security reasons, smart cards using the embedded chip system developed by EMV (Europay, Master Card, Visa) are replacing traditional credit and debit cards. As it will take time for all merchants to acquire the new point-of-sale card readers, initial card issues will be hybrids containing both stripe and chip. Industry experts expect ATM cards to follow suit.

As shown in Table 1-2, smart cards are used for a wide range of applications, some of which will be discussed later in this book. The use of smart cards as stored value cards, however, remains popular, as the cards are more convenient and safer than cash. In Tokyo, for example, more than 5.6 million people use smart cards to pay for their daily commute on the train.

Smart cards can be contact or contactless (Figure 1-13). A contact card must be swiped or inserted into a card reader. When a contact smart card is inserted into a card reader, the metallic pads of the card come into contact with the reader's metallic pins, thereby allowing the card and reader to communicate. The smart card and reader then are able to process the transaction. A contactless card, which only needs to come in close proximity to the card reader, uses a radio frequency to transfer information to and from the card and reader. The smart cards used for the commuter rail in Japan are contactless and work from up to four inches away from the reader. Most commuters do not even take the cards from their pockets or bags to pass through the turnstile.

Online Banking

In the past, a bank was largely a **brick-and-mortar business**, meaning that customers primarily conducted transactions in person at a physical location, over the phone, through paper-based communications, or, more recently, via an ATM. Today, many banks and credit unions are becoming **brick-and-click businesses**, that is, they offer online banking in

Figure 1-12 A smart card, which is comparable in size to an ATM or credit card, stores data on a thin microprocessor embedded in the card.

TABLE 1-2 Uses for Smart Cards

INDUSTRY/DISCPLINE	*APPLICATION*
Financial	▪ Credit and debit cards ▪ Prepaid card for small purchases using vending machines, laundry, or photocopy machines
Health care	▪ Card to carry medical information such as details of medical insurance coverage, drug sensitivities, medical records, and other information
Communications	▪ Prepaid card for phone calls ▪ Activation of programming for satellite TV ▪ Identifying caller on any GSM phone
Government programs	▪ Carry Food Stamp and WIC food benefits instead of paper coupons and vouchers
Information security and physical access	▪ Employee access card to protect access to computer systems ▪ Employee access card to protect access to facilities
Transportation	▪ Driver's license ▪ Prepaid card for mass transit fare ▪ Prepaid card for electronic toll collection systems
Retail and loyalty	▪ Consumer rewards card to track customer purchase and redemption

Smart cards have a wide range of applications in many industries and disciplines.

addition to the services provided at the physical banking facilities. A brick-and-click business is any business that allows customers to conduct business or complete transactions at a physical location, as well as online.

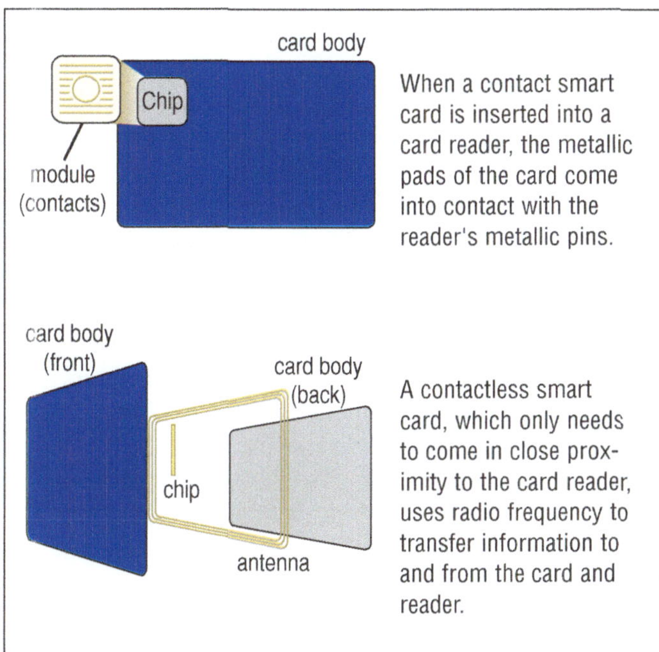

Figure 1-13 Smart cards can be contact or contactless.

By contrast, a cyberbank, such as NetBank, is a virtual bank that has no physical facilities and offers products and services solely on the Internet.

Online banking is easy, convenient, and fast. Using online banking allows you to complete banking activities, such as those listed in Table 1-3.

A common concern about online banking is the security of online banking transactions. While no online transactions are 100 percent secure and instances of fraud have occurred, the banking industry has been involved with securing electronic transactions for more than forty years, starting with electronic funds transfer (EFT) systems of the 1960s. Today, you can expect your online bank to use sophisticated security technologies to protect your personal information and to secure your online transactions. When shopping for an online bank, you should carefully review the bank's privacy policies and any security statements it provides.

BILL PAYMENT SERVICE Many financial industry analysts think the most valuable use of online banking is online bill payment. A **bill payment service** allows you to log on to a Web site and pay any number of bills from a range of vendors. In addition to online banks, e-businesses such as Fiserv CheckFree and PayTrust offer bill payment services.

TABLE 1-3

TRANSACTIONS AVAILABLE VIA ONLINE BANKING

- View real-time account balances and recent transactions.
- View a history of account activity.
- Search for individual transactions.
- Pay your bills.
- Transfer funds between accounts.
- Download transactions into personal financial management software such as Quicken and Microsoft Money.
- Issue a stop payment on a check.
- Order checks.
- Report a lost or stolen ATM card and request a replacement.
- Change personal information such as your address, phone number, and e-mail address.

Most online banking Web sites allow you to complete a wide range of transactions.

When you are ready to pay a bill online using an online bill payment service, you simply log onto your online bank or payment service's Web site, select a vendor from a list of vendors you created when you first established your account, and enter a payment amount and the payment date. On the scheduled payment date, your payment is debited from your bank account and transmitted to the vendor either by an electronic funds transfer or via a paper check. You also can set up recurring monthly bills, such as your cell phone bill or car payment, to be paid automatically on a specific day each month.

BILL PRESENTMENT More and more utilities, credit card companies, auto finance companies, and other businesses are using **bill presentment**, which is the process of sending bills electronically instead of mailing their customers paper bills or statements. Using bill presentment to send electronic bills, also called **e-bills**, can reduce substantially a company's billing costs. You can arrange to receive e-bills and then pay them electronically through your online bank account or bill payment service. Alternatively, you can pay your bill directly at the vendor's Web site.

COMPUTERS IN THE OFFICE

Offices are at the center of the action in business and many other organizations. In today's office, technology is an integral part of the business. Almost every employee has access to a desktop computer or laptop and a smartphone. Computers allow employees to store documents and spreadsheets on a network, so coworkers in different offices can review them at any time. Networked printers churn out high-quality presentations for the weekly board meeting. E-mail allow workers to communicate new advertising copy to a client, while receiving a signed copy of the latest contract.

Going Paperless

In the past, almost every activity in an office was recorded on paper. Memos were photocopied and distributed by hand, meeting agendas and handouts were distributed at the beginning of each meeting, and accounting information was kept by hand, in ledgers. For a creative department working on designs with a client, each iteration of the design had to be printed and shipped to the client for review – and then shipped back with comments.

Today, many offices have reduced paper in some areas of the business – and are working to be paperless. Archival information, such as tax returns and financial statements, are stored on disk or tape drives specifically designed for permanent storage. Paychecks are sent directly to individual's bank accounts using EFT and direct deposit. Many companies have corporate intranets (secure, online networks for employee use) that include online forms that employees can use to request vacations, send technical support requests, or update their address and contact information. Even the paper-laden process of completing a form for reimbursement of travel expenses is paper free: employees can fill out an online form from their computer or cell phone, to itemize expenses and request reimbursement. The creative department can send new advertising layouts to a client using a PDF file, so the client can see exactly how the ad will look on the back cover of a magazine.

PDF, which is short for **Portable Document Format**, is an electronic file format that preserves formatting, fonts, and layouts so files can be viewed and printed on a variety of computing devices using Adobe Acrobat Reader, or similar software. The PDF format also is greatly compressed, which means files are small enough to be sent quickly by e-mail or downloaded from the Web.

Many companies are creating annual reports in PDF for easy distribution to investors and shareholders. Others use PDF to make documentation for products, from cellular phones to washing machines, available to customers online (Figure 1-14). For creative publishing

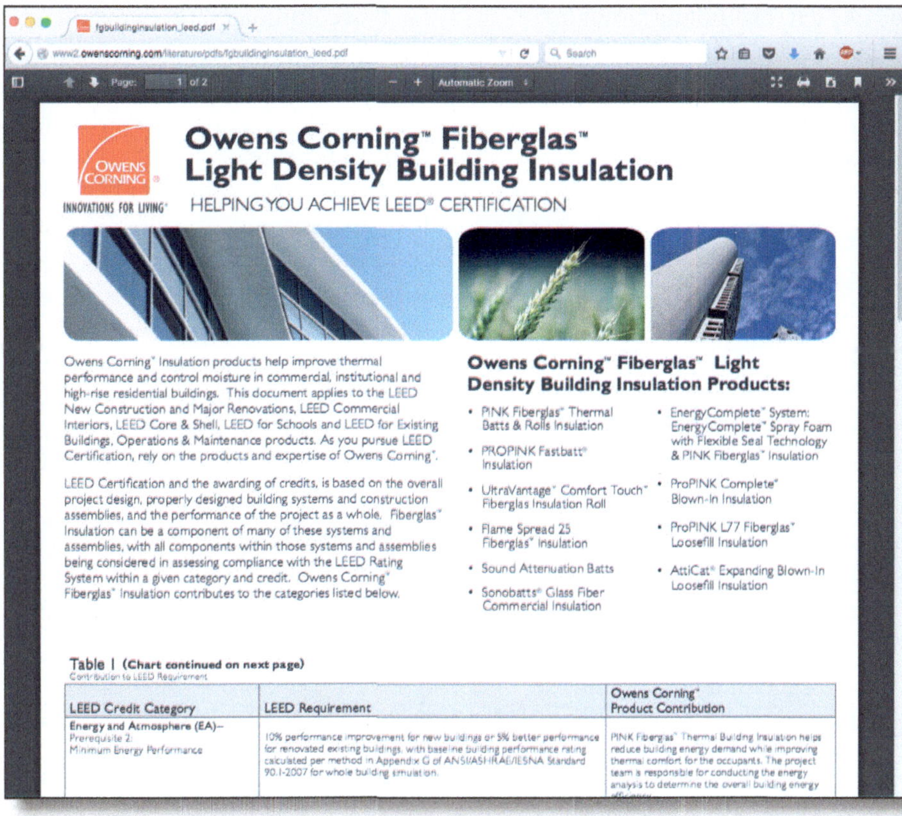

Figure 1-14 Many companies are using PDF files to make documentation for their products available online. Owens Corning, for example, allows you to view a PDF version of the product information guide for Light Density Building Insulation.

and advertising firms, PDF proofs can be e-mailed or posted to a Web site for download. Clients can make electronic comments directly in the file and e-mail them back in the space of hours, not days.

One of the first innovators in the move to a paperless office was Owens Corning, a fiberglass manufacturer. In 1997, the company designed its headquarters to be paper free. The office included no cabinets to file paper files; instead, they gave everyone computers with the same software so that everyone in the office could conduct internal business via an **intranet** (a private, inside-the-company internet) or e-mail. Memos, news, and policy announcements are sent via e-mail and posted on the intranet; all forms are on the intranet as well. Owens Corning estimated that its corporate intranet would save $50 million a year, mostly by reducing the need for filing and copying.

Despite the promise of a paperless office, however, most desks still are covered with documents and recycling bins are full of paper. Even Owens Corning still used paper for phone messages and, years later, found that the high cost of systems to support the paperless office offset some of the expected savings. Some studies show that, while technology could move offices closer to being paperless, the use of paper actually has increased. The use of the Web and e-mail, along with the ease of printing, has caused a rise in paper consumption of up to 40 percent in some offices. For many, e-mails and Web pages are easier to read when they are printed, which may be why employees, on average, print 33 Web pages each day.

Far from being obsolete, paper is the perfect medium for many work activities and provides a complement to digital documents. For now, the paperless office may remain more of an aspiration than a reality.

Telecommuting

One of the unique changes in the office brought about by computers is telecommuting. **Telecommuting** is a work arrangement in which employees work away from a company's office or other workplace, and communicate with the office using technology, including computers, video and telephone systems, e-mail, and high-speed network connections.

As shown in Table 1-4, telecommuting provides many advantages. For employees, telecommuting:

- Reduces commuting time, allowing employees to work during the time they normally would spend in a car
- Offers employees flexible schedules, which decreases absenteeism
- Allows employees to work for a company anywhere in the world
- Increases productivity and improves quality, especially for jobs that demand a high degree of privacy and concentration; fewer interruptions can lead to better, faster results
- Creates higher morale and reduces stress by giving employees a sense of control over their work life

Telecommuting does have its disadvantages. Because their efforts are not directly visible to coworkers, a CEO might not appreciate the efforts of a telecommuter as much as the employee who arrives an hour early to the office each morning. Telecommuting also requires discipline. In the home, the distractions are numerous: housework, television, pets, and family. Employees who are successful working remotely must be self-motivated, able to focus, and comfortable defining their own work schedules to ensure projects are completed successfully. If telecommuters do not maintain regular contact with the office, managers also may feel they do not know what the worker is doing. To help combat this, telecommuters may believe that they need to work longer and harder than employees in the office, as a way of proving their value.

TABLE 1-4

ADVANTAGES	DISADVANTAGES
■ Reduces commuting time	■ Out of sight, out of mind to boss and coworkers
■ Provides flexible schedule and decreases absenteeism	■ Requires discipline and focus
■ Global employment opportunities	■ Puts onus on employee to initiate regular contact
■ Increased productivity	■ Perceived need to work hard to prove value
■ Creates higher morale	■ Reduces the social interaction of the office
■ Reduces stress	■ Initial cost to employer for set up
■ Reduces need for office space dedicated to individual employees	■ Often have to handle your own tech support

Telecommuting has several advantages and disadvantages.

Telecommuters also miss the social interaction of an office and can experience feelings of isolation. Telecommuters also miss out on office gossip, which may mean being out of touch with important, but unofficial, matters that affect a company or a project. Telecommuters often also have to provide their own technical support. Even if the company has Help desk resources available, troubleshooting a computer or network problem must happen over the phone, rather than in person.

For many, a pure telecommuting job with no time in the office is not the ideal; instead, many workers want to work at home for only one or two days a week to focus on core projects or to handle personal responsibilities.

HUMAN FACTORS AND THE WORKPLACE

While computers and technology have had many positive impacts on the work world, using a computer also creates some new health issues and safety hazards. Problems such as repetitive stress injuries and computer vision syndrome are examples of some of the potential health problems caused by using computers for long stretches. Understanding these and other possible health risks – and how to prevent them – is a key step to healthy computing.

Ergonomics

The goal of **ergonomics** is to incorporate comfort, efficiency, and safety into the design of items in the workplace. Employees can be injured or develop disorders of the muscles, nerves, tendons, ligaments, and joints from working in an area that is not ergonomically designed.

Ergonomic studies have shown that using the correct type and configuration of chair, keyboard, display device, and work surface helps you work more comfortably and efficiently, while protecting your health. For the computer work area, experts recommend an area of at least two feet by four feet. Figure 1-15 illustrates additional guidelines for setting up your work area. Some also find that using desks where the desktop is thick glass and the monitor sits below the desk provides a comfortable work environment.

The way you organize the elements of your workplace to fit your individual needs is the most important consideration in working

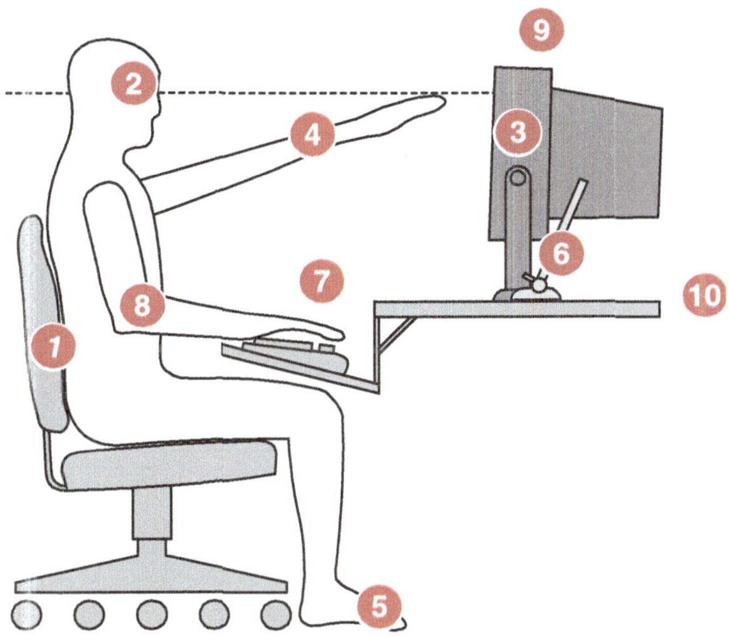

Figure 1-15 A well-designed work area should be flexible to allow adjustments to the height and build of individuals. Some other tips on setting up an ergonomically correct work area:

1. Use a good adjustable height chair with 4 to 5 legs for stability
2. Set the viewing distance to the monitor to 18 to 28 inches
3. Avoid glare on the screen (if needed, use an antiglare filter)
4. Sit at arms length from monitor
5. Place feet flat on floor or stable footrest
6. Use a document holder to place papers you are viewing as you work
7. Arms and wrists should be approximately parallel to the floor
8. Elbows should be relaxed, at about 90 degree angle to the floor
9. Center monitor and keyboard in front of you
10. Use a stable work surface and stable keyboard tray

comfortably. For instance, organize your desk to reflect the way you use work materials and equipment, so that the things you use most regularly, such as a mouse or telephone, are within easy reach. Above all, vary your tasks and take periodic breaks to help reduce the possibility of discomfort or fatigue.

Repetitive Stress Injuries

Many computer input and output devices have features that address ergonomic issues. For example, some keyboards have built in wrist rests, while others have a design specifically intended to prevent repetitive stress injuries. A **repetitive stress injury (RSI)**, such as carpal tunnel syndrome, is caused when muscle groups complete the same repetitive actions, over and over again. In the past, RSIs were common among factory workers who performed the same task on an assembly line for hours a day. Today, RSIs are just as common among office workers. Computer keyboards are a major source of RSIs, resulting from constant typing at fast speeds. Mice and trackballs also cause injuries from the long periods spent using the input device. Other health problems caused by poorly designed work areas include back, neck, shoulder, and foot pain.

Symptoms of an RSI include stiffness or burning in the hands, loss of strength in the hands, and pain in the upper back, shoulders, or neck. Correct typing technique and posture, the right equipment setup, and good work habits are important for prevention of RSIs. These and other preventative tips are listed in Table 1-5.

Computer Vision Syndrome (CVS)

Studies show that from 50 to 90 percent of computer users experience the symptoms of computer vision syndrome (CVS) at one time during their lives. CVS is caused by screen glare, improper lighting, monitor settings that are hard on the eyes, and even a need for glasses. Symptoms of computer vision syndrome include eyestrain or eye fatigue, dry or burning eyes, increased sensitivity to light, blurred vision, headache, and pain in the shoulders, neck, or back.

The symptoms and problems of CVS, however, usually can be alleviated by good eye care and changes in the work environment. Some tips for reducing CVS include using a high-resolution monitor, positioning the center of the monitor about 18 to 28 inches away, arranging the light to avoid glare, and stopping periodically to rest your eyes. Although blinking is a reflex, you blink less often when looking at a computer than when reading or performing other tasks. Remember to blink often when using your computer to avoid dry eyes or blurred vision. Regular visits to an eye doctor to check your vision also can help you avoid eyestrain while working at your computer.

QUALITY OF WORK LIFE

Many believe that technology has, in general, improved the overall quality of life and, in particular, increased the quality of work life. Technological change has decreased work time and reduced danger for workers, while creating better goods

TABLE 1-5 Tips for Healthy Computer Use

TIP	*DESCRIPTION*
Use correct posture.	You should not have to slouch or stretch to reach the keys or read the screen. Anything that creates awkward reaches or angles in the body will create problems. Relax and shift positions frequently.
Increase your font sizes and use easy-to-read colors.	Small fonts encourage you to hunch forward to read. Use color schemes easy on the eyes, particularly shades of gray for text documents.
Type gently.	Do not press hard on the keyboard; use a light touch. Also, use two hands to perform operations with two keys (such as CTRL+X).
Keep a light grip on the mouse.	Hold the mouse lightly; don't grip it hard or squeeze it. Place the pointing device where you don't have to reach up or over very far to use it; close to the keyboard is best
Take a break.	Take time to stretch and relax. This means both momentary breaks every few minutes and longer breaks every hour or so. Pace and plan your computer work.
Listen to your body.	If you are experiencing pain, it could be a first sign that your work area is not well-designed. Stop and evaluate the pain; take time to learn what is comfortable for you as you work.

These simple tips can help you avoid RSIs from working at a computer.

and services at lower prices for consumers. Employees can use technology to gain access to information from around the world; telecommunications makes working from anywhere at any time a reality.

Technology also has had a negative impact on the quality of work life. Employee monitoring, for example, reduces morale and causes employee stress, while new technologies force entire sets of workers to find their skills no longer are current. This section reviews a few aspects of work life altered by technology: employee monitoring, skilling and deskilling, worker autonomy, and the blurring of boundaries between work and home.

Employee Monitoring

Employee monitoring involves the use of computers to observe, record, and review an employee's use of a computer. Employee monitoring can track communications such as e-mail messages, the Web sites an employee visits, the amount of time an employee spends away from the computer, and, with keystroke monitoring, how many keystrokes per hour the employee is performing. Many software programs exist to help employers monitor their employees. Further, *it is legal for employers to monitor your use of their computer equipment and how you use your time at the workplace.*

As more employees are granted Internet access, more companies also are using employee monitoring tools to help ensure network security and guarantee that employees are not using computers in a way that might damage the company's reputation. Other employers use monitoring to help manage productivity. For example, employers can place time limits or other restrictions on Internet access to ensure that employees do not waste time sending personal e-mail or browsing the Web.

E-mail is a hotly debated topic when it comes to workplace privacy. Laws relating to the privacy of your e-mail at work are not well defined, but several workplace privacy court cases have been decided in favor of the employer, stating that if an e-mail system is used at a company, the employer owns it and is allowed to review its contents. Messages sent within the company, as well as those sent outside of the company, can be subject to monitoring by your employer.

Because the topic of monitoring is a sensitive one, many companies publish policies explaining that they have the legal right to monitor employees' computer use and that, by accepting employment, employees acknowledge that right. Most companies do not abuse their right to monitor employees; they only want to protect themselves from any illegal or harmful use of their network and computer systems.

Skilling and De-skilling

Computers and technology are at the core of a debate about whether the use of technology in the workplace helps increase the skill of workers by allowing them to learn and utilize constantly changing technology, or results in the deskilling of workers, due to automation that creates highly rigid jobs with narrow scopes. **De-skilling** is the process by which the tasks that workers do are fragmented to a point where a worker loses sight of the larger purpose of the job – he or she simply executes the task.

Many espouse the de-skilling side of the debate, arguing that managers exploit new technologies to help them control workers. This idea, first brought forth by the Marxist Harry Braverman in the early 1970s, remains popular today with those who believe managers computerize the workplace in order to tighten controls at every turn. They also suggest that computerization degrades work at the lowest levels of the office hierarchy, where jobs are the most routinized and the division of labor is the most rigid. Data entry clerks, such as telephone travel agents, insurance claims clerks, and word-processing specialists, for example, are forced into jobs that use one type of software for a single job task – jobs that are unsatisfying, uncreative, and monotonous.

Others emphasize the potential for computers to upgrade work and enhance employee skills. For them, an office rich in computer technology is one rich in opportunity. Instead of spending time on routine tasks, office workers can use computers and other technologies to speed through these tasks – and then focus on more interesting and creative work. For examples, office workers and professionals can use word processors to create mailings quickly and spreadsheets to track sales accurately. E-mail allows workers to communicate faster; the Internet and a company's databases place information at workers' fingertips. By helping to speed these routine tasks, office workers can focus on bigger-picture questions, such as how to analyze sales data to map regional sales trends or create a new advertising campaign for the latest product.

Worker Autonomy

Autonomy is self-directing freedom, and especially moral independence. In the workplace, worker **autonomy** is the freedom of workers to contribute to the overall goals of the organization, as well as to their own personal goals.

The extent to which computers help to foster or inhibit worker autonomy varies by industry, sector, and occupation. For manufacturing workers, better technology in the workplace has benefits and drawbacks. In some places, workers are more autonomous. State-of-the-art information technology at one Harley-Davidson plant, for example, allows workers on the factory floor to make production decisions that previously only would have been made by managers. The plant also gives network access on the shop floor to update workers on time and attendance, quality control issues, and the plant's production level. The end result is that workers are engaged in the process and feel a sense of personal responsibility for the results.

Others suggest that the use of technology in the factory strips employees of their autonomy. By using production-scheduling systems to define exactly what tasks are next in a particular process, employers can standardize activities and keep a tight rein on workers to drive maximum efficiency.

In service work, computers give employees more access to the information they need to complete their jobs. Customer service or Help desk employees now have large databases of information immediately available to help them quickly retrieve a customer's account information and determine the most appropriate way to handle the customer issue. Further enhancing autonomy in the service sector is the fact that many companies outsource their customer service to telecommuters, who connect to the company network remotely. These same workers, however, often find technology confines them to routine jobs with little opportunity for creativity.

Blurred Boundaries

As tablets, cell phones, and computers become more powerful and more portable, you may find that you depend on them in unanticipated ways – quickly looking up a phone number while away from your desk, getting an e-mail that the shipment of new inventory has arrived, or checking your voice mail on the way home. These tools significantly change the way individuals work and live, extending the employees' focus on work and allowing them to work from anywhere, at any time. That, however, can be precisely the issue: today's technologies make it increasingly difficult for people to separate themselves from work, as the boundaries between work and home life become blurred.

Recent research found that 20 percent of workers keep in touch with the office while on vacation. Cell phones, laptops, and pagers are the most common devices used. 77 percent of workers aged 22 to 34 check personal e-mail while on vacation; 39 percent check work e-mail. 60 percent of people over 60 check e-mail on vacation. Other studies showed that employees who use the Internet regularly work longer hours in the office – and are more likely to work additional hours at home.

We are so used to being available at any time that we must be reminded to turn off our cell phones and pagers before church, movies, concerts, or school classes begin. More seriously, the time that individuals used to have for themselves is encroached on by work. Evenings once reserved for family and friends now often include at least one visit to the computer to check e-mail. Coworkers, managers, and clients can contact you on the weekend, on vacation, in the middle of dinner, and just about anywhere else, all as part of the ethic that dedicated employees always are accessible via their "electronic leash." On the surface, it looks as if individuals are being highly productive, but the reality is that employees risk burning out. What's interesting is that over half of U.S. workers do not take all their vacation time each year, yet 77 percent report feeling burned-out on the job. Workers wonder if the office will survive without them, if they'll be replaced while away, or whether co-workers who aren't vacationing will be resentful. At the other end of the spectrum, though, are those employees who don't want to be reached. Nine percent of workers have lied to their employers, claiming they couldn't be reached on vacation, to minimize the guilt associated with not checking in while gone.

Employers are starting to realize that employees and the self-employed need to have down time to recharge – and that the "always on" lifestyle causes more stress and strain than individuals realize. Employees also are recognizing that, because technology lets you accomplish your work more efficiently, many people end up taking on too much and thus always feeling rushed or behind. As is increasingly clear, the key is to reach a balance. As shown in Table 1-6, individuals can take steps to re-establish boundaries between work and home – first and foremost, simply by turning off the technology for a while.

TABLE 1-6

TIPS TO CREATE WORK-HOME LIFE BALANCE

- Turn off the technology. Define the times when you are working – and when you are not. Also allow for a middle area, where you are less accessible, but not completely out of contact (for example, during your commute). During the times when you are not working, turn off the smartphone, computer, or tablet.
- Discuss your availability with your boss, coworkers, and clients. Create a proposal and, as needed, modify it to meet your needs and your coworkers' needs.
- If possible, do not bring work home. If you must, set aside a specific time frame during which to work on it.
- Work with your team members to set agreed upon boundaries. If everyone agrees to not check e-mail on vacation, it makes it easier to maintain that behavior.
- Create time for yourself at least once or twice a week. Take time to fully disconnect all of your technology gadgets and take a walk with the dog, read, or go see a show.
- Take your lunch break. A break during the day can be a terrific stress reliever.

Several simple actions can help you reestablish the boundaries between your work life and home life.

LOOKING AHEAD

The work world of today looks far different from how it looked 50 years ago – and it is difficult to imagine what the workplace will look like another half century from now. In a perfect world, technology and the Internet will greatly improve the world of work, so that individuals never have to commute to work, robots handle any dangerous factory jobs, and a computer recording a conference call generates memos and status reports automatically. For many, the workplace of the future offers much opportunity for highly productive and satisfying work, aided by computers and technology. For others, the future and the new economy do not hold such hope.

Employment and Unemployment

Technology constantly changes both existing and emerging jobs. When computers originally were introduced into all facets of the factory, the office, and the retail store, many low-skilled production and service jobs requiring less education vanished – causing some to suggest that technology creates a condition of increasing unemployment.

No one can deny that technological change has displaced workers. As new technology makes the old obsolete, the new technology completely changes job descriptions and can eliminate occupations – but, in turn, it creates new opportunities. Over the last century, declines in the number of production jobs have been offset by increases in office and service jobs. Instead of machinery, these workers' tools are the telephone, the computer, e-mail, and the Internet.

The U.S. Department of Labor projects that 8 of the 10 fastest growing jobs between now and 2022 will be computer related. The demand for computer-related occupations will continue to increase as a result of rapid advances in computer technology and the ongoing demand for new computer applications, including those for the Internet and intranets.

Other jobs – even those considered to be nontechnical – will require an understanding of how to use technology. Administrative workers must understand word processing, accounting, and human resources software, along with how to set up teleconferences and book travel reservations online. Truck drivers use global positioning systems to determine the fastest route to their delivery destination. Food service workers use computer terminals to input customer orders and generate end-of-day sales numbers. According to the U.S. Bureau of Labor Statistics, more than half of all American jobs require some degree of computer technology skill, and that percentage is forecast to grow to more than 75% by the end of the decade.

For the remaining Americans not working in technology-rich jobs, however, wages may continue to fall as the only work available to them may be low-paying service-sector jobs with few advancement opportunities. Even today, this trend is seen in many major U.S cities, and the problem continues.

Technology can significantly improve the lives of those who have the skill and education to adopt it – and further separate those who do not. This gap between those who have access to computers and those who do not is referred to as the **digital divide**. Some liken it to the days of the Industrial Revolution, when unskilled workers were forced into dangerous, tedious, low-paying jobs in factories. Today, however, underskilled workers are force to accept underpaid jobs in service industries instead of in factories. The social, ethical, and legal implications of the digital divide will be discussed later in the book.

A New Economy?

In the end, the solution to the problem is difficult. Technological change is a key part of progress for any society. Going as far back as the Agricultural Revolution and the Industrial Revolution, new technology has always created change. Along with the change will be the inevitable shifts in available jobs and the skills required to hold those jobs. In the early 1800s, England saw a protest movement against the new factories, called Luddism. **Luddites** were mostly craftsmen whose jobs were replaced by machines, and they tried to fight back by destroying those machines and the factory buildings which housed them. Can you imagine life today if we held back from light bulbs out of consideration for the candle makers? Although the movement failed, the term "luddite" is still used to describe anyone who opposes the introduction of new technologies. Paradoxically, the jobs that the Luddites so feared they would lose to the new machines did not vanish – by the end of the nineteenth century, textile mills were employing at least one hundred men for every one employed at the beginning of the century.

The challenge for all of us is to keep our work skills as current as the available jobs.

Today the Information Age has brought its own revolution, resulting in an entirely new set of rules in the economy.

The old sources of competitive advantage – access to raw materials, transportation routes, or customer markets; low costs; and a large labor pool – are becoming less important. In an economy in which information is the raw material and the best selling product, these other factors are less key. Instead, the most important factors are having networked computer systems that provide efficient access to information to help foster innovation and creativity, and the educated workforce to use these systems.

Finally, the most valuable input for many firms is the skills and talent of their workforce. In the past, workers often held one job and followed a company from location to location. Today, you are likely to hold many jobs over your lifetime, each for a shorter period. Each time you change a job, you have the opportunity to move ahead and redefine your work. In today's technology-rich new economy, your ability to move up the corporate ladder is helped by a solid understanding of computers, technology, and their applications.

CONCLUSION

In this chapter, you learned about the transition from an agricultural to an industrial and, finally an information-based economy, and the changes that transition has brought. You learned about the use of computers in business and industry, including the use of computers in the factory, in retail sales and marketing, in banking, and in the office. After learning how ergonomics can help minimize health issues related to computing, you then were introduced to the various ways computers impact the quality of work life. Finally, you learned more about how computers may change work in the future, creating new jobs that require a solid understanding of computers, technology, and their applications.

Key Terms

acquirer
automated clearing house (ACH)
automated teller machine (ATM)
autonomy
bar code
bar code scanner
bill payment service
bill presentment
brick and mortar; brick and click
computer-aided design (CAD)
computer-aided engineering (CAE)
computer-aided manufacturing (CAM)
computer-integrated manufacturing (CIM)
credit-authorization system
database marketing
de-skilling
digital divide
direct deposit
e-bills
electronic funds transfer (EFT)
employee monitoring
encrypted
ergonomics
Information Age
information economy
inventory control system
job-scheduling system
just-in-time manufacturing
Luddite
manufacturing resource planning (MRP)
opt in
opt out
PDF (Portable Document Format)
point-of-sale (POS) system
production-scheduling system
repetitive stress injury (RSI)
smart card
social media
social media marketing
spam
telecommuting
3D printing
UPC (Universal Product Code)
warehouse management system (WMS)

Chapter Review

Multiple Choice

Select the best answer.

1. _____ integrate various production and process control systems into a single computerized system.

a. Computer-aided design (CAD) systems
b. Point-of-sale (POS) systems
c. Computer-aided engineering (CAE) systems
d. Manufacturing resource planning (MRP) systems

2. A(n) _____ helps factory managers decide when to initiate production based on the supplies on hand and customer demand.

a. inventory control system
b. job-scheduling system
c. distribution system
d. warehouse management system

3. _____ use(s) the UPC (Universal Product Code) to identify different items.

a. Retail and grocery stores
b. Libraries
c. The United States Post Office
d. all of the above

4. Spam is _____.

a. an organization that collects credit-authentication requests
b. the use of bill presentment to send electronic bills
c. unsolicited, junk e-mail sent as part of an electronic mass mailing
d. a science that incorporates comfort and efficiency into workplace design

5. An ATM (automated teller machine) allows you to _____.

a. withdraw cash and deposit money
b. transfer funds
c. inquire about an account balance
d. all of the above

6. Unlike a magnetic striped credit card, a smart card _____.

a. has a magnetic stripe that stores data that cannot be changed
b. stores data that can be changed
c. is large and immoveable
d. cannot interact with computers or other automated systems

7. _____ is an electronic file format that preserves document integrity so files can be viewed and printed on a variety of platforms using reader software.

a. ACH
b. PDF
c. WMS
d. EFT

8. For the computer work area, ergonomics experts recommend having _____.

a. two feet by four feet
b. four feet by eight feet
c. eight feet by sixteen feet
d. sixteen feet by thirty-two feet

9. A _____, such as carpal tunnel syndrome, is caused when muscle groups complete the same actions over and over again.

a. posttraumatic stress injury (PSI)
b. computer vision syndrome (CVS)
c. repetitive stress injury (RSI)
d. workplace pathology syndrome (WPS)

10. Employee monitoring involves the _____.

a. use of computers to observe, record, and review a worker's use of a computer
b. electronic transfer of funds to a worker's bank account
c. use of computers to mine worker databases and create marketing lists
d. practice of working away from an office and communicating via technology

Computers in Government 2

Nowhere are computers more pervasive than in the government, law enforcement, homeland security, and the military. The federal government — which most consider to be a paper-laden bureaucracy — is using technology to launch a new paperless era, in which you can do anything from tracking your Social Security benefits to submitting your tax return with a few mouse clicks. Law enforcement, which long has relied on human intelligence to solve crimes, is applying computer technology to help local, state, and federal agencies more effectively prevent and solve criminal cases. For departments focused on providing homeland security and military protection, computers are indispensable tools, supplying key information quickly in a crisis, while offering tools to help protect citizens and soldiers during war.

In this chapter, you will learn more about how the government uses computers to streamline the electoral process, speed the delivery of mail, help gather and analyze census data, and handle millions of tax returns. After reviewing how law enforcement officials use computer technology to track evidence, enforce traffic laws, and locate stolen goods, you will see how other technologies help officers find missing children and route emergency help to any 911 caller. The chapter also looks at how computers help ensure homeland security, by tracking visitors to the country, offering collaborative tools for crisis management, and providing surveillance at the country's borders. Finally, you will learn about the use of cutting-edge computer technologies by the military. Later chapters will discuss how different levels of government are active in other economic sectors, such as transportation, science, and medicine.

COMPUTERS AND GOVERNMENT

Government – including local, state, and federal – is the largest user of computers in the world. Like other businesses, the government uses computers and software to streamline office functions, make information available to citizens via Web sites, manage budgets, handle employee payroll, and process vast numbers of applications and forms for government benefits, driver's licenses, passports, change of address, and more. In addition, the government collects, stores, and analyzes huge quantities of data, including labor statistics, laws and regulations, trademarks and patents, every book indexed in the Library of Congress, and the American Memory collection of primary source materials concerning the history of the United States (Figure 2-1). The federal government (along with state and local governments) also uses computers for many specialized tasks, such as supporting elections, sorting and posting millions of packages at the U.S. Postal Service, collecting and storing Census Bureau data, and handling tax returns at the Internal Revenue Service.

The Election Process

In the past, federal, state, and local elections relied on hand-counted paper ballots or, more recently, mechanical lever-based machines. To get their message out to voters, candidates held public debates or purchased television time for advertising.

Today, computer technology is used to support and automate many aspects of the electoral process. For example, in any campaign headquarters, campaign staff members use text messaging and e-mail to communicate with each other and possible voters, while employing desktop publishing software to create flyers and mailings to send to potential supporters. Other staff members might use accounting software to monitor the amount of money spent on advertising, travel, and staff payroll, or to forecast the total donations needed to support future campaign expenses. More specialized programs, such as fundraising software, allow candidates to track donor's names, addresses, e-mail addresses, and gift amounts and create the mailing lists used to send appeals for more funds.

Outside headquarters, computers are used in almost every aspect of the electoral process, including conducting campaign polling, providing information to potential voters via Web sites, blogs, podcasts, text messaging, and e-mails, researching an opponent's record, registering voters, and predicting voting results. Computerized voting systems also are used to record votes, count ballots, and tally outcomes.

CONDUCTING POLLS The practice of conducting polls to gauge public opinion on an issue dates back to the 1960s, when President John F. Kennedy conducted polls to determine the best way to present his civil rights agenda. At that point, polling was so unusual that Kennedy took precautions to keep the polls and the results quiet. Since then, polling has become a mainstay of the political process before, during, and after elections.

In general, **political polling** is a process funded by candidates, in which a small group of qualified voters are asked questions specific to the topic about which pollsters want to gather data: an issue, a candidate, or an upcoming election. The answers given by the voters then are used to predict how a larger group of voters will act.

Figure 2-1 The government uses computers to help complete a wide range of tasks, from handling internal tasks to making information available to the public.

The process of developing and responding to poll results relies heavily on computers. For example, to start the polling process for a congressional campaign a polling consultant uses software to design, create, and edit surveys for paper and the Internet (Figure 2-2). The consultant uses the software to input the types and content of the questions, the order of the questions, and how they should appear on paper or on screen. The output is a completed survey to use in a poll.

In the past, the polling took place in person, by mail, or, most likely, by telephone. However, as more individuals screen or block unknown telephone calls, pollsters are turning to e-mail and the Internet to conduct polls. For example, during a campaign season you might receive an e-mail from Harris Interactive, a leading market research firm, inviting you to participate in a poll. The e-mail includes a link to an online poll, where you answer questions presented on Web pages. Unlike telephone surveys, the online questionnaires can incorporate graphic, audio, or even video clips. Your responses are collected in a database and, as needed, merged with results gathered via telephone or mail.

With the data collected and entered into a database, the consultant uses opinion polling software to analyze the data and determine how specific demographic groups (such as single women under 35, registered Republicans under 40, or Latino men living in Essex County) responded to questions about certain issues. The system generates views of the data and other reports. Based on these results or output, the candidate can craft and deliver multiple campaign messages targeted to each group.

Many people, however, are critical of the validity of polls, especially Internet polls. The critics note that input gathered online comes from a group limited to those with computer access, and thus does not reflect the reactions of a true cross-section of voters. For instance, Americans aged 65 or over are most likely to vote – but only about half of that group is online.

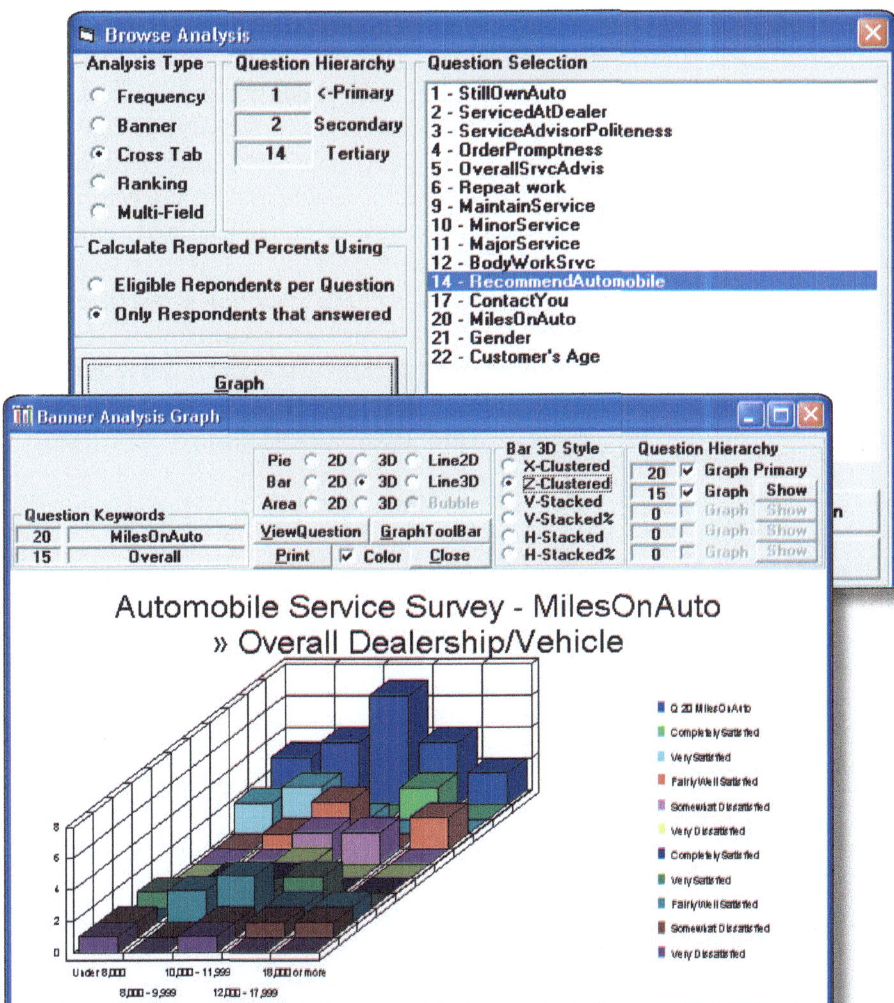

Figure 2-2 Survey software packages are used to (a) create the questionnaires used in polls, and then, (b) help analyze and chart the results.

COMMUNICATING WITH VOTERS

Computers and the Internet have changed the political process by making it easier than ever to communicate with voters. The use of Web sites to reach voters first gained popularity when Republican nominee Bob Dole ended his closing remarks at the initial presidential debate of 1996 by referring people to his Web site. For many, this was the first time they considered getting campaign information from a candidate via the Internet – and the response was huge. Traffic to the Dole Web site increased to 2 million hits the day after the debate and traffic remained high throughout the campaign.

In every political season since then, candidates have increasingly relied on Web sites, e-mail, and chat rooms to keep voters updated on their view and the latest news. Web sites provide information on their career histories and political positions, and encourage their supporters to sign up for volunteer work, donate money online, and pass along e-mail endorsements to friends and newspapers. Chat rooms allow voters to pose questions directly to a candidate, so they can learn more concerning specific subjects about which they are concerned. The White House, for example, regularly holds chat sessions to allow you to pose questions directly to key members of the presidential staff.

Many political Web sites also provide interactive tools to help engage citizens. For example, to promote a tax cut plan a politician can create a Web site with an online calculator that allows visitors to see how much the tax cut would save them each year.

RESEARCHING CANDIDATES The Web simplifies the process of researching information on a candidate. For example, at C-Span's Web site you can check the voting records for any member of Congress, as well as search a campaign finance database to see who has donated money to federal candidates. The Web site also has bulletin boards that allow you to share your thoughts on a candidate or learn how other people reacted to a recent debate (Figure 2-3).

Voters are not the only ones using the Web to learn about candidates; candidates themselves can use the Web to learn more about their opponents. Web sites, such as www.thomas.loc.gov, list any bill introduced into Congress, along with the bill's supporters. Using this information, candidates can highlight the voting records of opponents and spotlight any contradictory statements or positions that an opponent has had in the past, or, based on poll results, might be currently communicating to voters. Members of a candidate's staff also can read numerous news sources in print and online to cull quotes that might be used to discredit an opponent. Having collected this information, staff members use word processing, collaboration, or database software to organize and store the information for use later in the campaign.

CASTING A BALLOT: COMPUTERIZED VOTING SYSTEMS In the country's early history of elections, voting systems largely were paper-based or used mechanical devices, such as the machines with levers you pulled to indicate your vote. Today, although hand-counted paper ballots continue to be used, most voting is electronic.

Until 2000, most polling places used computer-readable punch card devices. With a **punch card system**, you mark your paper ballot by punching out bits of paper, called chads, using a stylus. With the chads removed, the punch card then is fed into a computerized counting machine that records the vote. However, in 2000 the electoral process for the U.S. Presidency was brought to a halt by hundreds of hanging chads – small pieces of thick paper not entirely punched from the card – that could cause a computer to read a vote incorrectly. After the winner was finally decided almost one month later, most state and local governments moved quickly to introduce more sophisticated, computerized voting systems.

Newer types of computerized voting systems include optical mark recognition, direct recording electronic (DRE) machines, and Internet-based voting systems (Table 2-1). With **optical mark recognition systems** (also called optical scanning systems or mark-sense systems), you fill in circles, squares, or other shapes printed on a paper ballot to indicate your vote. An optical mark recognition device scans the paper, detects the darkest mark for each question on the ballot, and records that as the vote. Similar systems are used widely for standardized college entrance exams.

Direct recording electronic (DRE) machines are specialized computers that allow you to enter your vote by pushbutton, touch screen, or dial (Figure 2-4). Keyboards also are included with the DRE machines to allow you to type write-in votes. Votes are counted by a computer, and results are available almost instantly at the end of Election Day. To eliminate potential fraud with DREs, you may be given an electronic

Figure 2-3 The C-SPAN Web site includes community bulletins boards that allow you to share your thoughts on election events.

TABLE 2-1

VOTING SYSTEM	*DESCRIPTION*	*PROS AND CONS*
Punch Card	Voters mark their ballots by punching holes in paper cards using a stylus. Punch cards then are fed into computerized counting machines.	***Pros:*** Easy to use, most voters are accustomed to using such cards ***Cons:*** The bits of paper that are removed when a card is punched, called a chad, often do not become completely detached from their cards when prescored cards are used. These hanging chads can work their way back into place in the punch card, thus blocking holes and causing the computer to read the vote incorrectly
Optical Mark Recognition	Paper ballots printed with circles, squares, or other shapes that voters fill in to mark their votes. Optical scanning technology is used to detect the marks on each ballot.	***Pros:*** Easy to use, most voters are accustomed to using such cards. Scanning machine can notify voters if their ballot is improperly marked, giving them an opportunity to remark their ballots. ***Cons:*** May require specific type of writing instrument, such as soft lead pencil (most also require red ink to not be used).
Direct Recording Electronic (DRE) Machines	Computer terminals that allow voters to enter their votes by pushbutton, touch screen, or dial. DRE machines can display images as well as text.	***Pros:*** Easy to use, if well designed. More accessible to illiterate or disabled, because graphics can be used to support text. System does not allow voter to make unambiguous choices; thus no questions on intended vote can arise. ***Cons:*** More expensive than punch card and mark-sense systems. Also, because there are no physical ballots that can be recounted or examined manually, a DRE system must be thoroughly tested prior to an election to ensure proper operation. Votes also must be recorded on two or more backup devices, in the event the system is corrupted. Power outages can bring the system down; the system should be capable of running on batteries or emergency generators.
Internet-Based Voting	Allows users to cast a vote from any computer connected to the Internet (either at home or at a polling place). The ballot then is transferred via the Internet to a centralized tallying center.	***Pros:*** Can eliminate the expenses associated with setting up and staffing remote voting locations, make voting more convenient for voters and eliminate the need for separate absentee ballot systems. ***Cons:*** Can raise security and privacy concerns, as well as concerns about people selling their right to vote to others. Finally, until everyone has Internet access and/or knows how to use a computer to vote, polling places will be required.

Several types of computerized voting systems are available today.

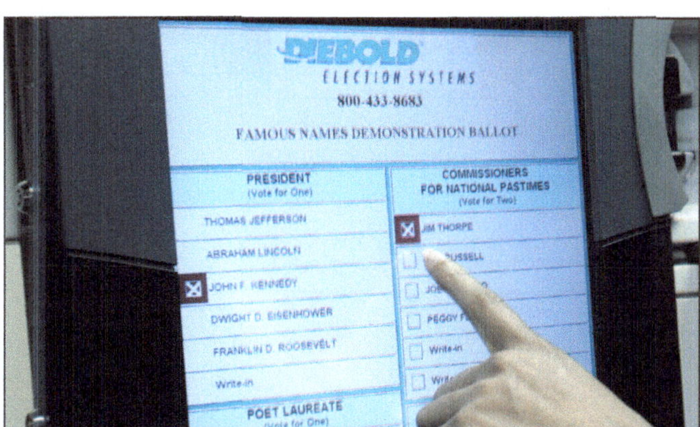

Figure 2-4 Direct recording electronic (DRE) machines allow you to enter your vote by pressing buttons or touching images on a touch screen.

card when you sign in at the polling place. Before casting your vote, you must swipe the card in a card reader connected to the DRE. DREs also can maintain a paper or electronic backup in case of later audit or recount.

In the future, you may provide your vote via some type of **online voting system**. Since 1986, the federal Uniformed and Overseas Citizens Absentee Voting Act (UOCAVA) has given overseas U.S. residents and military personnel the right to both register and vote in all federal, state, and local elections by email, fax, or web upload. But only Alaska extends this privilege to any eligible voter. Thus far, concerns about voter authentication and privacy, security of the election process, and auditability have blocked further action. Similarly abroad only a few countries use an Internet system for some or all voting, for example, Finland, some provinces in Canada, and some cantons in Switzerland.

As outlined in Table 2-2, computerized voting systems bring many benefits to the election process, including the ability to count ballots quickly, improve the accuracy of election results, and reduce election fraud. However, computerized voting systems also raise new apprehensions about security, reliability, the opportunity for fraud, and equal access. As you learned in Chapter 1, some Americans do not have access to the Internet – a concept called the digital divide – and this causes concern. For example, when the Democratic Party ran its presidential primary election in Arizona online, the U.S. Justice Department expressed anxiety about minority voters being locked out of the election process, simply because they did not have access to computers. To counter these concerns, polling places also remained open during the election, so that every registered voter could participate in the election process.

United States Postal Service

The United States Postal Service (USPS) handles some 155 billion letters, advertisements, periodicals and packages a year. Given the enormous volume of mail it must handle, the USPS relies on computer technology to streamline its operations, speed mail sorting, and offer better products and services to its customers.

For example, mail sorting has changed dramatically since the days when all mail was sorted manually. Today, machines and computers perform tasks necessary to sort the huge daily volume of mail. After you drop a letter in the mailbox, a mail carrier picks up the letter and delivers it to the closest sorting facility. A machine then separates your letter from thicker mail that must be sorted manually and moves it down a conveyor belt to an **optical character recognition (OCR) system**, which is a technology that relies on artificial intelligence to recognize patterns and read handwritten, typed, or computer-printed characters from documents and translate the images into a form a computer can process. The OCR machines at the sorting facility can read the addresses you have written on the envelope, look up the address in a database, and then apply an 11-digit POSTNET bar code that indicates the delivery address (Figure 2-5). Next, the letter moves on to a bar code sorter, which reads the POSTNET bar code and routes the mail to a different location in the facility, based on delivery address. Finally, the letter travels to a delivery point bar code sorter, which reads the 11-digit POSTNET bar code on your letter and places the mail into a carrier's mail bag in the order the carrier walks or drives the route.

By using sophisticated computerized equipment and bar codes, the USPS can process mail faster and more accurately, at less cost. Using these systems reduces the cost of processing 1000 pieces of first-class mail from $40 to $2.50. To pass these savings back to customers, the USPS offers discounts to companies that include POSTNET bar codes on the mail before it arrives at the sorting facility.

TABLE 2-2 The Benefits of Computerized Voting Systems

BENEFIT	*DESCRIPTION*
Simplify and streamline the voting process	Can reduce the time it takes to count ballots and obtain election results. Results can be calculated almost immediately after the polls close.
Improve accuracy of election result	Can provide more accurate results than can be provided by hand count. Inaccuracies introduced as a result of voters' unclear ballot marks can be eliminated.
Reduce election fraud	Unlike paper ballots, electronic ballots cannot be lost or destroyed before they reach the tallying location. Computerized voter registration logs also make it easier to identify people who should not be registered or who attempt to vote using someone else's registration.

Computerized voting systems can bring many benefits to the election process.

Figure 2-5 The USPS uses 11-digit POSTNET bar codes that indicate the delivery address to help route mail to its correct location quickly.

In addition to using computers to help sort mail and ensure delivery, the United States Postal Service uses computers to provide better products and customer service. For example, at the USPS Web site, you can find ZIP codes, locate nearby post offices, calculate postage costs for a package, change your address, or make arrangements to have the post office hold or forward your mail. You also can buy stamps and have them shipped to your home or link to a licensed PC Postage vendor, such as Stamps.com, that allows you to buy and print stamps or shipping labels directly from your computer. If you'd rather customize your stamps with photos of your family, pets, wedding, or recent vacation, authorized vendor www.photo.stamps.com will do the job and ship your stamps directly to you via – what else? – the USPS (Figure 2-6).

Figure 2-6 Licensed digital postage vendors such as photo.stamps.com can create unique stamps using customers' own photos

Census Bureau

Mandated by the Constitution, every ten years since 1790 the U.S. government has counted its population. Census results impact a wide range of matters, from congressional representation to Federal assistance for states, cities, and schools. Therefore, great efforts are made to count every person. In 2010, you or your family probably received a census form in the mail from the U.S. government. After completing the form, which asked questions about who lives at your address you mailed it back. By law, the Federal government must keep your personal census data secret for 72 years. However, it can aggregate, or group, your data with other households in your area, and make those results public.

For Census 2010, the Census Bureau was challenged with counting over 300 million Americans in six months and making the results available to citizens via the Bureau's official Web site (Figure 2-7). To do this, the Census Bureau outsourced the project to Lockheed Martin Corp., which used more than 10,000 computers, ranging from PCs to a supercomputer. To speed the process of inputting the data, the Census Bureau used optical mark recognition forms that could be scanned electronically. Once the data was entered, powerful computers tabulated the data collected by the census questionnaires. The bureau also used an image-capture system to store scans of forms and help process poorly completed forms, allowing census workers to access forms electronically to deal with bad handwriting or poorly marked bubble choices (instead of having to find one original paper form among millions).

For the 2020 census, the Census Bureau intends to augment these activities by providing its questionnaire online for citizens to answer. The Census Bureau also plans to supply a data-collection app which Census field workers could download and use on their personal smartphones and tablets. As they travel door-to-door interviewing citizens, the census worker will be able to input data, for upload to the main Census Bureau database.

Internal Revenue Service

The Internal Revenue Service, like the US Postal Service, handles huge volumes of information, in the form of around 230 million tax returns each year. The IRS relies on computers for numerous activities, including processing returns, reviewing returns for possible audit, accepting payment, and providing refunds using direct deposit.

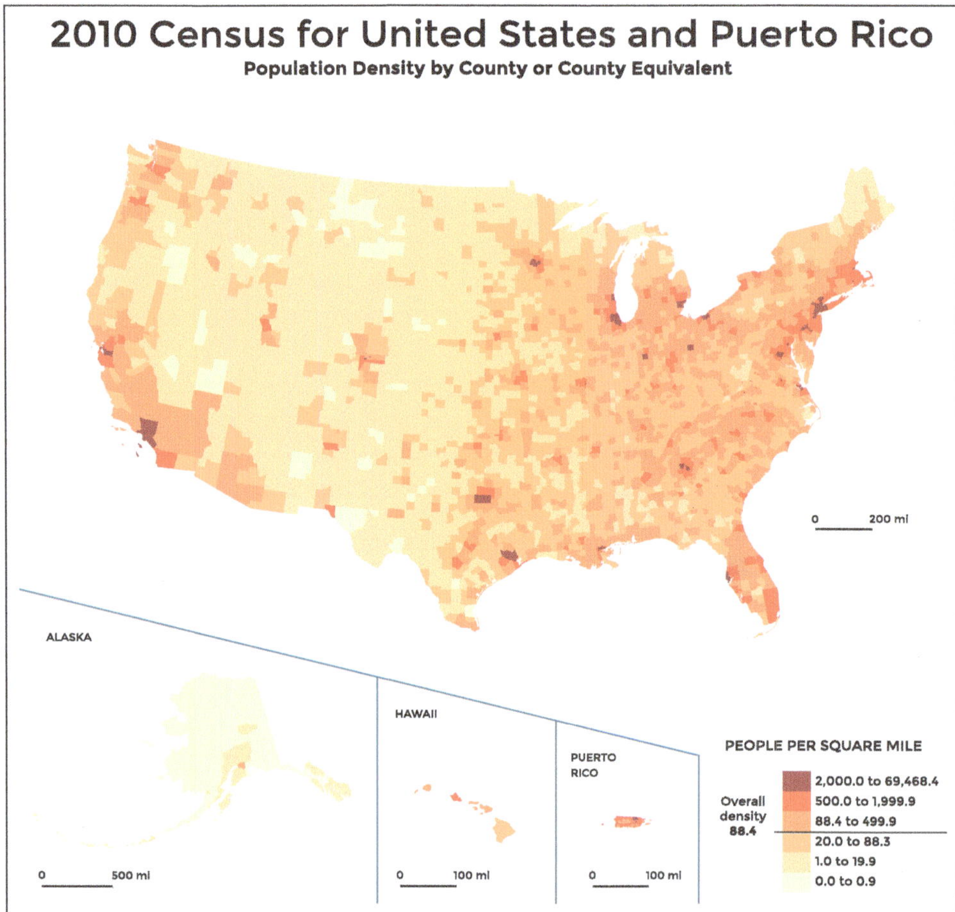

Figure 2-7 All of the Census 2010 results are stored in searchable databases accessible via the Census Bureau Web site, which also provides data organized geographically in maps.

Computers have changed the way taxpayers work with the IRS. In the past, Americans had to complete their tax returns by hand, using paper forms. Today, **tax preparation software** guides individuals, families, and small businesses through the process of filing taxes (Figure 2-8). Tax preparation software programs, such as Intuit TurboTax or H&R Block ask you a series of questions and then create your completed tax forms. The software also analyzes the forms to search for potential errors or places where you may have missed deductions.

If you mail in a paper copy of your tax return, an IRS employee enters every piece of information on your tax form into a computer system (Figure 2-9). The system checks returns for correct Social Security numbers and mathematical accuracy; if the returns are correct, this information then is stored in large magnetic tape machines. A second file that includes refund information is sent to disbursing centers, which handle the process of sending you your refund.

IRS **e-File** allows you to complete and submit your tax return over the Internet. With e-File, you can complete your tax return using tax preparation software and then submit the final forms electronically. Alternatively, you can complete your entire return online, via a tax preparation Web site, and then submit the completed return over the Internet to the IRS. Because the IRS does not have to reenter all of the data from your paper return into its system, using e-File typically means you will get your refund faster. Approximately 91% of taxpayers used the electronic filing process in 2015.

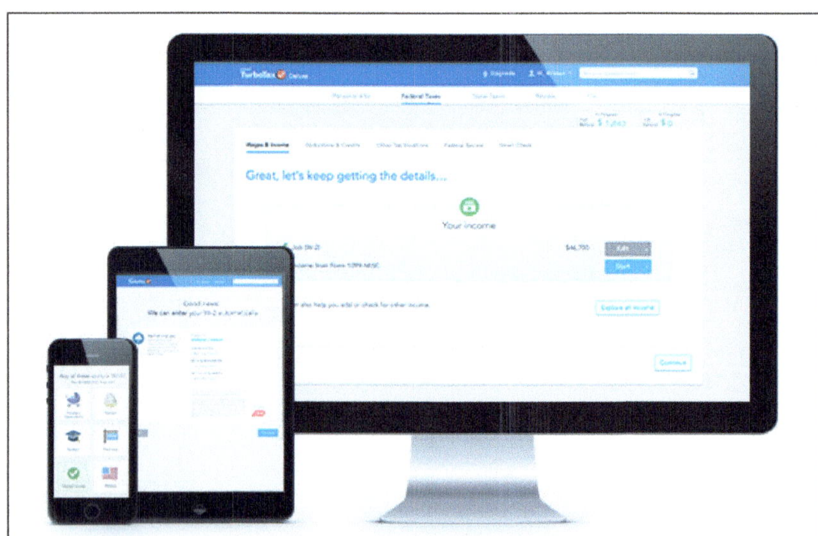

Figure 2-8 Today, tax preparation software, such as Intuit TurboTax and H&R Block's TaxCut, guides individuals, families, and small businesses through the process of filing taxes.

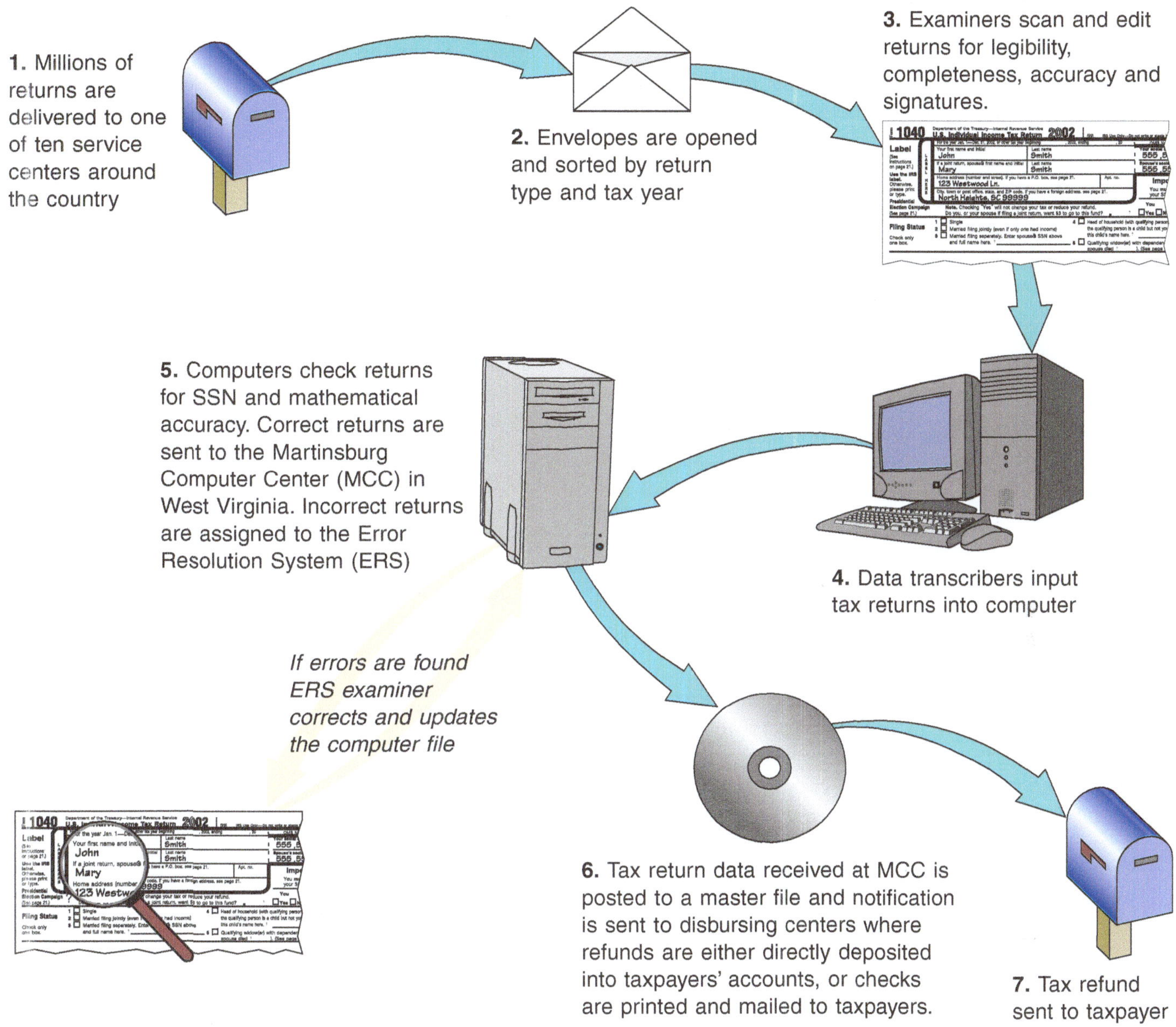

Figure 2-9 If you mail in a paper copy of your tax return, the IRS processes the form, reviews it for accuracy and then, as needed, sends you a refund using the above steps.

The IRS plans to spend close to $410 million during the next few years to modernize its information technology infrastructure to make the process of managing its business easier. The IRS projects that this investment will lead to increases in annual revenue of $699 million – more than paying for the project's cost.

Using computer technology also helps the IRS process refunds more efficiently. For example, as you learned in Chapter 1, you can specify that you want to receive your refund via direct deposit, which means the IRS transfers the refund electronically straight to your bank account. The IRS.gov Web site also includes a feature that allows you to track the status of your refund, using your Social Security number and file status information.

The IRS relies on its Web site to provide helpful information and tools to taxpayers, such as federal tax codes and forms available in PDF format, information on where to find your local IRS office, tax calculators to help you determine what you owe, e-File information, and more. In recent years, during the height of the tax season right before April 15, the IRS.gov Web site receives almost 200 million hits.

The IRS also uses computers to determine if returns should be audited. A computer program numerically scores every individual tax return and some corporate tax returns to determine if they should be reviewed manually. If your return is selected and has an error, the computer automatically prints and addresses a discrepancy notice that is mailed to inform you of the error.

Regulatory Environment

By legislation and regulation, governments can encourage both the development and use of computer applications. For example, to be in compliance with the 1990 Americans with Disabilities Act (ADA), Apple, Google, and Microsoft have developed smartphone apps for the visually impaired. These apps vocalize whatever displays on a smartphone screen, or announce whatever screen object the user touches. There are also apps that verbally identify denominations of US currency, and some of those programs even work with non-US money, such as euros.

Another example stems from the growing use of drones in many countries around the world. While clearly a technology with many possible benefits to society, drones also can also threaten security, safety, and privacy. In the US, the Federal Aviation Administration (FAA) has the duty of regulating the use of drones so that, for example, they do not endanger private or commercial aircraft. Some experts view the problems caused by drones as similar to the situation more than a century ago when automobiles started appearing on streets dominated by horse-drawn vehicles and pedestrians. Then, it took time to understand better the behavior of automobiles and the humans who drove them, before suitable regulations were in place. This may also prove to be the case with drones and their regulation.

COMPUTERS IN LAW ENFORCEMENT AND FIRE SAFETY

In today's police force laptop computers have been standard in most squad cars (and even on some motorcycles). Attached to in-vehicle base stations providing power and connectivity, these devices display valuable information while on the road, such as warrants, restraining orders, driving records, and criminal histories. The laptops also help officers file accident reports and complete other routine work. When writing tickets, many officers use a handheld computer which includes a scanner for reading the bar code on driver's license, a camera, and a thermal printer for generating the citation.

Computers also are used by law enforcement officials to support a wide range of tasks, including tracking evidence and criminal records, enforcing traffic laws, quickly communicating information about missing children, and ensuring a rapid response to 911 emergency calls.

Tracking Evidence

A crime scene can have thousands of pieces of physical evidence: a bullet casing, a scrap of cloth, or a crumpled receipt. Any one of these pieces of evidence may be the key to constructing a criminal case, and the evidence needs to be kept safe, organized, and accessible. Further, police and courts have a legal and ethical responsibility to record, maintain, and protect the **chain of custody** for all evidence, to prevent tampering or accidental contamination.

Today, police departments manage chain of custody using evidence-tracking systems – a collection of computer software, databases, and other supporting technologies (ex., bar scanners). As each item of evidence is brought in, police enter complete documentation about it into a handheld computer, which wirelessly transmits the information to the evidence database. The handheld computer then prints out a bar code sticker that the officer affixes to the evidence container. Once this label is in place, a quick scan of the bar code will access the evidence database and display information about what the item is, what case it belongs to, and where and by whom it was collected. Each time the item is scanned, the scan is logged in the database so officials can know exactly who handled the evidence at any point in time, in case questions about possible evidence tampering arise.

Databases also are used to monitor other types of evidence, including DNA. For example, the FBI's Combined DNA Index System (CODIS) is a database with three levels of DNA data: local, state, and national. When DNA evidence is gathered from a crime scene, the DNA profile is entered into the CODIS system. CODIS uses two key indexes: the forensic and offender indexes. The forensic index contains DNA collected as crime scene evidence, while the offender index includes DNA profiles of individuals convicted of violent crimes. CODIS allows federal, state, and local crime labs to compare DNA profiles electronically, so that they can better identify and convict previous offenders.

Another incredibly valuable database system used by law enforcement is the Integrated Automated Fingerprint Identification System, usually referred to as AFIS (pronounced *ay-fis*). The system allows law enforcement officials to search for and match fingerprints collected from previous arrests. Today, instead of using ink and fingerprint cards to take fingerprints, a scan system captures fingerprint images electronically. After capturing the image, an officer enters the data normally found at the top of a fingerprint card – name, date of birth, and arrest information – using the scan system keyboard. This data, along with the digital fingerprint images, is transmitted to a central AFIS system that can be accessed by officials around the country to identify the owner of fingerprints left at the crime scene.

Storing Criminal Records

Technology has made searchable databases of criminal records widely available to law enforcement agencies, including officers on the street. For example, the FBI's **National Crime Information Center (NCIC)** database is a computerized index of criminal justice information, such as criminal records and information on fugitives, stolen properties, and missing persons. After arresting a subject, law enforcement officials can access the database to see if other warrants for the subject's arrest are open or if the subject's name is connected with other crimes.

Another FBI system – the **National Instant Criminal Background Check System (NICS)** – was established to help gun and explosives dealers perform background checks on prospective buyers to ensure that convicted felons, among others, cannot buy these items from a dealer. When a customer wants to buy a gun, the firearms dealer calls a toll-free number that connects the dealer with the state Bureau of Identification. An operator then runs a query for the purchaser's name. The query searches through several different databases, including a state criminal database, the federal NCIC, an outstanding warrant database, and a few other state databases. To ensure the full effectiveness of the system, records in the database must be updated and as accurate as possible – a delay in entering data could mean that a criminal leaves a store with a new gun. For this reason, many states have waiting periods before a customer can actually take a gun from a store, just to be sure that all of the latest data has been entered in the database. Historically, the denial rate is around 1.4% of total applicants.

Other databases are used to make relevant information about sexually violent offenders available to the public. The murder of seven-year old Megan Kanka led to the passage of **Megan's Law**, which requires people convicted of certain sexual offenses to register with local law enforcement agencies, for the rest of their lives. Information in the database includes the offender's name, aliases, photograph and physical description, ethnicity, date of birth, scars, marks and tattoos, registered sex offenses, and county and zip code based on last registered address. In order to make this information available to the public, many communities make the sex offender database available online (Figure 2-10).

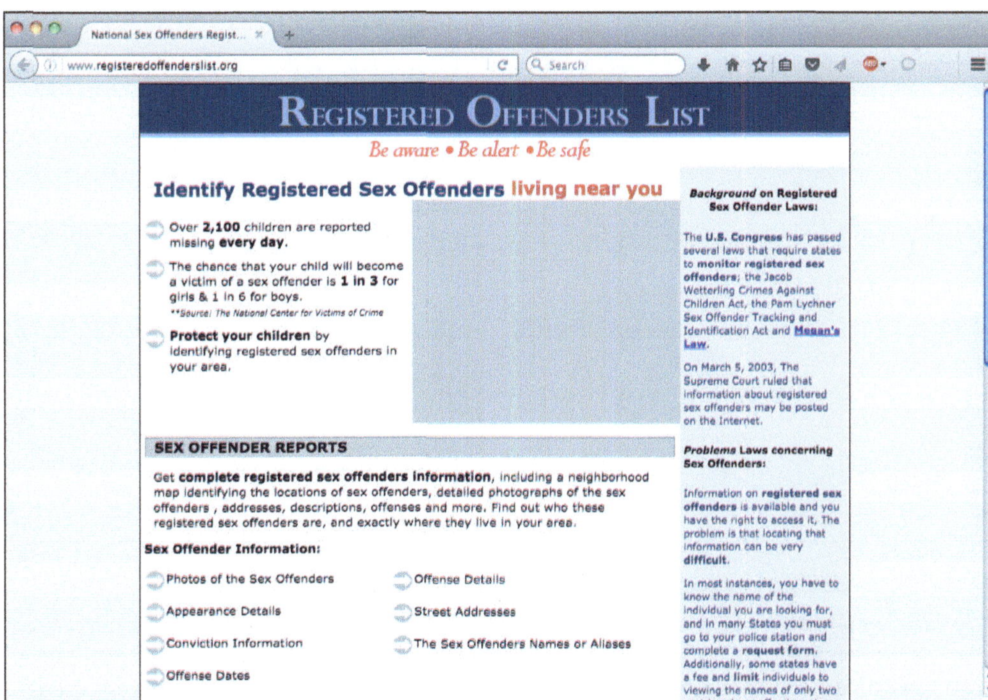

Figure 2-10 Sex offender databases available online as part of the response to Megan's Law.

Enforcing Traffic Laws

Even traffic lights are using computer technology to ensure that you (or other drivers) do not run a red light. **Red-light systems** include three key elements: one or more digital cameras, one or more triggers, and a computer. In a typical system, cameras are positioned at the corners of an intersection so they can photograph cars driving through the intersection (Figure 2-11). Each red light has a trigger, or a sensor loop, which is a length of electrical wire charged with an electrical current to generate a magnetic field. When a car passes over the sensor loop, it changes the magnetic field and sets off the trigger.

The computer is the core of the system: it is connected to the cameras, the triggers, and the traffic light and constantly monitors the traffic signal and the triggers. If your car moves over the sensors loops at a particular speed when the light is red, the computer instructs the cameras to take two pictures to document the violation – one as you enter the intersection and one when you are in the middle of the intersection.

To document the violation fully, the computer adds the date, time, intersection location, and other information to the digital photo. With this information and photos of the infraction, the police have everything they need to charge you for running the red light.

If you do get a citation for running a red light, speeding, or parking next to a fire hydrant, at least computers make paying your fine easier. You can access information regarding your citations and parking tickets

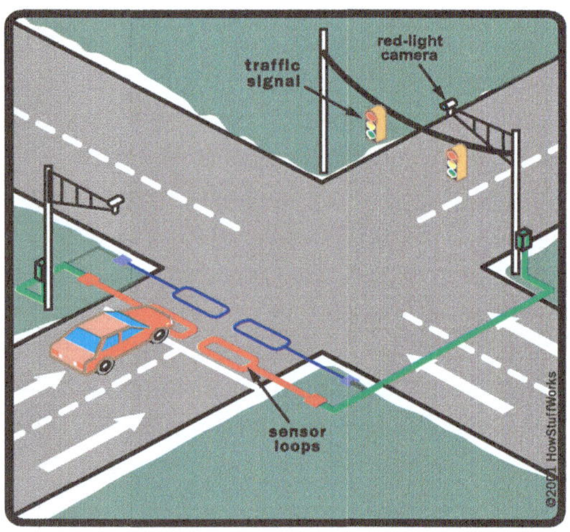

1. Each traffic light has a trigger, or a sensor loop, a length of electrical wire buried just under the asphalt with an electrical current to generate a magnetic field.

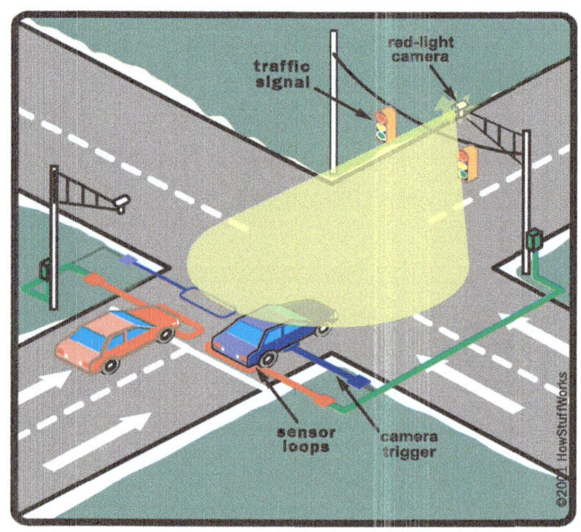

2. If your car moves over the sensor loops when the light is red, the computer automatically instructs the camera to take two pictures to document the violation – one as you enter the intersection –

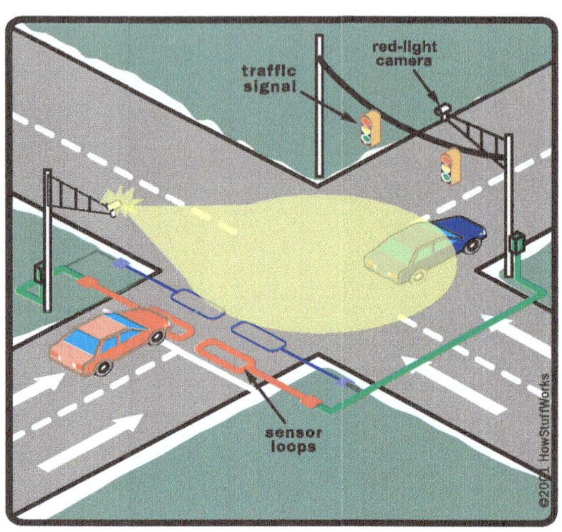

3. – and one as you are in the middle of the intersection to capture your car proceeding through the intersection (and your license plate number).

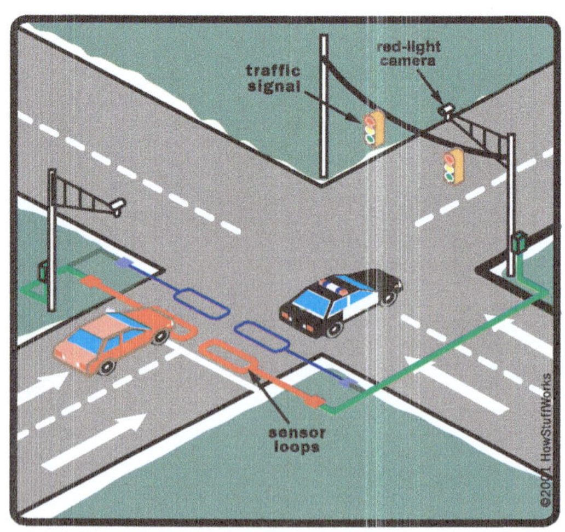

4. With the photos, along with information on date, time, and the intersection, the police have everything they need to charge the driver or the car owner.

Figure 2-11 Red-light systems rely on computer technology to catch drivers who run red lights.

online by going to a Web site and entering your citation number (Figure 2-12). If there is a balance due on the citation, you can enter your credit card information and submit payment online.

Tracking Stolen Vehicles

Motor vehicle theft is the most expensive property crime in the United States: the 700,000 vehicles stolen annually cost consumers more than $4.1 billion. You can protect your car from thieves using a stolen vehicle recovery system, for example **LoJack**. With the LoJack system, a wireless radio-frequency transceiver about the size of a chalkboard eraser is placed somewhere in your car (the installer does not tell you where the transceiver is located). When you report your stolen car to the police, the incident is entered into the National Crime Information Center database, which allows police to match the vehicle identification number of your car with your LoJack device and then automatically send a signal to the device on a special FM frequency. This signal activates the LoJack device hidden in your car, which in turn sends out a homing signal to a special tracking computer in police squad cars. The tracking computer displays a map with arrows to show police which way to steer their cruiser to locate the stolen vehicle.

You can further protect your car from theft by purchasing a system that uses a motion sensor and a uniquely coded key pass to detect unauthorized movement of the vehicle. When you are driving the car, the key pass identifies you as an authorized user. If the vehicle is moved without the key pass present, however, a notification is sent to you via phone or email.

Finding Missing Persons

Computers also are being used in the race to find missing persons. The **AMBER Alert** system, for example, is a missing child alert system created to issue an immediate notification to the public so they can help recover missing or abducted children and teenagers before they can be harmed. All 50 states now have participation plans in place.

While the AMBER (which is short for America's Missing: Broadcast Emergency Response) Alert programs are relatively new, the technology that underlies the system is not. The technology is the Emergency Alert System (EAS), which is known to most television viewers as a loud beep followed by a weather warning or the "This is only a test" warning message.

When a law enforcement agency decides to issue an AMBER Alert, an officer sends key information – pictures of the missing child, the suspected abductor, a suspected vehicle and any other information available – to radio and television stations designated as primary stations under the Emergency Alert System. These stations immediately interrupt their programming to broadcast the alert on the air.

Other AMBER Alert messages are displayed on dynamic message signs that enable transportation officials to type in any information they want, including an alert on a child kidnapping (Figure 2-13). Law enforcement officials and staff from the **National Center for Missing and Exploited Children (NCMEC)** also provide alerts via e-mail, mobile phones, and as headers on Web sites, with the message content pushed from central servers to each Web server hosting a Web page with the AMBER Alert header. Another example of

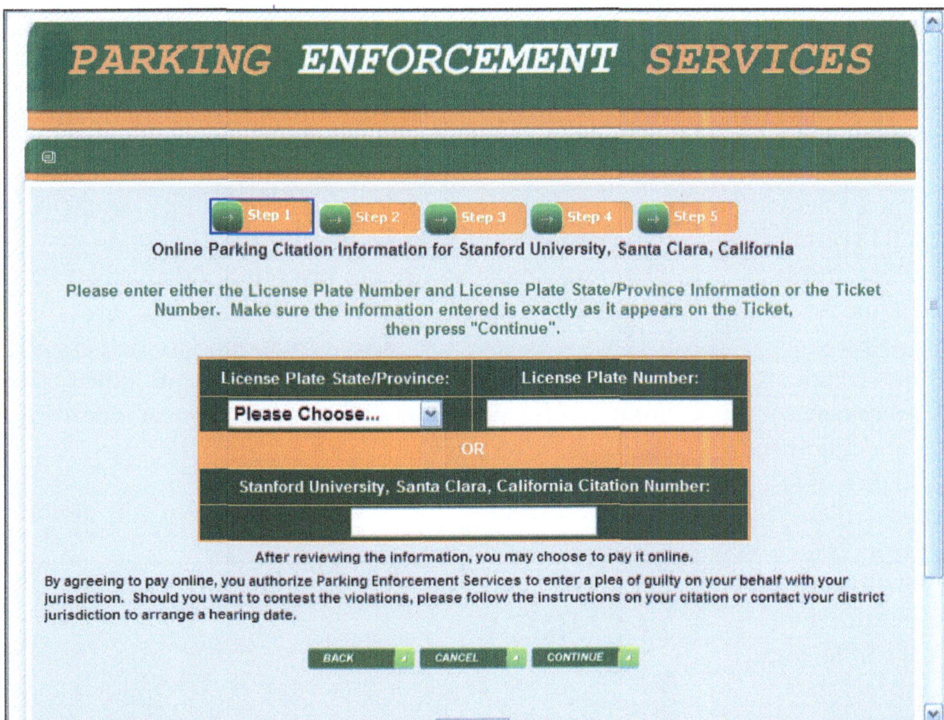

Figure 2-12 Computers even have made paying your citations simple, allowing you to access and pay your citations and parking tickets online.

Figure 2-13 Amber Alert messages are displayed on dynamic message signs that enable transportation officials to type in a child kidnapping alert.

this type of computer application is Silver Alert, which notifies the public about missing persons suffering from Alzheimer's disease or other forms of dementia.

Providing Wireless 911

For years, individuals have dialed 911 to connect to emergency personnel. When you dial 911, the call automatically is forwarded to a public-safety answering point (PSAP), also called a 911 call center. The operator takes key information, such as the type of emergency and your location, and then dispatches the appropriate emergency personnel. **Enhanced 911 (E911)** computer software helps emergency-response operators. E911 automatically displays two key pieces of information – your telephone number and the address where your telephone is located – on the 911 operator's computer monitor as he or she answers the call. The Enhanced 911's automatic number identifier (ANI) and automatic location identifier (ALI) databases provide these two pieces of information.

But suppose the 911 request comes from a mobile phone, or a phone using an Internet VoIP (Voice over Internet Protocol) service? Mobile phones are not associated with one fixed address; callers can be located just about anywhere. In 2014, approximately 240 million calls were made to 911; depending on community, anywhere from one-third to half of 911 calls are wireless.

With the E911 system, the GPS receiver in the phone receives signals from GPS satellites. When you make a 911 call from your cell phone, the operator's computer links to the automatic location identifier (ALI) database to get specific address information based on the latitude and longitude data from the GPS receiver, so that the operator can send emergency personnel right to your location. The FCC now requires all wireless carriers to ensure that 95% of their customers' phones be E911-capable. However, it remains difficult for 911 responders to bring help when a caller uses an Internet phone. Currently the FCC can require only those VoIP services connecting to traditional land lines to support E911. Ultimately the burden is on the subscriber to keep their address current with their chosen VoIP provider.

Fire Safety

Computers offer many different applications when fighting fires. For example, just as with police cars, in-cab laptops can provide critical information to fire crews, such as best routing to the scene. Also, many vehicular and industrial fires involve on-site chemicals and other toxic substances that could endanger both crews and the surrounding community. The number of these dangerous agents is easily in the thousands. The possible threats are not just physical hazards (ex., flammability, reactivity, corrosion) but also health hazards (ex., carcinogenicity, irritation). Fire fighters use computers to identify mystery chemicals and other unknown substances as well as to develop an appropriate response strategy.

COMPUTERS AND HOMELAND SECURITY

After the attacks in New York on September 11, 2001, homeland security became a renewed focus for the government and citizens alike. Computer technology is playing a key role in keeping the country safe, by helping to track citizens and visitors to the country, to provide good communication during national crises, and to protect the United States' borders.

Tracking Citizens

Beginning in 2005, the U.S. State Department began issuing passports to U.S. citizens bearing an **RFID (Radio Frequency Identifier)** chip (Figure 2-14). The chip contains an identification number and a digital signature – numbers assigned to the chip when the passport is issued – in addition to a digital facial image and all the personal data currently found on the information page of a passport. All this data is stored in a central government database. Once the chip is printed and embedded in the passport, it cannot be altered. When citizens present their passports at U.S. ports of entry using the special readers needed to collect the data, the system makes note of the entry. Critics contend that chips can be read by unauthorized scanning devices from as far away as 30 to 65 feet, without the passport holder's knowledge or consent. Government officials state that the chips are readable only when in close proximity to their chip readers. Damage to the chip, via tampering or exposure to water, can render it useless, requiring processing the "old fashioned" way.

Tracking Visitors

Tracking U.S. citizens is just one concern for homeland security officials. One of the biggest problems is one that has been aggravated by the use of computers: the easy availability of fake identification documents. Using high-quality laser printers and desktop publishing software, counterfeiters can create credible passports, Social Security cards, birth certificates, and driver's licenses. Of the many millions of people who visit the United States each year, it can be difficult to know who is using real documents and who is using fake.

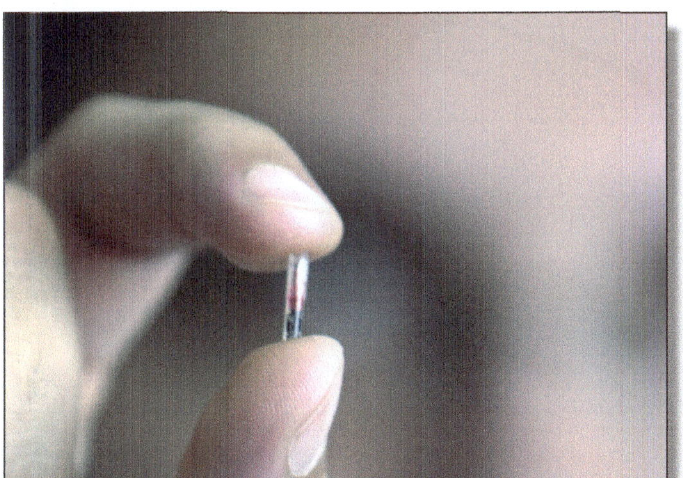

Figure 2-14 After your medical and personal information are encoded on the rice-sized microchip, the VeriChip is implanted under the skin with a large needle device.

To thwart the use of counterfeit documents, the United States implemented the US-VISIT (Visitor and Immigrant Status Indication Technology) management system, which is designed to make it easier for legitimate tourists, students, and business travelers to enter the country, while making it more difficult to enter illegally.

The core of the US-VISIT system is a database of biometric identifiers. The system would require foreign students, tourists, and business travelers to supply two **biometric identifiers** – digital fingerprints and a digital photograph – when entering and leaving the country. The biometric identifiers are stored in the US-VISIT database, along with information on the visitor's visa, nationality, and other personal data. Each time visitors use a passport or visa to exit or enter the country, their identifiers are matched against those in the database to verify their identity. The tracking system is intended to make it easier for immigration officials to spot visitors whose 90-day visas have expired and help tourists, students, and business travelers enter the United States more quickly by using biometric identifiers to verify their identities.

International students with visas attending schools in the United States also must provide personal information to the Web-based SEVIS (Student and Exchange Visitor Information System), which is administered by the Student and Exchange Visitor Program (SEVP). SEVIS is intended to help the government to ensure that foreign students and exchange visitors enroll and stay enrolled in courses at the school. Prior to SEVIS, colleges and universities had to submit paperwork for each student attending their schools. With the SEVIS system, administrative staff at a school can input student data and print bar-coded forms via the SEVIS Web site – or the school can upload student data in a batch, directly from the school's computer systems to the SEVIS systems. The SEVIS database will alert SEVP if students who enter the country fail to enroll at the school they are supposed to attend or if students drop out of their programs. Many have expressed criticism of the new system, fearing invasion of privacy. Others note that the system has experienced technological problems including data transfer issues that result in lost information, delays in processing simple forms, and personal information being sent to the wrong individuals.

Surveillance Using Computer Vision Systems

The U.S. Bureau of Customs and Border Protection is stepping up security on the U.S. and Canadian border – the longest international border in the world – by implementing a computer vision system at ports of entry along the border. The computer vision system, which is a new type of video surveillance system, uses hundreds of digital video cameras along the 3,987 mile border to see and analyze unusual activities or movements in real time. The surveillance system software uses artificial intelligence to analyze the data gathered by the video cameras. The software reviews the digital video feeds in real time for any unusual objects or activity – perhaps a large truck without license plates or people climbing over a fence. If the system identifies something suspicious, it immediately sends alerts to computers and wireless devices so that enforcement agencies can respond promptly. Other applications of computer vision systems like this include monitoring restricted areas, such as parking lots, for unauthorized vehicles, packages, or other objects, and controlling access to secure locations by checking movement around entrances and exits.

Crisis Management through Collaboration

Emergency management systems are computer programs used by local, state, and national agencies to respond appropriately to a wide range of natural or human-caused events. Linked together by wireless, Internet, or other technologies, the software can run on both laptops (for incident response teams) or as part of a general crisis management system installed in an emergency operations center. In addition to supporting command, control, and communication among a variety of responding agencies, the software also offers tools for weather modeling (ex., smoke plume behavior in a city), resource management, and geographical maps containing multi-layered data (Geographic Information Systems).

A Web-based collaboration system allows everyone involved to share critical information in real time (Figure 2-15). Authorized users can enter information about specific incidents, so that others can view information related to the event. Once the incident is logged into the system, it is placed on a map along with an incident report. The system also provides comprehensive situation reports for all agencies, status and damage reports for critical facilities, and even staffing assignments to handle recovery and response efforts.

Another benefit of this software is the ability of emergency response personnel to use its modeling and simulation features to practice and improve their efforts. **Computer models** can represent just about any object, organism, or structure. A **computer simulation** uses software (and sometimes hardware) to imitate the behavior of a process or system over time. Many different parts of our economy test or explore products or ideas using computer models inside computer simulations.

COMPUTERS IN THE MILITARY

The world's first electronic, digital, programmable computer (named *Colossus*) was built by the British during World War 2 for deciphering messages encoded with the German Enigma machine. Militaries around the world have used computers ever since. The United States military is continually working

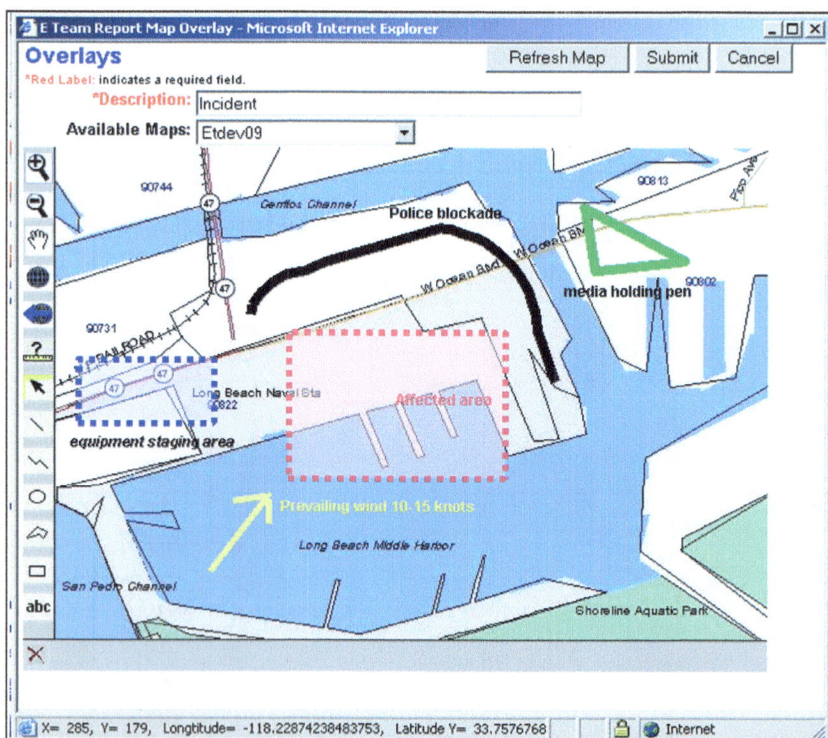

Figure 2-15 To help aid crisis management, the Homeland Security Department and other agencies use a Web-based collaboration system to share computerized incident maps in real-time.

with research universities and companies to improve the technologies behind military equipment and systems. Historically, wars and conflicts have brought many new products into commercial use by citizens. For example, in the 1970s the U.S. military developed the **Global Positioning System (GPS)** – a network of geostationary satellites that beam location and time information to receivers on Earth – to guide troops and vehicles accurately in all kinds of weather and at night. Today GPS is used by all aspects of the transportation sector, by hikers and other sport participants, and by smartphone apps that do everything from geotagging your photographs to offering location-aware travel advice.

Today's military continues to set trends in the computer and technology field, with interesting spin-offs to the civilian sector. This section will discuss drones, autonomous vehicles, robots, computer-based simulations for training, and cybersecurity.

Remote-Controlled Drones

A **drone** is an **unmanned aerial vehicle (UAV)**; it has no human pilot onboard. Instead, people operate drones remotely using sophisticated computer hardware and software. Drones have been experimented with and used by the U.S. military since at least the 1960s, but it was only in the 1990s that hardware miniaturization and sensor improvements made these complex devices practical. Today there are many types of military drones used for a wide range of purposes, including reconnaissance, combat, and cargo transport. These lightweight, remote-controlled drones use GPS for navigation and one or more miniature cameras (black-and-white, color, or infra-red night vision) that feed (often by satellite) live video images to the pilot and other ground receivers who might be half-way around the globe. Eventually, the military will introduce completely autonomous drones. For example, the U.S. Navy's X (for eXperimental)-47B is an unmanned, autonomous aircraft that can take-off from and land on aircraft carriers. Whether these self-flying drones will supplement drones that are human-piloted, or completely replace them, is yet to be seen.

In the 2010s, further technology improvements allowed drones to enter the marketplace. Today, many different varieties of drones can be purchased or rented. Ranchers use drones to check on livestock and range fencing. Farmers use drones to identify places in fields needing more water or fertilizer (Figure 2-16). Oil companies use drones to check pipelines for leaks. Scientists use drones to fly over active volcanoes. Film makers use drones for capturing unique views of their story. The range of applications continues to grow.

At the same time, drones have invaded personal privacy, endangered commercial aircraft, and entered restricted airspace. Governments around the world are scrambling to respond to problems such as these. In the U.S., for example, the Federal Aviation Administration

Figure 2-16 Unmanned aerial vehicles (UAVs) can be used to provide surveillance. UAV's can be equipped with a miniature camera that relays live video images to the operator.

(FAA) has placed restrictions on how high private drones may fly, and requires all drones over half a pound to be registered.

Remote-Controlled Robots

Another major field for military research is robotics. Remote-controlled robots provide the military with eyes, ears, and feet in small or hazardous locations where it is impossible or unsafe for soldiers and emergency personnel to go. For example iRobot, the manufacturer of Roomba vacuum robots, also builds a small, general-purpose machine called PackBot (Figure 2-17). The military can equip PackBots with a variety of sensors, cameras, and arms to "sniff" for explosives or poison gasses; locate and dispose of IEDs (Improvised Explosive Devices); collect biological, chemical, or radiological samples; probe ruined buildings for trapped victims; and locate snipers. Over 2000 PackBots were deployed to Afghanistan and Iraq.

Many of these same technologies are also available on PackBots sold to civilian emergency responders and research scientists. After the Fukushima, Japan, nuclear power plant complex was severely damaged by tidal wave in 2011, PackBots were the first robots to enter the radioactive facility.

The military is also studying the use of remote-controlled robots to move cargo or heavy weapons over rugged terrain. One example of robotic "pack mules" is the LS3, a 4-legged cylinder that can tote 400 pounds over 20 miles of widely varied terrain, following a sensor attached to a human soldier. Some of this technology has migrated into the health sector to improve patient mobility (Figure 2-18).

Autonomous Vehicles

Scientists currently are working on a different type of military robotic system that can steer a vehicle without human help – an autonomous vehicle. In peacetime, these self-driving vehicles could deliver humanitarian aid, or be used on long, tedious runs where boredom could make human drivers careless. In wartime, these robots could drive trucks in convoys vulnerable to enemy attack or ambulances returning wounded for care. These robots would rely on **neural networks** – software designed to mimic the operation of a human brain – trained to pilot the vehicle, as well as GPS, an array of sensors, and digital cameras to help the robot locate its position, evaluate its immediate environment, and drive correctly. Google, Tesla, and other companies around the world have adapted much of these technologies for their own experiments with autonomous cars and trucks.

Computer Simulations

As noted earlier a computer simulation uses software (and sometimes hardware) to imitate the behavior of a process or system over time, given certain conditions. During World War II, the Manhattan Project gave rise to the first computer simulation, the process of nuclear detonation. Since then, defense forces around the world have used computer simulations to model vehicle designs, military strategy, and many other subjects.

Effectively training soldiers for combat involves giving them an opportunity to experience the time spent in complicated and expensive military vehicles. However, live training inside battle tanks, aircraft, and ships can be dangerous and extremely

Figure 2-17 Remote-controlled robots, called PackBots, were used in Operation Iraqi Freedom to crawl through buildings and look for signs of ambush.

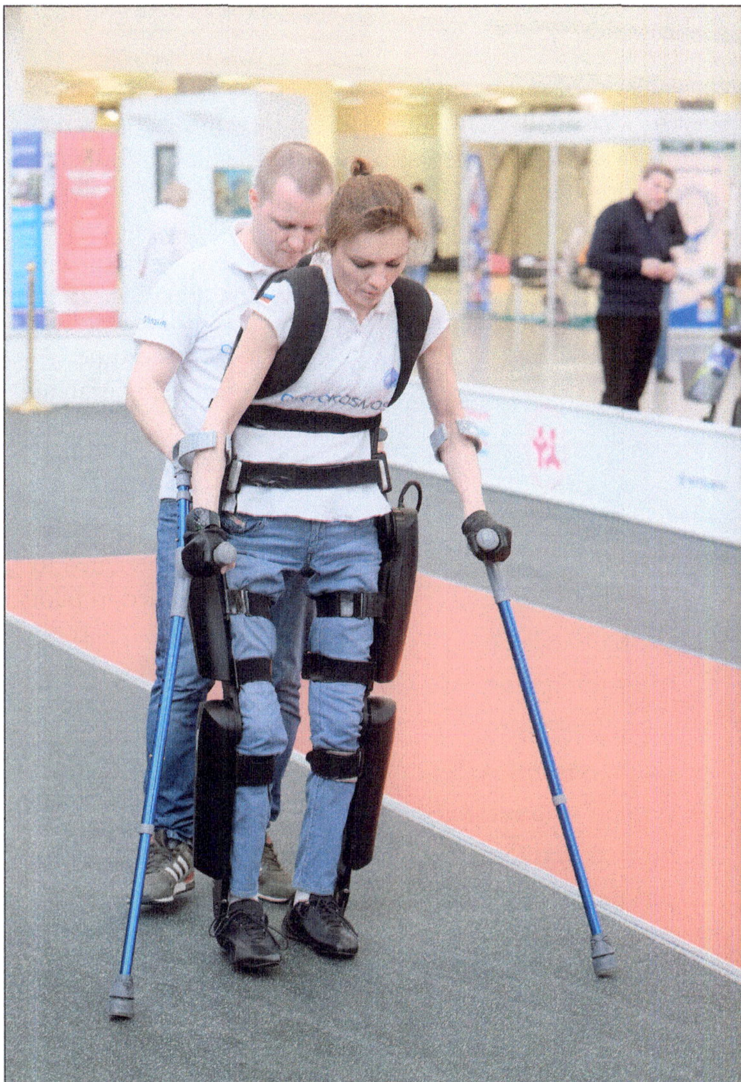

Figure 2-18 Demonstration of an exoskeleton at an exhibition of the rehabilitation equipment for disabled people.

expensive. Computer simulation, on the other hand, can provide many of the same benefits as live training without the associated risks and costs. The primary goal of the computer simulations used by the military is to provide a realistic representation of battle conditions, so that soldiers trained by simulation can apply their experience to an actual battlefield.

Typically, a military training simulation involves modeling the experience of being inside a tank, helicopter, jet fighter, or naval vessel. A single computer simulates each military vehicle. By connecting two or more computer simulators, a soldier training in a tank simulator in California can fight against a soldier training in an Apache helicopter simulator in Connecticut. With thousands of soldiers participating from computer simulators, entire battles can be replicated.

Using computers for training simulations has several benefits. First, soldiers can practice a scenario repeatedly and learn from mistakes without additional cost or danger. Further, the computer simulator records every event in sequence, so that supervisors can review and replay portions of the exercise to offer feedback and analysis. Finally, with many simulators a supervisor can change variables in real time – for example, by adding a sandstorm to a simulated battlefield – to test soldier's reactions and response time. The realism of a simulation, however, depends on the accuracy of the assumptions provided by experts and the algorithms coded by programmers. If the assumptions and algorithms are incorrect, the simulation itself may create an unrealistic situation, which has little value as a training exercise.

As you will learn in future chapters, computer simulation is a tool widely used in many different fields beyond education and training. Vehicle designers use computer simulation to test their concepts. Architects use computer simulation to model different room designs and orientations for customers. In medicine, computer simulations model the behavior of diseases or how a given disease can spread within a human population. Scientists often use simulations to prepare forecasts, model storm behavior, or analyze other environmental developments. And in film, computer simulation forms the basis for modern computer animation.

Cyber Command

Cyberspace is the global environment within which computers and other electronic devices communicate with each other. Although the Internet is a part of it, cyberspace is a much larger set of networks. And cyberspace continues to grow as computer applications affect more and more of our work and personal lives. Rogue groups and some nations view cyberspace as a new opportunity for spying, threatening, intimidating, or even controlling their opponents. For example, many nations use networked computer systems to manage their power distribution grids. Someone could attack that part of the global cyberspace to disrupt the flow of electricity. In America, the United States Cyber Command is an inter-service agency that coordinates cyber defense and cyber response activities by the Army, Navy, Air Force, Marines, and Coast Guard. Established in 2009, Cyber Command's mission is to "ensure US/Allied freedom of action in cyberspace and deny the same to our adversaries."

CONCLUSION

In this chapter, you learned how computers have changed the electoral process. You discovered how key government branches and agencies, such as the United States Postal Service, Census Bureau, and Internal Revenue Service, use computers to streamline their processes and provide better service to citizens. You also learned how law enforcement uses computers and technology to maintain databases to track evidence and criminal records, enforce traffic laws, communicate information about missing children quickly, and incorporate GPS technology into cellular phones to ensure a quick response to a 911 emergency call. After reviewing how computers are used to help ensure homeland security by tracking visitors to the country, you also learned about the government's use of Web-based collaborative tools to share information in a crisis and how computer vision systems help to protect the country's borders. You learned that the military has been in the forefront of computer research, with innovations such as GPS, remote-controlled drones, remote-controlled robots, autonomous vehicles, and computer simulation. You learned about cyberspace and the United States Cyber Command.

Key Terms

biometric identifiers
chain of custody
computer models
computer simulations
cyberspace
direct recording electronic (DRE) machines
drone/unmanned aerial vehicle (UAV)
e-File
Emergency management systems
Enhanced 911 (e-911)
Global Positioning System (GPS)
Internet-based voting systems
neural networks
online voting systems
optical character recognition system (OCR)
optical mark recognition systems
political polling
punch card system
red-light camera systems
tax preparation software

Chapter Review

Multiple Choice

Select the best answer.

1. Critics of the validity of online polls note that the polls _____.
   (a) cannot incorporate graphic, audio, or video clips
   (b) collect only voter responses without any demographic information
   (c) gather input from a group limited to those with computer access
   (d) all of the above

2. When sorting mail, the USPS uses a(n) _____, which relies on artificial intelligence to recognize patterns and read handwritten, typed, or computer-printed characters from documents and translate the images into a form a computer can process.
   (a) optical mark recognition (OMR) systems
   (b) magnetic-ink character recognition (MICR) systems
   (c) optical character recognition (OCR) systems
   (d) bar code scanning (BCS) systems

3. The Internal Revenue Service (IRS) Web site provides taxpayers with all of the following assistance *EXCEPT* _____.
   (a) federal tax codes and forms in PDF format
   (b) analysis of forms for errors or discrepancies
   (c) the address of a local IRS office
   (d) tax calculators to determine what is owed

4. The _____ was established to help gun dealers perform personal history checks on prospective buyers to ensure that convicted felons cannot buy guns.
   (a) Combined DNA Index System (CODIS)
   (b) National Instant Criminal Background Check System (NICS)
   (c) Automated Fingerprint Identification System (AFIS)
   (d) National Crime Information Center (NCIC) database

5. A key element of red-light camera systems is a trigger, which is a _____.
   (a) digital camera mounted on a light standard
   (b) computer database that stores information on traffic violators
   (c) stylus that adds pertinent information to the digital photo
   (d) length of electrical wire buried just under the asphalt

6. The _____ is a missing child alert system, created to issue an immediate alert to help recover missing or abducted children.
   (a) Amber Alert system
   (b) LoJack system
   (c) Emergency Broadcast System (EBS)
   (d) Automatic Number Identifier (ANI) system

7. The core of the U.S. VISIT system is a database of _____, such as digital fingerprints or iris or retinal scans.
   (a) bar codes
   (b) global positioning systems
   (c) artificial intelligence
   (d) biometric identifiers

8. New passports issued to U.S. citizens contain _____ which holds, among other things, personal data about the passport holder.
   (a) a bar code
   (b) infrared sensors
   (c) an RFID chip
   (d) digital fingerprints

9. _____ is software designed to mimic the operation of a human brain.
   (a) expert system
   (b) GPS
   (c) neural network
   (d) Roomba

10. Which of the following is NOT a part of cyberspace?.
    (a) Internet
    (b) WiFi
    (c) corporate intranet
    (d) artificial intelligence (AI)

Computers in Medicine 3

The disciplines of medicine and science involve similar steps, such as making an assessment of the cause of an occurrence — whether a new disease or a hole in the ozone layer — and then collecting and analyzing data to understand better why that occurrence happened. After confirming the reason for the occurrence, a course of action typically is recommended. In medicine, the recommendation might involve a physician telling a patient to exercise and take a prescription drug for a few weeks.

Over the last few decades, computer technology has transformed the discipline of medicine — completely altering the way data is collected, analyzed, communicated, and stored. In this chapter, you will learn more about the use of computers in medicine to maintain patient histories and manage the medical practice, as well as to improve patient diagnosis and monitoring. After looking at technology in the operating room and seeing how telemedicine is making health care available at a distance, you will learn how computers are used in medical research and training. Finally, you review the problem of how to assess the credibility of medical Web sites.

COMPUTERS IN MEDICINE

When you visit your physician for a routine examination, he or she is likely to greet you carrying a laptop or tablet computer, along with a stethoscope. As you review your medical history and the reason for the current visit, the physician may enter notes into a software application. After your visit, the physician might print and hand you a sheet listing prescription information together with any special instructions, along with an e-mail address you can use to send any questions you might have.

In today's technology-rich field of medicine, the doctor's office and hospital are filled with computers, printers, and other technology devices. This explosion of computer usage in the world of health care often is referred to as **medical informatics** – the application of computers, communications, and information technology to all fields of medicine, including medical care, medical education, and medical research. Using computers in medicine and health care helps doctors more effectively manage their practices. Both doctors and patients can use computers to collect and interpret data, and make subsequent actions as a result. For example, physicians and pharmacists can access online drug databases to learn more about possible side effects of a new prescription drug or view results from the latest clinical trials. Patients can access Web sites to learn more about health and wellness or find out how to cope with an illness. Furthermore, e-mail has completely changed communications among physicians and between physicians and their patients, making doctors accessible at any time, even from miles away.

Maintaining Patient History

One of the biggest challenges of any medical practice or hospital is keeping accurate and up-to-date patient records. For years, health care professionals relied on paper-based patient records to track patient visits, prescriptions, medical history, and recommended follow-up care. With paper-based patient records, your medical history evolved as a series of written notes from a physician, along with data, such as laboratory test results.

As medicine became increasingly advanced and specialized, however, the use of the paper-based record became progressively more inefficient. First, a patient record only can be at one place at one time. If a doctor takes the patient records to review with a specialist, a lab technician does not have access to the records that might alert her to possible adverse reactions to certain tests. Paper-based patient charts also have to be pulled and re-filed every time a phone message, lab report, or accounting update needs to be documented. In many cases, the result of having charts handled by many different people may be misplaced medical records.

Computers can help change this slow, costly, and error-prone part of the medical process into a relatively streamlined procedure. An **electronic health record (EHR)** is a computer-based record of a person's health status and medical care over time. It allows all data on a patient to be stored in one place (Figure 3-1). An EHR includes a patient's medical history, prescriptions, and health insurance information. Because it is electronic, it also can include digital X rays, video of recent surgery, or recorded notes from the physician. All EHR records are entered, stored, and maintained using documentation management software designed for the health care industry. Starting in 2014, Medicare and Medicaid require US hospitals and doctors to use EHR,

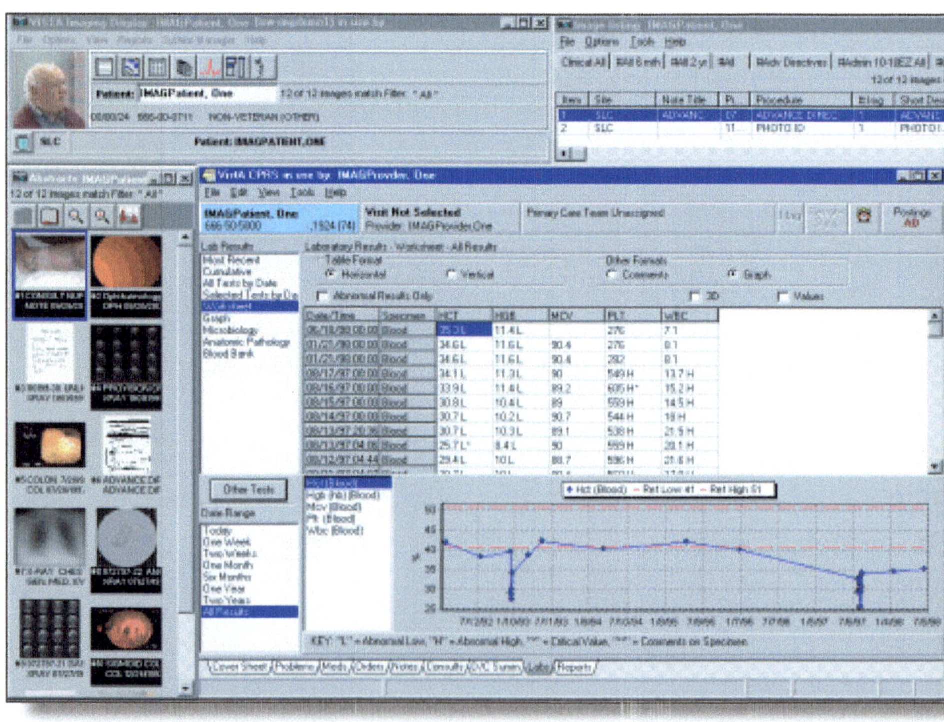

Figure 3-1 Electronic health record (EHR).

so it will become common for patients of all ages to have an EHR.

If you are the patient, the experience of visiting a physician using an EHR system is apparent as soon as you walk into the waiting room. Instead of photocopying an insurance card, the receptionist scans your insurance card, along with the new patient datasheet that forms the basis of your chart. Examination rooms include computers, conveniently positioned so that both you and the doctor can view and discuss your chart and medical history. The physician also can pull up any other pertinent documents, such as X rays or referral-letters that have already been scanned and stored in the practice's main database. If your visit involves lab work, the physician can connect to the computer system at the lab to pull up your results.

If the physician prescribes a new medication, the EHR system automatically generates a list of potential drug interactions. After a physician enters the prescription data, the EHR system can calculate drug dosage based on your weight, write the prescription, and print it, so you can pick it up as you leave the office. The EHR system also generates a sheet that you can take home regarding your diagnosis and any special instructions – a huge help in keeping you and other patients safe.

A growing number of consumers are using applications offered by insurance (ex., Blue Cross/Blue Shield) or commercial firms (ex., Microsoft HealthVault) to create and maintain their own **personal health record (PHR)**, independent from their physician's or hospital's EHR. Useful as a check on a patient's EHR record, these applications can also help organize complex medical histories as well as keep track of a family's medical records and stats (Figure 3-2).

Managing the Medical Practice

Running a medical practice involves much more than providing health care to patients; it also involves billing, handling insurance claims, scheduling, and more. An **electronic medical record (EMR)** system helps a physician address some of these needs. The physician can sit at the com-puter and enter all information into the chart during the examination. The EMR then links the information with the appropriate codes for the billing department. Using the EMR system cuts out the time-consuming process of dictation, transcription, and coding for billing and insurance claims. The claims manager can also use the already coded records from the EMR system to file claims electronically.

In addition to EMR, billing, and insurance systems, physicians also use scheduling systems to schedule patient appointments and automatically print out reminder cards to mail to patients. Some physicians rely on laptop or tablet computer software that permits mobile input of new patient chart data, review of clinical records, and review and entry of schedules, patient demographics, procedure or diagnosis codes, billing, and more. The technology frees the medical practitioner from paper-based documentation and the need to spend time checking in with the office or running between locations to get vital information. Reporting is another key element in medical practice management software. Reports generated from the medical practice management software can help the physician monitor patient outcomes over time; other reports can help billing and insurance managers track completed or overdue payments.

Finally, as part of the on-going effort to control medical costs and improve service, many health care providers now offer their customers a **patient portal**. This is a secure website that gives patient access to some

Figure 3-2 Personal health record formatted for use on a tablet computer.

medical records and test results, as well as request appointments or prescription refills, and email their doctor. Some portals go beyond this to offer patients a variety of wellness information and health monitoring tools, such as a body mass index calculator or food diary.

Improving Patient Diagnosis and Monitoring

Computers have revolutionized patient diagnosis, making available new tools and machines to allow for the capture and analysis of patient data to help determine the source of a health problem. Computers also are at the heart of improved patient monitoring, where numerous new developments help ensure a patient's vital statistics can be monitored continuously, either in the hospital or at home.

CLINICAL DATA CAPTURE AND MEDICAL IMAGING Today, many diagnostic tools widely used in medicine rely on computer technology to provide accurate and detailed clinical data to allow physicians to make a sound diagnosis. Further, by capturing their observations from the patient digitally, these tools make it easy to store results in an EHR system, and to share this data with other physicians for consultation. Table 3-1 describes several of these tools. For example, computers allow for the automatic capture of the electrical activity of the heart and the brain. **Electrocardiograms (EKGs)** are used to record the electrical activity of the heart, show any abnormal rhythms, or detect heart muscle damage. The systems typically consist of a screen to monitor the heart functions (Figure 3-3a), along with a printer

TABLE 3-1 Medical Tests that Use Computer Technology

DIAGNOSTIC TEST	*DESCRIPTION*
Electrocardiogram (EKG)	A test that records the electrical activity of the heart, shows abnormal rhythms, and detects heart muscle damage.
CT scan	Computed tomography is an imaging test in which many X rays are taken of a part of the body from different angles. A computer combines these images to produce cross-sectional pictures of internal organs.
Magnetic resonance imaging (MRI)	A method of taking pictures of the inside of the body. Instead of using X rays, MRI uses a powerful magnet and transmits radio waves through the body; the images appear on a computer screen as well as on film. Like X rays, the procedure is physically painless, but some people find it psychologically uncomfortable to be inside the MRI machine.
Ultrasound	A method of gathering images using reflected sound waves to produce a picture of organs and other structures inside the body. During an ultrasound test, a small handheld instrument called a transducer (that emits and detects high-pitched sounds beyond the range of human hearing) is passed back and forth over the area of the body being examined. A computer analyzes and converts the reflected sound waves into a picture on a video monitor. The images produced by ultrasound are called a sonogram, echogram, or scan. Pictures or videos of the ultrasound images may be saved for a permanent record.
Electroencephalography (EEG)	A method to record the electrical activity of the brain. Sensors (electrodes) are attached to the head and connected by wires to a computer. The computer records the brain's electrical activity on paper as wavy lines. Certain brain abnormalities can be detected by observing changes in the normal pattern of the brain's electrical activity.
Digital X-rays	A method of gathering images that uses a sensor placed next to the X-ray site. Within seconds, the X-ray is displayed in sharp, vivid detail on a computer screen. Because of this short exposure time, the amount of X-ray radiation is reduced by as much as 90 percent. Once the X-ray image is on the computer, it can be enhanced for a more precise diagnosis, saved for later use, or sent to insurance companies or specialists, as needed.

Today, many diagnostic tests and tools use computer technology to provide accurate and detailed clinical data.

for obtaining hard copy results. EKG systems may also contain databases to archive patient results.

Other computer devices used in the diagnostic process include machines focused on obtaining medical images. Using **ultrasound**, for example, a computer analyzes sound waves reflected back from structures in the body (Figure 3-3b). **Magnetic resonance imaging (MRI)** provides a way to take images inside the body by using a powerful magnet and transmitting radio waves through the body (Figure 3-3c). The resulting images appear on a computer screen for viewing by the physician. Even the often-used X ray has benefited from advances in computer technology, which allow a **digital X-ray** to be taken. Using a digital X ray means a health care professional does not have to wait for the film to be developed; instead, the physician or radiologist can look at an image as it is being taken and make an immediate diagnosis (Figure 3-3d). Moreover, digital x-rays use lower radiation dosages and the images can be enhanced to reveal better details such as soft tissues.

Computed tomography (CT) can be used for "whole body scanning," a technique for capturing a digital picture of the patient's entire body in one session. Considered somewhat controversial by the FDA (which does not certify or approve technologies associated with whole body scans) and some in the medical profession, this type of scan can provide a virtual diagnostic view inside the patient without using surgery or other invasive means to make a diagnosis. Most of the controversy does not surround the technology itself, but rather the benefits and its role in effective detection of disease. In some cases, abnormalities detected are not life-threatening yet create undue stress and concern for the patient.

As technology continues to advance, even more unique diagnostic tools are available to health care professionals. For example, a pill-sized camera that patients swallow allows doctors to travel virtually through a patient's small intestine to detect ulcers and tumors. More effective than CT scans or X rays, and much less invasive than previously available diagnostic tests, the pill camera can allow doctors to find and repair problem areas before the patient experiences major problems.

COMPUTER-AIDED DETECTION **Computer-aided detection (CAD)**, sometimes called computer-aided diagnosis, is the use of computer programs designed to aid health care professionals with interpreting medical images. These programs combine digital imaging capabilities with artificial intelligence tools such as neural networks or expert systems (see Morley, Chapter 8).

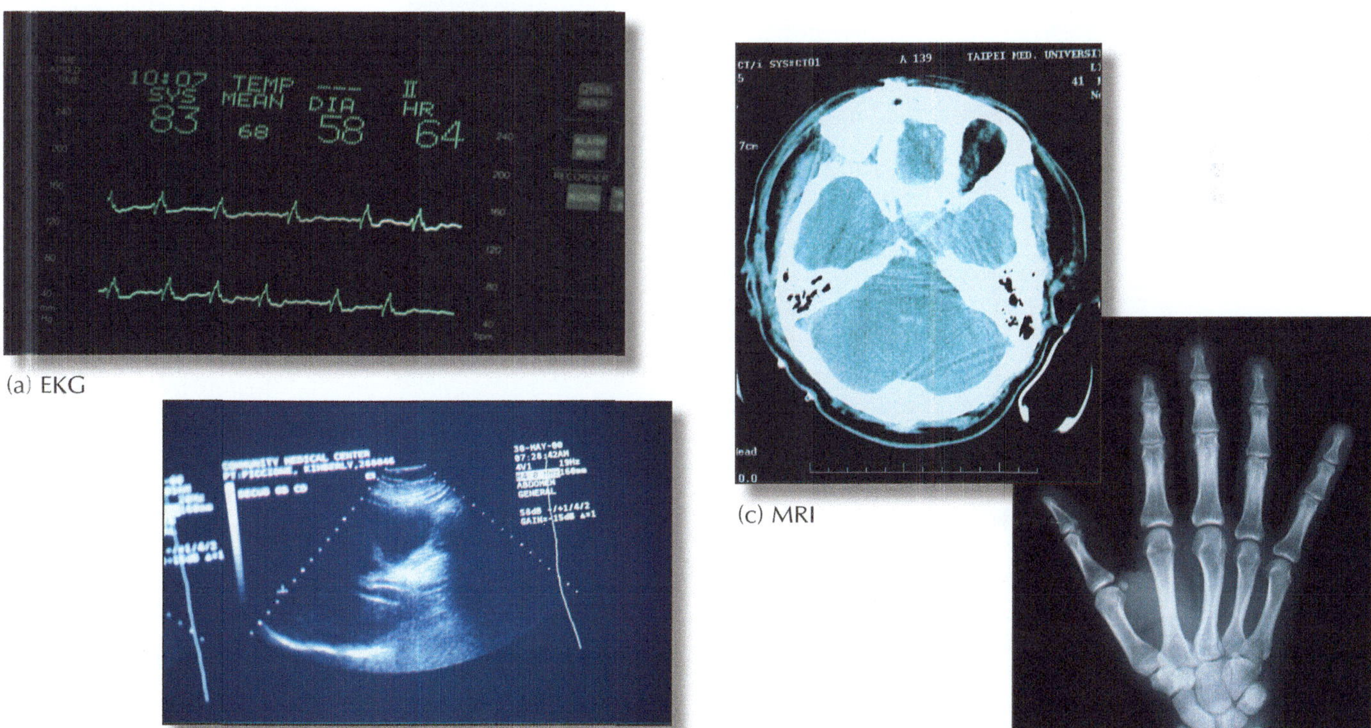

(a) EKG

(b) Ultrasound

(c) MRI

(d) Digital X ray

Figure 3-3 In the diagnostic process, computers allow for the capture of clinical data, such as the electrical activity of the heart and the brain or views of bones, tissue, and other structures.

A typical application is examining a patient's digital imagery for a tumor (Figure 3-4).

Medical images, such as MRIs or even photos, are difficult to analyze because they contain structures without well-defined edges or corners. To simplify the process, a CAD system can help physicians better detect irregularities by highlighting those features in color, or by comparing the newest image with a previous one.

As a patient, you might worry that a computer is performing the work of the doctor, all the while knowing computer systems are susceptible to errors resulting from programming issues or outright failure. It is important to recognize that while CAD systems are designed to improve the process and outcome of clinical decision making, they cannot replace or overrule a physician's judgment or a physician's diagnosis.

COMPUTER-AIDED THERAPY When faced with a complex disease such as cancer, it has often been challenging for patient and doctors to identify the right treatment with the best chance of success. In response, hospitals like the MD Anderson Cancer Center are starting to use **IBM Watson**, a computer technology trained in natural language understanding and data analysis, to help oncology clinicians find, monitor, and adjust the best therapy. Watson does this by integrating the patient's MHR and other information with a massive data warehouse of global laboratory results and research outcomes. The goal is to offer each patient a customized therapy plan for battling their cancer.

ACCESSING PHARMACEUTICAL AND MEDICAL INFORMATION Every day, physicians must make informed decisions on a wide range of prescription drugs and other pharmaceuticals, based on disease treatment options, drug interactions, and drug cost. In the past, physicians relied on books, such as the *Physician's Desk Reference* (PDR), to research specific prescriptions. The printed materials, however, often were out of date as soon as they were printed.

Today, much of this content is available on the Web, which provides an up-to-date and more easily searchable form of the content in the book volumes. For example, all of the content in the *Physician's Desk Reference* now is available online at physician.pdr.net. Doctors and nurses can use the Web site to decide what to prescribe based on illness, patient history, drug cost, and drug characteristics – including drug interactions and side effects. The Web site also includes a tool to search for possible drug interactions and the latest news on drugs recently approved by the Food and Drug Administration (FDA). A simplified version of this website is available as an app for mobile devices.

Just as technology has made pharmacy databases more available, it also has made medical research and medical databases from a number of reliable, reputable sources more accessible, as shown in Table 3-2. The MEDLINEplus Web site, for example, provides a database of references and abstracts from the world's largest medical library,

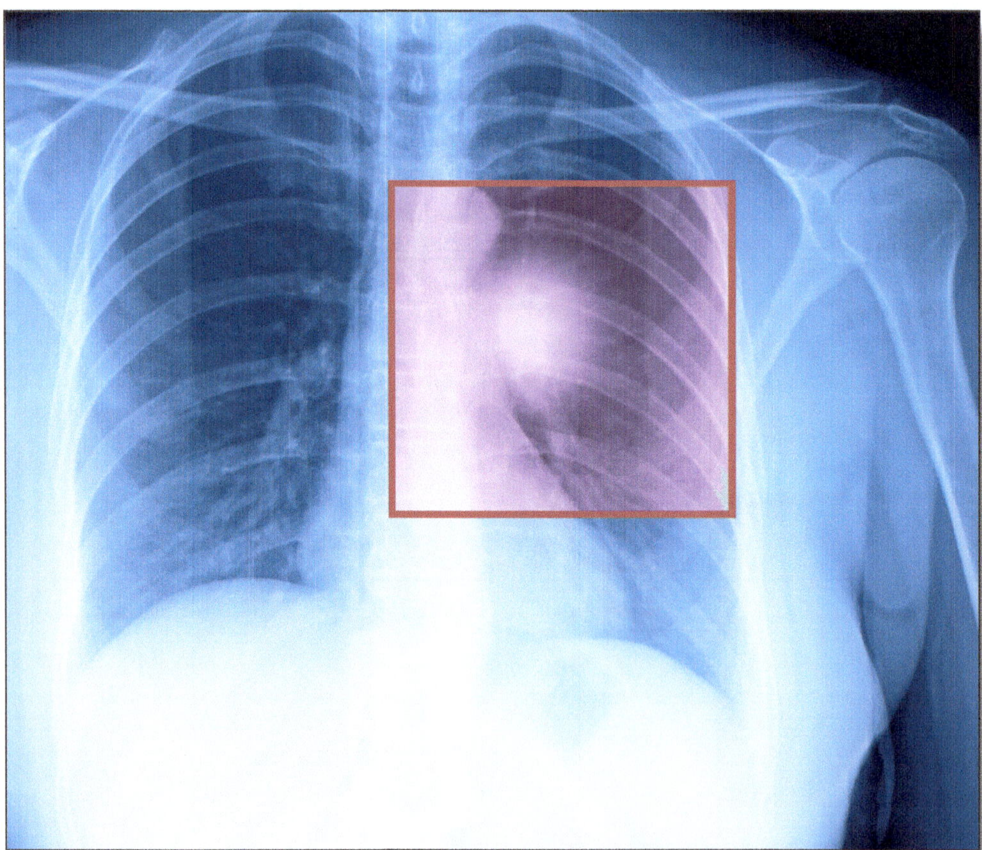

Figure 3-4 Computer-aided detection of lung cancer.

TABLE 3-2 Some Popular Web Sites for Medical Information

WEB SITE	ADDRESS	DESCRIPTION
PDR.Net	physician.pdr.net	Provides an online, searchable database of drug information and potential drug interactions, along with news and information on recent approvals of new drugs
MEDLINEplus	nlm.nih.gov/medlineplus	Provides a database of references and abstracts from the world's largest medical library, the National Library of Medicine. The Web site provides information on over 950 diseases and conditions, lists of hospitals and physicians, a medical encyclopedia and a medical dictionary, and links to thousands of clinical trials
TOXNET	toxnet.nlm.nih.gov	Provides several integrated toxicology and environmental health databases, information on hazardous substances, how to handle human exposure, waste disposal, and more
Centers for Disease Control and Prevention	www.cdc.gov	Provides a wide range of information on new and existing diseases; traveler's health information on specific destinations; health data; and news for physicians and patients
healthfinder	healthfinder.gov	Provides patient-friendly information from the Department of Health and Human Services, covering prevention and wellness, diseases and conditions, alternative medicine, and more
OncoLink	oncolink.org	Provides content focused on helping cancer patients, families, and health care professionals get accurate information on cancer causes, treatments, and coping resources
WebMD	webmd.com	Provides easy-to-understand information on a wide range of health, wellness, and nutrition information, along with tools for managing your health and supporting those with illnesses

Medical Web sites can be an excellent source of information for physicians and patients alike.

the National Library of Medicine. Other Web sites are focused on specific areas of medical practice. OncoLink, for instance, is focused on cancer treatment.

Patients also can use the Web to become better informed about their illnesses – whether to verify what doctors tell them regarding a course of treatment or prescription drugs, to educate themselves before they go to the doctor so they know what to ask, or to find others experiencing the same illnesses in chat rooms. Web sites, such as WebMD and MedlinePlus, provide easy-to-understand information so that patients and their families can better understand and cope with an illness.

HOSPITAL PATIENT MONITORING AND CARE Computers also provide new tools to help monitor patients after diagnosis, during surgery, and throughout the course of treatment. For example, after a patient has a stroke, slight changes in basic vital signs can cause long-term damage. To ensure continuous, real-time monitoring, hospitals can replace the labor-intensive process of monitoring patients' vital signs with sophisticated mobile monitors. The monitors measure heart rate, blood pressure, temperature, respiration, and blood oxygen levels, displaying the results on a screen and sounding an alarm if any levels go outside the normal range. The data from the monitors also is stored in a computer database for later analysis.

In the emergency room, operating room, and recovery area, one of the most useful monitors is the **pulse oximeter**, which is used to monitor a patient's blood oxygen levels and pulse rate (Figure 3-5). The pulse oximeter consists of a probe attached to the patient's finger or earlobe, which is linked to a computer that displays blood oxygen saturation and heart rate.

Other computer applications are making their way into hospital patient rooms. To facilitate communication, staff can use hand-held or bed-mounted language translators. To avoid medication errors, many patients receive their prescribed drugs from a **computerized provider order entry (COPE) system**, which also uses barcodes to ensure that the right patient gets the right medicine in the correct dosage. Improved sensors allow computerized dosage pumps to administer IV medications more accurately. To battle hospital-acquired

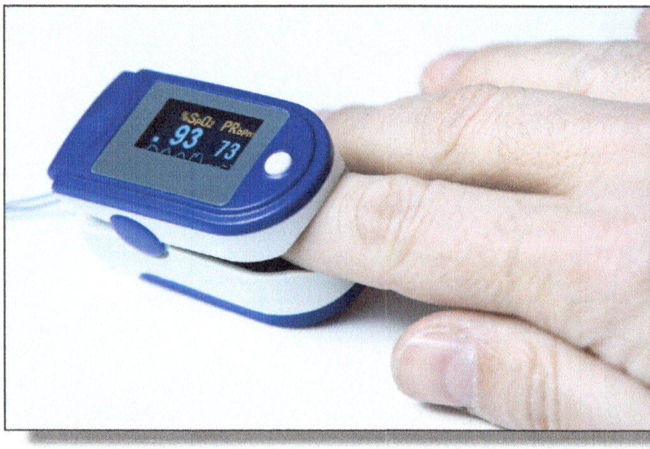

Figure 3-5 Pulse oximeters are used to continuously monitor a patient's blood oxygen levels and pulse rate. Handheld devices can be equipped with pulse oximeter software and a probe to provide a fully functional and highly portable pulse oximeter.

infections, computer-controlled air handlers disinfect and scrub the air, while ultraviolet disinfectors sterilize each patient's room after discharge (Figure 3-6).

Once a patient leaves the hospital, monitoring may continue. For example, it may be necessary for cardiac (heart) patients to use a **Holter monitor**, a portable pocket-sized EKG that continuously records the heart's electrical activity for a period of 24 to 48 hours (Figure 3-7). Other computerized tools serve diabetes patients, who have used finger prick tests for years to monitor and control their blood sugar levels. Some of these testing meters now integrate with monitoring apps on mobile phones, offering greater flexibility for patients as well as better record-keeping and data sharing with physicians. Patients with severe diabetes may use a continuous glucose monitor (CGM), a tiny sensor embedded under the patient's skin which can either alert the patient via a smartphone app, or instruct a small insulin pump carried by the patient to administer a certain dose (Figure 3-8). Tiny programmable computers also manage operation of implanted pacemakers, defibrillators, hearing aids, and neurostimulators.

Sometimes discharged patients require physical therapy. The motion-capture systems pioneered by film and video game industries (see Chapter 5) are being used to help rehab patients, ex., recovering stroke victims, improve their physical motion. The data captured by this technology, ex., movement time or smoothness, help both patient and medical professional understand what needs improvement and thus better target rehabilitation therapy (Figure 3-9). Also, playing specialized video games can help patients improve motor functions and eye-hand coordination.

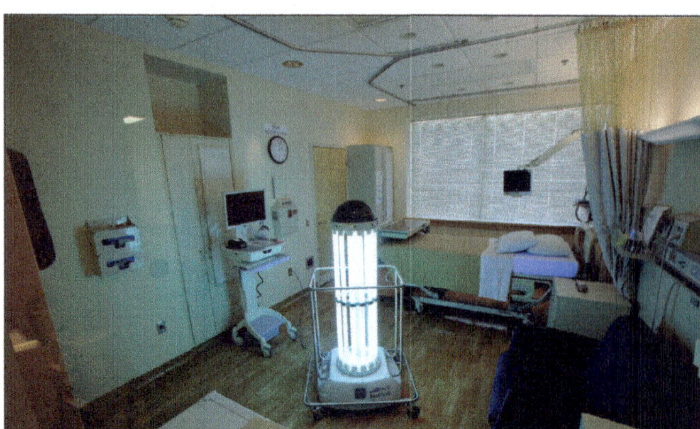

Figure 3-6 Ultraviolet disinfecting robot sterilizing a patient room.

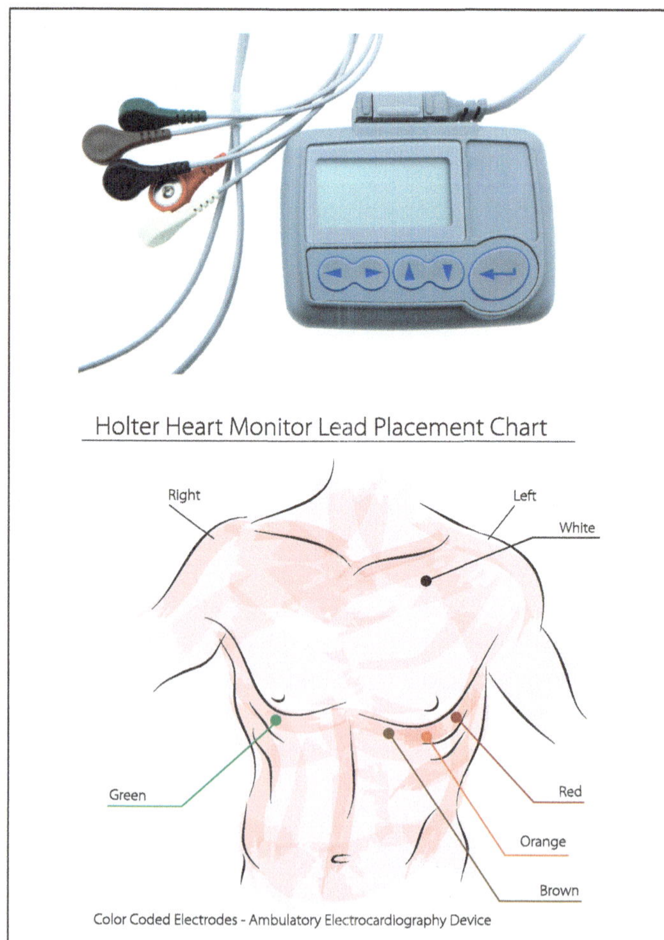

Figure 3-7 Holter heart monitor and chart showing placement of sensors on a patient.

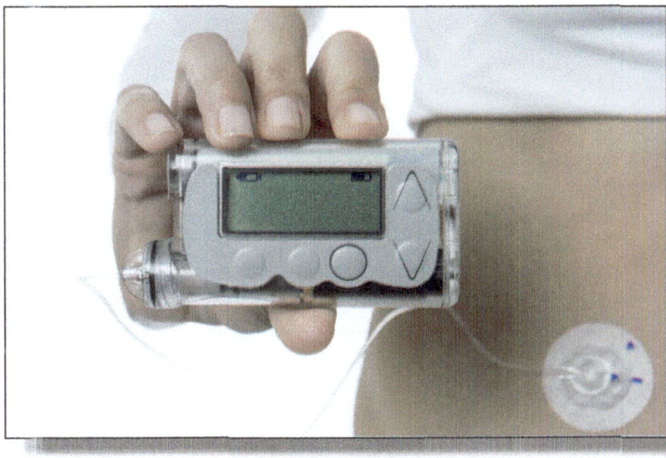

Figure 3-8 A portable insulin pump.

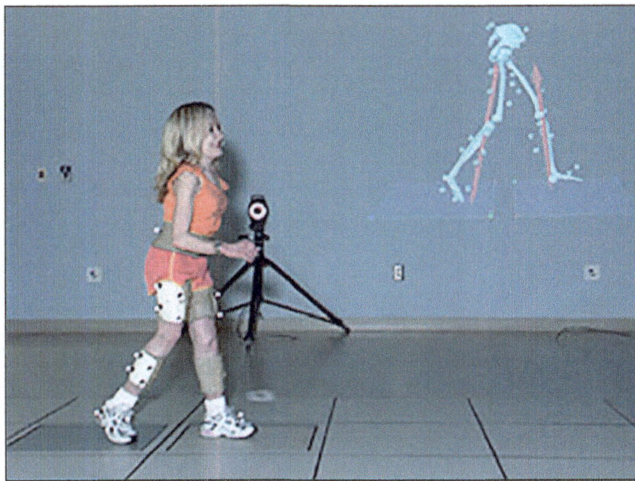

Figure 3-9 Motion capture for physical therapy.

Technology in the Operating Room

Along with the diagnostic, monitoring, and therapy tools already described, the operating room of any hospital relies on numerous technological advances to ensure the highest quality of patient care. **Computer-aided surgery (CAS)** involves the use of computers and other technologies to assist a surgeon at all points in the process, including pre-operative strategy, surgical navigation (ex., tumor location), and the surgical procedure itself. The goals of CAS are to minimize invasion of the patient's body and to reduce the trauma associated with surgery, thereby speeding patient recovery.

For example, with **image-guided surgery** surgeons can use preoperative MRIs, CT scans, and other images to locate in three dimensions target tissues or to avoid hazardous parts in a surgical area (Figure 3-10). In very delicate surgery, such as neurosurgery on the brain, such techniques allow for less invasive and shorter procedures and reduce the risk that regions of the brain might be compromised. The software can even take into account possible changes in the shape of tissues during the operation (ex., swelling) and distort the images accordingly. Some systems can also project onto the patient's body imagery of the target, and change the projection in real time.

Endoscopy is a medical procedure in which a doctor looks inside a patient using a computerized, fiber-optic device called an endoscope. During the procedure, the physician watches a video screen while maneuvering the endoscope that supplies the images. In addition to a tiny camera and strong light, the end of the device often has a cutting tool used to perform minor surgery, such as removing polyps. **Keyhole surgery** is the use of endoscopes and other small, flexible, computer-assisted tools to operate on patients without major incisions (Figure 3-11). This can speed patient recovery and so reduce costs.

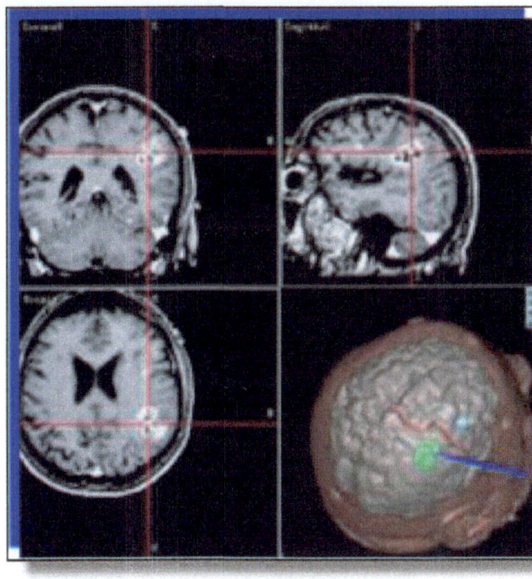

Figure 3-10 Image-guided neurosurgery.

Another example of CAS are **robotically-assisted surgery (RAS)** devices, which permit the surgeon to maneuver and use a great variety of surgical instruments through one or more tiny incisions (Figure 3-12). Still other CAS systems involve the use of robots to help perform very delicate procedures. For example, a surgeon might sit at a computer console and use table-mounted robotic arms to repair cardiac valves.

Hospitals also use **operating room management systems**. These programs can schedule surgeries, track tissue and device implants, support anesthesia care, and track the use of surgical instruments, sponges, and other materials employed in the OR. They also can share data with the patient's electronic health record (EHR).

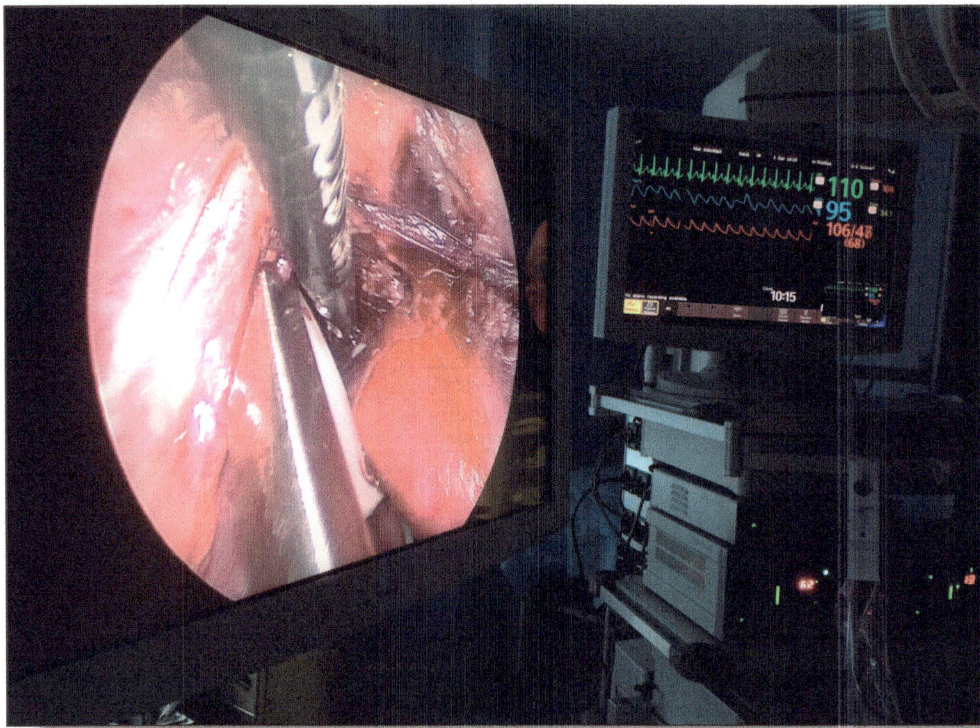

Figure 3-11 Keyhole surgery using endoscopy.

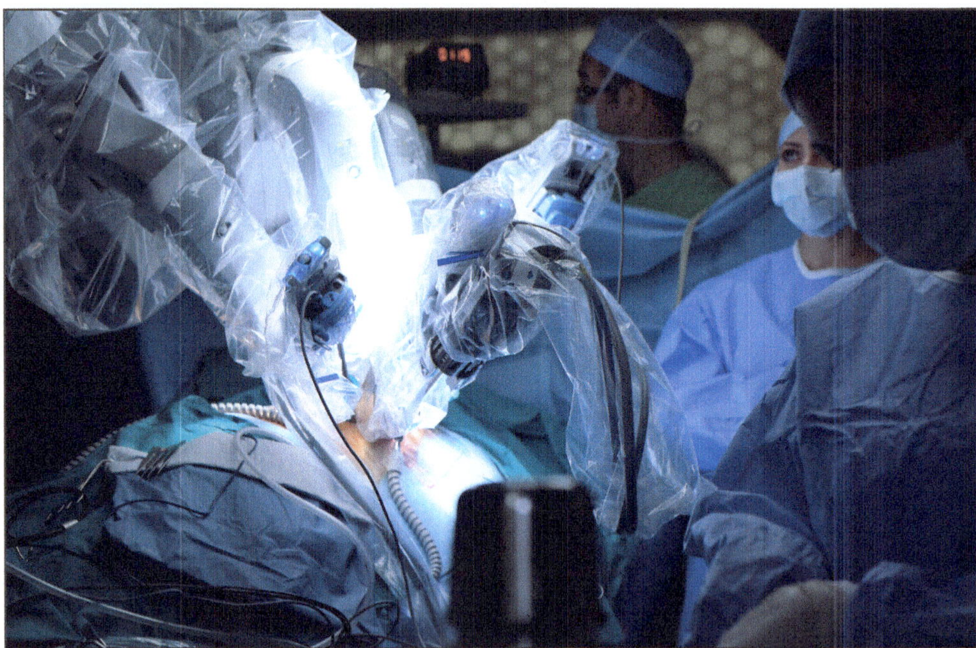

Figure 3-12 Robotically-assisted surgery.

Telemedicine and Remote Surgery

Imagine if a surgeon could be transported instantly from a hospital to a rural area, a battlefield, or an accident site. This scenario is becoming a reality with telemedicine and remote surgery. **Telemedicine** is the use of advanced computer technology and telecommunications to provide health care remotely. Telemedicine makes it possible for doctors and nurses to serve patients at a distance. Telemedicine also allows health care professionals to consult with each other and work together on cases, regardless of where the patients, medical professionals, and relevant clinical data are located. With telemedicine, physicians can use live Internet and videoconferencing technologies to share digitized images such as X-rays, CT scans, and EKGs (Figure 3-13). Because these images can be electronically stored and transmitted worldwide by computer, mobile clinics can go to remote areas to give examinations and take digital X-rays, which can be transmitted back to the main hospital for immediate diagnosis.

One of the most valuable uses of telemedicine is that it allows doctors in remote areas, such as rural locations or a battlefield, to consult with specialists at medical centers. For example, in a recent application of telemedicine, physicians in Virginia assisted with the anesthesia in a gall bladder surgery performed on a patient in Ecuador. The telemedicine was made possible by a satellite link from a clinic in Ecuador to an anesthesiologist in Virginia, who watched the patient's vital signs on her computer screen while communicating with the anesthesiologist who was in the operating room.

Still other telemedicine applications involve Internet-based remote monitoring systems for patients with chronic illnesses. These patients can use standard Internet connections and online forms to submit measurement results, such as blood pressure, body weight, or blood sugar levels, along with digital photos of problem areas, such as burns or other wounds. A patient can avoid numerous trips to the hospital, but the doctor or nurse still can track the patient's progress daily.

Remote surgery, also called telesurgery, allows a surgeon to use a RAS device in a patient location that is distant, or hard-to-reach, or in a combat zone, or exposed to very dangerous disease. Although the potential of remote surgery is great, many problems have blocked significant use, such as international agreement on standards for telesurgery equipment, protocols, and training.

Medical Research and Training

Computer systems also contribute to the learning process in the field of medicine – whether training students on new procedures or helping to recognize patterns of disease within a city or around the world.

RECOGNIZING PATTERNS OF DISEASE In our incredibly mobile world, disease can travel quickly from one city or country to another. **Epidemiology** is concerned with the distribution, cause, and control of disease across time and geography in human populations. Today, thanks to computer technology, data regarding a specific disease outbreak can be collected into a database. Computers can process and analyze this vast quantity of data to look for infected persons and find patterns in the spread of the disease. This activity is critical for breaking the chain of disease transmission and stopping an epidemic.

One such tool is Epi Info, a free, public-domain statistical program developed by the US Centers for Disease Control and Prevention (CDC) (Figure 3-14). Over 180 countries use this tool to create health surveys, enter data, and run analyses. Epi Info can also accept **add-ins** (software accessories) customized for particular diseases, such as the Viral Hemorrhagic Fever add-in developed for West African Ebola.

Larger cities and health centers are developing computer systems to recognize patterns of disease associated with outbreaks or epidemics. For example, since 2001 The New York City Syndromic Surveillance System has monitored emergency room visits to the city's many hospitals. The system tracks both seasonal increases of disease (ex., influenza) and sudden outbreaks from natural or human causes. Each day, the system analyzes more than 50,000 pieces of data, including calls, emergency room visits, and drugstore

Figure 3-13 Physicians can use live Internet and videoconferencing technologies to share digitized images such as X rays, CAT scans, and EKGs.

Figure 3-14 Epi Info main screen displays incidence of a disease by U.S. county. Smaller screens displaying other information, ex., clusters of disease, form a touch menu on the left.

purchases, sifting them by symptom, time, and place for patterns that might escape human notice. The system routinely picks up patterns of disease that never would have been caught by human analysis alone.

The Internet also assists in the data collection process, as health care providers around the world can rapidly share information with each other – and can share prevention tips with individuals around the world. As discussed later, however, one should take the time to evaluate the credibility of medical information on the Internet – especially as related to outbreaks, which tend to cause high levels of concern – before acting on the information.

IMPROVING MEDICAL TRAINING Computer technology fundamentally has changed the nature of medical training and education. **Virtual reality (VR)** applications model something real when working with the original is not possible or practical. VR can simulate a patient for medical students or nurse trainees. The simulator has sensing instruments that detect the user's movements. The program then computes the changes and projects the correct response onto the screen. As the user works with the VR training system, the computer can collect data on the user's performance for later review.

While VR does provide excellent visual training, in many medical applications, a surgeon relies upon both visual and haptic feedback to complete an operation successfully. **Haptic feedback** is based on the sense of touch, such as the feel of a surgical scalpel on tissue. Newer training simulators use haptic feedback to recreate how injecting a needle into a patient actually feels – thus better preparing the student for the actual act.

In an even more realistic form of training with haptic feedback, Army medics training at Fort Sam Houston learn to deal with realistic wounds inflicted on a high-tech mannequin, known as SimMan 3G (Figure 3-15). A human patient simulator, SimMan 3G is life-sized and has an artificial pulse, mechanized lungs, and plastic bones. Plastic veins in the simulator bleed fake blood from wounds, while plastic bones stick out from a broken leg. The device can also display neurological (ex., brain trauma) symptoms. Each simulator has wireless connectivity with a laptop computer that monitors and changes vital signs and then challenges trainees by dropping blood pressure or collapsing a lung. Each time the medic touches the body, the computer records what procedure was performed and what effect it had. For example, administering drugs causes a realistic reaction to the drug. Spending time in the classroom with these patient simulators is good practice for saving real soldiers in combat.

All of these training tools, whether virtual reality or simulations, allow surgeons to practice hundreds of procedures prior to patient contact, and the practice carries no risk to live patients. Since doctors with less experience are more likely to make errors, using computerized tools

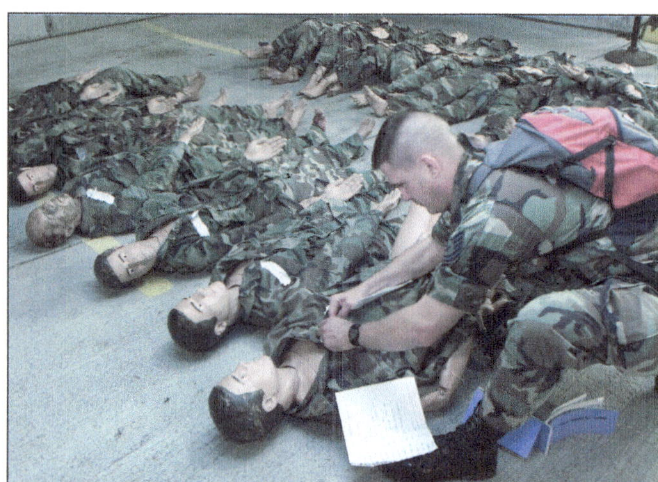

Figure 3-15 Army medics get to practice their skills on SimMan, a high-tech patient simulator that trains them to deal with battlefield injuries and humanitarian needs, such as delivering a baby.

for training can lead to a more highly skilled and better prepared staff of medical professionals.

Credibility of Medical Information

The number of Web sites about health care information has grown quickly, providing information on how to find a good physician, eat a healthy diet, and get the proper exercise. Other Web sites allow you to review information about a specific illness or medical condition. Your primary source of health care information should be your doctor or other health care professional. However, if you are looking for health information online, you can choose from hundreds of Web sites.

In addition to researching specific medical, health, diet, and fitness topics, you can review Web sites to look into hospital services, to evaluate enrollment options and coverage of health insurance providers, and fill prescriptions at online drugstores. Web sites such as WebMD Physician Directory or AMA DoctorFinder can help you find a local doctor. The Web sites of health care organizations such as the National Cancer Institute and American Stroke Association also provide information about how to find support groups for a particular illness or disability.

As you browse through all of these Web sites, however, be aware that not all online information is accurate or up to date. Many health-oriented Web sites have substantial gaps in the availability of key information, as well as conflicting information. Others fail to provide information about the authority and credentials of the individuals offering health advice, or do not clearly state possible commercial interests behind their claims.

With these concerns in mind, how should you evaluate health-oriented Web sites? The credibility of the content at these Web sites first should be evaluated using the basic steps outlined in Table 3-3, which involve identifying the sponsoring organization or author, establishing that the content is timely and objective, and comparing the content with that from other, similar sites.

TABLE 3-3 Tips for Evaluating Health-Related Web Sites

AUTHORITY	■ Examine site addresses and Web page headers and footers to determine the sponsoring organization or author of the site and then determine whether the sponsor or author has authority or expertise in the area. ■ Look at the date the site published or last updated the information. Out-of-date pages may not present the most recent developments or up-to-date information. ■ Look for primary sources. A primary source is any document, item, or other data that comes from a first-hand, authoritative resource. ■ Do not assume that government or education sites are always authoritative. For example, sites with the .edu top-level domain represent educational institutions, but a Web page may be the work of a student rather than a researcher or expert.
OBJECTIVITY	■ Determine whether the information is fair, whether any biases are stated clearly, or if the information is skewed toward commercial interests. ■ Look for links to other sites, and read background information about the author or organization. For example, when looking for information about a new prescription drug, you should weigh whether the site bases its recommendations on scientific evidence or whether the site profits by promoting the sale of the drug.
SCOPE	■ Evaluating the scope of a site — that is, the depth of coverage and the amount of detail provided — can help determine the value of its information. Although not a perfect approach, you can judge the accuracy of information on one site by comparing its scope with several other sites. ■ One technique for determining scope is to compare several sources on the same topic. If a Web site is missing information or conflicts with numerous other sites on a particular topic, it may be a less valuable source of information. ■ Look for detail and depth of coverage, as well as citations or references to other sources.
DESIGN AND FUNCTIONALITY	■ Pages that display mistakes in grammar or spelling, poor organization, or broken images and links may indicate a poor quality source.

Because the Internet offers anyone the opportunity to publish information, you must assess the credibility of the information presented on the page carefully — especially when it is health-related information.

Most people who go online to find health information rely on popular search tools to locate health-oriented Web sites; yet, some health care professionals suggest you should ask a trusted source, such as your doctor or nurse practitioner, to recommend health-oriented Web sites. Another alternative is to look for accredited Web sites, such as those accredited by the Geneva-based Health On the Net Foundation (HON) or the American URAC (Utilization Review Accreditation Commission). The Web site standards required by these independent, non-profit agencies include an editorial review process to ensure content accuracy; internal processes to guarantee privacy, security, and Web site quality; and the full disclosure of possible relationships with manufacturers or other commercial interests.

Another resource to help you evaluate medical Web sites is the Medical Library Association's CAPHIS (Consumer and Patient Health Information Section) Web site. CAPHIS evaluates consumer health sites based on a number of criteria, including credibility, disclosure, sponsorship and authorship, and design, and then lists the highest-rated Web sites as part of the CAPHIS Top 100.

As you review information on the Web, watch out for false health care reports and health hoaxes. Unfortunately, it is all too easy to circulate false information via the Internet. You can find a list of current false health reports and health hoaxes at the Centers for Disease Control and Prevention (CDC) Web site. Finally, before acting on any information you gather from a Web site, consult a physician to ensure that the information you have gathered is accurate, effective, and will keep you on the road to good health.

CONCLUSION

In this chapter, you learned about how the use of computers in medicine has fundamentally changed the process of data collection, analysis, and communication. You learned how computers are used in medicine to maintain patient history and manage the medical practice, as well as to improve patient diagnosis and monitoring. After learning more about how computer technology contributes in the operating room and how telemedicine is making health care available at a distance, you learned how computers are used in medical research and training. You also learned more about how to assess the credibility of health-oriented Web sites.

Key Terms

add-ins
computed tomography (CT)
computer-aided detection/computer-aided diagnosis (CAD)
computerized provider order entry (COPE) system
computer-aided surgery (CAS)
digital x-ray
electrocardiogram (ECG) or (EKG)
electronic health record (EHR)
endoscopy
epidemiology
haptic feedback
Holter monitor
IBM Watson
image-guided surgery
keyhole surgery
magnetic resonance imaging (MRI)
medical informatics
operating room management system
patient portal
personal health record (PHR)
pulse oximeter
remote surgery / telesurgery
robotic-assisted surgery
telemedicine
ultrasound
virtual reality (VR)

Chapter Review

Multiple Choice

Select the best answer.

1. An electronic health record (EHR) is a patient record maintained by computer that includes _____.
(a) a patient's medical history
(b) prescriptions
(c) health insurance information
(d) all of the above

2. Using a(n) _____ system cuts out the time-consuming process of dictation, transcription, and coding for billing and insurance claims.
(a) CAD
(b) EMR
(c) CAS
(d) PHI

3. Computer-assisted diagnosis often is supported by _____ systems.
(a) decision support or expert
(b) scheduling or billing
(c) virtual reality or haptic feedback
(d) all of the above

4. Which of the following diagnostic tests uses a powerful magnet?
(a) MRI
(b) EKG
(c) CT
(d) EEG

5. Endoscopy is a surgical technique that involves the use of _____.
(a) preoperative images to understand the shape of tissues in a surgical area prior to the surgery
(b) a special viewing instrument that allows a surgeon to see images of the body's internal structures
(c) satellite links for communicating with anesthesiologists in the operating room
(d) simulators that allow medical trainees to believe that they are interacting with a patient

6. One of the most valuable uses of _____ is that it allows doctors in remote areas, such as rural locations or a battlefield, to consult with specialists at medical centers.
(a) epidemiology
(b) telemedicine
(c) haptic feedback
(d) computer simulation

7. Newer training simulators use _____ to recreate how injecting a needle into a patient actually feels — thus better preparing the student for the actual event.
(a) epidemiology
(b) telemedicine
(c) haptic feedback
(d) computer simulation

8. COPE is responsible for _____.
(a) disinfecting hospital rooms
(b) telesurgery consultations
(c) delicate surgery in the OR
(d) correctly prescribed drugs for patients

9. What medical technology can project a picture of the problem area on the patient's body during an operation?
(a) CT
(b) image-guided surgery
(c) RAS
(d) keyhole surgery

10. Tiny programmable computers manage operation of _____.
(a) hearing aids
(b) pacemakers
(c) continuous glucose monitors
(d) all of the above

Computers in Science and Engineering 4

The disciplines of medicine and science involve similar steps, such as making an assessment of the cause of an occurrence — whether a new disease or a hole in the ozone layer — and then collecting and analyzing data to understand better why that occurrence happened. After confirming the reason for the occurrence, a course of action typically is recommended. In a scientific study, the recommendation might involve scientists suggesting regulations to limit the release of greenhouse gases into the atmosphere.

Over the last few decades, computer technology has transformed science — completely altering the way data is collected, analyzed, communicated, and stored. In this chapter, you will learn more about the use of computers in science to help with observation and data collection, data classification and analysis, and data modeling and simulation.

Likewise, improvements in computer technology have allowed engineers to tackle structural problems earlier thought impossible to solve. You will learn about some of these projects later in this chapter.

COMPUTERS IN SCIENCE

Science involves the pursuit of knowledge about the world around us, from the smallest particle of physical matter to the vast expanse of stars and galaxies that make up the universe. The process of science generally follows a series of steps known as the **scientific method**, a procedure by which scientists work to construct an accurate representation of the world. The scientific method involves:

1. Observing some occurrence or aspect of the world or identifying a problem
2. Developing a hypothesis to explain this occurrence
3. Determining how to test the hypothesis
4. Collecting data and then analyzing data to prove or disprove the hypothesis
5. Concluding whether or not the hypothesis was correct

Over the past few decades, computer technology has revolutionized science and the research process defined by the scientific method. Computer technology has given scientists powerful new tools to support the basic activities of the scientific method, including observing the world, collecting data, and then classifying or analyzing that data. Computers also allow scientists to create highly accurate models or simulations of the real world to test their ideas.

The speed and power provided by computers lets scientists tackle scientific questions that they previously never would have been able to investigate, such as mapping the entire set of genes that define humans or searching for signals from extraterrestrials. Today, computer technology plays such an integral role in science, it is unlikely you could find a scientist or a research project that did not use computer technology in some way to support or further the research process.

Observation, Discovery, and Data Collection

As noted above, a key part of the scientific method is observing and collecting data to better understand some aspect of the world. Computers and communications devices have transformed the data collection process, making it possible to gather data automatically and store or transmit it for immediate analysis. Computers even allow researchers to gather data around the clock from remote locations around the globe, under the seas, and outer space.

COLLECTING WEATHER DATA The weather is an extremely dynamic, global system that has a profound impact on all life. Collectively, nations spend billions of dollars each year trying to predict weather behavior. All weather forecasts begin with observations of what the weather is currently doing all over the world. The data collected from low-tech devices such as rain gauge buckets, along with computer-based devices such as weather balloons, Doppler radar, and satellites are used as the basis for weather forecasts updated continuously each day.

For example, weather balloons are launched daily from over 800 sites around the world. The weather balloons travel high into the atmosphere, carrying high-tech instrument packages, called **radiosondes**, which that collect data about the upper atmosphere (Figure 4-1). The radiosondes measure temperature, humidity and air pressure at various altitudes, along

Figure 4-1 A weather balloon helps measure basic weather information. The weather balloon works by:
(1) Lifting a radiosonde about 20 miles into the atmosphere
(2) The radiosonde measures temperature, humidity, and air pressure.
(3) The balloon pops and the radiosonde is carried back to earth by parachute.

with wind speed and direction. They then transmit this data via radio waves to a receiving station that receives and stores the data in a computer database. After about a 2 hour flight, the radiosonde returns to earth by parachute. The National Weather Service launches close to 70,000 radiosondes annually.

Doppler weather radar also helps to collect weather data, by sending out a beam of energy and then measuring how much of that beam is reflected back. Rain, snow, sleet (even clouds of grasshoppers) reflect back more of the beam and are indicated by various colors.

Weather satellites, referred to as **Geostationary Operational Environmental Satellites (GOES)**, orbit the Earth about 22,000 miles above the equator (where their speed will exactly match the Earth's rotation) and gather even more precise data. Each GOES has a sounder that measures temperature and humidity at various altitudes, along with a camera that takes and then sends back the photos that accompany the evening weather forecast and the weather updates on Web sites like NOAA.gov and weather.com.

HUNTING HURRICANES Having computers to help collect data automatically is of enormous value to the meteorologists and atmospheric scientists seeking to learn more about what happens during a hurricane. Any time a hurricane endangers a location in or near the United States, the National Oceanic and Atmospheric Administration (NOAA) sends out its hurricane hunters – airplanes that routinely fly into the types of weather most pilots avoid. The planes essentially are scientific laboratories with wings: the planes include a probe at the front to take in air for measurement; a cone at the rear that includes Doppler weather radar; and numerous instruments to collect basic weather data such as temperature, humidity, and wind speed and direction, as well as the amount of water and ice in clouds. From under the aircraft, the crew can launch **dropsondes**, devices very similar to radiosondes. The plane itself houses computer workstations for up to ten scientists, who can analyze the collected data in mid-flight (Figure 4-2). Using satellite links, the hurricane hunter planes transmit the collected data back to the National Hurricane Center near Miami, Florida, along with radar photos that show details of the hurricane's structure. Meteorologists and scientists use this data to assess the hurricane's movement and determine any possible impacts.

REMOTE SENSING The GOES satellites also play an important role in data collection by using remote sensing. **Remote sensing**, which is the use of aircraft, satellites, or other distant devices to collect and record data, gathers a wide range of data, including hazardous waste emissions, beach erosion, wildlife populations, and atmospheric and weather changes and patterns.

The National Science Foundation's Antarctica Automatic Weather Station (AWS) project supports meteorological research and climate prediction. Each of the 63 AWS units measures air temperature, air pressure, wind speed, and wind direction (Figure 4-3). The AWS unit is controlled by a small computer, which updates the data approximately every ten minutes and then later transmits the data to a polar-orbiting NOAA satellite, which receives the data and stores it in a data collection system. The data then is relayed to ground stations around the world for communication to scientists and meteorologists.

Remote sensing also is used by many countries to track the behavior of the oceans. NOAA's National Data

Figure 4-2 A hurricane hunter resembles a cargo plane, except for the radar dome on the belly of the plane. Inside, the plane houses computer workstations for scientists, who can analyze the collected data in mid-flight.

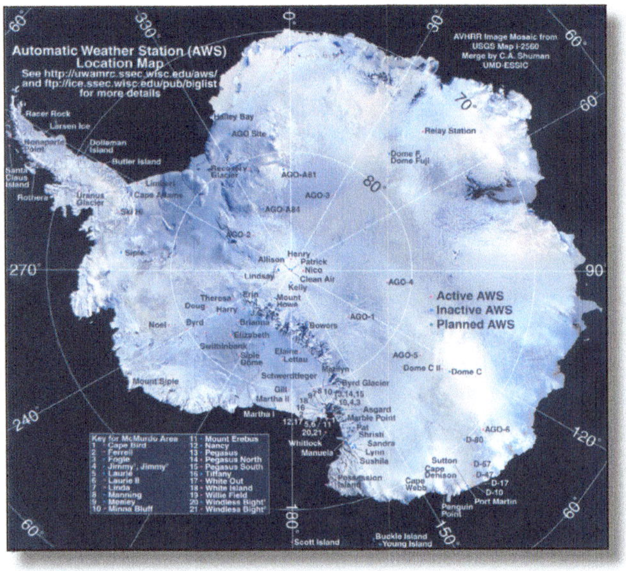

Figure 4-3 Hundreds of automatic weather stations located across Antarctica measure weather data and transmit it back to a data collection center.

Buoy Center (NDBC), for example, maintains and monitors about 150 buoys and Coastal-Marine Automated Network (C-MAN) stations that serve as weather sentinels of the sea and coasts (Figure 4-4). The moored buoys and C-MAN stations measure wind speed, direction, and gust; barometric pressure; and air temperature as well as sea surface temperature and wave heights. Each hour, the buoy or C-MAN relays the data via satellite to a ground station, which sends the data on to the National Weather Service, which then sends the data over the Internet to world meteorological centers and interested scientists and individuals via the Web.

The Center is also operates the DART (Deep-ocean Assessment and Reporting of Tsunamis) system, which uses about 50 moored buoys with seismic sensors at the bottom of the Pacific, Atlantic, and Indian Oceans to track the earthquakes that trigger tsunamis. These huge tidal waves are a major threat to coastal communities: once they reach shore, tsunami waves can be up to 100 feet high. Each moored buoy in the DART network has a device called a bottom pressure recorder (BPR) that measures the water surface levels (Figure 4-5). Every hour, the computer device attached to the BPR transmits the data to the surface buoy. The surface buoy retransmits the data to a satellite, which transmits the data to a ground station and on to the Tsunami Warning Centers. With the data from the DART system, the warning centers can identify tsunamis early enough to issue warnings or start evacuating coastal towns.

Finally, the NDBC has responsibility for the Tropical Atmosphere Ocean (TAO) project, which uses over 50 buoys in the equatorial Pacific to monitor El Niño and La Niña events.

REMOTE OBSERVATION Modern astronomy and space exploration could not exist without the many tools computer technologies provide. For example, computers direct the activities of both optical and radio telescopes, as well as all space telescopes, spacecraft (ex., *Cassini* orbiting Saturn), and exploratory robots (ex., *Curiosity* on Mars). Software aims these instruments at targets

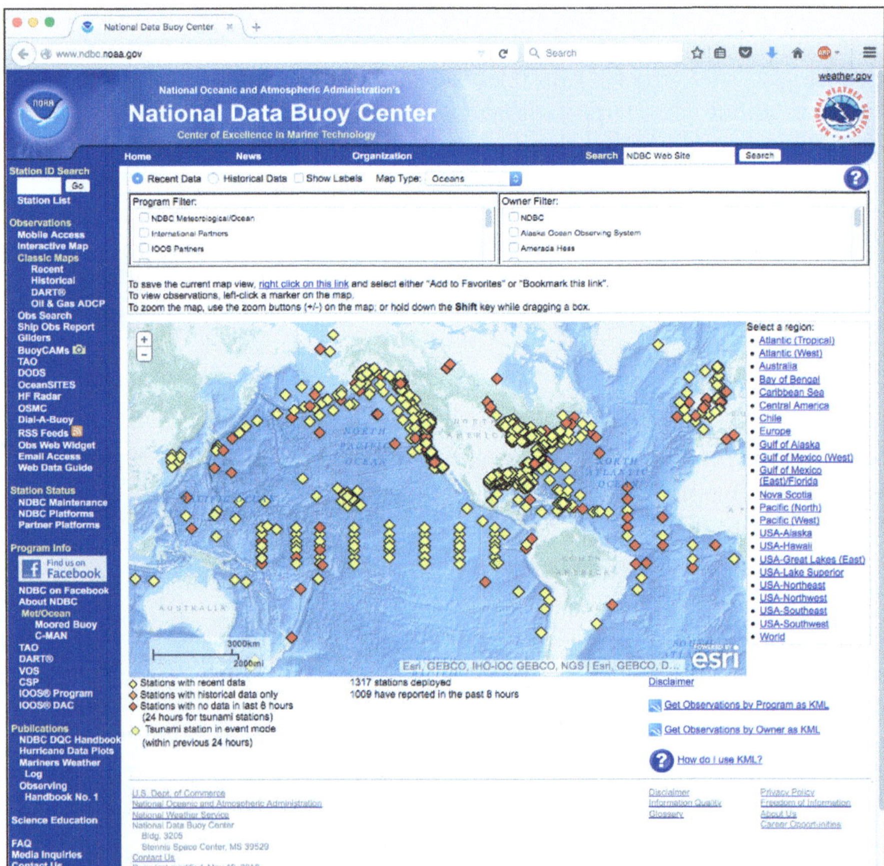

Figure 4-4 Real-time data from the buoys and C-MAN stations is posted on the National Data Buoy Center Web site for use by scientists, fishermen, boaters, surfers, and others.

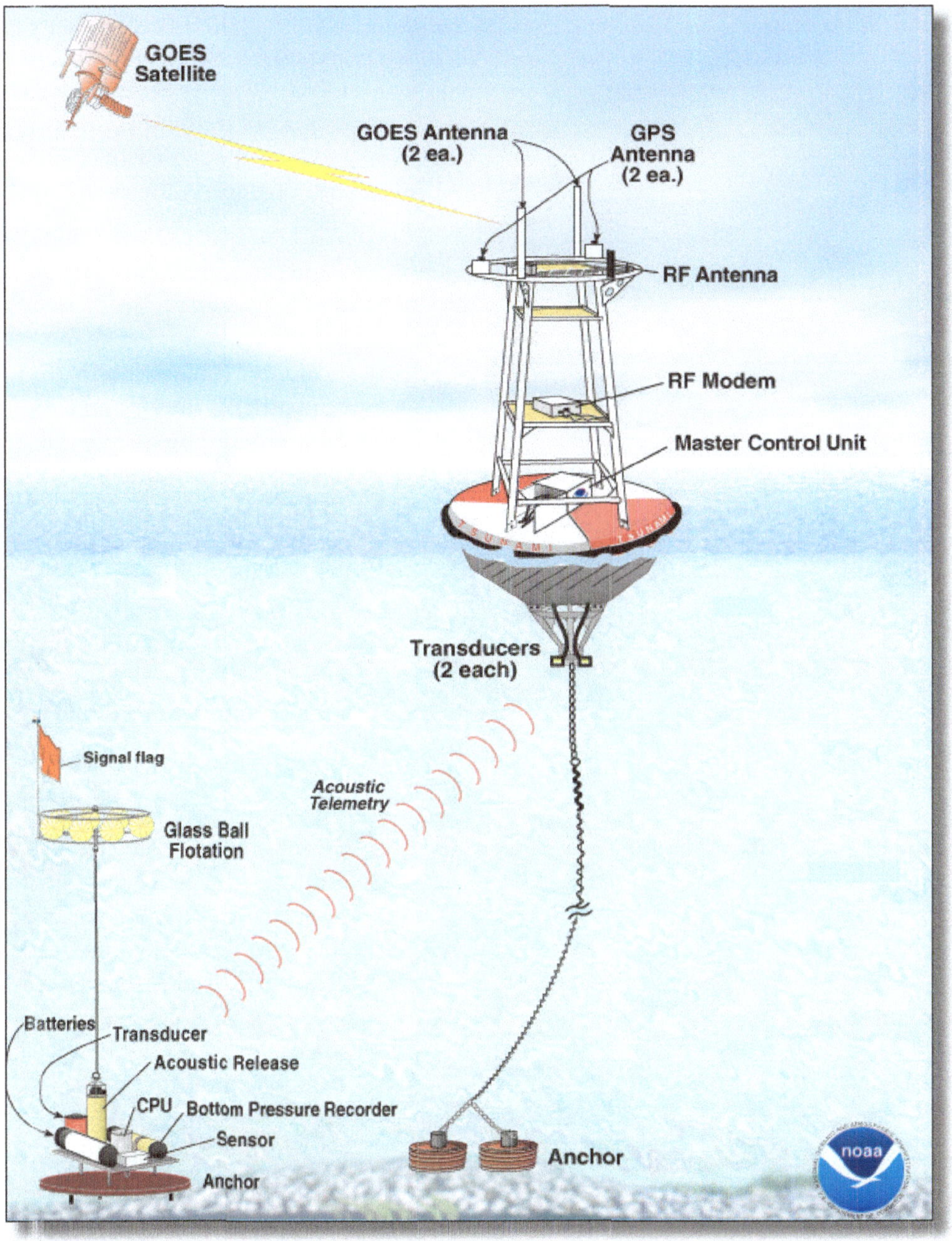

Figure 4-5 Each moored buoy in the DART network has a bottom pressure recorder that measures the water surface levels and then transmits that data across an acoustic link to the surface buoy hourly. The surface buoy retransmits that data to a satellite, which finally transmits the data to a ground station.

requested by scientists, and then records the collected images and/or other data. In the case of ground-based optical telescopes, scientists use special programs to remove from collected images the optical distortions caused by viewing through Earth's atmosphere.

Some computer-controlled satellites record images in wavelengths unseen by the human eye, such as infrared or x-rays. The most famous of these instruments is the Hubble Space Telescope. Its infrared camera has detected many extrasolar planets by photographing the heat radiation they give off (Figure 4-6). **Multispectral imaging** goes beyond this and captures optical data simultaneously from many different parts of the electromagnetic spectrum that are beyond human perception. This particular technology has also been used here on Earth to recover 'invisible' details from prehistoric rock art, ancient documents, as well as to document the pigment composition of paintings and any restoration intervention (Figure 4-7).

Data Classification and Analysis

After data is collected, it must be organized, or classified, so that it can be analyzed. Computers have provided scientists and researchers with the power to classify and analyze vast quantities of data more quickly and accurately than ever before.

DNA SEQUENCING A **genome** is the blueprint for an organism, encompassing the organism's entire set of DNA, including its genes. A **gene** defines a characteristic of any organism, including how you look, how you behave, and even how you fight off a cold.

DNA is made up of similar chemicals, or **bases**, that are repeated billions of times throughout an organism's genome. The human genome, for example, has around three billion pairs of bases in each cell. The order of the bases defines the diversity of the biological universe – dictating whether an organism is a person, an ear of corn, or a golden retriever.

Automated DNA sequencing is a computer-driven process for identifying the internal composition of a strand of DNA. This analysis and classification process is extremely important for many different fields of study,

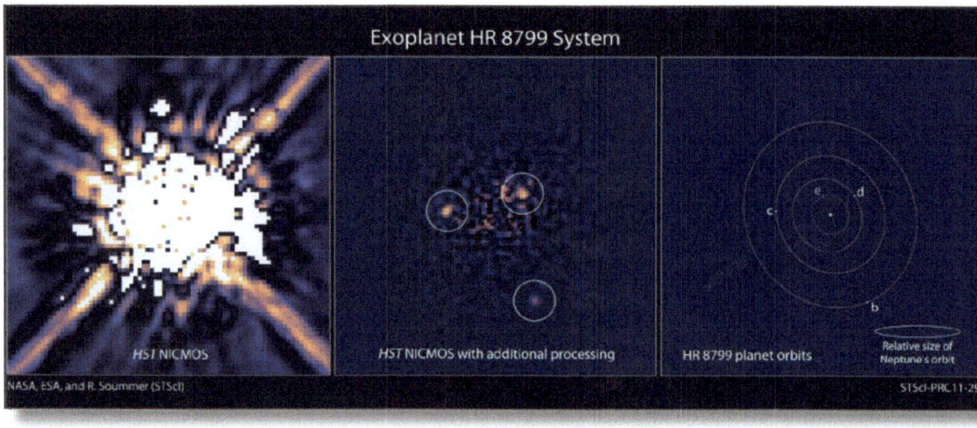

Figure 4-6 Extrasolar planets revealed by the heat they radiate into space.

Figure 4-7 Multispectral imaging of a 2,100 year-old papyrus reveals its Greek text.

from criminal investigation to identifying possible causes of disease to archaeological forensics to paleobiology. Knowledge about the effects of DNA variations among individuals can lead to revolutionary new ways to diagnose, treat, and someday prevent thousands of illnesses, such as diabetes, cancer, multiple sclerosis, schizophrenia, and more. It also might allow physicians to screen patients to determine if they are at risk for certain diseases or whether they might react adversely to a particular drug.

Knowledge about the effects of DNA variations among individuals can lead to revolutionary new ways to diagnose, treat, and someday prevent thousands of illnesses, such as diabetes, cancer, multiple sclerosis, schizophrenia, and more. It also might allow physicians to screen patients to determine if they are at risk for certain diseases or whether they might react adversely to a particular drug. Additionally, governments use DNA analysis to identify unknown persons. And archaeologists have used DNA, which persists in the enamel of teeth, to identify the remains of King Richard III and Pharaoh Akhenaten.

VOLUNTEER COMPUTING

Sometimes data classification and analysis can be done by people volunteering their computer time. **Distributed computing** divides a large problem among a series of networked computers which communicate with each other and coordinate their processing. **Volunteer computing** is a subset of distributive computing that relies upon owners of personal computers to donate some of their computer's resources to a distributive computing project. One example of volunteer computing is the SETI@home project. **SETI**, which is an acronym for the Search for Extraterrestrial Intelligence, specifically involves the search for radio or light signals from other civilizations in the universe.

In the SETI@home project, the Arecibo radio telescope in Puerto Rico continuously collects radio signals from space and has gathered massive amounts of data. The data, however, still must be analyzed to determine if any of the signals are, in fact, signals from extraterrestrials. Instead of spending the money to have one huge computer evaluate each radio signal, the SETI@home project turned to volunteer computing.

The Project distributes for free a simple data analysis program, called BOINC (Berkeley Open Infrastructure for Network Computing), in the form of a screen saver which individuals can run on their personal computers. Whenever the computer is idle, BOINC connects with the SETI@home server at the University of California, Berkeley. BOINC downloads a batch of radio data, called a work-unit, analyzes the data, reconnects with the SETI@home server to transfer the results of the analysis, and then downloads another work unit.

Figure 4-8 Laboratory assistant analyzes DNA sequence on a computer.

This solution has proven so successful that volunteer computing advocates use BOINC software for a wide array of projects, such as rendering 3D animations for artists, improving climate prediction models, understanding the structure and behavior of proteins, and detecting earthquakes (using the accelerometers inside many laptop computers).

Data Modeling and Simulation

As noted in Chapter 2, many different parts of our economy use computer-based modeling and simulation to test or explore products and ideas. For instance, instead of crashing a new car into a wall, it is more cost efficient and safer to build a computer model of the car and then develop a computer simulation of the crash.

Models and simulations also are useful when it is physically impossible to view the data firsthand. For instance, meteorologists must rely on computer models of how the weather will behave in the next week, because they cannot observe the future's weather. The same is true of models and simulations used to predict the impacts of pollution on the coastal areas or earthquakes along fault lines.

FORECASTING THE WEATHER Weather forecasts provide critical information about the weather to come. There are many different techniques involved in weather forecasting, from relatively simple observation of the sky to highly complex mathematical models run on computers.

As previously noted, all weather forecasts begin with observations of what the weather is doing all over the world. The collected data is then fed into supercomputers that use mathematical models of the atmosphere to make predictions. In the United States, the National Weather Service operates these computers, and refines the computer models continuously to make them as accurate as possible. Almost all U.S. weather forecasts use the predictions resulting from these models. However, even with the most refined models and fastest computers, meteorologists cannot forecast day-to-day weather for more than about a week ahead of time. The atmosphere is just too complex.

Other weather models developed in the U.S., Europe, Japan, and elsewhere try to forecast and understand the behavior of hurricanes, thunderstorms, and other severe weather events (Figure 4-9).

ENVIRONMENTAL IMPACT MODELING Computers also model the impacts that various occurrences, such as hurricanes or human actions, have on the environment. For example, NOAA's Geophysical Fluid Dynamics Laboratory (GFDL) has pioneered computer modeling research for two decades, with the goals of better understanding weather phenomena, such as El Niño/La Niña, as well as to model the progress of ozone depletion and global warming.

Over the past few decades, scientists have noticed an increase in ocean heat, which is one of the key characteristics of global warming. Using computer models, the scientists at GFDL were able to pinpoint greenhouse gases introduced into the atmosphere by

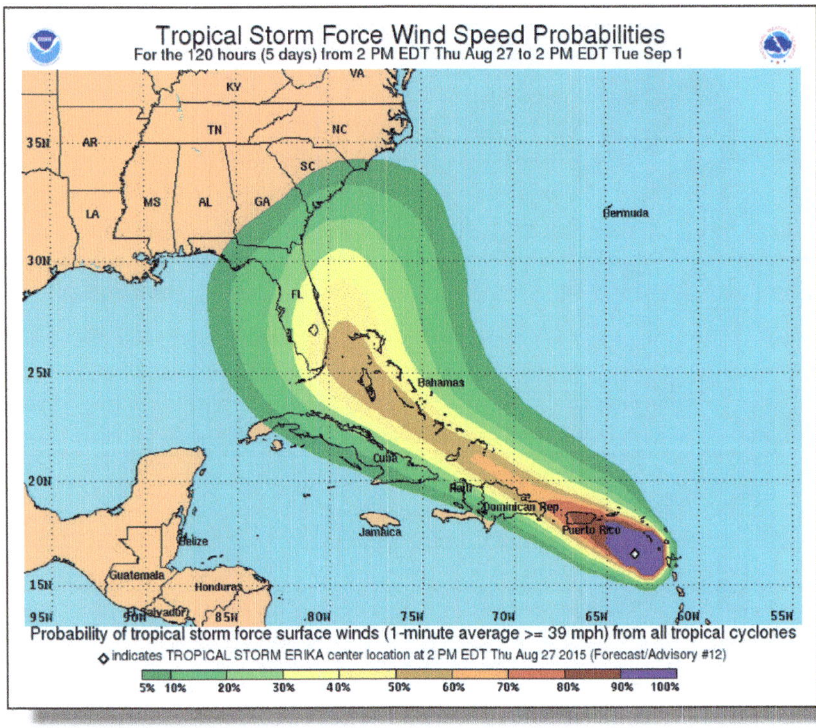

Figure 4-9 A computer-generated prediction of wind speeds for a tropical storm.

emissions from cars, factories, and so on as a significant factor in global warming.

GFDL then went on to create computer simulations of how the increase in ocean heat will affect the earth over the long term. In response to greenhouse gas warming, the water in the world's oceans will expand from ice melt, thus causing sea level to rise. (For reference, the volume of ice in the Greenland and Antarctica ice sheets, if melted, is equivalent to a sea level rise of 23 feet and 240 feet respectively). GFDL's computer simulations show that, as greenhouse gas levels double or quadruple, the sea level would gradually continue rising for centuries, rising about one to two meters (approximately three to six feet) after 500 years. Figure 4-10 illustrates the effect of a hypothetical sea level rise of one, two, four, or eight meters. The red areas in Figure 4-10 indicate regions of the southeastern United States that would be below sea level under such sea-level rise scenarios.

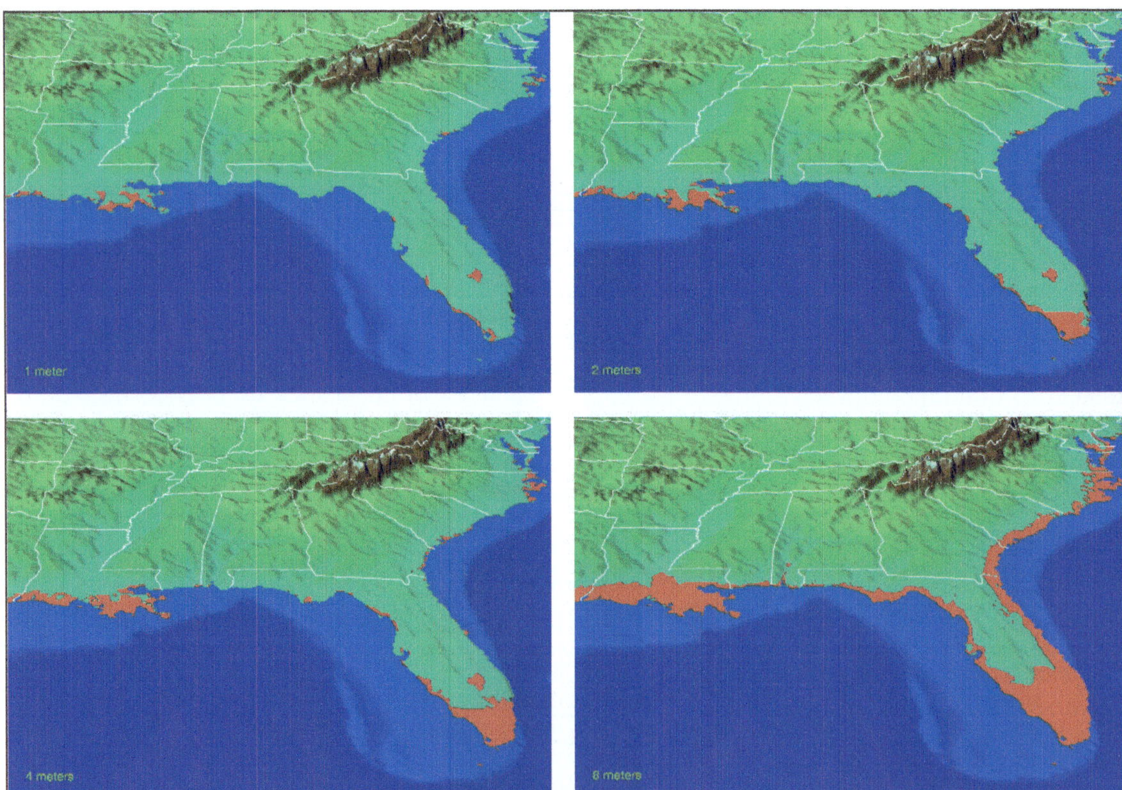

Figure 4-10 Computer models are used to simulate the effects of sea level rise caused by global warming. The graphical model shows how a sea level rise of one, two, four, and eight meters would leave the areas in red under water.

GEOGRAPHIC INFORMATION SYSTEMS Many problems have a site-related component. A **geographic information system (GIS)** is a computer system capable of assembling, storing, manipulating, and displaying data identified by location. A GIS associates *where* things are – the geographic information – with *what* things are – the descriptive information. Unlike a flat paper map, a GIS can present many layers of descriptive information laid out over geographical terrain. Each layer of a map in a GIS represents a different set of data (Figure 4-11). For example, a baseline layer might be a seafloor map of the Puget Sound area; the next layer might show the fish population based on commercial catches; a third layer might show water temperature variations; a fourth might show water pollution levels; and so on. Using the GIS, you can add and remove layers to control the amount and type of information on the map at one time. This allows you to combine various data points to study possible relationships.

A GIS can be used in a wide range of spatial applications, including crisis management (as seen in Chapter 2), natural resource management, scientific research, and development planning. For instance, a GIS can help emergency planners to calculate response times in the event of an earthquake by mapping out the best routes for rescue personnel to get in and the best evacuation routes for citizens to get out.

Geographic Information Systems have been used to analyze whether the use of pesticides or other toxic chemicals may have contributed to the number of breast cancer cases in the Cape Cod area of Massachusetts. Government agencies, such as the Arizona Department of Environmental Quality, use geographic information systems to analyze air and water quality, including possible groundwater contamination. Real estate agents in large metropolitan areas have used geographic information systems to help potential home buyers narrow their searches to appropriate communities based on housing costs, commute times, air quality, schools, and other factors. And restaurant chains depend on GIS analysis of traffic patterns, community demographics, location of competition, and planned roadway construction to determine what street corner is best for their next outlet.

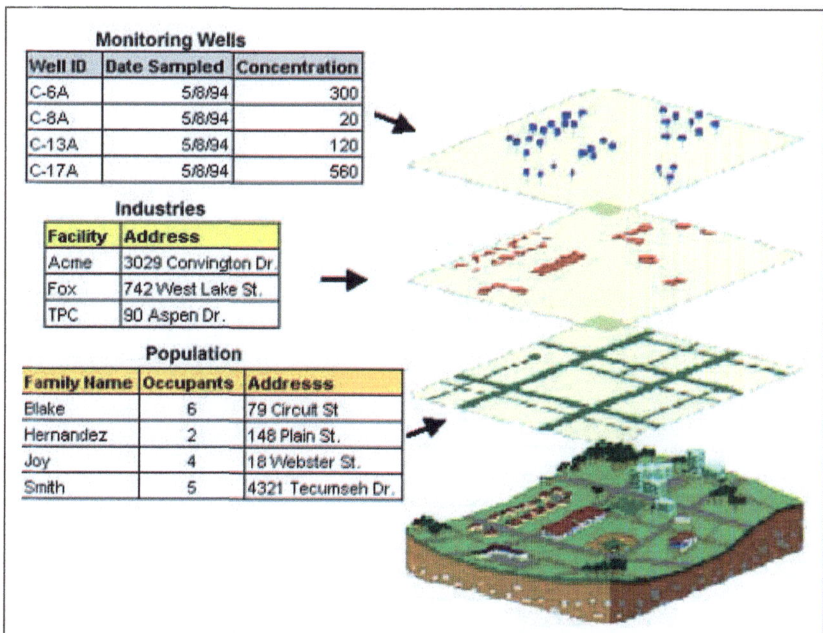

Figure 4-11 Each layer in a GIS map can represent a different set of data. Using the GIS, you can add and remove layers to combine various data points to study possible relationships among layers.

Sample Applications in Science

ARCHAEOLOGY Archaeology is the study of how people lived in the past, based on the physical remains they left behind. Those remains are often not readily visible. To help find hidden sites, archaeologist can use a variety of computer-based tools. For instance, **lidar** is a remote-sensing computer technology that bounces laser beams off a target, in this case the earth's surface, and analyses the returned light. Aircraft and satellites can use lidar to create highly detailed maps of any desired terrain, especially dense forests, swamps, and other hard-to-access places. This technology can highlight elevational differences due to hidden ruins, roads, canals, or other artificial structures (Figure 4-12).

Ground-penetrating radar (GPR) is a computer-based technology that sends radio pulses unto the ground and evaluates the echoed results. In addition to revealing subsoils, ground water, and buried utilities, GPR can help archaeologists locate buried roads, walls, cemeteries, and other physical remains.

During excavation, archaeologists use applications on tablets and laptops to record the site survey (made with GPS), as well as the identity, characteristics, and grid location of all discovered artifacts. To help with identification, excavators can turn to online databases, email, and video consultations using a program like Skype. Once enough information about a site is available, archaeologists can use CAD software to create 3D models of how an ancient temple, palace, or house looked in its day.

Figure 4-12 Lidar in Archaeology.

GEOLOGY Geology is the study of the Earth's rocks and the factors which cause those rocks to change over time. One branch of geology explores for natural resources in the ground that can be extracted by mining or drilling. Computer software (some of it free from governmental agencies such as the U.S. Geological Service) can identify underground stratigraphy based on survey results, build assay databases, create 2D and 3D sectioning and contouring maps, and calculate financial return from estimated volume. If a company decides to open a mine, it will rely for profitability on other computer systems to help manage the extraction. For example, Analytical Spectral Devices offers FieldSpec, a family of portable mineral spectrometers to analyze cuttings on site in real time (Figure 4-13).

Volcanoes can be terrifying, destructive, and deadly when they erupt. A volcanic eruption in Columbia, for example, wiped out an entire town and killed over 25,000 inhabitants. But the chaos and economic disruption caused by a false alert, say to the 3 million people living around Italy's Mt. Vesuvius, would also be very bad. So another branch of geology studies the behavior of volcanoes to learn better when it is time to evacuate. Volcanologists focus on changes in a volcano's ground deformation, gas emissions, and earthquake generation, and they use computers in their work. In addition to portable seismometers and GPS stations, volcanologists also place a variety of sensors in a communications network around and inside a volcano. A major group of these devices sniff for volcanic gases like sulfur dioxide and identify both type and rate of emission. Sometimes small robots or drones are used to collect samples, especially when conditions are dangerous. And like archaeologists, volcanologists can use data returned from lidar-equipped satellites and aircraft.

Figure 4-13 FieldSpec tool in use.

PLANETARY SCIENCE Planetary science is a subdivision of astronomy that studies solar systems – the origin, composition, and behavior of planets, dwarf planets, moons, asteroids, and comets. This chapter has already discussed computer applications with both earth-based and space-based telescopes. The focus here is on robotic applications for space exploration.

All unmanned spacecraft use onboard computers to run power, navigation, and scientific equipment. If the mission of the spacecraft will take it beyond near-Earth space, an additional consideration for engineers and scientists is messaging time lag. The farther away from Earth, the more time it takes to receive a message. For instance, even travelling at near-light speeds, a radio signal takes between 4.3 and 21 minutes to reach Mars from Earth, depending on the given distance between the two worlds; a response would take the same amount of time. For Pluto, the one-way transit time is more than 4 hours! Because a lot can happen during the intervening time, deep space probes travel with onboard artificial intelligence software for crisis response.

For planetary science, there are three basic types of spacecraft: probes, orbiters, and landers. Probes have no braking rockets and thus can only fly-by their targets. Their principal job is initial exploration, and their scientific payload will vary with the target. Two common instruments are a digital camera and a spectrometer for atmosphere or surface analysis. Among currently active probes are *Voyagers 1* and *2*, and *New Horizons*.

Orbiters have computer-controlled braking rockets to slow the spacecraft enough for gravity to pull the vehicle into orbit around the target. Common equipment includes several different kinds of digital cameras, a spectrometer, and surface-probing radar. Presently, orbiters are active around Venus, Mars, and Saturn. *Cassini*, the Saturn orbiter, dropped a small lander on the moon Titan, which sent images and data via Cassini back to Earth.

Landers are the most sophisticated planetary spacecraft. Except for course corrections and software updates, the entire mission-to-target is computer controlled. Minimally they consist of two parts, a "bus" which pilots the vehicle to the planet, and the lander itself which separates from the bus before entering the atmosphere. Landers reach the surface either inside protective air bags, by firing retro-rockets, or lowered by a rocket-powered "sky crane." Once on the ground, landers deploy a series of scientific equipment which often includes a robotic arm and drill. An automated chemistry lab processes retrieved samples. On Mars several landers have released robotic explorers and two are presently active: solar-powered *Opportunity* and nuclear-powered *Curiosity* (Figure 4-14). Both rovers use navigation cameras and artificial intelligence software to help determine their routes.

ZOOLOGY Zoology is the study of Earth's animal kingdom in all of its dimensions. A major problem is discovering the migration habits of different species of wildlife, as well as monitoring over time any changes in those patterns caused by, for example, global warming. One way to do this is to attach a special collar or harness containing a GPS receiver, data recorder, and communications gear (cellular, VHS radio, or satellite), all battery-powered (Figure 4-15). On-board software controls how often to record the host's location, when

Figure 4-14 NASA Curiosity selfie.

Figure 4-15 Cheetah wearing a tracking collar.

to transmit data, and in some cases when to detach the collar or harness. In some cases, tracking devices are implanted into horn or tusk for longer duration studies. When VHS radio is used, scientists carry into the field a small computer attached to a hand-held antenna to receive data. If a tracking device is not possible because an animal is very rare and hard to find (ex., Siberian tigers), scientists can install computer-controlled cameras, listening devices, and other sensors in places they suspect the animal might appear.

With sea life, GPS trackers are much less effective as they cannot receive the timing satellite signals underwater. Instead, data from sea turtles, whales, sharks, and other animals large enough to carry the equipment broadcasts to multiple satellites and surface buoys that are part of the international **Argos system**. Computing centers in the United States and France receive the data, process it, and distribute results to scientists. Customized sonar is an available tracking method for fish too small to wear devices.

COMPUTERS IN ENGINEERING

Engineering is the use of science, mathematics, and other disciplines to design, build, and operate structures, machinery, or other products and systems. Engineering has many different subdivisions, such as aeronautical, chemical, civil, electrical, and mechanical. Today, all branches of engineering rely heavily on using computer systems that run mathematical models and help design, test, construct, and operate a variety of projects. In fact, engineering applications have some role to play in all of the other chapters in this book.

The engineering process consists of a series of phases:

1. Research – clearly identify and understand the problem and its requirements; brainstorm possible solutions and select a promising one.
2. Plan – develop a strategy for implementing the idea, including a work schedule and a list of specifications and materials.
3. Prototype – build a working model, at least in a computer simulation; review the design and develop a testing schedule.
4. Test, Revise, Test Again – iterative improvement of the prototype, with consequences for the Plan phase as more is learned.
5. Submit Proposal to Build or Produce – demonstrate as needed; if approved, then...
6. Build Project or Commercialize Product.

As an example, the semiconductor industry designs and manufactures a wide range of computer chips, including **central processing units (CPUs)**, the "brains" of a computer. Market demand today is for powerful CPUs that are small, use less electricity and, in consequence, radiate less heat – perfect for smartphones, tablets, and other thin computing devices.

The engineering process starts by a design team working with potential customers to identify their device's computing needs, power constraints, and other factors related to modern CPUs. Brainstorming helps the team evaluate different layouts for the CPU – where to locate the memory components, where to put the datapath (pipeline) routes, where to locate the logic circuits, and so forth (Figure 4-16). Once they have agreed on a promising design, the team assembles a working development strategy and list of required resources. If approved, the team builds a working prototype and subjects it to a battery of tests, such as measuring power consumption and heat dissipation under various computational loads. The team makes design adjustments as needed and retests. If the prototype meets or exceeds

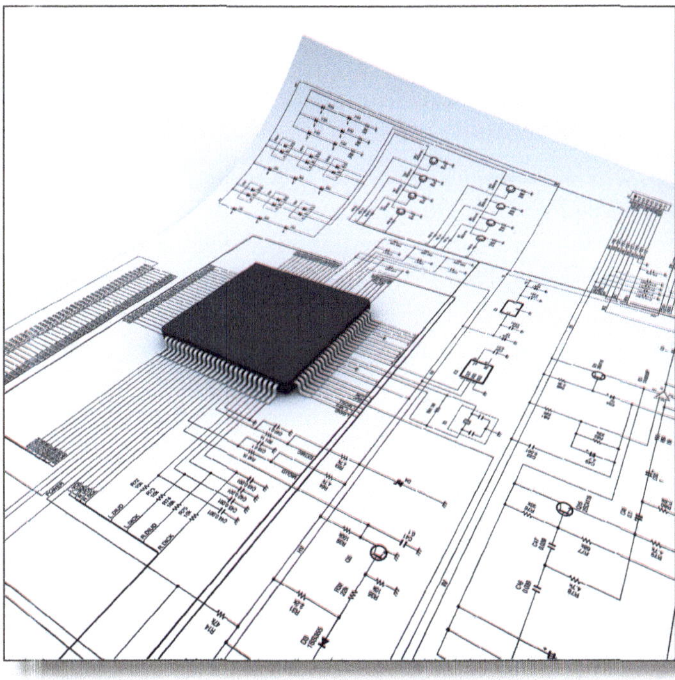

Figure 4-16 Microchip design.

specifications, the team requests permission to move the design into production. Ultimately, as a consumer you might purchase a smartphone or tablet with this CPU inside.

Software and the Engineering Process

The computing tools used by engineers can vary by subdiscipline. Civil and mechanical engineers might use AutoDesk's AutoCAD, while architectural engineers might use Bentley's AECOsim. But all engineering contains a strong mathematical component, and here the industry leader for numerical computing is Mathworks' MatLab, which also supports data analysis and visualization. Once the design is finalized, the specifications need to go to contractors for bid and eventual construction. At this point, different software tools may appear at the factory and job site. For instance, residential and commercial construction companies might use Windows desktop or tablet versions of MiTek's Sapphire to speed assembly and installation of structural frames.

Engineering projects are frequently group endeavors involving people from many different engineering subfields. Consequently the software tools used must facilitate this collaboration by, for instance, allowing multiple people to work on the same project at the same time. And it is also important, especially for large projects involving many vendors, that the tools use standardized file formats permitting electronic data exchange between companies. As an example, Autodesk sells Product Design Suite, a collection of software tools based on its AutoCAD product that support the entire engineering process.

When the project involves buildings and other structures, increasingly engineers and their clients are using **Building Information Modeling (BIM)** software like Graphisoft's ARCHICAD. The philosophy behind these products is the need to document and manage *the entire life-cycle of a building or structure*, not just its design and construction phases. Thus engineering software must support facility operations and maintenance, any future repurposing, and eventual demolition (Figure 4-17). BIM software can simulate the entire construction process before work actually starts, identifying constraint choke-points, materials shortages, and other problems. The use of BIM products has become so important that both the project build team and the client will have BIM managers on staff to participate in management activities such as cost, construction, and operations.

Sample Applications in Engineering

THE SALVAGE OF THE COSTA CONCORDIA

During the night of January 13, 2012, the Italian cruise ship Costa Concordia struck an underwater rock near Giglio Island, Italy, causing the liner to

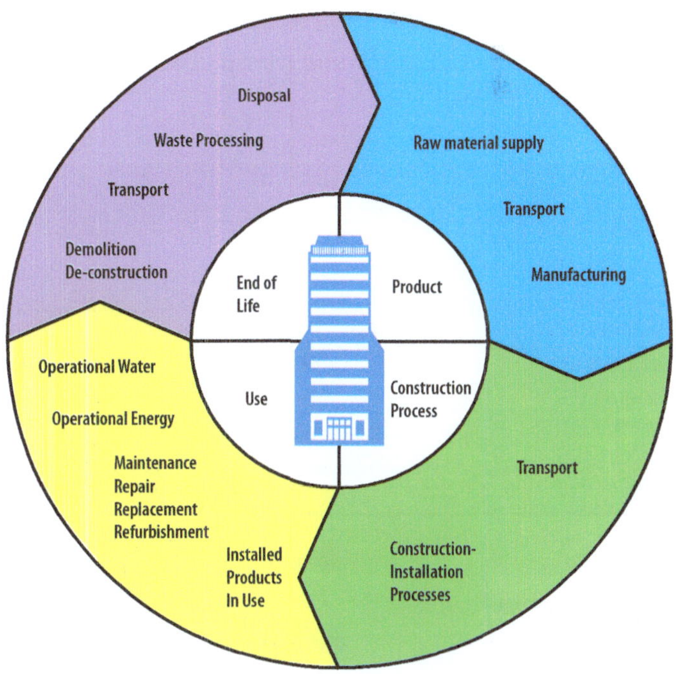

Figure 4-17 The life cycle for a building.

capsize on its starboard (right) side with the loss of 32 lives (Figure 4-18). The waters around Giglio are part of an undersea marine sanctuary, and a popular destination for scuba divers. The wreck immediately raised fears of an ecological disaster, not only from toxic spills but also from the very real possibility that the ship would slide off the rock into far deeper water and become a pollution source for generations to come.

Over the next six weeks, thousands of tons of fuel oil and other toxic liquids were pumped out of the wreck. At the same time, an international team of engineers and marine scientists worked with Costa Cruises and the Italian government to develop a salvage plan. Various computer systems (including underwater robots) aided the group by recording visual and technical data about the ship's condition and by simulating different possible responses to this crisis. The key decision, which drove almost all other planning, was to minimize chances of environmental destruction by removing the ship intact from the wreck site.

The final plan identified these major tasks:

a) Securing the wreck with cables, and always monitoring them so that the ship would not slide into the abyss;
b) Attach metal floats to the port (left) side, while at the same time building underwater steel platforms to hold the ship when righted;
c) Rotating the wreck onto the platforms;
d) Attaching metal floats to the starboard side;
e) Floating the wreck and transporting it to the port of Genoa;
f) Dismantling the wreck in an environmentally safe manner; and
g) Clearing and cleaning the wreck site, as well as replanting marine flora as needed.

The *Costa Concordia* was 952 feet long, had 13 decks, and weighed 114,000 gross tons. No salvage plan of this magnitude and complexity had ever been attempted. The work involved many different branches of engineering, including civil, chemical, nautical, and mechanical. All engineers made heavy use of computer systems to run calculations and simulations, identify, order, and track needed materials, and control thousands of sensors used for monitoring toxic spills, cable stresses, steel integrity, and so on. In September 2013, the salvage consortium used special engineering software to control the slow rotation of the wreck (Task c), as the slightest error could have ripped the ship apart. When the vessel was finally towed to Genoa in July 2014, Italian salvage firms had in place a detailed strategy, built with computer support, for carefully dismantling the wreck. Initially budgeted at $300 million, the entire stabilization and recovery actually cost $1.2 billion.

THE DESIGN AND CONSTRUCTION OF THE BURJ KHALIFA For a number of years the tallest building in the world, Dubai's Burj Khalifa stands 2.723 feet tall, contains 432,000 cubic yards of concrete and 43,000 tons of rebar, and took six years to build. Engineers conducted over 40 wind tunnel tests (many computer-generated) to identify the pressures and stresses of winds on the massive structure and the towering cranes needed to build it. The resulting design was a "Y"-shaped structure, which guaranteed that at least one arm at all times would remain unstressed and able to support the rest of the building. Engineers also used computers to simulate and design the building's air duct systems so that heavier, colder air would not pool at the bottom levels, where its pressure could crack materials and threaten the building's structural integrity. No one had ever pumped concrete to such heights before, so once again engineers had to use computer systems to design, test, and construct innovative concrete delivery systems. The completed

Figure 4-18 Costa Concordia.

building has tens of thousands of sensor devices in it, starting with the foundation, to help both humans and dedicated computer systems monitor and manage the structure (Figure 4-19). And in case of danger, separate computer systems pressurize and air-condition "refugee areas" located every 25 floors.

DESIGNING EARTHQUAKE-RESISTANT STRUCTURES

Some authorities consider earthquakes to be the worst type of natural disaster because they strike without warning. When the underground stresses on rock finally give way, the resulting violence – up and down or side to side – reshapes the land. The shaking can also do tremendous damage to buildings and other structures, either directly or by causing avalanches, rock falls, and tsunamis. In major earthquakes like the 7.8 tremor that hit Nepal in 2015, structural failures kill or injure many people. Earthquake engineers analyze this destruction, seeking ways to reinforce old buildings and design new ones that are more earthquake-resistant. Using computers, they can simulate earthquakes in software, or with a hydraulically powered shake table, and test designs for degrees of failure or resistance. Experiments show that using inexpensive wire mesh in the adobe brick walls found in many countries, or in the rock-and-mud-mortar walls built in Nepal, can significantly improve earthquake resistance. Many buildings in cities can benefit from seismic dampers made of rubbery disks or large springs (Figure 4-20). And using suspended, large, concrete blocks or steel pendulums near the top of tall skyscrapers can steady those buildings in strong winds or earthquakes.

Figure 4-19 Burj Khalifa tower, Dubai.

THE VENICE TIDE BARRIER PROJECT

Rising sea levels have been slowly, but steadily, destroying the city of Venice. After decades of debate, the response is the world's largest flood prevention project. The lagoon within which Venice and other towns sit will be protected from the Adriatic Sea by a series of 78 gates divided between the lagoon's three inlets. Each gate is a hollow, box-like structure 92 feet long, 65 feet wide, 15 feet thick, and weighs 300 tons. 125-foot long steel and concrete pilings attach each gate to the lagoon floor. At rest, a gate contains sea water and lays on the bottom. When needed, compressed air inflates the gate, which rises to the surface and blocks the incoming waves (Figure 4-21).

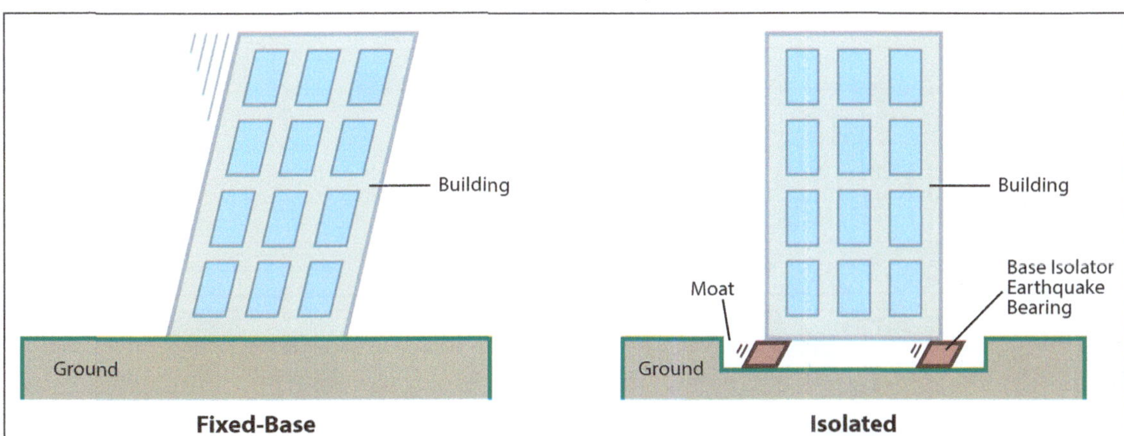

Figure 4-20 Earthquake bearings can help protect both a building and its occupants from damage caused by earthquakes.

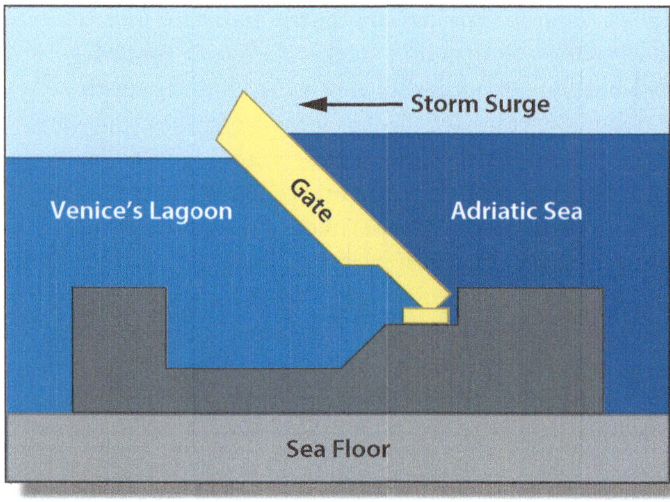

Figure 4-21 Venice Tidal Barrier Project.

Before construction, engineers used computers to design and test both the structure and operation of the gates, as well as to design special floating vessels to transport, position, and install each gate. A computer-based control system operates each gate as needed.

THE BELLAGIO FOUNTAINS The Bellagio Hotel and Casino in Las Vegas wanted 8 acres of water fountains to welcome and entertain guests (Figure 4-22). The sheer size of the attraction dwarfed anything attempted before. The attraction uses 5,000 LED lights, a fog generator system, and four different types of water jet "shooter" devices: 798 minishooters send water 100 feet high; 192 supershooters push water 240 feet into the air; 16 extreme shooters can send water as high as 460 feet; and 208 robots (called "oarsmen") that can make the water change direction. Custom computer software, networked by 135 miles of wire and cables, monitors and controls every aspect of operation and performance. Only a change of program is needed to put on a different water show.

Hydraulic, civil, mechanical, and electrical engineers collaborated on the project. Computer applications were used on all aspects of the design and construction, from CAD to project management. Approximately 30 engineers keep it operating daily, and all have diver training because they need to be in or under the water for much of their work.

Figure 4-22 Bellagio Hotel Fountains.

ROACH ROBOTS Not all engineering applications are large-scale; most are actually quite small. When a building collapses from poor construction, tornadoes, explosion, or earthquakes, the pressure is on rescuers to find and extract survivors before they die from injuries, dehydration, or other factors. But collapsed buildings are extremely difficult, and dangerous, to explore. One answer might be to send in the CRAMs (Compressible Robot with Articulated Mechanisms). CRAM 'bots mimic cockroaches (Figure 4-23). If you can put aside the ick factor, you will appreciate that roaches are a marvel of natural engineering. In addition to their speed and maneuverability, roaches can move through crevices less than a quarter of their height by compressing their exoskeletons. Yet that same exoskeleton can withstand compressive forces almost 900 times the roach's weight. Perfect for invading your home or workplace — but also perfect for exploring collapsed buildings. Researchers used computer-controlled cameras and sensors to make detailed measurements of live cockroach movements during a variety of tests. They also used mathematical models and ran simulations. The hardest work proved to be designing an artificial exoskeleton; the rest could be built using off-the-shelf parts, 3D printing, and custom computer software. The prototype cost less than $100.

Figure 4-23 Robot cockroach and friend.

CONCLUSION

In this chapter, you learned about how the use of computers in science has fundamentally changed the process of data collection, analysis, and communication. You learned how computers help scientists with observation, discovery, data collection, classification, analysis and modeling/simulation. After learning about sample applications in science, you moved on to the role of computers in engineering. You learned about the engineering process and how computer applications can be of help. Finally, you learned about some sample computer applications in engineering.

Key Terms

ARGOS system
automated DNA sequencing
bases
Building Information Modeling (BIM)
central processing unit (CPU)
computer model
distributed computing
doppler weather radar
dropsondes
gene
genome
geographic information system (GIS)
Geostationary Operational Environmental Satellite (GOES)
ground-penetrating radar
lidar
multispectral imaging
prototype
radiosondes
remote sensing
scientific method
SETI
volunteer computing

Chapter Review

Multiple Choice

Select the best answer.

1. The first step in the scientific method involves _____.

(a) collecting data and then analyzing data to prove or disprove a hypothesis
(b) concluding whether or not a hypothesis is correct
(c) observing some occurrence or aspect of the world or identifying a problem
(d) developing a hypothesis to explain an occurrence

2. Weather balloons travel high into the atmosphere, carrying high-tech instrument packages, called _____, that collect data about the upper atmosphere.

(a) radiometers
(b) satellites
(c) radiosondes
(d) radiographies

3. Key components of a geographic information system are _____.

(a) tools for entering geographic information such as addresses
(b) a database management system (DBMS)
(c) tools for inputting or using graphics files to use as baseline maps
(d) all of the above

4. NOAA is responsible for which remote-sensing project?

(a) National Data Buoy Center (NDBC)
(b) Coastal-Marine Automated Network (C-MAN)
(c) DART (Deep-ocean Assessment and Reporting of Tsunamis)
(d) all of the above

5. Which computer-controlled satellite has detected the heat signatures of extrasolar planets?

(a) Kepler
(b) Cassini
(c) Voyager 1
(d) New Horizons

6. SETI@home uses what free computer program?

(a) Excel@home
(b) BOINC
(c) Genome
(d) none of the above

7. The third step in the engineering process involves _____.

(a) commercialize product
(b) develop a list of specifications and materials
(c) build a prototype
(d) brainstorm possible solutions

8. BIM is a tool used for _____.

(a) collecting EL Niño weather data
(b) recording the lifecycle of a building or other structure
(c) exploring the surface of other planets
(d) discovering buried ruins

9. Wind and air pressure simulations confirmed that the shape of the Burj Khalifa had to be a _____.

(a) square
(b) waveform
(c) oval
(d) Y

10. Which engineering field ran computer simulations for the salvage of the *Costa Concordia*?

(a) mechanical
(b) civil
(c) nautical
(d) all of the above

5 Computers in Arts and Entertainment

The idea of computers as a core part of the arts is new for some. Art, in the view of many, is a creative and often physical process that is free-form, and thus cannot benefit from the inherently logical processing of a computer. Today, however, computers and other technologies are an integral part of the arts and entertainment world, helping artists to translate a world full of information into unique creative works or polished music videos. The computer serves as a tool in the artistic process. A costume designer can use a computer to help in drawing patterns, while a sculptor might use it to create 3-D models of a new project. A composer can use software to create new music and then produce printed sheet music to share with the quartet that will play the new concerto. Photographers can capture images digitally and edit them into entirely new scenes, while television and movie producers can create a vast range of special effects and script parts for completely computer-generated characters.

In this chapter, you will learn more about the use of computers in arts and entertainment. After reviewing the process of converting analog data to digital data, you will learn how computers affect music, from creating new music to recording and distributing the music around the world. You also will learn how dance, theater, and sculpture are changed by the use of computers to enhance and refine the craft. After discussing the use of computers in art conservation and preservation, the chapter moves on to examine computer graphics and digital photography and videography. Next, you will learn how cutting-edge computer technologies are used in the television and movie industries, including software to edit footage, add new special effects, colorize older movies, and create animated characters. Finally you will learn how computers are used in sports to help athletes and officials improve their performances.

COMPUTERS AND THE ARTS

Artist is a broad term – it includes visual artists, theater artists, dance artists, musicians, sculptors, and more. As noted earlier, for these artists the computer is a tool to aid in producing drawings, to place notes on a music staff, to add special visual effects to a digital photo, or to insert a unique sound in a musical composition. Sculptors also use computers to help create models before the artist begins the process of making the 3-D physical form.

Digitization: Analog to Digital Conversion

Before exploring the use of computers in the arts, you must understand the difference between analog data and digital data, as well as the process of converting between the two formats. Recall that data are "things" which, by themselves, have no meaning. When humans apply their knowledge to data, these things acquire meaning. Meaningful data becomes useful information.

Through the five senses, the human body receives and processes analog data, i.e., data in its original, natural format. This format is continuous (i.e., not sampled) but varies by magnitude or direction. For example, light and sound are continuous wave patterns of data received by the eyes and ears. People hear sounds when their ears pick up pressure waves created by vibrating objects. They see objects and color when light waves interact and strike their eyes. Originally, photography, recorded sound, radio, television, and film all used analog technologies to capture, store and transmit data, such as a song, an episode of a weekly program, or a motion picture. Sheet music, LP records, audio cassette tapes, VCR tapes, and 35mm film are all examples of analog media (as are paintings and sculptures).

Analog media are readily understandable by humans, and have served well, in some cases for thousands of years. By contrast, all electronic computers use digital data, formatted as bits (0s and 1s) that represent an off or on state. Unless specially trained, the vast majority of humans cannot understand digital data. So if sound and light waves are analog and a computer is digital, how does a computer record a photograph of a stunning landscape, play music through speakers, or show the car chase in your favorite action movie on a computer screen?

A computer samples all analog input and converts it into digital values before further processing the data. To supply human-understandable information, the computer must convert the digital data back to its original analog form.

To experience analog-to-digital conversion, try using the Windows 10 Voice Recorder to record a digital audio clip of your analog voice. Whether a separate device or embedded in the computer, the microphone is an analog input source. The diaphragm in the microphone captures analog sound waves and converts them into a continuous electrical signal (also analog). The signal flows to the computer's **analog-to-digital-converter (ADC)**, which converts the signal into digital (binary) data of 1s and 0s. The digital data flows to the **digital signal processor (DSP)**, which compresses the data to save storage space. Finally, the DSP sends the compressed data to the central processor, which stores the data in WAV, MP3, or other audio file format.

To play a digitized sound, such as a WAV, an MP3, or a CD track, the computer reverses the process. The central processor retrieves and sends the digital data to the DSP to be decompressed. The DSP sends the decompressed data to the computer's **digital-to-analog converter (DAC)** which converts the digital data back to an analog voltage for output via a speaker or headset. This process happens very quickly, seeming almost instantaneous to a listener.

Throughout the chapter, you will see how the use of computers in the arts requires analog-to-digital conversion and the reverse, in order to capture the motion, sound, and sights of the real world into the art forms of music, dance, theater, sculpture, graphic arts, and photography.

Music

Computer technology is becoming an integral part of nearly every aspect of music. Musicians use computer technology to create, compose, and perform music. The digital recordings of a musical performance can be manipulated and processed down to the level of individual notes – allowing a producer to edit out slight imperfections in an artist's voice or remove background noises. For example, if you have listened to a live concert recording, the background crowd noise probably has been edited out, using audio editing software, to enhance the performance. The finished digital recording can be distributed via broadcast, the Web, or other media.

COMPOSING MUSIC The process of composing music is an iterative one. Artists may write a few notes on paper, play those notes on a guitar to listen to the melody, change the notes to a slightly different key, try humming those bars, and so on. While some artists complete the composition process entirely before performing a song, others might improvise a song first and then later transcribe that performance into a set of sheet music. With computer hardware and software, artists have the flexibility to compose and create music in almost any fashion they choose.

Music notation software, such as Sibelius and Finale, allows you to create sheet music electronically. You can use notation software to produce new compositions, such as a jazz tune. To compose the song using notation software, you first set up a **score**, which is a series of staves (the five horizontal lines) on which all the different instrumental or vocal parts of a musical work are written. Using the software, you can select any number of instruments or voices and a time signature (Figure 5-1). For the jazz tune, you might decide to choose several instruments, such as the trumpet, a string bass, a piano, drums, and a saxophone, and a time signature of four beats per measure. The software automatically sets up the score based on your input.

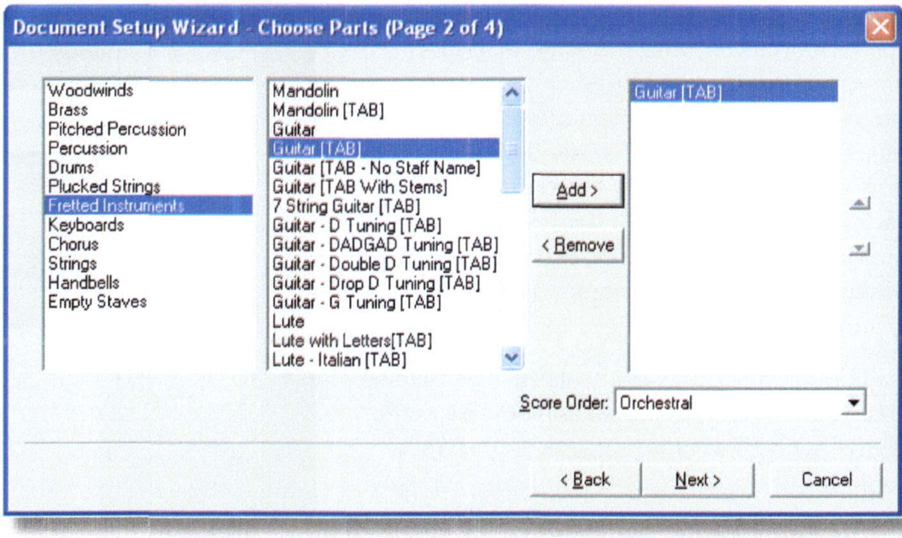

Figure 5-1 Using notation software, you can select any number of instruments or voices and a time signature for your new composition.

Figure 5-2 Some notation software allows you to scan printed sheet music, such as a Brahms song, which you then can edit, print, or post to the Web.

Next, you enter notes for the song. Typically, notation software allows you to input notes by:

- Clicking note buttons and then clicking them on to a staff in the score
- Typing notes on your computer keyboard or playing a tune on a MIDI keyboard (see below) connected to the computer
- Importing existing MIDI files
- Scanning printed sheet music, such as an existing classical tune (Figure 5-2)

As you enter notes for a melody for the lead saxophone, the software automatically will harmonize your melody and create your piano, string bass, and drum accompaniments, adding a nice jazz rhythm to your tune. Guitarists and other instruments with frets use a unique type of notation, called TAB or tablature, which uses notation for chords instead of standard music notes on a score. Many notation software packages also support creating TAB. Musicians enter notes as they would any other score – by entering via keyboard or mouse or connecting a MIDI guitar – so that that the notation software automatically can create the TAB.

Most notation software also allows you to type lyrics directly onto the score or import full verses from a text file. After you have entered the notes for each instrument in the song, you can use the software to play the tune so you can hear your new creation, and then edit it, as needed. Once you are satisfied, you can save and print the score – and even publish directly to the Web (Figure 5-3).

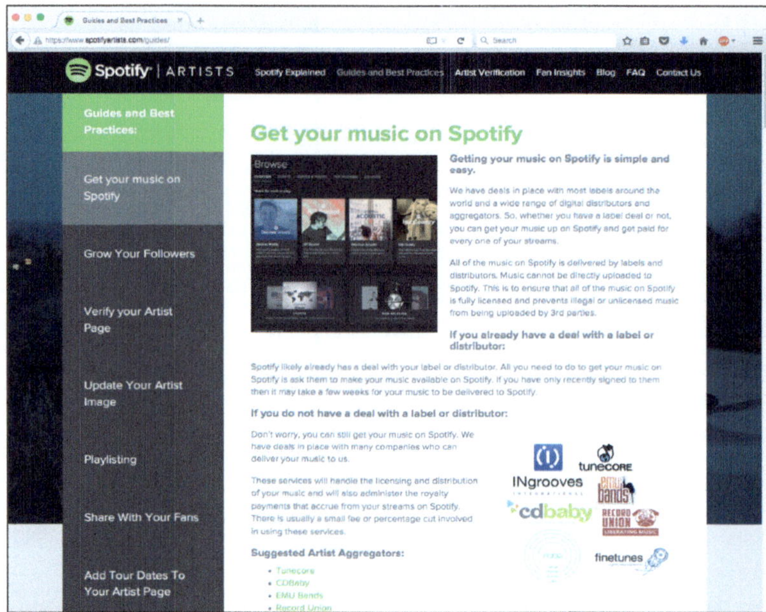

Figure 5-3 Files created using notation software can be posted to the Web as HTML files or to special Web sites, such as the Finale Showcase, where artists can post sheet music files for shared viewing, playing, transposing, and printing.

PLAYING AND RECORDING MUSIC

Traditional musical instruments such as pianos, guitars, and trumpets are analog devices that rely on sound waves to transmit sound. In a studio setting, artists play instruments and sing into microphones that transmit the sound to a computer. Inside every microphone is a diaphragm that collects the sound waves and creates movement in a plate, wire, or other component that converts the sound wave into an electrical voltage that can be digitized by computer. Each performer or artist has his or her own microphone, and the sound of each voice or instrument is recorded as a separate track, or unique stream of digital sound.

Some of the sounds in today's music are not just recorded on computers – they are created using computers. For example, using a synthesizer, musicians can generate the complex tones of many instruments. A **synthesizer**, which can be a hardware device or a computer or a chip, creates sound from digital instructions input by the user, either by a standard computer keyboard or by devices resembling musical instruments.

The signals from a synthesizer are fed into the computer via a MIDI port. A **MIDI port** is a special type of serial port that connects the computer to an electronic musical instrument or other input device, such as an electronic piano keyboard (Figure 5-4). **MIDI** (pronounced *MID-dee*) is short for **Musical Instrument Digital Interface** and is the music industry's standard for how to represent music in digital form, as well as for how devices, such as sound cards and synthesizers, represent sounds electronically. MIDI actually has three components: a MIDI port to connect an input device, the MIDI protocol or language, and the file format, called Standard MIDI.

As noted, a computer with a MIDI port has the capability of recording sounds (data) that have been created by a synthesizer and then processing the data to create and output new sounds. The **MIDI protocol** is a series of instructions or messages that describes the action of a musical performance. The MIDI message encodes these actions, such as pitch and volume, as bytes of digital information. Each message instructs the synthesizer which sounds to use, which notes to play, and how loud to

Figure 5-4 An electronic piano keyboard is an external MIDI device that allows users to record music, which can be stored in the computer.

play each note. For example, to sound a note in MIDI language you send a Note On message; you can turn off the note by sending a Note Off message. Other MIDI messages include those to tell an instrument to change volume or change the sound (for example, from a guitar sound to an organ sound). The synthesizer then generates the actual sounds.

When the MIDI messages are saved so you can play them back later, they typically are saved in a format called the Standard MIDI format. The Standard MIDI files differ from the raw MIDI instructions in that they are time-stamped to ensure they play back in the correct sequence. Standard MIDI files typically are the primary source of music for many popular computer and online games, as well as your cellular phone's ring tones.

A **sequencer** is a software program or dedicated device that records, processes, edits, and plays back MIDI data through a MIDI instrument or computer speaker. To record a MIDI file, you play a note on a MIDI keyboard, guitar, or other instrument connected to the computer (Figure 5-5). The sequencer records the data, including the length, volume, pitch, and other information about that note. Sequencing software allows you to record MIDI data in multiple tracks for a single recording, such as the bass, guitar, and keyboard.

Figure 5-5 MIDI instruments allow a range of controls and features that are not available on conventional instruments. For example, you can set each drum pad to generate a different drum sound or special effect. Buttons on a MIDI wind instrument allow you to change the octave or even change the sound from a clarinet to a saxophone or flute.

Most film and TV scores, as well as popular recorded music, are written and performed using electronic keyboards and other MIDI-equipped musical instruments. Thanks to advances in digital sampling and synthesis technologies, the orchestra playing behind that big-screen blockbuster movie is more likely to be the product of MIDI than a real orchestra with dozens of instruments.

EDITING MUSIC Each day thousands of musicians, composers, engineers, and producers use audio-editing software to record and master albums, score and post soundtracks for film and television, and create music for the Internet. **Audio-editing software** lets you modify audio clips, including music, and produce studio-quality soundtracks and songs (Figure 5-6). Audio-editing software works like a musical word processor, in that it has cut, paste, copy, and other editing functions that allow an artist to modify a track in any song. Most audio-editing software also includes features of a sequencer to allow you to edit, mix, and incorporate MIDI tracks with other audio tracks.

With audio-editing software, you can combine multiple tracks of songs and create special effects such as reverb, delay, or a looped sound of a chorus behind a melody. The software also can generate rhythms that complement the melody of a song. You can adjust the song by changing the speed or tempo; adding or changing notes; or modifying pitch, tone, and timbre to create an entirely new sound. For example, you can play a song on a MIDI keyboard at 60 beats per minute, but then play in back at 120 beats per minute using audio-editing software. Because MIDI messages contain individual instructions for playing each individual note of each individual instrument, you actually

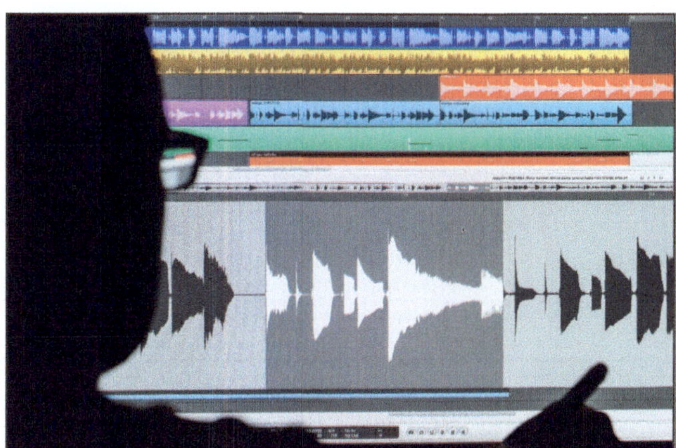

Figure 5-6 Audio-editing software lets you combine multiple tracks of songs and create special effects such as reverb, delay, or a looped sound of a chorus behind a melody.

can change just one note in a song or orchestrate an entire song with entirely different instruments. With live artists, you would have to bring the entire band back into the studio to rerecord any needed tracks. The end result of the recording and editing process is a final song, soundtrack for a video game, or television score, which then is printed as sheet music for performance or recorded to the Web or other medium for distribution.

PERFORMING MUSIC Computers are helping artists in the performances of their art as well. Computer-controlled amplifiers and speakers, for example, output sound from their instruments, while computers at the soundboard are used to balance the sound, ensure microphone volumes are correct, and create special lighting and sound effects.

Computers also help train musicians to perform better. In a unique application of technology to music, a facility at Arizona State University uses technology to help students learn the subtle movements required to be a world-class conductor. The system, known as the Digital Conducting Feedback System, gives students a chance to practice conducting without a live orchestra. During each training session, you stand in front of a mirror and a digital video camera records your conducting. You then put on a customized set of spandex sleeves that have pockets to hold four pairs of electrodes. These electrodes are placed in precise locations designed to capture key points of arm movement.

As you start to conduct a song, a computer algorithm monitors the movements of your arms. Based on your movements, the computer generates the sound of an orchestra. If your movements are technically correct, the digitally created orchestra sounds in perfect harmony and pitch. By experiencing the response of the digital orchestra in the lab, you learn to adjust your movements to generate the best sounding output from the orchestra. The electrodes also transmit your movement data to the computer, where your conducting performance is recorded for later analysis.

DISTRIBUTING MUSIC Computer technology has made distributing and accessing music easier than ever. Online vendors such as Amazon or iTunes often make samples available to entice customers. Users can purchase a single song or an entire album online and download MP3 or ACC files directly to local storage, allowing them to listen immediately from their smartphone, tablet, or desktop computer.

Dance

In the world of dance, computers increasingly play an important role, allowing dancers to choreograph dances; reproduce their movements using computer notation and digital video, and use motion capture technology to create virtual dance partners and musical scores.

CHOREOGRAPHY AND NOTATION Just as music involves a series of notes, dance involves a series of steps. Choreography is the art of designing how dancers will move during a performance. Choreographers can use a computer program, called **dance notation software**, which captures movement as a series of symbols so that it can be shared with others. A dancer uses a dance score just as a musician uses a music score; the dance score allows each artist to learn the work without being influenced by someone else's artistic interpretation, and allows the dance to continue to be performed.

Several different methods of dance notation are in use today – including Eshkol-Wachman Movement Notation, Benesh, and Labanotation. Software products created for each of these methods allow choreographers and dancers to use the computer keyboard and mouse to input notation for a particular dance. LabanWriter and LabanDancer, for example, include tools to allow choreographers and dancers to notate their works using the Labanotation dance notation (Figure 5-8). The completed notation provides guidelines for future staging of the work.

Choreographers use animation software modified to create choreographed animations of dances. For example, DanceForms software

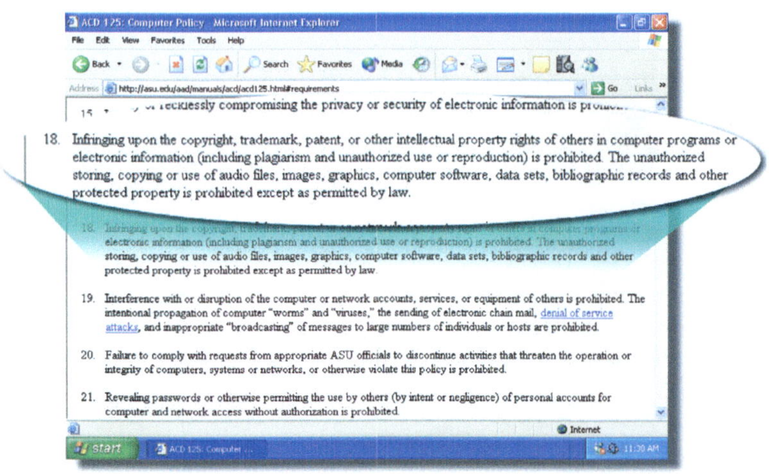

Figure 5-7 Many colleges and universities post acceptable use policies on their Web sites to communicate with students that any activity that infringes on copyrights is not acceptable use of campus computing resources.

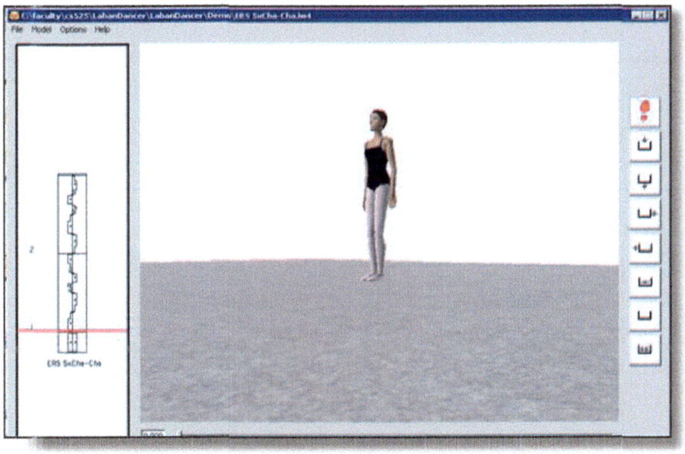

Figure 5-8 Software helps dancers notate dances for future reference. Using a special version of the AutoDesk AutoCAD software, called CALABAN, users can notate a dance called The Workers' Quarters using Labanotation symbols.

includes templates of basic dance moves and tools to create mirror images of dancers, as well as 100 ballet positions and transitions that are used to script ballet choreography. Using DanceForms the choreographer can plan the movements of individual dancers, view the interactions of all the dancers from different perspectives, and adjust each dance sequence in relative time (Figure 5-9).

In addition to capturing choreography using dance notation and animation, dancers can use other computer-based tools to document a dance fully. Computer technology allows any aspect of a dance – including electronic documents outlining the historical basis, the costumes, and production information such as costume, set, and light designs; digital audio of the musical score; and digital video of the performance – to be recorded and stored digitally. The dance notation even can be synchronized to the digital video to show exactly the

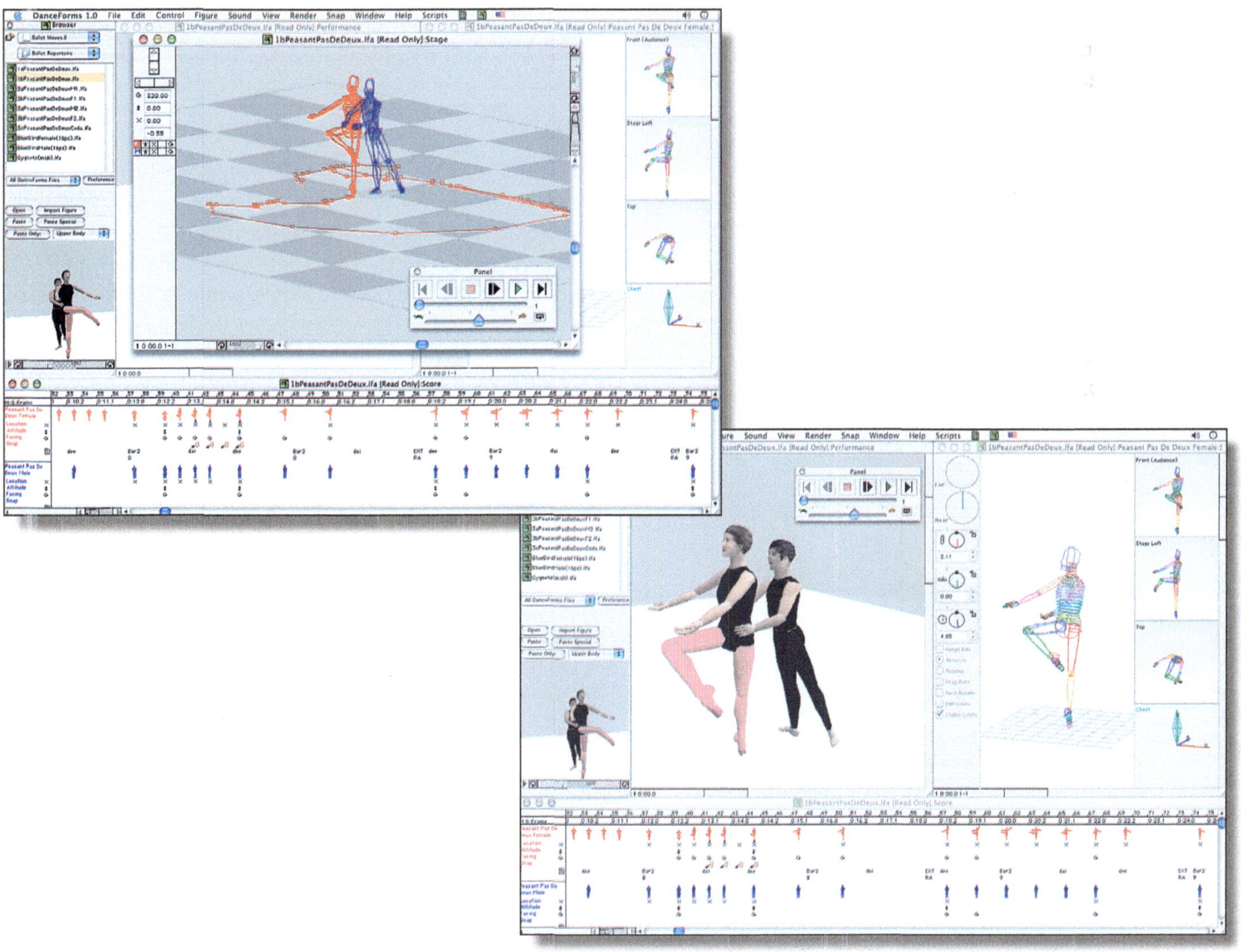

Figure 5-9 Using LifeForms software, a choreographer can plan the movements of dancers using computer-generated animations.

steps that created a particular move. This documentation process results in a complete electronic record of a dance, so that future performers have all the information needed to recreate a performance.

MOTION CAPTURE Dancers also rely on a computer technology borrowed from cinema called **motion capture** to record and analyze their dance movements, and even create virtual dance partners and musical scores based on those movements. People began studying the movements of humans and animals in the 19th century, using multiple still cameras attached to a set of trip wires. But it was not until the past few decades that computer applications have revolutionized this field.

Several different tracking technologies are available for motion capture, including mechanical, optical, and magnetic. Optical tracking is the most common method used today. Almost every tracking technology uses markers fixed to the subject, ex., at elbows, knees, and other joints. These markers might be passive (ex., reflective) or active (i.e., powered). To simplify the whole process, performers often wear a motion capture body suit which has trackers already applied (Figure 5-10).

In recording a dance, for example, the motion capture system tracks the position and orientation of each marker over 100 times per second to identify the location of the performers' bodies in space. This rapid tracking records every bodily motion and provides highly accurate capture of movements such as a leap, a pirouette, a rond de jambe, or a two-step.

Figure 5-10 Dancers and athletes rely on a technology called motion capture to record and analyze their movements. Computer animators apply this same technology to 3-D models to create lifelike animation.

Using this technology, moreover, one human dancer can dance with 3-D computer-generated models of another dancer based on the movements acquired from a real dancer using motion capture. As the real, live performer dances, the 3-D generated dancer can appear on a screen behind the dancer. Using a 3-D computer model allows a choreographer to use movements a human cannot complete, such as diving into the floor and vanishing from sight. Other applications of motion capture use sensors to transmit the position of a dancer's body to a computer. The computer software interprets the movements and then uses the information to control sound, lighting, and other effects. A particular leap by a dancer might cause lights to brighten, while a slower fluid movement of the arm could trigger a specific audio file to play as background music. A dancer defines the timing and action of those effects, based solely on his or her movements. While using such technology during a live performance, timing is critically important. If the timing of the dance if off slightly, the computers may not be able to adjust and thus the music and effects will be out of sync with the performers.

Theater

Computers are used in many aspects of theater, allowing the production crew to design, model, and test key elements of a theatrical performance – lights, sets, costumes, and sound. This saves both time and, especially, money. For example, using computer-aided design (CAD) software, set designers can create 3-D models of sets and then use these models as guides as they create the physical objects, either by hand or using computer controlled machines like 3D printers (Figure 5-11).

Stage lighting also relies on computer technology, including CAD software. For years, creating lighting effects was labor intensive and slow, requiring many technicians to adjust and move lights manually. Computers have automated much of the stage lighting process, allowing changes to unfold as slowly or quickly as possible to make effects, such as a sunrise or an explosion, more believable. A click of a button instructs computer-controlled lights to move into position for the next cue. Today, lighting technicians and designers also can use CAD software to design a lighting scheme and then play it back to watch the resulting effects, without even setting foot onstage.

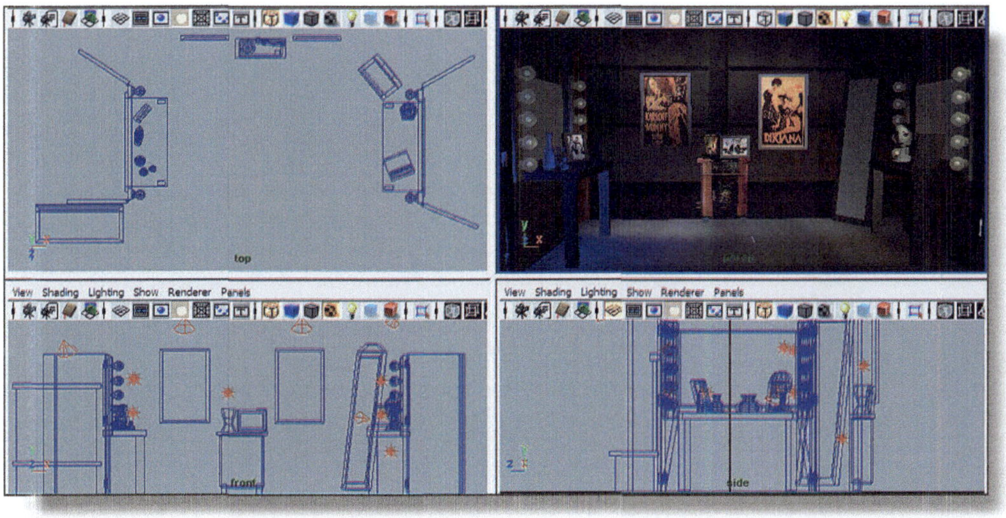

Figure 5-11 Set design software.

design, and other types of 3-D modeling software to create a digital model of an object that they want to sculpt. That 3-D model then serves as a guide as the sculptor creates the art in a physical medium, such as marble.

As a sculptor, you also can use 3-D scanning hardware and software to record an existing object and then recreate that object in a different medium. Once the object is scanned, you can use CAD or 3-D modeling software to enlarge, reduce, or alter the object's digital model.

Computers also help sound designers, who use a computer-controlled soundboard and software programs that manage multiple input tracks and effects, allowing operators to balance sound more effectively and create stunning effects. During scene changeovers, the sound designer can cover the noise by cueing digital music to play through speakers placed throughout a theater. The software also knows when performers are offstage and automatically turns off their microphones.

For the costume designer, cast measurements are stored in the computer so that, for the next production, the designer can plug the correct measurements into CAD software and then design and print a pattern for any part of the costume needed.

Theater box offices also use software to handle ticket sales. Either via telephone or over the Web, the software allows customers to specify the show they would like to see, select seats from a seating chart, and pay for the tickets. Box office staff can use the same software to report by day on sales or available seats for a particular show; to print labels to mail customers their tickets; or to calculate commissions earned by promoters.

Sculpture and 3-D Media

Sculpture is another art form that has benefited from the use of computers. In the past, a sculptor created a work using only a medium such as wood or marble, the appropriate tools needed to shape the medium, and a trained eye. Today, as a sculptor, you may rely on computers to help with several aspects of the artistic process. Sculptors can use CAD software, like that used in product

Once you have created the model for your sculpture, you can use a 3D printer or CNC (computer numerical controlled) milling machine to shape your desired medium. The manufacturing industry uses CNC milling machines for complex manufacturing of items such as jet engines and car parts. In sculpture, CNC milling machines use CAD models or 3-D models as the input to the CNC milling machine. The software reads the models and determines the geometry of the object. After you enter some milling parameters (type of cutting tool, required accuracy, and so on), the CNC system software automatically calculates the milling paths and then guides the tools on the milling machine to sculpt the object, as defined by the model. CNC milling machines can range in size from desktop versions that can mill smaller objects such as bottles and jewelry to large machines used to mill larger objects. The Chicago Field Museum, for example, relied on a large CNC milling machine to create sculpted bones to replace foot bones that were missing from the original fossil set of the Tyrannosaurus Rex (Figure 5-12).

Art Conservation and Preservation

Art and architecture form part of the tangible cultural heritage of a people. They are vulnerable to "the ravages of time," even if protected in a museum. Organizations around the world use various computer systems and applications to record, stabilize and protect art and architecture for future generations. For example, a 3-D scanning system was used in the Digital Michelangelo project, to record all of Michelangelo's sculptures and architecture. These 3-D scanners sweep a fine line of laser light across the sculpture's surface (Figure 5-13). The scanner captures the shape of the laser line as it curves across the unique features and chisel marks of the sculpture. This information is stored in computers as 3-D coordinates for later processing into a surface model of the sculpture. For larger sculptures, such as Michelangelo's *David*, the scanner head must be placed on a rolling assembly that allows the scanner to move around the object so each side of the object can be scanned. In addition to creating an archive for study, these data serve as a "base line" for future conservators to identify and remedy deterioration.

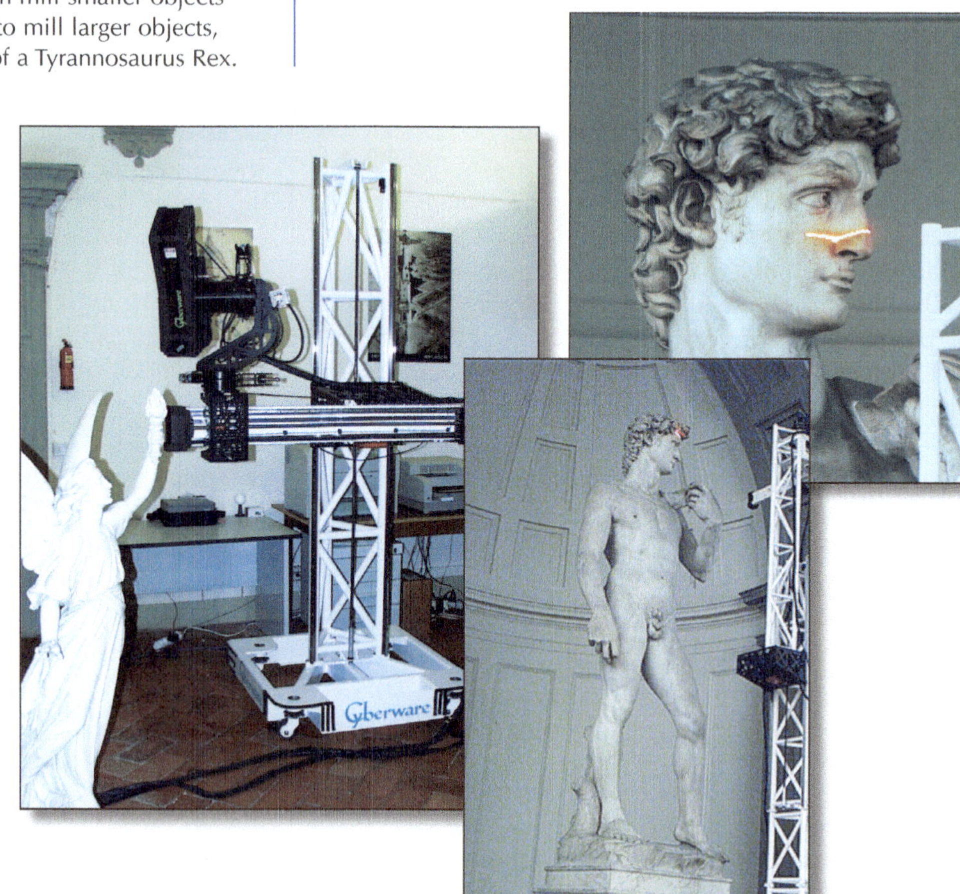

Figure 5-13 In order to create 3-D scans of larger statues, the 3-D scanning system includes a vertical truss, a horizontal arm for vertical movement, a pan-tilt head for horizontal movement, and the scanner head – all on a rolling base.

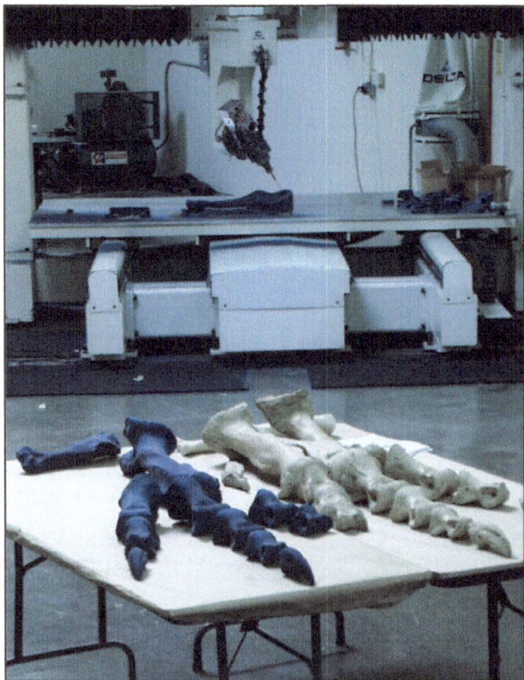

Figure 5-12 CNC milling machines can range in size from desktop versions that can mill smaller objects to large machines used to mill larger objects, such as the foot bones of a Tyrannosaurus Rex.

Graphic Arts

Graphic arts, also simply called graphics, is the collective term for two-dimensional work such as drawing, painting, calligraphy, and printing. Although computer graphics encompasses a wide range of artistic expression, it essentially involves drawing pictures and surface features on computers, a process also called **rendering**. The graphics created on a computer can be illustrations, cartoons, simulations, designs for new products, logos, backgrounds for a music video, or stylized art. Using computers, graphic artists can create pictures of realistic objects or items that do not yet (and may never) exist.

Some suggest that creating art on a computer means the computer does the work. In reality, the artistic process is executed on a computer, but only at the direction of the artist. When creating graphics using a computer, the activity is similar to creating art using pen and paper or paintbrush, oil, and canvas – the artist envisions the image, plans the approach to create the image, and then uses software (instead of pen or paintbrush) to create the graphic. **Illustration software**, such as Adobe Illustrator, allows you to draw and render digital art using a finger, mouse, or graphics tablet, just as you would use a pencil, brush, or pastels to create traditional art. The software has the computer equivalents of all the tools that an artist would use manually: brushes, pencils, spraying tools, erasers, different types of paper, and so on. Using the software, you also can add effects with special filters or edit and retouch a graphic, picture element, or "pixel," by pixel.

Other unique types of graphics software include software for creating fractal art. A **fractal** is a geometric pattern that is repeated at ever smaller (or larger) scales to produce irregular shapes and surfaces that cannot be represented by classical geometry. A fractal has symmetry of scale, which means you can zoom in on part of a fractal shape an infinite number of times and it still looks the same. A **computer-generated fractal** is a unique art form that uses mathematical formulas to create art with a vast range of structure, detail, color and light (Figure 5-14). The fractal essentially is a graphical image that represents the behavior of a mathematical equation repeated over and over. The formula used determines how each of the millions of pixels in the image is formed and colored. Artists then can modify the formulas and change color algorithms to create unique images of abstract shapes or representations of waves, plants, landscapes, and planets.

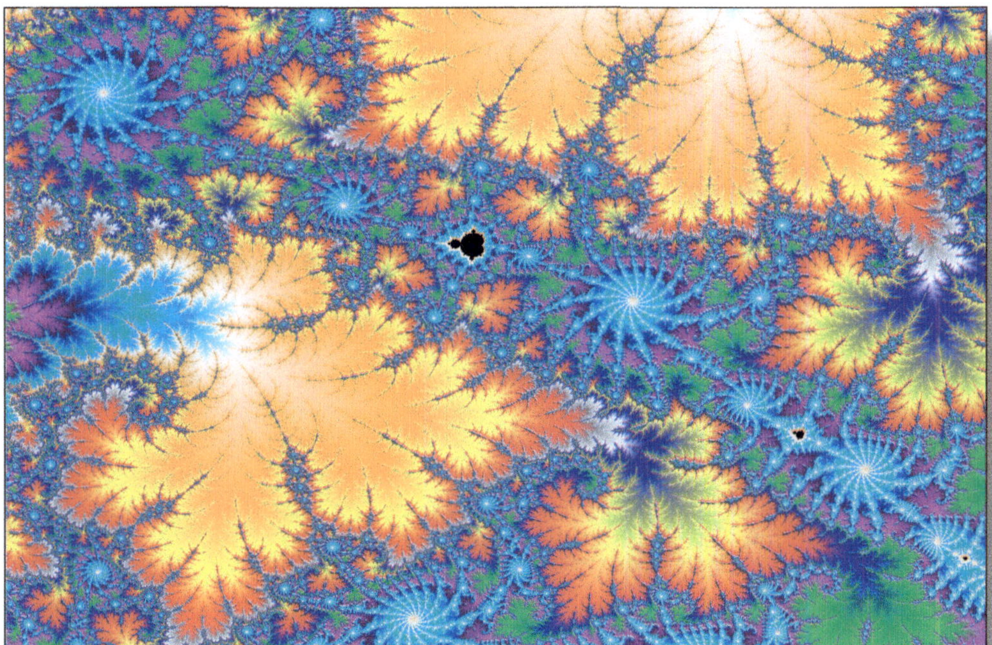

Figure 5-14 Software used to create fractal art provides tools to allow artists to define what mathematical formulas to use to create the art, set color schemes, define geometrical patterns – and even distribute calculations over a group of networked computers.

Photography and Videography

Today, photography and movie production rarely use traditional analog film media. Instead, a **digital camera** allows users to take still pictures or video electronically and store images in memory, on a removable storage card, or on the Web ("in the cloud"). Digital cameras appeal to a wide range of users, including professional photographers. For example, real estate agents use digital cameras so they can easily post images to a Web site for review by clients and customers. Or you might use a digital camera to share quickly images with friends and family via e-mail and Web sites. Photojournalists and professional photographers use digital cameras to take photographs and then refine the images using editing software, like Adobe Photoshop, before creating prints on high-quality paper or posting them to an online gallery on the Web.

Digital cameras are available in many different formats, and almost all support both still photography and video recording (Figure 5-15). Smartphones, laptops, and tablets use very tiny cameras called **webcams** intended for taking quick, convenient photos or videos for uploading to the Web. Ruggedized, compact cameras like GoPro are useful for capturing outdoor or underwater activities. Both of these formats offer little or no physical enhancements such as zoom lenses or filters.

A **point and shoot camera** fits easily in the hand and offers zoom hardware. It is a good choice for casual users who want some control over how they can take images and video. A **prosumer camera** offers most of the control features of a professional digital camera, but the lens system remains fixed to the camera body. These cameras appeal to serious photographers or videographers who cannot afford costly, professional-grade equipment. Finally, there are **professional-grade cameras**, which offer interchangeable lenses and perform as well or better than their analog film counterparts.

(a) webcam

(b) point-and-shoot

(c) prosumer

(d) professional-grade

Figure 5-15 Several types of digital cameras are available on the market, with features designed for specific types of users.

BEHIND THE SCENES: DIGITAL PHOTO AND VIDEO CAPTURE All photography begins by capturing light, and light is an analog medium. Figure 5-16 illustrates how one type of digital camera transforms the captured image into a screen display. As you point the camera lens towards the image you want to photograph and click the button to take the picture, light passes through the lens of the camera to one or more chips called **charge-coupled devices (CCD)**. For the best picture quality, professional digital cameras have three CCDs to capture three different light spectra (red, green, and blue). Each CCD generates an electrical signal that represents the image; this analog signal then is converted to a digital signal by an analog-to-digital converter (ADC). A digital signal processor (DSP) adjusts the quality of the image and stores the digital image on the storage media in the camera.

DIGITAL PHOTO EDITING Using software, the images captured on a digital camera can be viewed, edited, incorporated into documents, and printed. Some digital cameras allow users to review and edit images while they still are stored on media in the camera. Most users, including professional photographers and photojournalists, prefer to download a copy of the images from the digital camera to a computer's storage drive, or to the cloud. With some digital cameras, you can download images using a cable that connects between the digital camera and the USB port or FireWire port on the system unit. If the camera stores photos on storage media, such as an SD card, you can insert the media into a reading device that connects wirelessly or attaches to a USB port in the system unit (Figure 5-17). Many newer computers also come with built-in card readers to make it easier to transfer and store images. Still other cameras can transfer content using WiFi or Bluetooth technologies.

Once the photos are stored on a computer, a photographer can edit the images using **photo-editing software**, such as Adobe Photoshop. These programs vary greatly in capabilities and cost (from free to thousands of dollars). With these tools, you can adjust the contrast and brightness and correct lighting problems (Figure 5-18a), remove red-eye, crop an image and remove unnecessary or unwanted elements (such as your

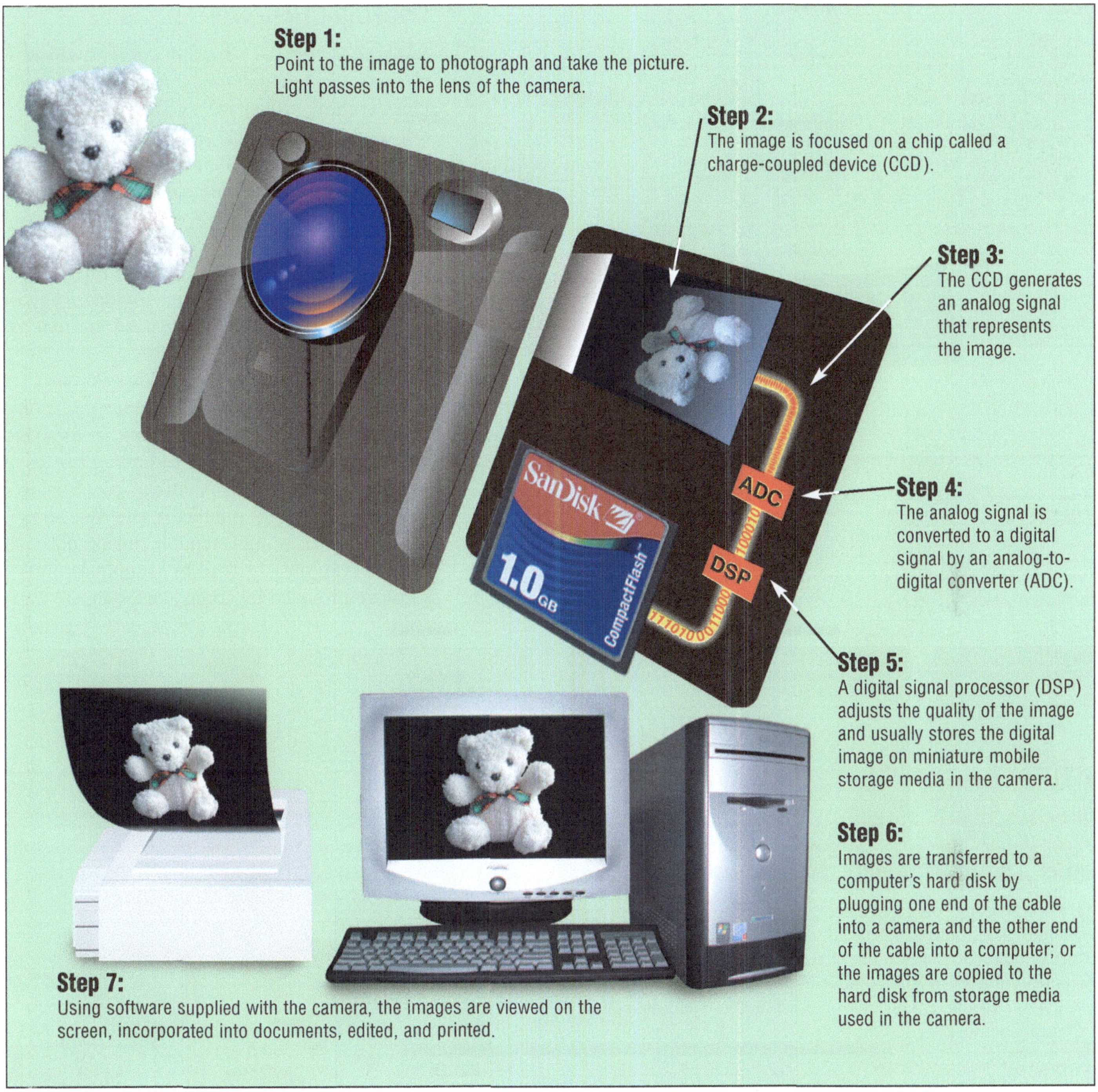

Figure 5-16 How a digital camera works.

thumb or the random stranger in the background). You also can use photo-editing software to add color to black-and-white photos and even remove blemishes and wrinkles (Figure 5-18b). Professional artists use photo-editing software to create stunning images by adding special effects or to transform a single photo into a digital image that looks like an oil painting or an entirely new artwork (Figure 5-18c).

You also can use photo-editing software to print photographs or create electronic photo albums. Home photographers often post their digital photographs to online photo sharing and printing sites, such as Instagram or SmugMug. Professional photographers and photojournalists often post their photos to online galleries that showcase their work, as well as to their own Web sites.

Figure 5-17 To download digital photos, you can insert the media, such as an SD card, into a reading device that connects wirelessly or attaches to a USB port in the system unit. You even can get a mouse with a built-in card reader.

Copyright Concerns

A **copyright** – a legal document which protects any tangible form of expression – gives authors and artists exclusive rights to duplicate, publish, and sell their materials. Because digital photos and computer graphics are easily shared and transferred over the Internet, they raise unique copyright concerns. One way to ensure that copyrighted photos, graphics, and animations are used only by those who have permission is to add a digital watermark to the files before posting them to the Internet.

Digital watermarking allows you to embed a digital code or other pattern in audio, images, video, and documents. Sometimes the watermark is faintly visible to human eye, as when a stock photo agency like Getty Images displays its holdings online for sale. But often the watermark is imperceptible during normal use, and can only be read by computers and software provided by companies such as

(a) Photo-editing software, such as Adobe Photoshop, allows you to edit digital photographs to adjust the contrast and brightness. For example, the photo on the left has a yellowish color. After balancing the levels, the contrast improves (middle) but the color cast is still visible. Finally, after balancing the color, the yellowish cast is removed and the true bright colors of the peppers come through.

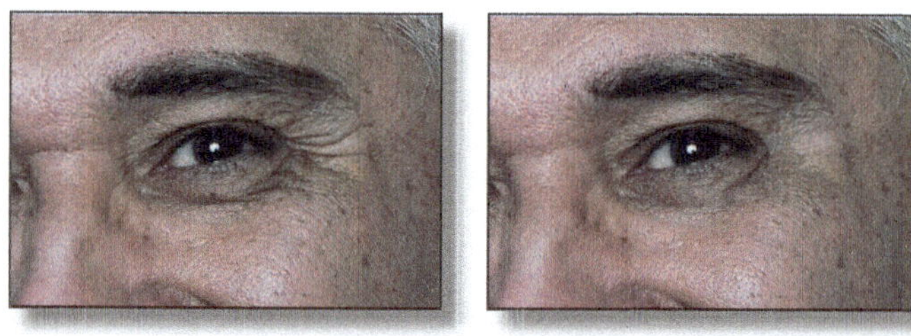

(b) Photo-editing software allows you to remove blemishes and wrinkles from a photograph. Here, for example, the wrinkles below the eye are removed digitally.

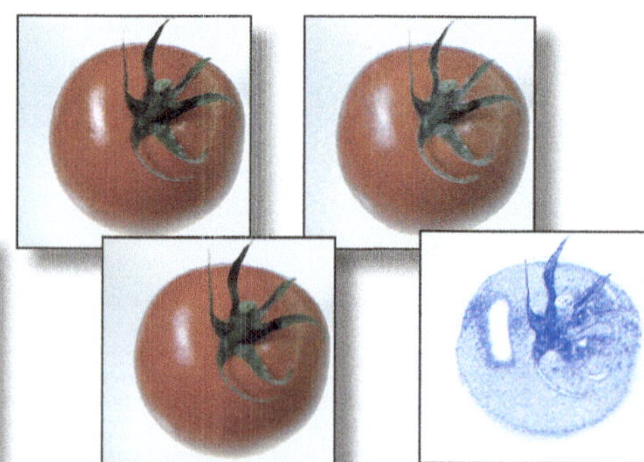

(c) Professional artists can create stunning images by adding special effects, such as the steam rising from the pizza in the first image. Photo-editing tools also allow you to take a digital photo of a tomato and create new versions that look like an oil painting or an entirely new artwork.

Figure 5-18 Sample editing capabilities of Adobe Photoshop.

Digimarc. To create an unseen digital watermark, you can use Digimarc's software to make subtle changes to the data that is part of the original digital content. The changes made by the software cannot be seen by the human eye (Figure 5-19). Yet, the digital watermark can be recognized by simple reading devices or applications enabled with the appropriate Digimarc software.

What You See May Not Really Be True

In addition to copyright problems, the fact that both digital photos and video can be easily edited means that what you see may not really be true. For example, to promote tourism Washington State once paid for a tourism ad showing an impossible view of Seattle – but how would anyone not familiar with Seattle know the picture was false? Sometimes the edits are obviously fake, such as inserting a beer bottle on an image of the Martian surface, or a famous person's head on a different body. Other times the edits require investigation to uncover the truth. When North Korean leader Kim Jong Un purged his uncle, digital editors removed the uncle from appearing in any photographs (Figure 5-20). Also, state-run or religious-run media may edit original images to emphasize leaders or de-emphasize something else, for instance the participation of women in a protest march.

Image without watermark Image with watermark View of imperceptible watermark

Figure 5-19 Digimarc's software embeds a digital watermark by making imperceptible changes to the data of the original digital content. The first photo shows the original image; the second the image with the watermark, which cannot be seen by the human eye. The third image shows the changes made to the image to embed the watermark, which includes information on the copyright owner, contact information, and more. This calculation is made by subtracting the original image from the watermarked image.

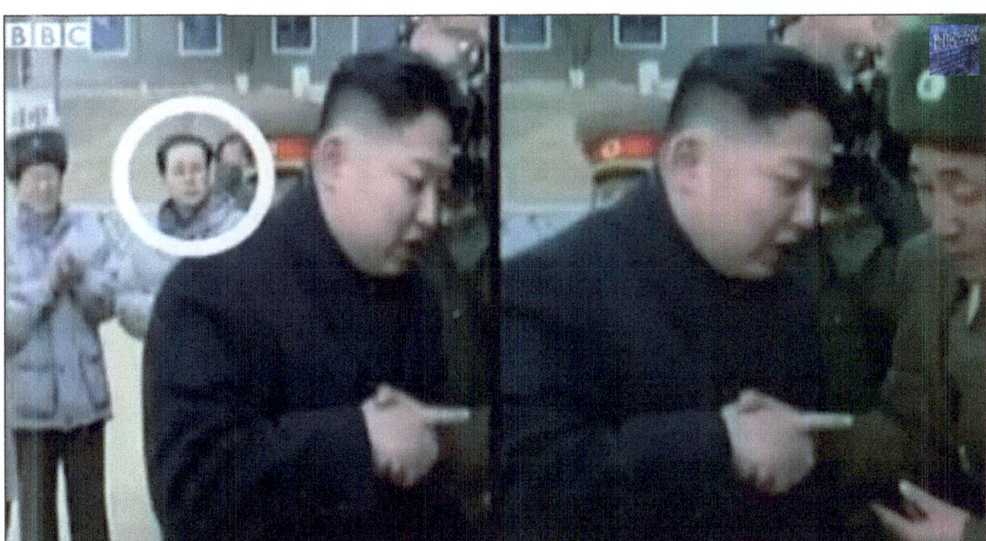

Figure 5-20 Jang Song-thaek has been removed from the photo on the right.

Reputable news organizations may alert the public to these altered images, but ultimately it is up to each of us to evaluate carefully any still or moving imagery of importance to us. For example, do parts of an image look jagged, misaligned, or suspiciously out of focus? Do the visible shadows agree with the light source(s) or is something mismatched?

COMPUTERS IN ENTERTAINMENT

Computers have changed the world of entertainment in ways unimaginable just a few years ago. For example, movies and television shows once were shot on rolls and rolls of film that had to be developed at the end of each day of shooting. In 2002, *Star Wars Episode II: Attack of the Clones* was the first major motion picture shot, distributed (via satellite), and shown in purely digital format.Today digital projection is normal in most theatres. Film makers like this method of exhibition because it allows them to make changes almost until viewing time. Theater owners like digital projection because every showing is pristine – no film breaks, no color fading, no scratches, hair and other dirt. No bulky shipments of reeled film; instead a hard drive plugs into the digital projector. Moreover, the projection systems in the theaters (and stadia) can display almost any digital content. So owners profit from exhibiting big sporting events, concerts, operas, or Broadway productions – and pull in an entirely new type of audience.

In the area of television and movies, computers have allowed for advances in video editing, colorization, animation, and motion capture. Computers also have changed sports, from the CAD-created equipment to the simulators used to train athletes.

Television and Movies

As noted, technology developments in film and television have shifted the industry from a film-based world to a digital one. Directors can use special animation software to plan the sequences of camera angles and individual shots for an entire movie or TV show, a process called **storyboarding**. Digital cameras allow both directors and actors to evaluate their work immediately after recording, instead of having to wait hours for analog film to be developed and printed as "rushes" or "dailies." And instead of literally cutting unwanted scenes from analog film and splicing the cut ends back at the correct point, video editors use powerful software such as Adobe Premiere Pro CC (Figure 5-21) to complete postproduction editing of raw footage digitally and add titles, soundtracks, and special effects to produce even higher-quality results.

DIGITAL VIDEO EDITING The first step in the editing process is **splitting**, which involves segmenting the video into smaller pieces, or scenes, that you can manage more easily. Most video-editing software automatically splits the video into scenes. After splitting, you would cut out unwanted scenes or portions of scenes, and possibly save them for inclusion as extras in the home video release. This process is called **pruning**.

When you have all of the scenes you want to use in the final production, you would then edit each individual

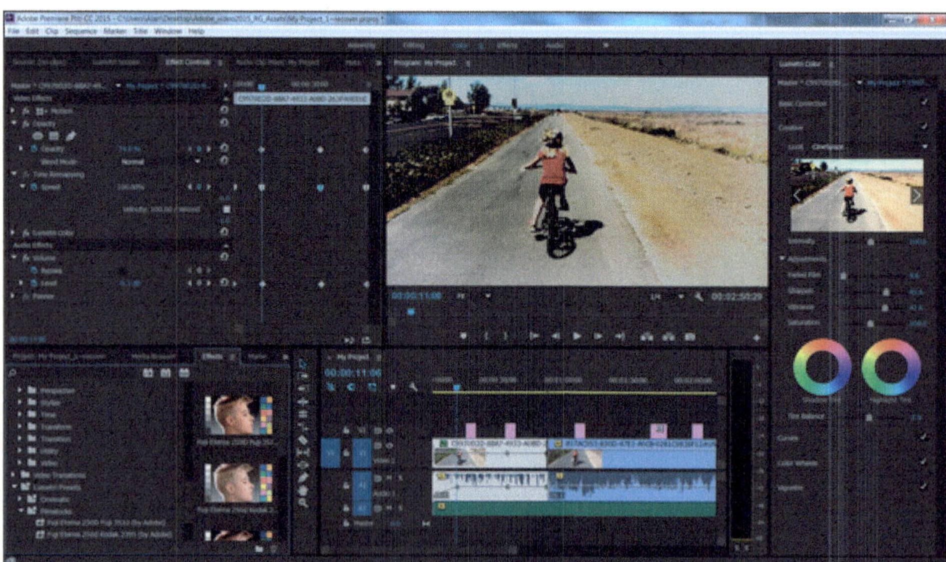

Figure 5-21 Adobe Premiere Pro CC video editing software.

scene. You can crop, or change the size of scenes to cut out irrelevant footage, and correct any lighting issues. If video has been recorded over a long period – and some movies can take years to make – using different cameras under different lighting conditions may result in digital video with varied lighting. Using color correction tools help you analyze the video and match brightness, colors, and other attributes of video clips to create a smoother look to the video.

After editing all of the scenes, you can add logos or titles to scenes. For a foreign film, for example, you could add subtitles to translate the film into English. You also can add opening and closing credits, as a simple credit roll or a highly animated sequence. Video editing software provides templates for titles and credits, so that you can select a template as a baseline and then customize the font, color, shadows, and more. Some video-editing software even allows you to import text files listing credits to save production time and avoid misspellings.

You may want to add special effects, such as warping, zoom motion, or morphing. **Morphing** is a special effect in which one object or actor is transformed into a different object or actor over the course of several seconds of video, creating the illusion of metamorphosis (Figure 5-22). Early morphing, as seen in *Terminator 2: Judgement Day* (1991) was very computer-intensive, costly, slow, and thus rarely used. Today, massive improvements in both computer hardware and software have made morphing simple and frequently seen in both movies, TV shows, and advertising.

Video composition – the process of integrating two or more elements into one complete scene – allows you to make a given scene more interesting. Video composition software, such as Adobe After Effects, provides tools that allow you to include visual effects – such as sunlight, rain, or animated characters – sound effects, and transitional effects, such as fade-in or fade-out. In creating the *Lord of the Rings* trilogy, editors used video composition software to integrate numerous visual effects, including live action from the set; computer graphics elements such as water, smoke, pine needles; digital lighting; and even the computer-created character Gollum. Some shots featured as many as 400 separate elements, which were integrated using video composition.

Video composition also is used to integrate special effects created using a background screen of a uniform color not appearing on a foreground actor or object. This **green screen technique** overlays the motion of the main subject against a bright green background. The actual background scene can be substituted digitally in real time or later. This technique allows actors and scale models to find themselves in totally imaginary situations – hurtling through the atmosphere in space ships, flying through the air, or scaling walls (like The Avengers) – and have it look completely real on television or in the theater. The same technique also is used to project a weather map full of computer graphics behind the meteorologist and to make news reporters look as if they are on location, when they never left town (Figure 5-23). Finally, this technology can be used

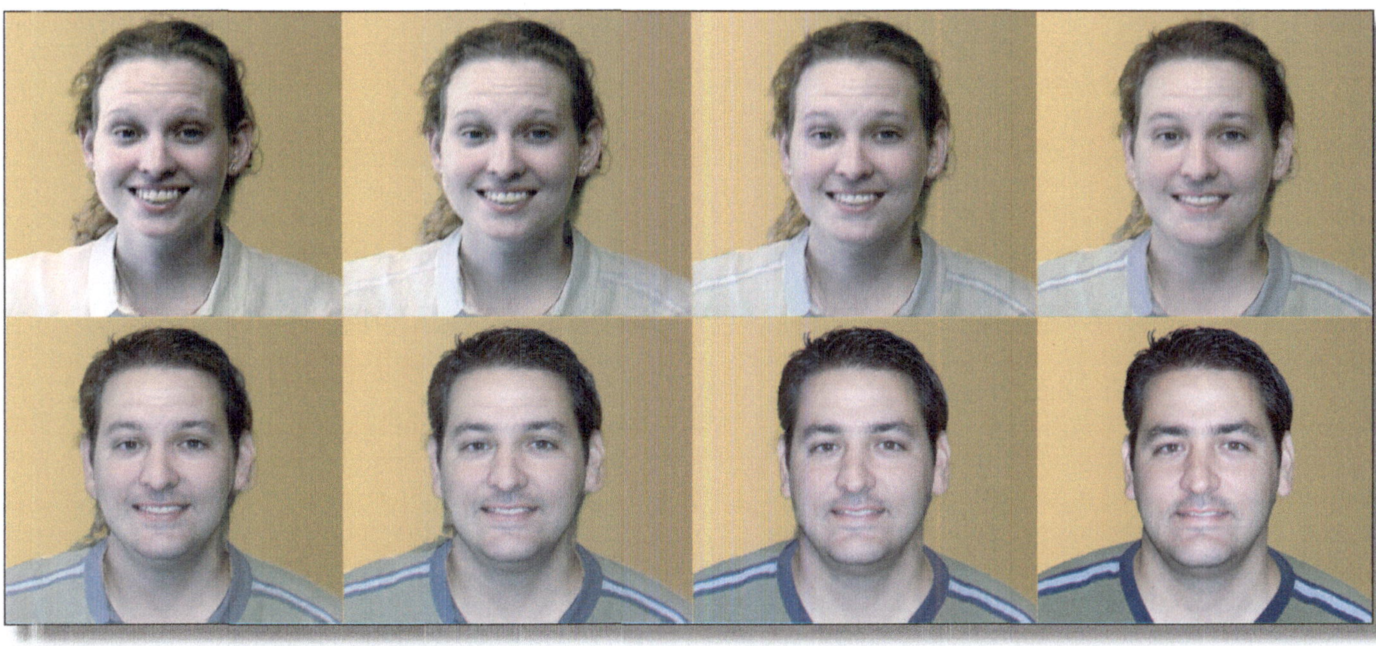

Figure 5-22 Morphing creates the illusion of metamorphosis over time, to allow for unique special effects in film and music videos.

Figure 5-23 Actors preparing for a scene in front of a large green screen. The director will overlay an appropriate background either in real time or as part of the postproduction process.

for **virtual product placement**, which allows broadcasters to substitute different sponsored products in scenes every time a program is shown.

Video composition can also take place during live events. Broadcasters wanting to provide more information to viewers frequently use digital composition tools to generate **virtual signage**, displays superimposed on the standard video image. One example is the yellow first-down line seen in televised college and NFL football games.

COLORIZATION Computers also have been used to **colorize** – that is, to add color to – photographs and movies. There are several possible reasons for doing this. First, the original, analog, color dyes might have faded or changed hue over time, and thus need restoration. Second, colorization can help bring out details in old, historical, black-and-white photographs, thus enriching the viewer experience (Figure 5-24). Third, directors can use selective colorization to focus attention, as was done in *Schindler's List* with the girl in the red coat. Last, colorization "modernizes" a black-and-white movie or TV show, increasing its marketability to audiences accustomed to watching color entertainment.

This last practice is very controversial. Cinema enthusiasts argue that black-and-white movies have requirements for makeup, lighting, costumes, etc., very different from color, and that colorization ruins the visual messages directors and cinematographers want to send to the audience. Governments in some countries have responded to this dispute by authorizing their national libraries to archive important films in their original format. In the United States, the Library of Congress has responsibility under the 1988 **National Film Preservation Act** to save "films that are culturally, historically, or aesthetically important."

Colorization is an intensive process. To begin, the analog source is scanned into a computer to create a digital version. Next, the digital copy is cleaned to remove dirt, hair, and other debris, as well as scratches. The main technique for doing this is digital **cloning**, copying correct **pixels** (picture elements) and pasting them over damaged areas. Next, researchers will try to locate any artifacts and

Figure 5-24 Historic black and white photo that has been colorized.

costumes from the original shoot to register their original colors.

Now it is time to colorize. An editor slowly adds colors to each part of a photo. For a movie, an editor must color frame by frame, adding the colors one at a time to each part of the individual frame. Since one second of movie film equals 24 frames, this work rapidly becomes tedious.

To speed the process, an artist may add color only to **key frames** (frames defining a major change in motion or perspective in a sequence), and let the computer fill in the between frames using a process called interpolation. **Interpolation** involves having the computer software use algorithms to determine which colors to include between the manually colored frames and then automatically fill in the correct colors. As you will learn, computer animators rely on a similar technique – called tweening – to create realistic animations.

The opposite of colorization is **digital color grading**. Using special software, an original film image can be color-corrected to enhance a scene that was too dark when filmed, or change the color of an object or an entire scene. For example, digital grading was used in *The Lord of the Rings: The Fellowship of the Ring* to drain color from Boromir's face as he died. The technique has also been used to focus audience attention on the robots in *Pacific Rim* and to subdue terrestrial colors in *Elysium*.

Computer-Generated Imagery and Animation

Computer animation also called **computer-generated imagery (CGI**, or just **CG)** involves using a computer to give motion to a two-dimensional (2-D) or three-dimensional (3-D) object. CG was born decades ago when engineers and architects wanted to rotate their 2D designs on a computer screen. Today powerful systems offer computer graphic artists and animators many tools to create more vivid, lifelike, and fantastic animations.

As a 2-D animation artist, you draw an object or scene much as you would with illustration software. But to create a 3-D animation in CG, every object in the scene must be "sculpted" in 3-D to create a **wire-frame model**, a mesh-like set of lines ("wires") that follow the contours of the object. The wire-frame, and the polygons created by its intersecting wires, form the basis of an artificial object. In its simplest form various textures, like fine-grained wood, cover the wire-frame's polygons. If the object is to move, animators will insert motion-control points at key wire intersections, and program the behavior of each polygon. If the object is to be a character who can show emotion, animators will increase the density of programmable wire polygons around the eyes (for example). To heighten realism, an object can have different layers of wire-frame representing, for instance, skeletal, muscular, and skin behaviors. When completed, the animation software then generates the actual still image of the object and adds the appropriate effects, such as shadows and reflections (Figure 5-25). The act of applying all these textures and effects is called

Figure 5-25 In 3-D animation, the wireframe forms the basis for generating an artificial character or object. Skin, hair, human or reptile skin, or other textures can be mapped on to the wireframe to complete the digitally created character or object. After specifying texture, lighting, and other effects, you render the image to create the final 3-D object.

rendering, and is very computer-intensive work. This process is so demanding that animation companies like Pixar and Dreamworks use **distributive computing**, a software technology that allows many networked computers to work simultaneously on different parts of a large problem. For CG, the work divides among a large number of dedicated computers organized as a **render farm**. The size of the farm actually varies, since after hours the employees' desktop computers are pressed into render service.

Once you have the 2-D images or 3-D model, you must animate the sequence. A popular method called **key frame animation** is employed by most animation software, be it 2-D or 3-D. This technique requires the animator identifying the key frames in each sequence, and instructing the computer to generate all of the in-between frames, a process called **tweening**. Alternatively, you can use movements acquired using motion capture technology (discussed earlier) to provide lifelike movement for a 3-D animated character.

The entertainment industry rapidly has embraced the dynamic technologies of CGI, 3-D animation, and motion capture. For example, in the *Pirates of the Caribbean* trilogy, the crew members of Davy Jones' *Flying Dutchman* were all made possible with CGI (Figure 5-26). The computer-generated crew members were blended with live footage, using CGI software and video-editing software to integrate the live footage with the computer-animated creatures. Game programmers such as Ubisoft, Activision, and Microsoft Studios use motion capture to give the characters in serial tales like *Halo*, *Assassin's Creed*, or *Call of Duty* hundreds of body motions.

Sports

Over the last two decades, computers have become as much a part of sports as the arenas and equipment used by athletes. CAD software is used to design all types of sports equipment, from sneakers to baseball gloves to Formula One race cars. Computers also are used as virtual coaches and nutritionists. For example, using a specialized software program you can input details about your diet, exercise, and training plan, and the computer will output expert information on diet, fitness, and training schedules to help you improve your performance. Even the machines at the gym use computers to calculate the workout time, the calories burned, the effort expended, and so on.

Coaches and athletes use video cameras and motion capture to analyze and improve performance. With

Figure 5-26 In *Pirates of the Caribbean: Dead Man's Chest*, CGI crew members were blended with live footage to make it appear as if the Flying Dutchman's captain and crew were interacting with the humans.

baseball, for example, pitchers or hitters can record their performances on digital video and play the video in slow motion to look for the smallest movement that might be affecting performance (Figure 5-27). The attention to movement detail is even more intense for gymnasts, in a sport where the slightest shift in technique can be the deciding factor between a gold or silver medal. Using motion capture, a coach can track the exact movements of an athlete's body during an activity – such as throwing a curve ball, jumping a hurdle, or completing a back handspring – and then compare the athlete's actual movements with the optimum movements needed for the perfect throw, jump, or flip. Their training movements then can be analyzed over and over again until the athlete has the technique exactly right.

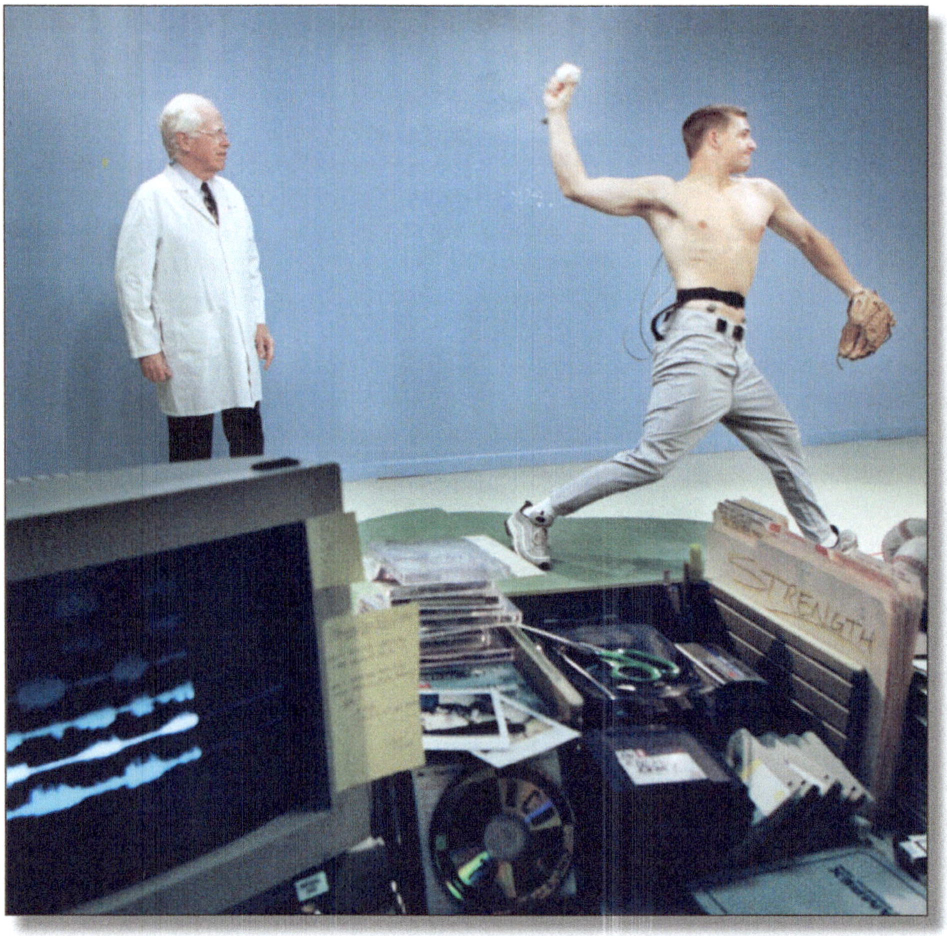

Figure 5-27 Using motion capture, a pitcher can track and analyze his exact movement during a pitch. The sensors are placed at key points to track movement which is then transmitted to and charted by a computer for analysis.

Computers also are found on the field and around a course. For example, to ensure that every clock on the Olympic courses are in sync, many Olympic venues rely on clocks coordinated by a GPS-based system that keeps every course on exactly the same time (except for the less than one second it loses every 20,000 years). Cross-country skiers, biathletes, and bikers have transponders strapped to their ankles or bikes to mark the time the athlete officially passes the finish line (Figure 5-28). The transmitters are synched with the GPS-based clock system to calculate an athlete's final time precisely; the same transponders are used to measure the split times along

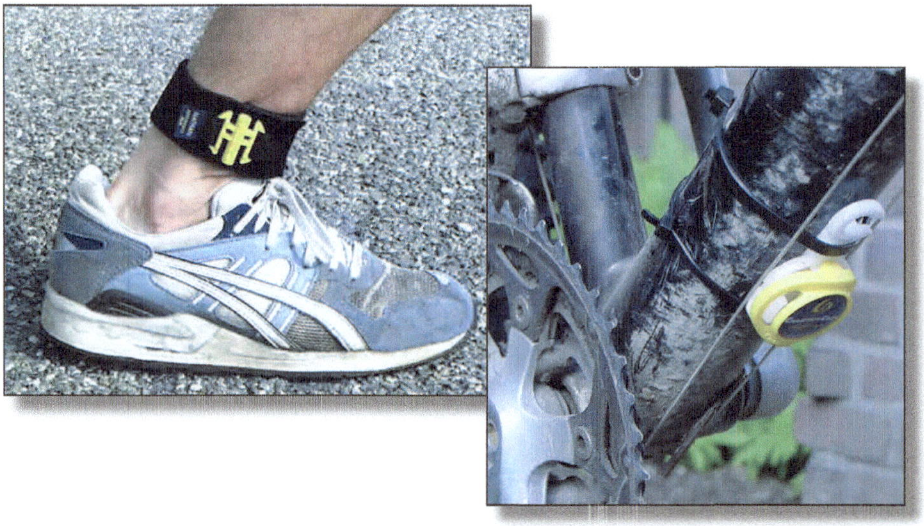

Figure 5-28 Marathoners and bikers rely on transponders strapped to their ankles or bikes to mark the time they officially pass the finish line.

the course, which can be miles long and far from any television camera.

Virtual reality is a form of computer-based simulation that creates immersive sensory experiences of places real or imagined. The U.S. Olympic bobsled team uses a virtual reality simulator so that they can practice their sport when no snow is on the ground. Virtual reality body suits also can allow you to learn new movements, such as a ski jump. The computer lets you rehearse a move by shifting your head to the left a fraction or tucking your elbows in just a bit. The virtual reality system adjusts to your actions and tells you when your moves would result in a crash or a perfect landing.

Some sports, such as downhill ski racing, are using computer technology to create "skiing ghosts" that race alongside the real skiers on the race course. In this case, footage from the fastest skier in a race is superimposed on the course alongside the skier actually racing to give a head-to-head view of how the leader and the current challenger stack up on the turns. For obvious safety reasons, this could never be done in real life.

CONCLUSION

In this chapter, you learned how computers are used in the arts and entertainment. After learning how computers convert analog data, such as music, to digital data, you learned how computers are changing every aspect of the music industry, from the way artists write and record songs to how they perform and distribute their music. The chapter also reviewed the use of computers in dance, and you learned how dance notation software, motion capture, and other computer technologies help dancers choreograph, record, and enhance their performances. You also discovered how computers are used in theater to help with set, costume, and lighting design, as well as ticket sales; and in sculpture to create 3-D models, control 3D printers and milling machines, and share telesculpture electronically. You learned how computers are used in the graphic arts to create a wide range of images, including computer-generated fractals. You also learned about digital photography, including how images are captured and edited to create unique photographic art, as well as the copyright and integrity concerns about digital media. You found out how computers are used in entertainment, with a focus on how television and movie creators use computers to capture and edit digital video, create computer animations, and colorize old photos and movies. Finally, you learned about the use of computers in sports, to create equipment, help athletes train, and to time results.

Key Terms

analog-to-digital converter (ADC)
audio-editing software
charge-coupled device (CCD)
digital cloning
colorize
computer animation
computer-generated fractal
computer-generated imagery (CGI)
copyright
dance notation software
digital camera
digital color grading
digital signal processor (DSP)
digital watermarking
digital-to-analog converter (DAC)
distributive computing
fractal
green screen technique
illustration software
interpolation
key frame animation
MIDI port
MIDI protocol
morphing
motion capture
Musical Instrument Digital Interface (MIDI)
music notation software
National Film Preservation Act
pixel
photo-editing software
point-and-shoot camera
professional-grade camera
prosumer camera
pruning
render farm
rendering
score
sequencer
splitting
storyboarding
synthesizer
tweening
video composition
video-editing software
virtual product placement
virtual reality
virtual signage
webcam
wireframe model

Chapter Review

Multiple Choice

Select the best answer.

1. A(n) _____ compresses digital data to save space.
(a) digital signal processor (DSP)
(b) analog-to-digital converter (ADC)
(c) musical digital interface (MDI)
(d) digital-to-analog converter (DAC)

2. Typically, music notation software allows notes to be entered by _____.
(a) typing notes on a computer keyboard or playing a tune on a MIDI keyboard
(b) clicking note buttons and then clicking them on to a staff in the score
(c) importing existing MIDI files or scanning printed sheet music
(d) all of the above

3. A _____ is a special type of serial port that connects the computer to an electronic musical instrument or other input device, such as an electronic piano keyboard.
(a) USB port
(b) MIDI port
(c) DAC port
(d) SCSI port

4. A sequencer is a software program or dedicated device that _____.
(a) generates an analog signal to represent the image
(b) uses mathematical formulas to create art with a vast range of structure, detail, color and light
(c) records, processes, edits, and plays back MIDI data through an instrument or computer speaker
(d) transforms one image into another image over the course of several frames of video

5. _____ captures movement as a series of symbols so that it can be shared with others.
(a) Dance notation software
(b) Audio-editing software
(c) Illustration software
(d) Image-editing software

6. Computer graphics essentially involves drawing pictures and surface textures on computers, a process also called _____.
(a) tweening
(b) morphing
(c) pruning
(d) rendering

7. A _____ offers many high-end features, but also has its lens fixed to the camera body.
(a) field camera
(b) point-and-shoot camera
(c) prosumer camera
(d) webcam

8. The first step in the digital video-editing process is _____, which involves segmenting the video into smaller pieces that can be managed more easily.
(a) pruning
(b) splitting
(c) rendering
(d) morphing

9. _____ is a process used in colorizing films that involves having computer software determine which colors to include between manually colored frames and then automatically fill in the correct colors.
(a) Green screen
(b) Video composition
(c) Interpolation
(d) Tweening

10. To create a 3-D animation, every object in a scene must have a _____, which is made up of a mesh-like set of lines that follow the contours of the object.
(a) MIDI protocol
(b) wireframe model
(c) digital watermark
(d) computer-generated fractal

Computers in the Transportation Industry 6

Every day, millions of people — including you — travel from home to work, school, the shopping mall, or across the country as part of their daily routine. No matter what transportation mode you choose — whether a car, train, ship, or airplane — computers are behind the scenes helping to control the basic functions of the vehicle, controlling traffic lights, or providing communication to air traffic control to land the plane safely on the runway. The transportation industry also relies on computers to help design, test, and manufacture the wide range of vehicles that travel along the roadways, tracks, and skies. In the near future, computers also will be at the heart of highways that can track traffic and help reroute cars to reduce congestion.

In this chapter, you will learn more about the use of computers in the transportation industry. First, you will learn about how computers are used to help design, test, and manufacture vehicles. Next, you will learn about the use of computers inside cars and trucks to help control basic systems, provide early warnings about possible collisions, provide safety features, and new entertainment options. You also will learn about the future of computerized cars, called smart cars, and review the potential downsides of relying on computer automation to guide a vehicle safely. After learning about how computerized mapping, onboard GPS systems, and telematics help you navigate safely to your destination, you will learn more about how computers help with route optimization for truck fleets, electronic toll collection, and intelligent highways. Next, you will learn about how computers are used in other transportation modes such as trains and ships. Finally, you will learn about the use of computers in the airline industry, to handle air traffic control, reservations and check-in, load and fuel calculation, and training.

DESIGN AND MANUFACTURING

Computers are used in all aspects of the design and manufacturing of automobiles, trains, planes, ships, and other vehicles. Using computer technology helps companies design, test, and produce a vast number of new vehicles each year. By relying on computers and other technologies to help support the production process, manufacturers can shorten development and manufacturing cycles, while lowering production costs and creating vehicles with better fuel consumption, task capabilities, and safety.

Design

As you learned in Chapter 1, computer-aided design (CAD) is the use of a computer and special software to assist in product design. Many vehicle engineers use CAD to create graphics and models of a new vehicle on screen, so that they can modify a design, dynamically change product features, and perform calculations to optimize the design for production.

Using computer-aided design allows automobile manufacturers to take a more efficient and flexible approach to product design. For example, instead of creating paper or clay models of a concept car, designers can use CAD software to create many different, highly detailed three-dimensional models, showing options with different headlights, hood shapes, tail lamps, or other features. These highly detailed models even can show how the sunlight reflects off the vehicle's sheet-metal panels. After getting feedback from customers and executives, designers quickly can add, subtract, or combine features of several car models and then again review it with key stakeholders in the design process. The ability to make design changes quickly not only reduces cycle time (the time from idea to shipping product), it significantly reduces costs involved in reworking physical models. Same or similar CAD practices are used by designers of trucks, buses, trains, aircraft and ships.

Testing

One of the major benefits of using computers in the vehicle design process is the ability to test the design of a car, plane, train, ship, or other vehicle before it is built. CAE software gives designers and engineers the ability to analyze designs in the early stages of the product development process, rather than after products are manufactured when changes are costly, time consuming, and even dangerous. Sophisticated CAE (computer-aided engineering) programs simulate the effects of wind, water, temperatures, weight, and stress on various components, to help engineers understand how the vehicle will handle certain operating conditions. For example, as discussed in Chapter 1, BMW engineers use CAE tools to analyze how components, such as axle links or wheels, will react under stress, before taking the time to build models of each component.

AERODYNAMICS TESTING Designers also use CAE to evaluate a vehicle as a total aerodynamic system. DaimlerChrysler, for example, has used computerized tools to help understand and redesign cars to reduce vibration noise caused by air being taken into and flowing around and through the car. To test aerodynamics of a car, plane, train, ship, or other vehicle, designers use several tools, including wind tunnel testing and Computational Fluid Dynamics (CFD). **Computational Fluid Dynamics (CFD)** involves programming specific equations into computers, running simulations, and allowing the computer to analyze how a fluid (such as air or water) flows over a shape. Using such models can help manufacturers create less wind resistant and more fuel efficient, quieter, safer vehicles.

A **wind tunnel** is a tube-like structure where wind is produced (usually by a large fan) to flow over the test object, such as a model of a car. The object is connected to instruments that measure and record the aerodynamic forces that act upon it. To use such a wind tunnel, designers quickly can create a small-scale prototype by using the CAD model as the input to a 3D printer or CNC milling machine. As you learned in Chapter 4, the software reads the models, automatically calculates the milling paths, and then guides the tools on the milling machine to cut the object, as defined by the model.

Physical wind tunnels are expensive to build, operate, and maintain; renting them is also expensive. To reduce development costs, engineers often conduct their preliminary tests using a computer-generated wind tunnel. A **virtual wind tunnel** is a software program that allows you to import a 3-D model of an object and then simulate the effects of wind as they would be in a physical wind tunnel (Figure 6-1). A virtual wind tunnel relies on CFD to predict how air will flow around a plane, car, or other vehicle.

For aircraft pilots or race car drivers, being able to predict the performance of any vehicle under stress is critically important. Because actual testing in live situations can be very dangerous, pilots and drivers first use CAE and simulations to test components and instruments. The simulation software even allows them to

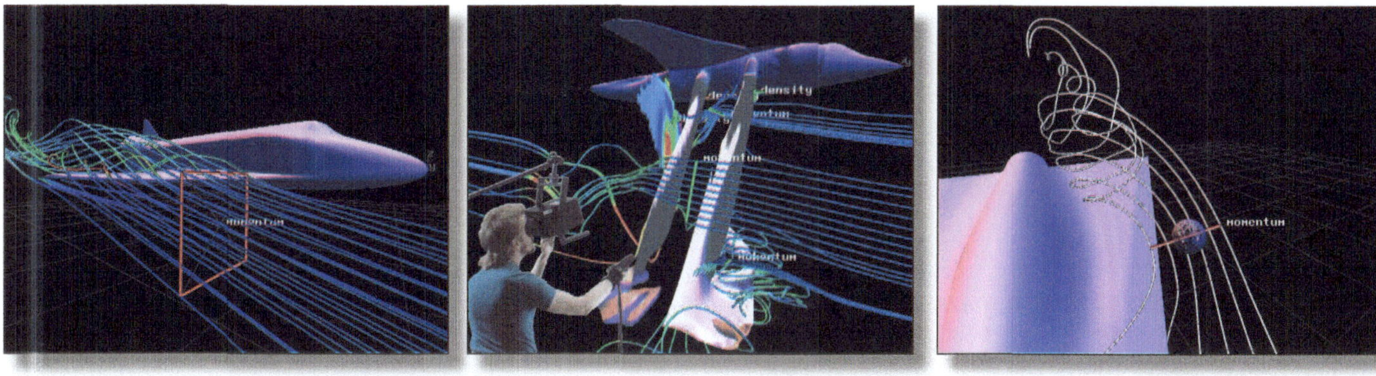

Figure 6-1 A virtual wind tunnel is a software program that allows you to import a 3-D model of an object and then simulate the effects of wind as they would be in a physical wind tunnel.

examine how individual flying or driving styles or a specific environment will affect performance. The drivers and pilots also use virtual wind tunnels and other training devices to ensure optimal performance.

CRASH TESTING Passing a real-time, destructive crash test is required by governments and insurance companies for most vehicle designs. As can be imagined, this test is very expensive, and today is conducted only as the last step. Before this point, far-less expensive computer simulations are used to test the damage a collision might cause to a vehicle and, more importantly, its passengers. In the case of automobiles, engineers create a very accurate computer model of the vehicle. They then can use the software to simulate the car crashing into another object, such as a tree, fence, or another car (Figure 6-2).

Running a car crash simulation, however, requires an enormous amount of processing power to take into account all of the possible inputs: acceleration, speed, road surfaces, car materials, number of passengers, types of restraints, air bag deployment, and so on. Most labs rely on **parallel processing**, in which the calculations are shared by two or more computers, in order to handle the processing load. A typical crash test might solve anywhere from five to thirty million equations simultaneously, so the parallel processing capability is essential. Additionally, some vehicle manufacturers will run close to 10,000 crash simulations a month, with most vehicle designs getting as many as 175 simulations. Using computerized crash testing also provides a much more controlled environment, so researchers can isolate specific variables.

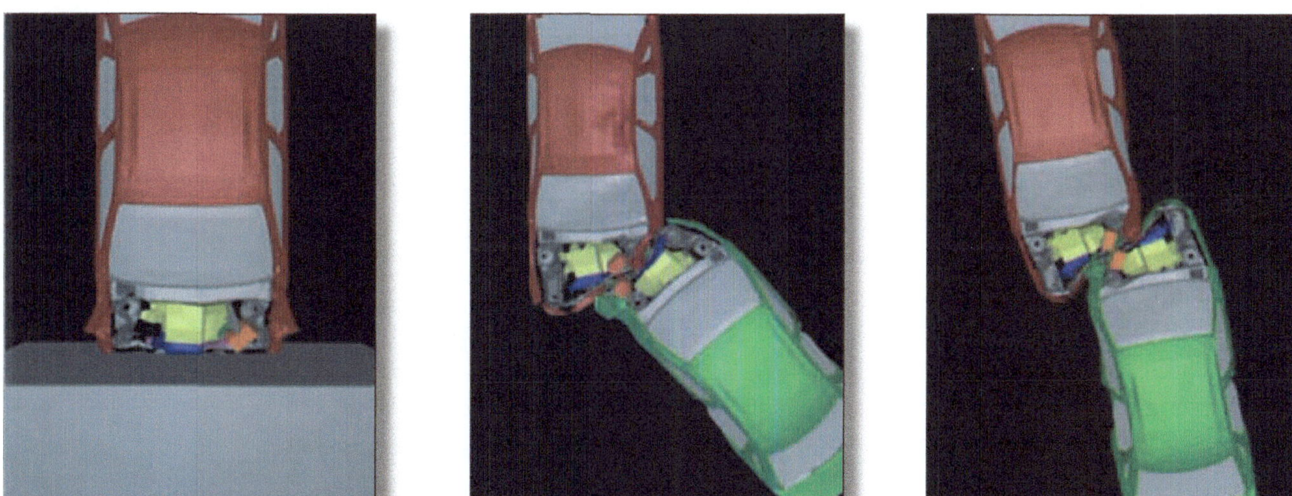

Results of a car crashing into a rigid barrier, such as a wall or post.

Results of a head-on collision between two cars.

Results of a collision between two cars in which the front of one comes in at an angle to the front of the other.

Figure 6-2 Computerized crash analysis helps to test the damage a collision might cause to a car and its passengers.

The National Highway Traffic Safety Administration (NHTSA) also uses car crash simulations, for example, to study the effects of collisions between sport utility vehicles and smaller cars and to determine the strength of guardrails. Similar crash analyses are used to better understand how lighter materials aimed at providing greater fuel efficiency can withstand crashes. If the models used in the simulations are sound, the computerized crash test results very closely match what will happen in the real world (Figure 6-3).

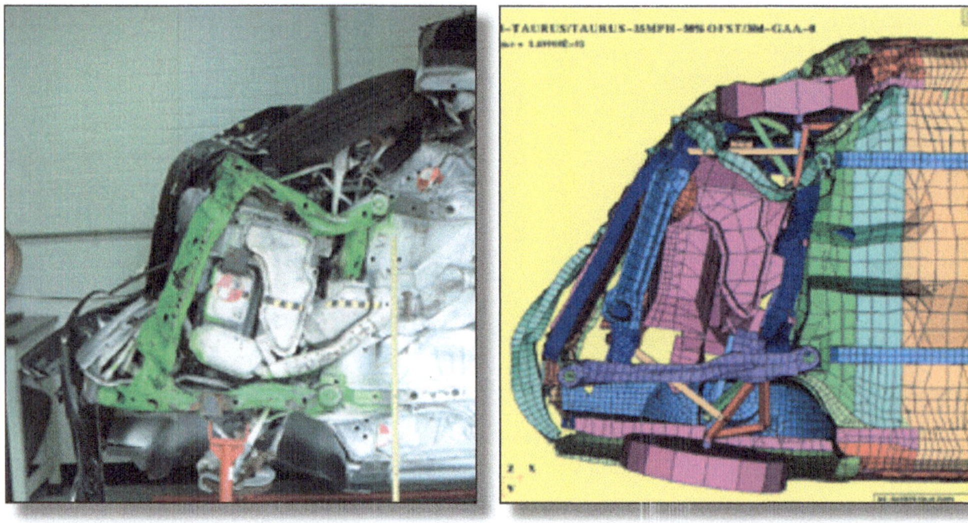

View of underside of test vehicle after two-vehicle crash. The tire at top is the driver-side tire.

Simulated result of the test vehicle after a two vehicle crash is almost identical to the real crash.

Figure 6-3 If the computer crash models are sound, the results of a simulated crash very closely match real-world results.

Manufacturing

Once a vehicle design is complete, fully tested, and approved for production, computer-aided manufacturing (CAM) helps speed the process of creating the actual vehicle. As you have learned, the manufacturing process also relies on computers to direct the machines that produce and assemble a product.

During the design process, digital assembly software shows the number of welds and the number of robots needed to assemble a vehicle, along with other tooling and fixtures. This allows the production lines to prepare adequately for the production of any vehicle. Further, the CAD design specifications can serve as inputs to CAM production equipment such as CNC milling machines, 3D printers, robots, software-controlled drills, welding, and tooling machines.

The assembly line in a vehicle manufacturing plant has changed fundamentally by the use of computers. Robots, for example, are used to help build various parts and assemble the finished vehicles (Figure 6-4). Robots are much more durable, faster, and efficient than humans and can complete tasks, such as welding or heavy lifting, that would be dangerous to humans. Although such robots are costly, the manufacturer benefits from the speed and reliability of the machines.

Inventory Control

As discussed in Chapter 1, a key challenge for a factory and its warehouse is to manage its inventory, so enough parts are available to continue production, but the warehouse is not left with overstocked parts that may become obsolete. Vehicle manufacturers rely on inventory control systems to track the current supplies of inventory and match this against anticipated future orders to ensure that enough components, such as rotors and engines, will be available to manufacture the shipment of new buses scheduled for delivery.

Vehicle parts suppliers and service technicians – including your local car repair shop – also rely on

Figure 6-4 A manufacturing plant uses robots to safely complete a wide range of tasks.

computerized inventory control systems to help them track thousands of parts for numerous makes and models (Figure 6-5). An automotive part inventory control system, for example, typically uses a database management system customized to keep track of each part, part number, stock on hand, inventory location, part manufacturer, unit cost, the selling price to the customer, and more. The inventory software generally also can store information on a specific collection of parts called a kit, which are needed to complete a job such as fixing worn out brake pads. By setting up a kit code, the repair shop can set up special prices for the kit, while being able to track the individual components in each kit separately.

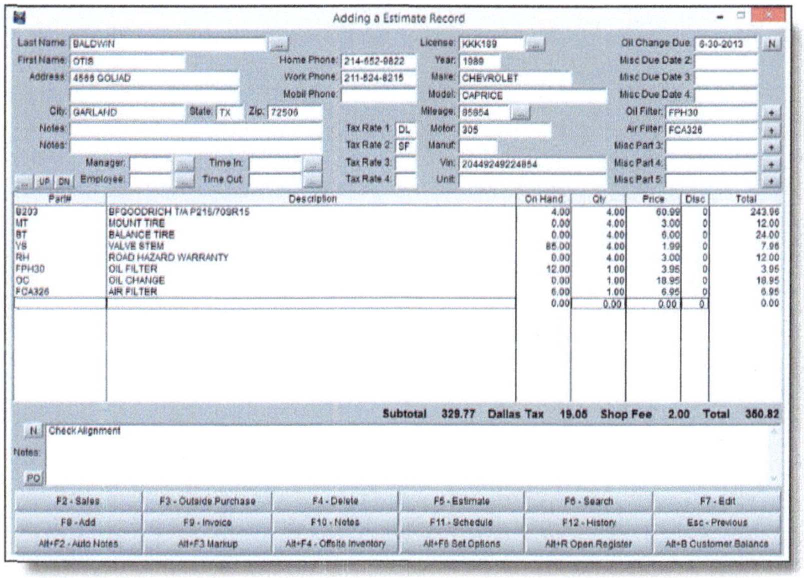

Figure 6-5 Automotive parts suppliers also rely on inventory control software, such as Auto Repair Boss, to help them track thousands of parts for numerous makes and models of cars.

AUTOMOBILES AND TRUCKING

Computers are not just used to design, test, and manufacture automobiles. They also are used to control numerous aspects of the car's basic functions. Computer-controlled devices in your car perform tasks such as ensuring the fuel is mixed with air in the correct amounts or displaying warning messages if you are about to back up into an object, such as a bicycle, parking meter, or another car. Other computer-controlled devices monitor your car's tire pressure to ensure they are inflated correctly. Soon computers may drive the car or truck, helping passengers avoid collisions and maintain a safe driving speed and distance.

Electronic Control Units

Although you might think of your car as a largely mechanical machine, cars today actually are highly sophisticated with many microprocessors (generically called **electronic control units (ECU)**) and sensors responsible for managing the vehicle. The ECUs and sensors communicate with each other using a **controller area network (CAN bus)**. The CAN bus also enables these systems to self-diagnose problems and report trouble codes when a mechanic links a reader to the network (Figure 6-6). Each ECU is responsible for a distinct system within the car. In turn, these system modules are connected to submodules, sensors, and user-operated buttons and switches. Figure 6-7 shows several of the key computerized modules used in today's automobiles; Table 6-1 lists each component, along with the functions it performs.

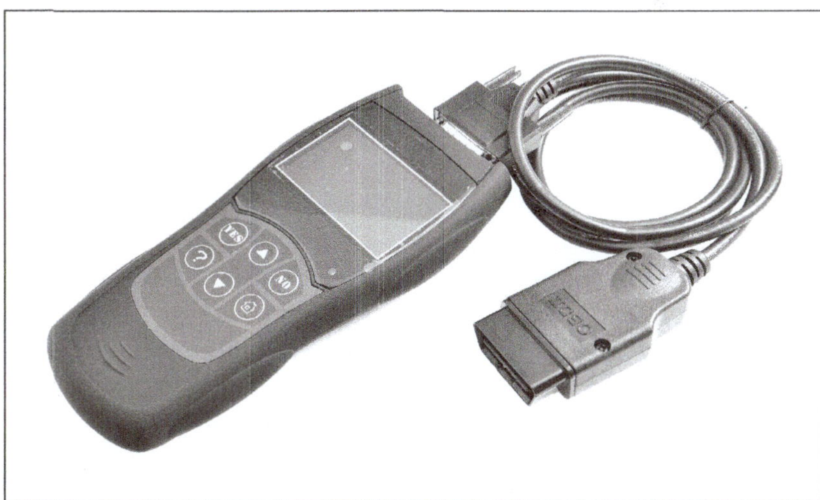

Figure 6-6 Each module in the car can report errors or faults to the Engine Control Module (ECM), which stores the data for a mechanic to read later using a device like this one.

Table 6-1 Responsibilities of Some ECUs in a Vehicle

ELECTRONIC CONTROL UNIT	*RESPONSIBILITY*
Engine Control Module	Manages operations such as fuel injection, ignition, throttle, lubrication, etc.; the most powerful single microprocessor in a car, it is responsible for on-board diagnostics
Body Control Module	Manages interior lights, door locks, power windows, power seats, and so on
Airbag Control Module	Manages deployment of all airbags; reports to Body Control Module
Driver's Door Module	Communicates commands from switches on door to Body Control Module
Cruise Control Module	Regulates speed while in cruise control; reports to Body Control Module
Instrument Panel	Manages gauges and indicator lights using data from the communications bus
Climate Control Module	Monitors interior temperature and manages heating and cooling systems; reports to Body Control Module
Antilock Braking System (ABS) Module	Manages antilock brakes and may handle traction control and stability control systems
Transmission Control Module	Manages automatic transmission; reports to Engine Control Module
Power Distribution Box Module	Manages relays in the power distribution box

In today's vehicles, ECUs (microprocessors) are at the heart of subsystems that provide safe, comfortable, and efficient driving. Trucks and inexpensive cars may have as few as 25–30, expensive cars may have as many as 100.

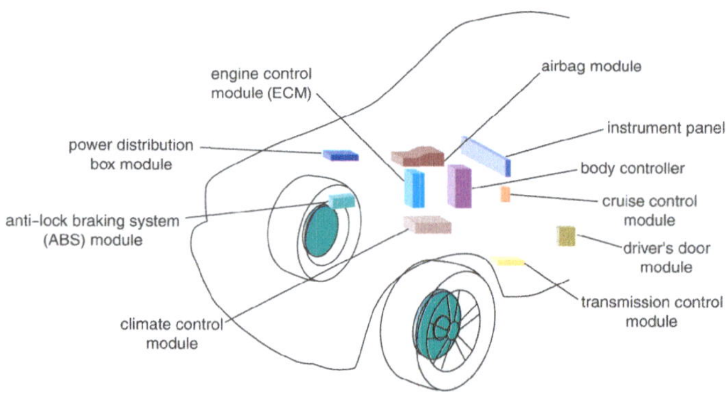

Figure 6-7 Today's cars use more than one hundred microprocessors to control various functions and subsystems.

Safety Systems

One of the major responsibilities of the microprocessors in electronic control units is passenger safety. For example, an **antilock braking system (ABS)** is designed to keep your wheels from locking up or skidding as you brake to slow down, so that you have more traction and control to steer the car out of harm's way. A simple ABS system relies on a microprocessor that serves as the ABS controller (Figure 6-8). The ABS controller continually watches the speed sensors, looking for rapid or unusual decelerations that indicate a car wheel is about to lock up and cause loss of traction. To help control the braking on any of the car wheels, the ABS controller sends messages to the brake valves to ensure the tire slows at the same rate as the car, which gives the car maximum braking power. With older cars, drivers were taught to pump the brakes to prevent the wheels from locking up. In a car with an ABS system, if you press your brakes hard in an emergency situation, you will feel a pulsing in the brake pedal as the ABS system rapidly opens and closes the brake valves, relieving the driver of the need to pump the brakes manually.

Although standard in many trucks, more and more cars also have **collision warning systems (CWS)** that alert the driver when the vehicle ahead is dangerously close or if the car is about to hit an object behind the car.

Cars and trucks equipped with a collision warning system have a central processor that sits above the engine block, as well as sensors on the bumper and below each door (Figure 6-9). The system uses radar to detect objects up to 350 feet ahead, while other radars on both sides of the truck's cab alert to objects in the blind spots alongside the vehicle. When the radar detects a potential hazard, the sensor sends the data to the central processor, which in turn sends signals to the small display unit inside the truck cab. The driver display unit outputs a warning in the form of lights and

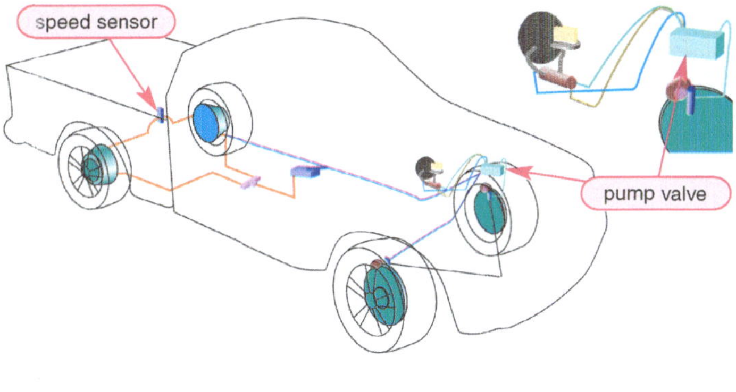

Figure 6-8 A simple ABS system relies on a microprocessor that receives input from the speed sensors and then triggers the appropriate action by the brake pumps and valves.

audible tones at quick intervals to warn the driver to maneuver the car to avoid an accident. Additionally, sensors in the front and rear bumpers can detect close-by obstacles, such as a bike or a child, and the display unit gives a warning. In support of the CWS, many automotive vehicles now include one or more video cameras that display surroundings either in a mirror or in the center dashboard.

Truck and other vehicle owners say that CWS can help to reduce accident rates by as much as 70 percent. Further, drivers report that over time, they become conditioned to maintain greater following distances. These systems quickly pay for themselves in the form of lower insurance premiums, fewer accidents and repairs, and lower fuel costs due to changes in the drivers' braking patterns.

Other work vehicles, such as snowplows, also will benefit from collision warning systems. In the midst of severe storms, drivers must navigate roads in low-visibility conditions that make road markings, guardrails, and even oncoming or stalled cars, almost impossible to see. Having CWS technology included in the snowplows helps warn drivers about potential hazards and helps to keep them safely driving down snow-covered roads.

Recently, new car manufacturers in Japan, the United States, and Europe have used CWS technology to offer **automatic parking**. A car with this option can self-park in a parallel space, and sometimes also in an angled space. This is another step on the road to the truly autonomous car of the future.

A few new car manufacturers also offer **automotive night vision** as an option. These systems use either an infra-red or thermal camera to display on a dashboard monitor or windshield a clearer image, in black-and-white, of what is ahead of a driver at night (Figure 6-10).

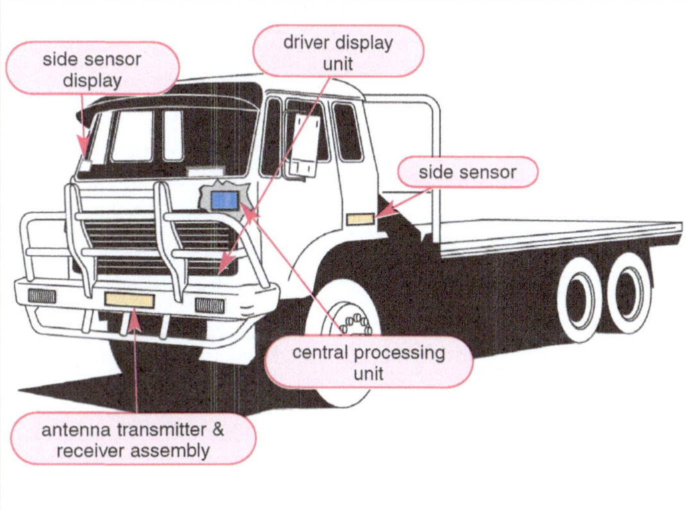

Figure 6-9 Collision warning systems (CWS), such as the Eaton Vorad Collision Warning System, can help warn cars and trucks about potential obstacles. The components include:

- Driver Display Unit: Installed in the dash or integrated into instrument cluster. Displays warnings and emits audible tones giving the driver additional time to take action.
- Antenna Transmitter and Receiver Assembly: Has a range of 350 feet to transmit information from sensors.
- Side Sensor Display: Displays lights on a pillar inside the cab and warns when a vehicle is alongside, out of the driver's view.
- Side Sensor: Detects vehicles alongside, out of the driver's view.
- Central Processing Unit: Determines if it should set off driver alerts at speeds from .25 to 100 MPH.

Figure 6-10 A night vision system, which generates a black-and-white image on a small LCD display, shows any obstacles that might be in the dark ahead.

In commercial vehicles, such as snowplows, even more sophisticated systems incorporate global positioning systems (GPS), radar, onboard databases, and display units to provide a virtual image of the road, including unseen obstacles. The GPS allows the system to locate the snowplow within 25 meters, while radar tuned to a system mounted on a nearby transmission tower, helps pinpoint the plow's position that is accurate to within a few centimeters. Using the location information, the system accesses the onboard unit to provide images of road features, such as turns, intersections, and medians. Inside the snowplow, these images appear on a display unit in clear view of the driver, who can use the virtual image of the road to help navigate the snowy road surfaces in the midst of a storm.

A major cause for automotive accidents is tire failure, and the primary source of tire failure is bad air pressure. An underinflated tire can cause great difficulty steering and braking the vehicle, not to mention reducing the tire's useful tread life and the vehicle's fuel economy. Consequently, governments in the United States and other countries now require all new cars, trucks, and motorcycles to have **tire-pressure monitoring systems (TPMS)**. You can also retrofit these systems into an older vehicle.

Most of these systems utilize a special wireless radio transmitter that is mounted to the tire rim (Figure 6-11). As you start to drive, an internal switch activated by the tire rotation turns on the battery-operated transmitters, which then transmit tire pressure and temperature to a receiver mounted in the car. When the pressure and temperature data sent from the sensors deviates from programmed levels, the receiver either illuminates a warning light, or displays a warning message along with identifying the problem tire. The early warning gives you time to safely pull over and address the problem, whether it is a slow leak that will eventually wear down the tire tread, or under-inflation that could cause a blowout.

In the future, motor vehicles may adjust tire pressure dynamically, depending on where you are driving. For example, logging trucks might have onboard computers that communicate via satellite to geographic information systems and weather databases. Depending on the terrain and weather conditions where the truck is driving, the system will be able to adjust the pressure in the truck's tires. By having tire pressure right for the road conditions, trucks can go faster and tires last longer (which means the system pays for itself in a few months).

Adaptive cruise control (ACC) is a system that maintains a safe driving interval between your car and other vehicles by changing gears or by applying the brakes. Current systems use sensors much like those used in collision warning systems to determine the relationship between your car and other vehicles (Figure 6-12). The sensors use either radar or lidar. **Lidar**, which is short for "light detecting and ranging," is a technology used to determine location, position, and speed, much like radar. The key difference is that lidar uses lasers, not radio waves, to determine the range to an object (Table 6-2).

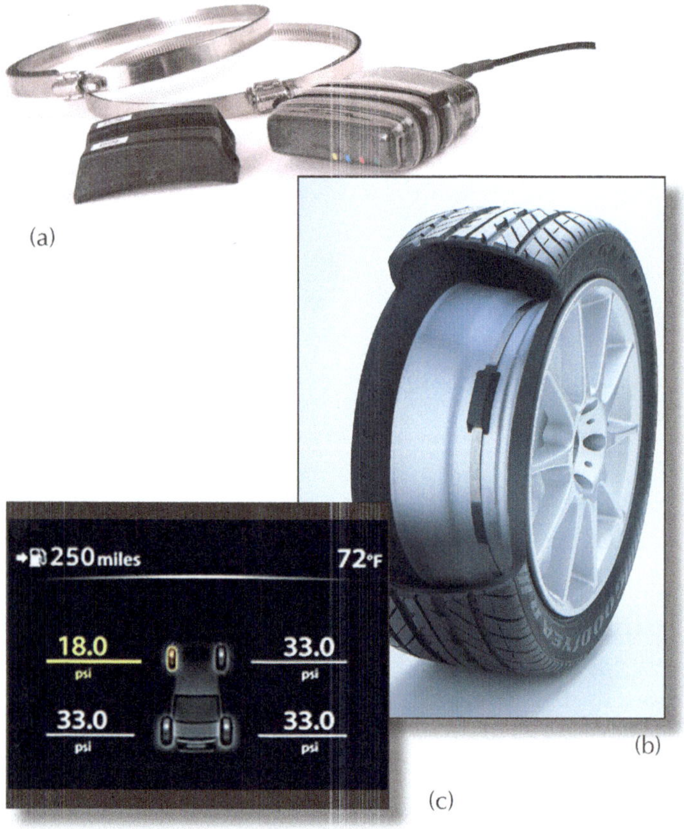

Figure 6-11 The SmarTire tire pressure monitoring system utilizes a special wireless radio transmitter (a) which is mounted to the tire rim (b) and transmits tire pressure and temperature to a receiver mounted in the car. The receiver communicates with a display module (c), that displays information about problems.

Whether using radar or lidar, when the sensors in the adaptive cruise control system sense an object is too close, it will send a message to the transmission or braking systems to change gears or apply the brakes. Although many high-end luxury cars already have adaptive cruise control systems, the technology is not foolproof. Radar is more expensive to install than lidar, but the laser-based system often mistakenly interprets rain and snow as oncoming vehicles.

Figure 6-12 To help maintain a safe distance between vehicles, adaptive cruise control uses forward looking radar or lidar and then electronically adjusts vehicle speed. When traffic clears, the vehicle returns to the set speed.

Table 6-2 Radar Versus Lidar

RADAR	*LIDAR*
Acronym for RAdio Detection And Ranging	Acronym for LIght Detection And Ranging
Radar transmits radio waves into the atmosphere at a target, which scatters some of the signal back to the radar's receiver.	Lidar transmits laser light at a target. Lidars operate at a higher frequency than radar, in the ultraviolet, visible, and infrared region of the electromagnetic spectrum.
Radar antenna sends out a short, high-power pulse of radio waves at a known frequency. The same antenna is used to receive the much-weaker signals that return.	The lidar's transmitter is a laser, while its receiver is an optical telescope.

Finally, a number of governments, research universities, and automakers are collaborating on the development of wireless communication between vehicles and with the infrastructure of highways. This technology, called **Vehicle to Vehicle (V2V)**, has the potential to greatly reduce collisions and traffic jams, although security advocates worry that, if implemented poorly, V2V could easily allow vehicle computer systems to be hacked.

ON THE ROAD

Computers and other technological improvements have made everyone's driving experiences on the road a bit safer, less stressful, and more efficient – helping to ensure you actually can enjoy the ride. For example, a number of governmental and commercial Web sites, such as Mapquest.com or, in the U.K., Frixo.com, provide updated traffic reports that highlight routes with congestion, construction, or accidents that might cause delays (Figure 6-13). Using computers allows you to generate printed maps customized to your specific route, rely on real-time directions communicated from your GPS system, or even contact a call center for directions to the nearest gas station; truck drivers even use computers to determine the most efficient route to their drop off location.

Other computer systems, such as electronic toll booths and sensors embedded in highways help you to move quickly – and safely – to your destination. These applications, and some of those discussed below, are a small part of an international movement toward

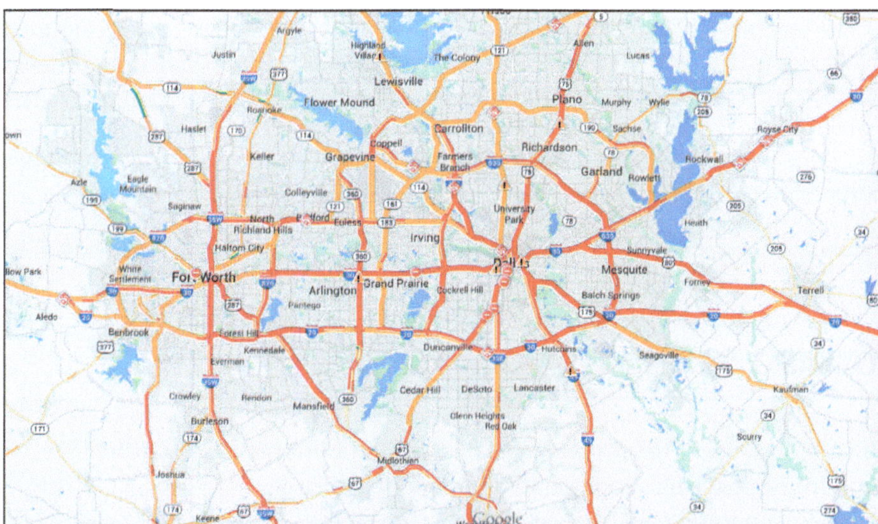

Figure 6-13 Web sites, such as Traffic.com, SmarTraveler.com, and local or state Web sites, provide updated traffic reports 24 hours a day.

Intelligent Transportation Systems (ITS), which is the application of computer, communications, and electronic technologies to help improve all modes of transportation by making them safer and more efficient.

Computerized Mapping and Directional Services

Planning an automobile trip used to require that you pore over printed maps and manually calculate the distance between your starting location and intended destination. Determining the actual mileage or driving time was difficult. You would have to reference a different resource to find overnight accommodations along the route. Now, you quickly can get directions from your starting point to your destination location using trip planner and map Web sites such as FreeTrip.com, Google maps, MapQuest, or Bing.com/maps (Figure 6-14). When you use one of these Web sites, you simply input a starting location and ending destination and then indicate your preference for either a scenic route or the shortest distance route. These Web sites use your input to query a vast database of geographical information and search for the most appropriate route to your ending destination. Further, these sites can show you scenic drives, restaurants, shopping, and motel, hotel, and bed-and-breakfast accommodations along the desired route. The resulting map then is displayed on the Web site for you to save, print, or share to a mobile or email address.

One of the features offered by new car manufacturers is a dynamic routing service (a part of telematics; see below). At the press of a button drivers can connect with a human agent to request directions to a desired location from their car's current position. The agent can download those instructions into the car's onboard navigation system. The route displays on screen and a computer-generated voice provides route guidance. Whether for a long trip – or simply to get directions to your friend's new apartment – online map sites have taken much of the guesswork out of driving from one place to another.

Onboard Navigation Systems

At one time onboard navigation systems, powered by a global positioning system (GPS), could be found only in luxury cars. Today they are widely available, even in economy cars, and as after-sale add-ons. The reasons are not hard to find. Using GPS, your car's current location can be tracked at any point, based on the signals received from the GPS satellites around the globe. With their location constantly updated and

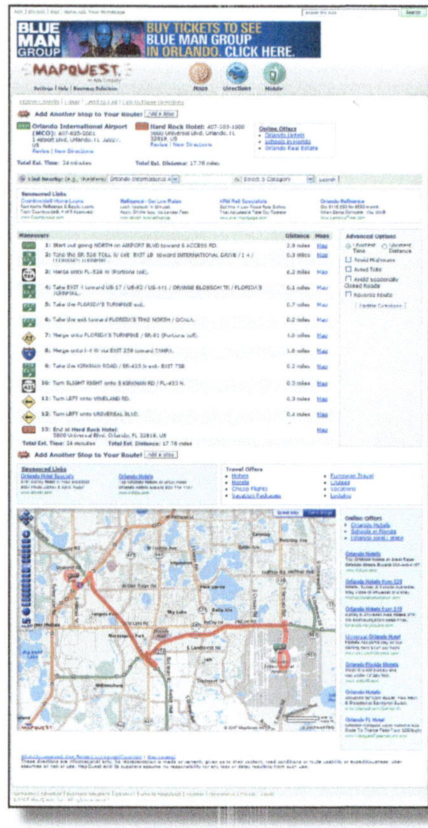

Figure 6-14 Map Web sites such as MapQuest allow the user to get driving directions between two locations — including tourist attractions, hotels, airports, and more.

shown on a display screen, drivers always know where they are. Additionally, onboard navigation systems provide turn-by-turn directions both on-screen and by automated voice, helping drivers keep their eyes on the road (Figure 6-15). If you make a mistake or decide to take a different route, the navigation system recalculates and offers new directions. And these systems can store selected destinations in an onboard database for easy retrieval and use.

Onboard navigation systems are also used to track fleets of commercial trucks as they haul goods to their destinations, freight and passenger trains, and ships at sea. The corporate office can track the location of any of their vehicles using a Web-based interface (Figure 6-16). Sometimes, this information is also made available over the Web to the general public, ex., cruise ship enthusiasts.

Telematics

Telematics is an emerging technology field that combines computers, location-sensing technology (usually GPS), and wireless data in a vehicle. Applications

Figure 6-15 A GPS system in your car includes a display unit to output key information about your location, as well as voice output, so you can keep your eyes on the road.

include vehicular, trailer, or container tracking, onboard navigation and hands-free mobile phone use.

One specific type of telematics, referred to as **call center telematics**, relies on a mobile phone built into a car. This allows the driver or other passengers to communicate directly with a call center staff person, who offers concierge-type services. Also, the system alert the call center if the car's air bags deploy (implying a serious accident), and can transmit trouble codes to the call center in case of vehicle breakdown. Many automobile manufacturers offer this technology service for an annual subscription fee. With General Motors' OnStar system, for example, you press a button in your car (often on or near the rearview mirror) to request a connection with an OnStar advisor in a remote call center (Figure 6-17). The advisor, who immediately can locate your car based on the GPS coordinates, can help by giving you directions to a nearby gas station, dispatch repair or emergency vehicles if you have an accident, or call ahead to make reservations at restaurants. If you are locked out of your car, you even can place a call to OnStar to have them unlock your car remotely.

Route Optimization

The next time you see a delivery truck or "18-wheeler," consider the job at hand: getting the load of goods to the right location in as timely a manner as possible, while minimizing the total distance traveled by company vehicles. Even a veteran truck driver cannot possibly know the best route to every delivery location. In the past, most truck drivers and dispatchers relied on a manual system for planning delivery routes – using paper maps and estimated travel times to determine the best delivery routes. A route-optimization program, however, can schedule drivers and display best routes based on customer locations and types, road network distances, vehicle costs and capacities, driver skills, time for delivery and more (Figure 6-18). The map databases utilized by the software also include information about underpasses or bridges that are restricted to certain weights or heights of vehicles. These programs calculate fuel consumption based on the suggested route, along with other costs, such as tolls. Finally, when confronted by mechanical problems or bad weather, dispatchers use this software to develop alternative ways to keep their shipments moving.

Figure 6-16 GPS devices also are used to track fleets of commercial trucks as they haul goods to their destinations. A simple GPS tracking device is placed in the cab or trailer. The office can track the location of any truck using a Web-based interface.

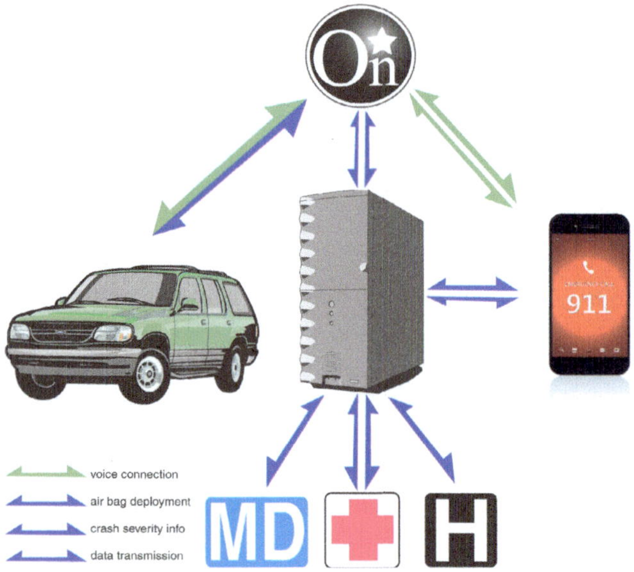

Figure 6-17 With the OnStar system, you press a button in your car to connect to an OnStar advisor over a cellular radio-based system.

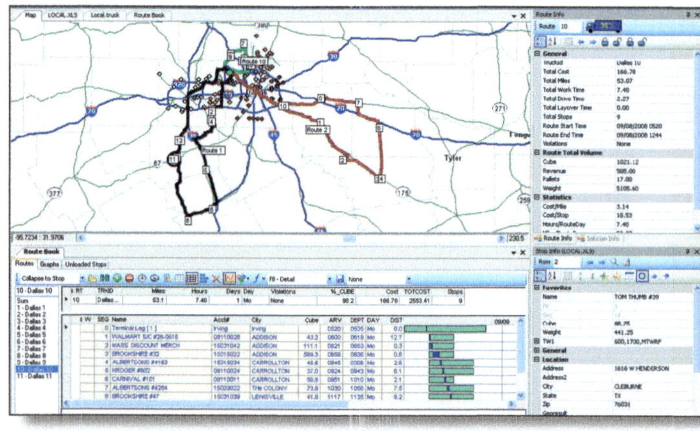

Figure 6-18 Trucking companies use computers and route optimization software such as Direct Route to ensure that their truck drivers are taking the best route to their locations and hitting locations in the appropriate sequence.

Electronic Toll Collection

In many states, charging tolls is a major source of revenue for maintaining and expanding transportation networks. To speed the collection process, many toll roads use a computerized toll-collection system that detects vehicles and processes their tolls electronically (Figure 6-19). An **electronic toll-collection system** uses a vehicle-mounted transponder that stores your account information. The **transponder** is a small, rectangular, plastic sticker which you attach to your car or truck windshield. Inside the plastic sheet is a passive **radio frequency identification (RFID)** unit. Unlike battery-powered, active RFIDs which broadcast continually, passive RFIDs broadcast nothing until, in this case, the vehicle comes within range of a toll station's radio signal. Then the passive RFID converts the station's radio signal into electricity and broadcasts back its identification number. At the same time, the toll station's optical recognition software images the vehicle's license plate. If the plate number matches the identity of the RFID, a program deducts the toll from your prepaid account. If not, the computer mails a bill to the address associated with the license plate.

Different states use various types of electronic toll-collection systems, including E-ZPass (New Jersey), Fastrak (California Bay Area), SunPass (Florida), and TollTag (North Texas), but all work in largely the same way. However, these systems are not always compatible with each other, so you may find yourself receiving a bill in the mail once you cross, for example, a state border.

(a)

(b)

Figure 6-19 Many of today's toll roads use an electronic toll-collection system that detects and processes tolls electronically (a). To use the system, you need a transponder (b) that stores basic account information, such as an identification number.

Intelligent Highways

The term **intelligent highways**, part of Intelligent Transportation Systems, refers to the application of computer systems to traffic management. As you drive to class or work, especially if you are on a major highway, consider various technologies in place to help track and control traffic. For instance, the wire **loop detectors** used to trigger a red-light system at an intersection also are placed in roads throughout the country to help determine traffic speed. The wire is charged with an electrical current to generate a magnetic field. When a vehicle passes over the sensor loop, it changes the magnetic field. By monitoring these changes and determining how quickly vehicles pass between sensor loops, transportation officials can determine traffic speed. This data on the number of vehicles and traffic speed is transmitted to a central computer, which is monitored by local transportation departments. If the data suggests that traffic volume is very high or vehicles are slowing significantly, the transportation department can watch live footage from video cameras along the road to understand exactly what the source of the problem is (Figure 6-20). Officials then can provide up-to-the minute messages on dynamic message signs (the same ones used to display AMBER alert messages) to alert drivers to congestion ahead and suggest alternate routes (Figure 6-21). In addition, some jurisdictions are using this same technology to adjust speed limits dynamically in response to traffic, weather, or other concerns. Intelligent highway data can also be shared with local radio and TV stations, as well as with cell phone applications which display traffic congestion.

Figure 6-21 With intelligent highways, transportation officials will be able to provide up-to-the minute messages on dynamic message signs to alert drivers to congestion ahead and suggest alternate routes.

Figure 6-20 From this room, the transportation department can watch live footage from video cameras along interstates for incidents that could create traffic problems. This immediate view helps provide better information on the source of the problem, which means better information can be communicated to travelers.

TRAINS

As with cars and trucks, computers are used inside locomotives and rail cars to control various systems, such as fuel injection, safety systems, instrument panels, and so on. Today, each train is a networked system that allows one car of a train to communicate with the others. For example, each car in a train has a computer system to control the brakes. Instead of having each system function as a stand-alone unit, many trains now use computerized braking systems in which all of the car computers are networked and take commands on when and how to brake from the locomotive. The engineer in the locomotive uses controls on the instrument panel in the locomotive to send these commands to the other cars.

A facility called a railyard, consisting of many parallel rows of track connected by switches, is where managers assemble and take apart freight trains. Computer programs, from Railroad Software or other vendors, help control this process (Figure 6-22). Operating on

Figure 6-22 An intermodal transportation facility in Vancouver, featuring a railyard in the foreground and a shipping container yard with mobile cranes in the background.

both desktop and tablet computers, these applications can identify and follow a given rail car out of thousands in the yard; assist with rail car inspections; and help manage transloading freight if the railyard is part of an intermodal center for trains, trucks, aircraft, or ships.

Engineers and dispatchers also use computers to determine the routes a train should take. When a dispatcher authorizes you to take the train over a specific route, a computer program assures that operations are safe and then transmits the route information to each active train via a radio frequency network. An onboard computer in each locomotive then displays the correct route to the locomotive engineer. GPS systems are used to track and locate the train at any point in its travels and the onboard computer accesses a database to compare the actual location and speed of the train with the information radioed by authorities. If the engineer attempts to steer the train along a route different than the one set by the dispatcher, the computer system will alert the engineer and, if necessary, stop the train.

At major airports like DFW, the operation of shuttle trains are almost entirely controlled by computers. If you board one of these airport trains, often called trams, you will notice that the trains have no human driver. Instead, the train movements are controlled by a computerized train control system, which instructs the trains to move along a preprogrammed path according to a set schedule and route. The trains are supervised automatically from a main control center, where humans can intervene and override the computer system, if something goes wrong. Such train systems typically use voice output to inform passengers that doors are about to close, or open at the next stop. The train systems also are linked to the passenger information displays over the train doors, which indicate the train's route.

SHIPS

Another transportation industry that depends heavily on computers is shipping. Naval architects and engineers use CAD/CAE/CAM technologies and naval simulators to design and build all varieties of ships. Today, many shipyards assemble merchant vessels or cruise ships from a series of built-out modules ready to connect (Figure 6-23). A part of the construction process is the installation of computer systems to help the future crew manage such complex functions as navigation, propulsion, cargo loading/unloading, and sewage recycling. If the new vessel is a cruise ship, additional computer systems will be required for operating what is in effect a mobile hotel and resort. Applications would include room management, entertainment, food logistics, and sea water desalinization. When a vessel is ready for her sea trials, special software can organize tests and log results. Once certified as sea worthy, the builder transfers vessel ownership and responsibility to the customer, and the ship is ready to begin its working life.

Figure 6-23 Modular assembly of a cruise ship.

The harbormaster is the person who has overall responsibility for the operation of a sea port. The harbormaster's staff use computer systems to track incoming and exiting vessels, as well as assigning harbor pilots and docking facilities to those ships (Figure 6-24). The staff also uses computer programs to handle customs and immigration duties, and conduct naval inspections. Canal authorities, for example at Suez or Panama, use similar harbormaster applications to manage transiting vessels.

Merchant vessels, like other commercial vehicles, do not make money when idling in port. Their crews use cargo management software to load, place, and unload cargo or containers as efficiently as possible (Figure 6-25). The software also helps the captain make special provision for hazardous cargo and evenly assigns loads so that the ship is less likely to capsize in heavy seas.

Once at sea, the bridge crew can steer modern ships by a joystick attached to a computer-control system (**steer-by-wire**) (Figure 6-26). GPS programs are often critical to the operation of the ship – beyond navigation. For instance, some industrial vessels require stationary or tightly controlled positioning when drilling into the sea floor, laying undersea cable and pipelines, or operating tethered robots for mining the sea floor. Guided by GPS signals, a computer system operates a series of onboard thrusters to maintain the desired position. Other ships require refueling at sea, for example military ships on patrol against pirates. Refueling at sea is a risky process for the two ships involved. Both vessels must move together in parallel at the correct separation distance: too far apart, and the lines and hoses break; too close and the water suction formed between the two ships can make the vessels collide. GPS-controlled autopilots solve this problem.

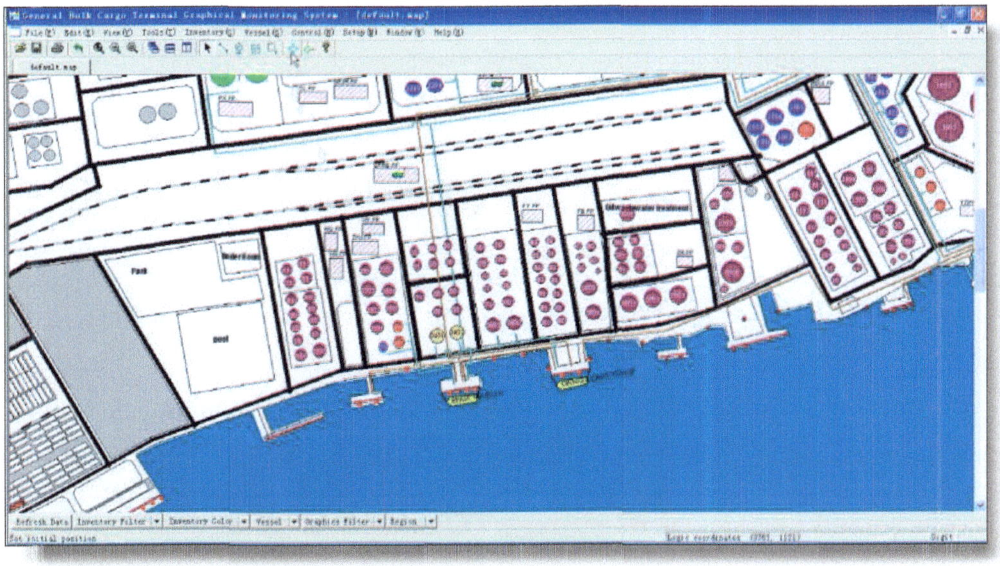

Figure 6-24 Port management software can track use of docking facilities, cargo storage, and intermodal services.

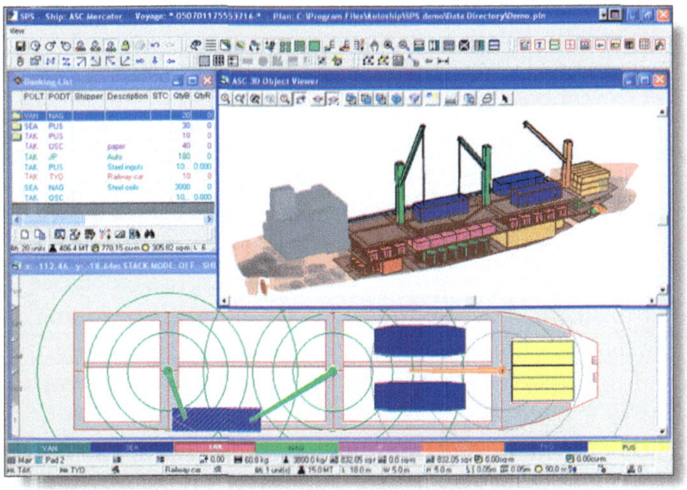

Figure 6-25 Load management software balances the weight of cargo and segregates for safety hazardous shipments.

Figure 6-26 Steer-by-wire controls on a modern ship.

AIRCRAFT

The modern airline industry depends on computers for almost every aspect of the business. Airplanes, like automobiles, are designed by using computers and computer-aided design and engineering. As with automobiles, simulations are completed in wind tunnel tests prior to manufacturing to ensure the plane designs are safe and efficient. The airplanes themselves rely on computers for system control (called **fly-by-wire**), communication back to air traffic control towers, and to provide customers with in-flight entertainment over small LCD screens. Numerous airport services are automated by computers, including the display screens that display flight, gate, and status information, the electronic announcements made over the intercom, and even car rental services. Pilots may also carry laptop or tablet computers with electronic versions of the dozen or so airplane manuals required on the flight deck.

In this section you will learn more about the use of computers to help train pilots on flight simulators, to manage ticketing and reservations processes, to support air traffic control, and to calculate the fuel required in each plane, based on its route and load.

Air Traffic Control

According to the Federal Aviation Administration (FAA), about 7,000 planes are in the sky above the United States at any given moment, which translates to about 90,000 flights per day carrying over two million passengers. As shown in Figure 6-27, having that many aircraft in the air at one time does not leave much room for error – especially at airports. The job of managing the take-off, flight, and landing of all of these commercial and private aircraft lies squarely in the hands of air traffic controllers across the United States. These air traffic controllers rely heavily on computers to help track the flight patterns of thousands of aircraft, ensure they are traveling at safe distances, and help reroute them around bad weather, while minimizing airport delays (Figure 6-28).

At the core of the air traffic control system is the Air Traffic Control System Command Center. The **Air Traffic Control System Command Center (ATCSCC)** oversees all air traffic control in the United States, including help manage regional centers where problems such as bad weather, or traffic overload, exist. The United States airspace is divided into 22 areas, as shown in Figure 6-29, each of which is subdivided into smaller airspaces. As your plane flies out of one airspace into another, the air traffic controllers from the new

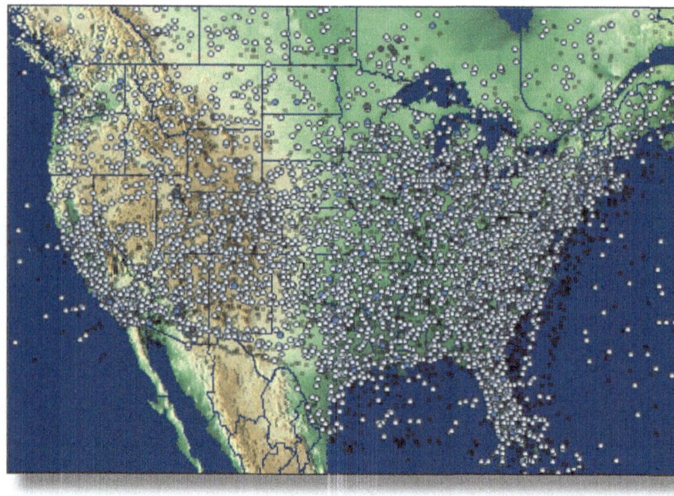

Figure 6-27 On a typical day, air traffic controllers monitor 90,000 flights over the United States. In this snapshot, each white dot represents a flight in the air.

Figure 6-28 Air traffic controllers rely heavily on computers to help track the flight patterns of thousands of aircraft to guide them to landing safely, while minimizing airport delays.

airspace take over monitoring the plane and giving instructions to the pilot.

Before any flight can take off, the pilot completes a pre-flight routine that includes transmitting a flight plan to the air traffic control tower. The flight plan includes the airline name, flight number, intended airspeed and cruising altitude, the flight route, and the unique beacon code assigned to that aircraft. In the air traffic control tower, a flight data person reviews the weather and enters the flight plan into the FAA host computer. The computer generates an electronic **flight progress strip**, which contains all of the necessary data for tracking that plane during its flight and will be constantly updated. Once the flight plan has been approved, the flight data

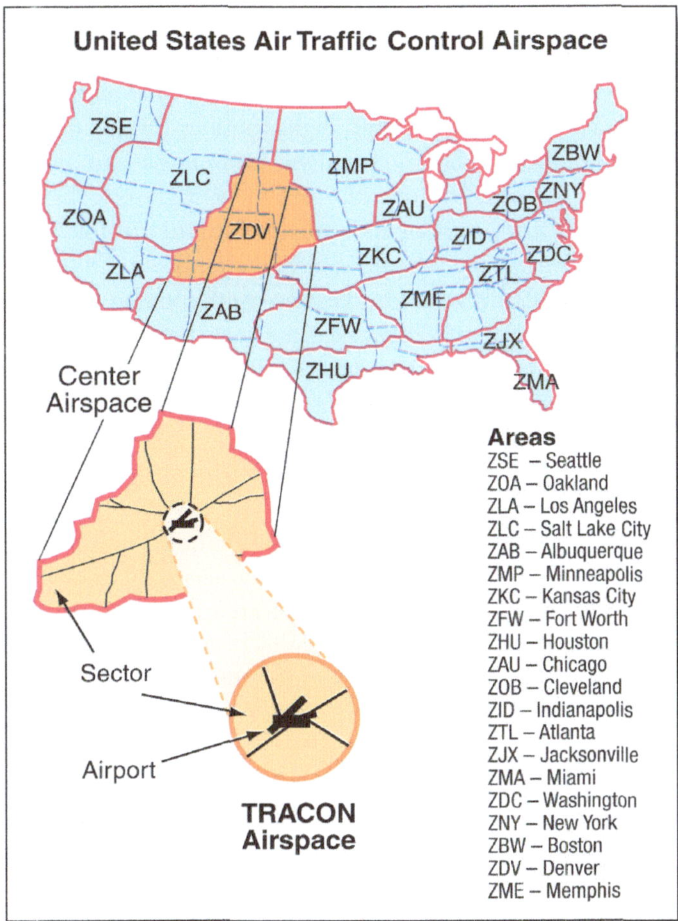

Figure 6-29 Excluding Alaska and Hawaii, this map shows 20 control areas, each of which is subdivided into smaller airspaces.

person gives clearance to the pilot and passes the strip to the ground controller in the tower, who guides the flight through take-off. As the plane moves from one airspace center to the next, the flight progress strip is passed from controller to controller, each of whom monitors the plane until it moves into the next airspace.

When the plane reaches the airspace for the destination airport, air traffic controllers will direct the plane to line up with other planes heading into the airport for a runway approach. Up until the point when the plane is 10 miles from the runway, all of the air traffic control has been based on information sent over radar and computers to air traffic control centers. Within 10 miles of the runways however, a local controller in the airport tower also will check the runways and the skies above the runways with binoculars and surface radar. When the local controller determines that it is safe, he or she gives the pilot clearance to land. Once the plane lands, a ground controller takes over, using ground radar information to direct the plane to the terminal gate.

As air traffic grows and technology improves, governments around the world strive to keep pace. Both Europe and the United States have started projects to modernize airspace systems. The FAA's initiative, called **NextGen**, is scheduled for completion in 2025. The primary focus of NextGen is precise tracking of aircraft over land or sea using GPS satellite signals, instead of radar signals, which can be blocked by topography and are limited over oceans. To participate in NextGen, both commercial and private aircraft will need new communication and navigation equipment.

Inside the airplane, computers help to give pilots another set of eyes. Systems such as the Automatic Dependent Surveillance-Broadcast (ADS-B) system and the Traffic Alert and Collision Avoidance System, or TCAS, use a special display screen to show the pilot the relative positions and speed of aircraft up to 40 miles away, thus allowing pilots to identify aircraft on conflicting flight paths. The system also sounds an audible alarm when it determines that another aircraft will pass too closely to another plane. TCAS provides a backup to the air traffic controllers systems used to separate planes in normal flight patterns. In addition to enhancing collision avoidance capabilities, the ADS-B and the TCAS allow pilots and controllers to work together to reduce delays.

Reservations and Ticketing

Airlines and travel websites use a **computer reservation system (CRS)** to query large databases and provide you with information about flights, hotels, rental cars, and other trip options. The CRS also helps the travel industry companies manage their inventories and frequent customer programs. Some travel websites specialize in providing information about a single topic. For example, SeatGuru.com evaluates the pros and cons of passenger seating on different models of aircraft, and relies in part on assessments provided by social media. Rarely are traditional airline tickets still used; instead passengers receive a barcode boarding pass that can be printed or sent to the customer's mobile phone.

Airport Security

Today, airports, harbors, cruise terminals, subways, and other major transportation systems use layers of security backed by computers. Managers use computer systems to vet prospective employees and track their activities while at work. In addition to supporting the telecommunications needs of security personnel, computer systems enable scanners and sensors to identify hazardous materials – metallic, chemical, biological, or radiological.

Facial recognition software evaluates security camera images of passengers and visitors. At airports, passengers, luggage, and cargo must pass through one or more computerized detection systems. Although many U.S. passengers arriving from abroad can use automated kiosks to speed their entry, all incoming passengers must have their passports scanned. The goal is to create a defense in depth against persons or organizations wishing to do harm.

Load and Fuel Calculations

Weight, and how that weight is distributed, impacts the performance of aircraft, ships, and other types of vehicles. Another important constraint is bad weather. The heaviest an airplane will be is when it takes off. Moreover, the price of jet fuel is the largest variable cost for any airline, other than labor. Airlines must work to ensure that planes carry the correct amount of fuel to fly safely to their destination. How can pilots ensure a safe take-off, flight, and landing when the onboard loads of fuel, passengers, luggage, and cargo can vary so much between flights, not to mention aircraft types?

These calculations are part of the daily routine of hundreds of pilots, flight engineers, and dispatchers. Crews must calculate the fuel requirements for each flight given forecasted weather conditions and the weight of passengers, luggage, and cargo. Additionally, they must decide where to position the luggage and cargo so that these weights will be balanced and not interfere with the control of the airplane while in flight. Computer programs process a number of complex formulas to generate the needed answers and instructions.

Flight Simulators

As you learned in Chapter 2, computer simulations often are used to give soldiers an opportunity to experience the time spent in complicated and expensive military vehicles. Similar types of computer simulations are used to train airline pilots, naval personnel, and others in the transportation industry to give them the benefits of live training without the associated risks and cost.

In the U.S., the FAA requires all commercial pilots to certify and periodically re-certify their competence to fly the aircraft types they are assigned, for example, Boeing 777 or Airbus 380. A **flight simulator** duplicates a specific airplane's cockpit and is capable of closely representing the actual aircraft through various ground and flight routines (Figure 6-30).

In addition to creating realistic modeling of an airplane's instruments, controls, and view, high-tech flight simulators also must be able to simulate the rumble of an uneven runway when the airplane lands or the thrust effect that occurs when brakes are used. During the training session, an instructor station system – typically a standard personal computer – monitors the pilot's flight and can instruct the simulator to replicate an instrument failure or turbulence; send commands from a simulated air traffic controller; or change the airport at which the pilot will land.

Using computers for training simulations has clear benefits. First, new pilots can practice scenarios repeatedly and learn from mistakes without additional cost or danger. Pilots also have a chance to become familiar with the instrumentation of a new type of plane, before actually getting in the cockpit. Further, because the flight simulator records every event in sequence, a flight training instructor can review and replay portions of the simulation to offer feedback and analysis. The end result is better-trained, more confident pilots, who can bring you safely to your destination.

Figure 6-30 A flight simulation involves modeling the experience of being inside the cockpit of a plane, with the flight deck that includes navigation, communications, and flight control instruments.

CONCLUSION

In this chapter, you learned about the use of computers in the transportation industry. First, you learned about the use of computers to help design, test, and manufacture vehicles, as well as the use of computers to control basic systems inside cars and trucks. You also learned how computers are used for ABS brakes, collision warning systems, night vision, and other safety features, as well as for new entertainment options. After a review of how smart cars could change your driving experience, you also learned about the potential downsides of relying on computer automation to guide a vehicle safely. After learning about how computerized mapping, onboard GPS systems, and telematics help you navigate safely to your destination, you also learned about using computers for route optimization for truck fleets, electronic toll collection, and intelligent highways. You also learned about how computers are used in trains and ships that are guided by computer systems. Finally, you learned about the use of computers in the airline industry, including air traffic control, reservations and check-in, fuel calculation, and training.

Key Terms

adaptive cruise control (ACC)
Air Traffic Control System Command Center (ATSCC)
antilock braking system (ABS)
automatic parking
automotive night vision
call center telematics
collision warning systems (CWS)
Computational Fluid Dynamics (CFD)
controller area network (CAN bus)
electronic toll collection system
electronic control unit (ECU)
flight progress strip
flight simulator
fly-by-wire
intelligent highway
lidar
loop detector
NextGen
parallel processing
radio frequency identifier (RFID)
steer-by-wire
telematics
tire-pressure monitoring systems (TPMS)
transponder
Transportation Security Agency (TSA)
Vehicle to Vehicle (V2V)
virtual wind tunnel
wind tunnel

Chapter Review

Multiple Choice

Select the best answer.

1. The _____, which is the most powerful electronic control unit in most cars, communicates with a wide range of vehicle components.
   (a) power distribution box module
   (b) computational fluid dynamic
   (c) flight progress strip
   (d) engine control module

2. A(n) _____ is designed to keep a car's wheels from seizing up or skidding as a driver slows down, so more traction is available to steer out of harm's way.
   (a) collision warning system (CWS)
   (b) intelligent transportation system (ITS)
   (c) antilock braking system (ABS)
   (d) computerized reservation system (CRS)

3. The key difference between lidar and radar in adaptive cruise control systems is that lidar _____.
   (a) is a technology used to determine location, position, and speed
   (b) uses lasers, not radio waves, to determine the range to an object
   (c) is more expensive to install than radar
   (d) all of the above

4. With a _____ device, also referred to as an onboard satellite navigation system, a car's current location can be tracked at any point, based on signals sent to and received from satellites around the globe.
   (a) CWS
   (b) GPS
   (c) ITS
   (d) ABS

5. _____ is an emerging technology field that combines computers, location-sensing technology such as GPS, and wireless data in a car.
   (a) transponder
   (b) communications bus
   (c) telematics
   (d) lane controller

6. The _____ system, which uses a cellular radio-based system to connect drivers with a live operator, is a GM-branded call center telematics system.
   (a) FreeTrip
   (b) SmarTire
   (c) OnStar
   (d) MapQuest

7. A _____ is a small, radio frequency identification (RFID) plastic sticker that you attach to your car windshield to use an electronic toll-collection system.
   (a) transponder
   (b) communications bus
   (c) telematics
   (d) lane controller

8. A/an _____ center is a place where computers help transload freight between trains, trucks, aircraft, or ships.
   (a) intermodal
   (b) railyard
   (c) harbormaster
   (d) robotics

9. NextGen refers to _____ .
   (a) railyard dispatch
   (b) air traffic control
   (c) canal management
   (d) none of the above is correct

10. A benefit of using computers for flight training simulations is that _____.
   (a) new pilots can practice scenarios repeatedly and learn from mistakes
   (b) pilots can become familiar with the instrumentation in a new type of plane
   (c) flight trainers can review and replay portions of a simulation to offer feedback
   (d) all of the above

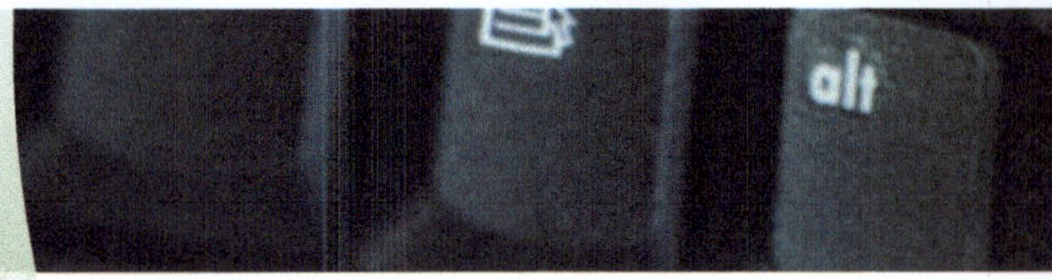

chapter 4

Network and Internet Security

After completing this chapter, you will be able to do the following:

1. Explain why computer users should be concerned about network and Internet security.
2. List several examples of unauthorized access and unauthorized use.
3. Explain several ways to protect against unauthorized access and unauthorized use, including access control systems, firewalls, and encryption.
4. Provide several examples of computer sabotage.
5. List how individuals and businesses can protect against computer sabotage.
6. Discuss online theft, identity theft, spoofing, phishing, and other types of dot cons.
7. Detail steps an individual can take to protect against online theft, identity theft, spoofing, phishing, and other types of dot cons.
8. Identify personal safety risks associated with Internet use.
9. List steps individuals can take to safeguard their personal safety when using the Internet.
10. Discuss the current state of network and Internet security legislation.

outline

Overview

Why Be Concerned About Network and Internet Security?

Unauthorized Access and Unauthorized Use
- Hacking
- War Driving and Wi-Fi Piggybacking
- Interception of Communications

Protecting Against Unauthorized Access and Unauthorized Use
- Access Control Systems
- Firewalls, Encryption, and Virtual Private Networks (VPNs)
- Additional Public Hotspot Precautions
- Sensible Employee Precautions

Computer Sabotage
- Botnets
- Computer Viruses and Other Types of Malware
- Denial of Service (DoS) Attacks
- Data, Program, or Web Site Alteration

Protecting Against Computer Sabotage
- Security Software
- Other Security Precautions

Online Theft, Online Fraud, and Other Dot Cons
- Theft of Data, Information, and Other Resources
- Identity Theft, Phishing, Social Media Hacks, and Pharming
- Online Auction Fraud
- Other Internet Scams

Protecting Against Online Theft, Online Fraud, and Other Dot Cons
- Protecting Against Data and Information Theft
- Protecting Against Identity Theft, Phishing, Social Media Hacks, and Pharming
- Protecting Against Online Auction Fraud and Other Internet Scams

Personal Safety Issues
- Cyberbullying and Cyberstalking
- Online Pornography

Protecting Against Cyberbullying, Cyberstalking, and Other Personal Safety Concerns
- Safety Tips for Adults
- Safety Tips for Children and Teens

Network and Internet Security Legislation

© iStockphoto/Petoo

OVERVIEW

As discussed in the last few chapters, networks and the Internet help many of us be more efficient and effective workers, as well as add convenience and enjoyment to our personal lives. However, there is a downside, as well. The widespread use of home and business networks and the Internet increases the risk of unauthorized computer access, theft, fraud, and other types of computer crime. In addition, the vast amount of business and personal data stored on computers accessible via company networks and the Internet increases the chances of data loss due to crime or employee errors. Some online activities can even put your personal safety at risk, if you are not careful.

This chapter looks at a variety of security concerns stemming from the use of computer networks and the Internet in our society, including unauthorized access and use, computer viruses and other types of sabotage, and online theft and fraud. Safeguards for each of these concerns are also covered, with an explanation of precautions that can be taken to reduce the chance that these security problems will happen to you. Personal safety issues related to the Internet are also discussed, and the chapter closes with a look at legislation related to network and Internet security. ■

WHY BE CONCERNED ABOUT NETWORK AND INTERNET SECURITY?

From a *computer virus* making your computer function abnormally, to a *hacker* using your personal information to make fraudulent purchases, to someone harassing you online in a discussion group, a variety of security concerns related to computer networks and the Internet exist. Many Internet security concerns today can be categorized as **computer crimes**. Computer crime—sometimes referred to as *cybercrime*—includes any illegal act involving a computer. Many computer crimes today are committed using the Internet or another computer network and include theft of financial assets or information, manipulating data (such as grades or account information), and acts of sabotage (such as releasing a computer virus or shutting down a Web server). Cybercrime is an important security concern today. It is a multibillion-dollar business that is often performed by seasoned criminals. In fact, according to the FBI, organized crime organizations in many countries are increasingly turning to computer crime to target millions of potential victims easily, and *phishing attacks* and other *Internet scams* (discussed shortly) are expected to increase in reaction to the recent troubled economy. These and other computer crimes that are carried out via the Internet or another computer network are discussed in this chapter. Other types of computer crime (such as using a computer to create counterfeit currency or make illegal copies of a DVD) are covered in Chapter 5.

TIP

According to a recent Norton Cybercrime Report, the total cost of cybercrime is now estimated to be $110 billion per year worldwide and nearly $21 billion in the United States alone with an average loss of $290 per person.

>**Computer crime.** Any illegal act involving a computer.

With some security concerns, such as when a spyware program changes your browser's home page, the consequence may be just an annoyance. In other cases, such as when someone steals your identity and purchases items using your name and credit card number, the consequences are much more serious. And, with the growing use of wireless networks, social media, cloud computing, mobile computing, and individuals accessing company networks remotely—paired with an increasing number of security and privacy regulations that businesses need to comply with—network and Internet security has never been more important. Consequently, all computer users should be aware of the security concerns surrounding computer network and Internet use, and they should take appropriate precautions. The most common types of security risks related to network and Internet use, along with some corresponding precautions, are discussed throughout this chapter.

UNAUTHORIZED ACCESS AND UNAUTHORIZED USE

Unauthorized access occurs whenever an individual gains access to a computer, mobile device, network, file, or other resource without permission—typically by *hacking* into the resource. **Unauthorized use** involves using a computing resource for unauthorized activities. Often, they happen at the same time, but unauthorized use can occur when a user is authorized to access a particular computer or network but is not authorized for the particular activity the user performs. For instance, while a student may be authorized to access the Internet via a campus computer lab, some use—such as viewing pornography—would likely be deemed off-limits. If so, viewing that content from a school computer would be considered unauthorized use. For employees of some companies, checking personal e-mail or visiting personal Facebook pages at work might be classified as unauthorized use.

FIGURE 4-1
A sample code of conduct.

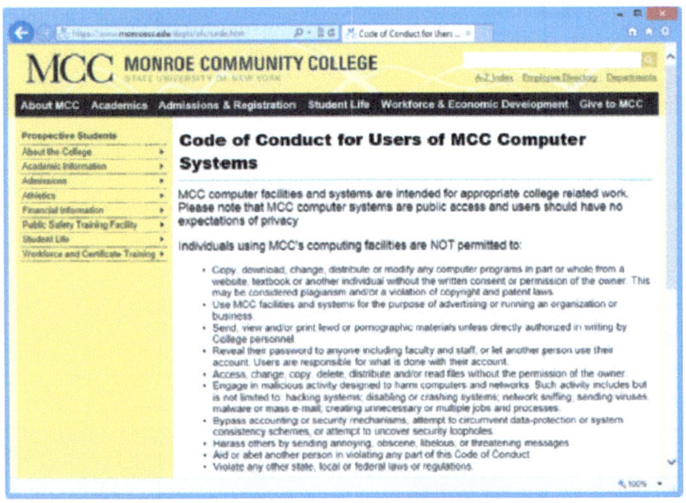

Unauthorized access and many types of unauthorized use are criminal offenses in the United States and many other countries. They can be committed by both *insiders* (people who work for the company whose computers are being accessed) and *outsiders* (people who do not work for that company). Whether or not a specific act constitutes unauthorized use or is illegal depends on the circumstances, as well as the specific company or institution involved. To explain acceptable computer use to their employees, students, or other users, many organizations and educational institutions publish guidelines for behavior, often called *codes of conduct* (see Figure 4-1). Codes of conduct typically address prohibited activities, such as playing games, installing personal software, violating copyright laws, causing harm to computers or the network, and snooping in other people's files.

Hacking

Hacking refers to the act of breaking into a computer or network. It can be performed in person by hacking into a computer the *hacker* has physical access to, but it is more often performed via the Internet or another network. Unless authorized (such as when a company hires a *professional hacker* to test the security of its system), hacking in the United States and many other countries is a crime.

>**Unauthorized access.** Gaining access to a computer, mobile device, network, file, or other resource without permission. >**Unauthorized use.** Using a computing resource for unapproved activities. >**Hacking.** Using a computer to break into another computer system.

Typically, the motivation for hacking is to steal data, sabotage a computer system, or perform some other type of illegal act. In particular, the theft of consumer data (such as credit card numbers) has increased dramatically over the past several years—more than 1,600 data breaches were discovered in 2012. Some of the most notable recent breaches include the 2013 theft of prepaid debit card numbers, which were then programmed with large balances and used in simultaneous ATM withdrawals by a gang of hackers and which resulted in a $45 million global heist; the 2012 theft of 3.6 million Social Security numbers, along with names, addresses, credit card numbers, and other sensitive information, from the South Carolina Department of Revenue computer system; and the 2012 *Zappos.com* data breach, which resulted in hackers gaining access to the names, addresses, phone numbers, and the last four digits of credit card numbers of 24 million customers. Another growing trend is to hack into a computer and "hijack" it for use in an illegal or unethical act, such as taking over an individual's computer, spying via a webcam, generating spam, or hosting pornographic Web sites. Hackers are also increasingly aiming attacks at very specific individuals, such as product designers and other individuals who have access to valuable corporate data.

TIP

According to a recent study, the total cost per data breach in the United States is $5.4 million—the highest of any country.

TIP

A number of recent data breaches have been performed by the *hacktivist* group *Anonymous.*

In addition to being a threat to individuals and businesses, hacking is also considered a very serious threat to national security in the United States. The increased number of systems that are controlled by computers and are connected to the Internet, along with the continually improving abilities of hackers, has led to an increased risk of *cyberterrorism*—where terrorists launch attacks via the Internet. Current concerns include attacks by individual terrorists, as well as by other countries, against the computers controlling vital systems; vital systems include the nation's power grids, banks, and water filtration facilities, as well as computers related to national defense, the airlines, and the stock market. In fact, President Obama and Chinese President Xi Jinping began serious discussion about cybersecurity in 2013 following a government report that found nearly 40 Pentagon weapons programs and almost 30 other defense technologies were compromised by cyber intrusions from China. President Obama has declared that "cyber threat is one of the most serious economic and national security challenges we face as a nation."

Today, hackers often gain access via a wireless network. This is because wireless networks are widely used and they are easier to hack into than wired networks. In fact, it is possible to gain access to a wireless network just by being within range (about 100 to 300 feet, depending on the Wi-Fi standard being used) of a wireless access point, unless the access point is sufficiently protected. Although security features are built into wireless routers and other networking hardware, they are typically not enabled by default. As a result, many wireless networks belonging to businesses and individuals are left unsecured. Securing a Wi-Fi network is discussed shortly.

ASK THE EXPERT

Courtesy ACM

Moshe Vardi, Rice University, Co-Chair of the ACM Globalization and Offshoring of Software Taskforce

Is there a national security risk to outsourcing/offshoring software development?

Offshoring magnifies existing risks and creates new and often poorly understood threats. When businesses offshore work, they increase not only their own business-related risks (e.g., intellectual property theft) but also risks to national security and to individuals' privacy. While it is unlikely these risks will deter the growth of offshoring, businesses and nations should employ strategies to mitigate the risks. Businesses have a clear incentive to manage these new risks to suit their own interests, but nations and individuals often have little awareness of the exposures created. For example, many commercial off-the-shelf (COTS) systems are developed offshore, making it extremely difficult for buyers to understand all of the source and application code in the systems. This creates the possibility that a hostile nation or nongovernmental hostile agent (such as a terrorist or criminal) could compromise these systems. Individuals are also often exposed to loss of privacy or identity theft due to the number of business processes being offshored today and managed under laws that are much less restrictive than in most developed countries.

War Driving and Wi-Fi Piggybacking

Unauthorized use of a Wi-Fi network is called **war driving** or **Wi-Fi piggybacking**, depending on the location of the hacker at the time. War driving typically involves driving in a car with a portable device looking for unsecured Wi-Fi networks to connect to. Wi-Fi piggybacking refers to accessing someone else's unsecured Wi-Fi network from the hacker's current location (such as inside his or her home, outside a Wi-Fi hotspot location, or near a local business). Both war driving and Wi-Fi piggybacking are ethically—if not legally—questionable acts. They can also lead to illegal behavior, such as individuals deciding to use data (credit card numbers, for instance) they run across while war driving for fraudulent purposes, as was the case with two men who illegally accessed a Lowe's wireless network during a war drive and later decided to steal credit card numbers via that network. War driving and Wi-Fi piggybacking can also have security risks, both for the hacker and the owner of the Wi-Fi network that is being used. For instance, they both risk the introduction of computer viruses (either intentionally or unintentionally) and unauthorized access of the data located on their computers. In addition, the owner may experience reduced performance or even the cancellation of his or her Internet service if the ISP limits bandwidth or the number of computers allowed to use a single Internet connection.

In some countries, such as the UK, the laws are clear that unauthorized access of a Wi-Fi connection is illegal. In the United States, federal law is not as clear, although some states (such as Michigan) have made using a Wi-Fi connection without permission illegal. In fact, a Michigan man was found guilty, fined, and sentenced to community service in 2007 for using the free Wi-Fi service offered to customers at a local café because he was using the service from his parked car located on the street outside the café to check his e-mail on a regular basis. And, at the time of this writing, Google was being accused, via a privacy class-action lawsuit, of collecting and storing private data (including e-mails, usernames, passwords, and documents) from unsecured home Wi-Fi networks in the United States and Europe while capturing data for its Street View mapping system.

Advocates of war driving and Wi-Fi piggybacking state that, unless individuals or businesses protect their access points, they are welcoming others to use them. Critics compare that logic to that of an unlocked front door—you cannot legally enter a home just because the front door is unlocked. Some wireless network owners do leave their access points unsecured on purpose and some communities are creating a collection of wireless access points to provide wireless Internet access to everyone in that community. However, it is difficult—if not impossible—to tell if an unsecured network is that way intentionally, unless the hotspot information states that it is a free public Wi-Fi hotspot. To help you locate public Wi-Fi hotspots, a number of services are available, such as browser-based mapping applications and smartphone apps that identify free and fee-based hotspots for a specific geographical location (see the Wi-Fi Finder app in Figure 4-2). Mobile apps have the advantage of automatically determining your geographical location to display information about hotspots in your current geographical area.

FIGURE 4-2
Wi-Fi finders. Online mapping services and smartphone apps can show you the available Wi-Fi hotspots for a particular geographic area.

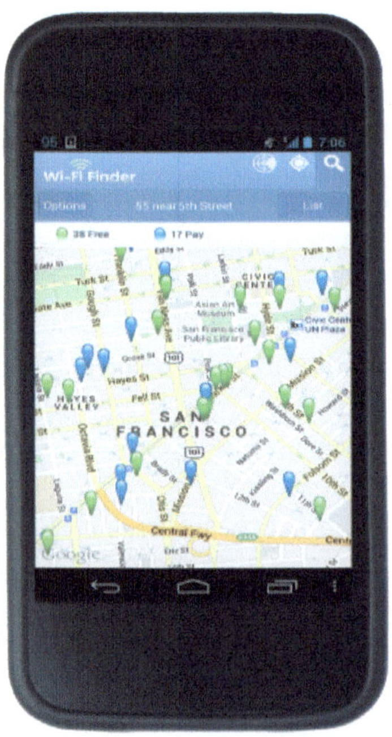

Some feel the ethical distinction of using an unsecured wireless network is determined by the amount of use, believing that it is acceptable to borrow someone's Internet connection to do a quick e-mail check or Google search, but that continually using a neighbor's Internet connection to avoid paying for your own is crossing over the line. Others feel that allowing outsiders to share an Internet connection is acceptable use, as long as the subscriber does not charge the outsider for that access. Still others believe that an Internet connection is intended for use only by the subscriber and that sharing it with others is unfair to the subscriber's ISP. This issue is beginning to be addressed by the courts and ISPs, and some answers regarding the legality of "Wi-Fi borrowing" and

>**War driving.** Driving around an area with a Wi-Fi-enabled computer or mobile device to find a Wi-Fi network to access and use without authorization. >**Wi-Fi piggybacking.** Accessing an unsecured Wi-Fi network from your current location without authorization.

Internet connection sharing will likely be forthcoming in the near future. However, the ethical questions surrounding this issue may take longer to resolve.

Interception of Communications

Instead of accessing data stored on a computer via hacking, some criminals gain unauthorized access to data, files, messages, VoIP calls, and other content as it is being sent over the Internet. For instance, *unencrypted* (unsecured) messages, files, logon information, and more sent over a wireless network (such as while using a public Wi-Fi hotspot or over an unsecured home or business Wi-Fi network) can be captured and read by anyone within range using software designed for that purpose. Once intercepted, the data can be used for unintended or fraudulent purposes.

Although it is unlikely that anyone would be interested in intercepting personal e-mail or text messages sent to friends and relatives, proprietary corporate information and sensitive personal information (such as credit card numbers and Web site logon information) is at risk if it is sent unsecured over the Internet or over a wireless home or corporate network. The widespread use of wireless networks with both home and office computers, as well as with smartphones and other portable devices, has opened up new opportunities for data interception. For instance, the data on mobile devices with Bluetooth capabilities enabled can be accessed by other Bluetooth devices that are within range and any sensitive data stored on a smartphone can be accessed by a hacker if the phone is connected to an unsecured Wi-Fi network. With an increasing number of smartphone owners storing sensitive data (such as passwords for online banking and social networking sites, and credit card account numbers) on their devices (and less than half of owners securing their mobile devices with a *password*, according to one estimate), the risk of that data being intercepted is increasing.

A relatively recent trend is criminals intercepting credit and debit card information during the card verification process; that is, intercepting the data from a card in real time as a purchase is being authorized. Often, this occurrs via *packetsniffing* software installed at payment terminals (such as restaurant cash registers or gas station credit/debit card readers) by hackers—the packetsniffing software gathers data during transactions and then sends it to the hackers, who may then use it for fraudulent purposes.

PROTECTING AGAINST UNAUTHORIZED ACCESS AND UNAUTHORIZED USE

The first step in protecting against unauthorized access and unauthorized use of a computer system is controlling access to an organization's facilities and computer networks to ensure that only authorized individuals are granted access. In addition, steps need to be taken to ensure that authorized individuals access only the resources that they are supposed to access.

Access Control Systems

Access control systems are used to control access to facilities, devices, computer networks, company databases, Web site accounts, and other assets. They can be *identification systems*, which verify that the person trying to access the facility or system is listed as an authorized user, and/or *authentication systems*, which determine whether or not the person attempting access is actually who he or she claims to be. In businesses, access control systems are often integrated into a comprehensive *identity management* (*IDM*) *system* designed to manage users' access to enterprise systems, such as to grant them secure and appropriate access to the systems they are allowed to access in as convenient a manner as possible. An emerging trend is to use *single sign-on* (*SSO*) systems that grant employees access to a number of secure resources with a single authentication. The three most common types of access control systems are discussed next, followed by a discussion of additional considerations for controlling access to wireless networks. Some emerging control systems are discussed in the Trend box later in this chapter.

TIP

To prevent a hacker from obtaining your logon info from an unused (*zombie*) online account, delete your old accounts if you are no longer going to use them.

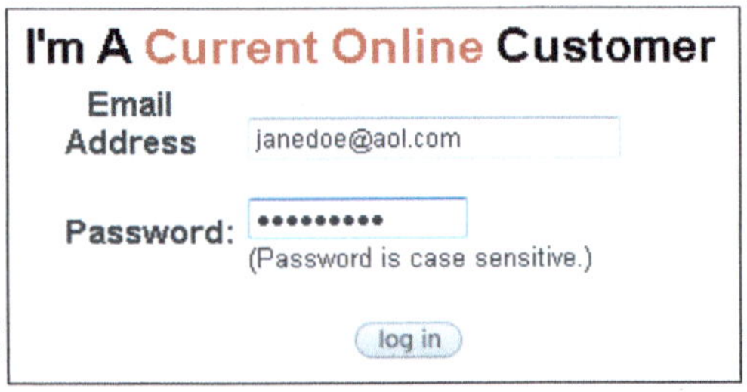

FIGURE 4-3
Passwords.
Passwords are used to log on to computers, networks, Web sites, and other computing resources.

Possessed Knowledge Access Systems

A **possessed knowledge access system** is an identification system that requires the individual requesting access to provide information that only the authorized user is supposed to know. *Passwords* and *cognitive authentication systems* fall into this category.

Passwords, the most common type of possessed knowledge, are secret words or character combinations associated with an individual. They are typically used in conjunction with a *username* (often a variation of the person's first and/or last names or the individual's e-mail address). Username/password combinations are often used to restrict access to networks, computers, Web sites, routers, and other computing resources—the user is granted access only after supplying the correct information. While usernames and e-mail addresses are not secret, passwords are and, for security purposes, typically appear as asterisks or dots as they are being entered so they cannot be viewed (see Figure 4-3). For some applications (such as ATM machines), a *PIN* or *personal identification number*—a secret combination of numeric digits selected by the user—is used instead of a password. Numeric passwords are also referred to as *passcodes*. Instead of traditional passwords, some systems (such as Windows 8 devices and smartphone *lock screens*) can use *picture passwords*—typically gestures or patterns drawn on top of an image, such as a grid of dots or a photograph.

One of the biggest disadvantages of password-based systems is that any individual possessing the proper password will be granted access to the system because the system recognizes the password, regardless of whether or not the person using the password is the authorized user, and passwords can be guessed or deciphered by a hacker or a hacker's computer easily if secure password selection strategies are not applied. For example, many hackers are able to access networking hardware and databases because the system administrator passwords for those resources are still the default passwords (the ones assigned during manufacturing) and so are commonly known; some insiders gain unauthorized access to systems using passwords written down on sticky notes attached to a user's monitor. In addition, passwords can be forgotten. Consequently, it is important to select passwords that are *strong passwords* but are also easy to remember without writing them down. Strong passwords are passwords that are at least eight characters long; use a combination of letters, numbers, and symbols; and do not form words found in the dictionary or that match the username that the password is associated with. Some strategies for creating strong passwords are listed in Figure 4-4.

A growing trend in possessed knowledge access systems is the use of *cognitive authentication systems* instead of, or

FIGURE 4-4
Strategies for creating strong passwords.

PASSWORD STRATEGIES

Make the password at least eight characters and include both uppercase and lowercase letters, as well as numbers and special symbols.

Choose passwords that are not in a dictionary—for instance, mix numbers and special characters with abbreviations or unusual words you will remember but that do not conform to a pattern a computer can readily figure out.

Do not use your name, your kids' or pets' names, your address, your birthdate, or any other public information as your password.

Determine a *passphrase* that you can remember and use corresponding letters and symbols (such as the first letter of each word) for your password. For instance, the passphrase "My son John is five years older than my daughter Abby" could be used to remember the corresponding strong password "Msji5yotMd@".

Develop a system using a basic password for all Web sites plus site-specific information (such as the first two letters of the site and a number you will remember) to create a different password for each site, but still ones you can easily remember. For instance, you can combine your dog's name with the site initials followed by a number that is significant to you to form a password such as "RoverAM27" for Amazon.com.

Do not keep a written copy of the password in your desk or taped to your monitor. If you need to write down your password, create a password-protected file on your computer that contains all your passwords or use a password manager program.

Use a different password for your highly sensitive activities (such as online banking or stock trading) than for other Web sites. If a hacker determines your password on a low-security site (which is easier to break into), he or she can use it on an account containing sensitive data if you use the same password on both accounts.

Change your passwords frequently—at least every 6 months.

>**Possessed knowledge access system.** An access control system that uses information only the individual should know to identify that individual.
>**Password.** A secret combination of characters used to gain access to a computer, computer network, or other resource.

in conjunction with, usernames and passwords. Cognitive authentication systems use information that an individual should know or can remember easily. Some systems use personal information about the individual (such as his or her city of birth, first school attended, or amount of home mortgage) that was pulled from public databases or the company database and the individual must supply the correct answer in order to be granted access. Other systems (such as the password recovery systems used by many secure Web sites to verify individuals when they forget their password) allow the individual to supply answers to questions when the account is created and then the individual can supply those answers again for authentication purposes when needed.

CAUTION CAUTION CAUTION CAUTION CAUTION CAUTION CAUT

Don't select answers for the cognitive authentication questions used in the password recovery process of many Web sites that a hacker may be able to guess based on information found on your Facebook page or other online source. Instead, supply answers that you can remember but that also follow secure password rules. For instance, if your dog's name is Spot, you could enter *MDN1s$pOT* as the answer to a question about your pet's name and remember it as "My dog's name is Spot."

Possessed knowledge systems are often used in conjunction with the *possessed object access systems* and *biometric access systems* that are discussed next. Using two different methods to authenticate a user is called **two-factor authentication**. Typically, the methods used are some type of possessed knowledge (something you know) along with either a *possessed object* (something you have) or a *biometric feature* (something you are). Two-factor authentication adds an additional level of security to an access control system because hackers are much less likely to be able to gain access to two different required factors. One emerging type of two-factor authentication uses a conventional username/password combination in conjunction with a *soft token* (an electronic object available via something you already carry with you, such as a smartphone or credit card, instead of using a *hard token*, such as a *USB key token*). A soft token can be generated by a mobile app or by pressing a button on a credit card; it can also be sent via text message. A soft token supplies a *one-time password* (*OTP*), which must be entered in conjunction with your username/password in order to log on to the account. Two-factor authentication systems are common in many countries and their use is growing in the United States. For instance, many banks offer two-factor authentication for online and mobile banking, and it is an option for Google, Twitter, and Facebook users. In Facebook, for example, once two-factor authentication (called *Login Approvals*) is enabled, you will see the security code screen shown in Figure 4-5 whenever you log in with your Facebook logon information using a new browser or device; you will need to enter the OTP sent to your phone before you will be logged into your Facebook account. The disadvantage of two-factor authentication for businesses is that only one individual can access the account, unless the site (like Facebook) supports multiple users for a single account.

FIGURE 4-5
Facebook two-factor authentication. The first time you log on with a new device, you must supply the OTP sent to your mobile phone in addition to your conventional username/password combination.

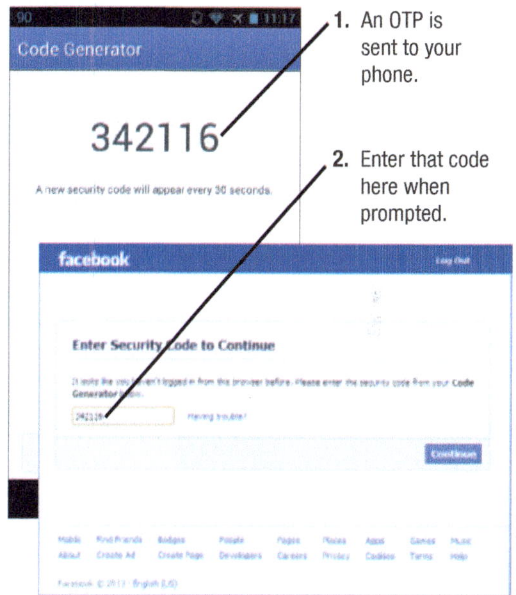

TIP

To enable Facebook Login Approvals, go to your *Security Settings* on that site.

Possessed Object Access Systems

Possessed object access systems use physical objects for identification purposes and they are frequently used to control access to facilities (called *physical access*) and computer systems (called *logical access*). Common types of possessed objects are smart

>**Two-factor authentication.** Using two different methods to authenticate a user. >**Possessed object access system.** An access control system that uses a physical object an individual has in his or her possession to identify that individual.

cards, RFID-encoded badges, magnetic cards, and smartphones that are swiped through or placed close to a reader to be read (see Figure 4-6)—emerging options include the use of an *NFC-enabled ring* or a Bluetooth app (as discussed in Chapter 8) to automatically lock and unlock your devices when they are within range. Possessed objects also include *USB security keys* or *tokens* (USB flash drives that are inserted into a computer to grant access to a network, to supply Web site usernames and passwords, or to provide other security features), access cards, smartphones, and other devices used to supply the OTPs used to log on to Web sites. An emerging option is integrating OTP capabilities into the hardware of devices, such as laptops that include Intel *Identity Protection Technology (IPT)*, in order to automatically authenticate the devices being used to log on to participating Web sites.

One disadvantage of using possessed objects is that they can be lost or, like passwords, can be used by an unauthorized individual if that individual has possession of the object. This disadvantage can be overcome by using a second factor, such as a username/password combination or a fingerprint or other type of *biometric* data.

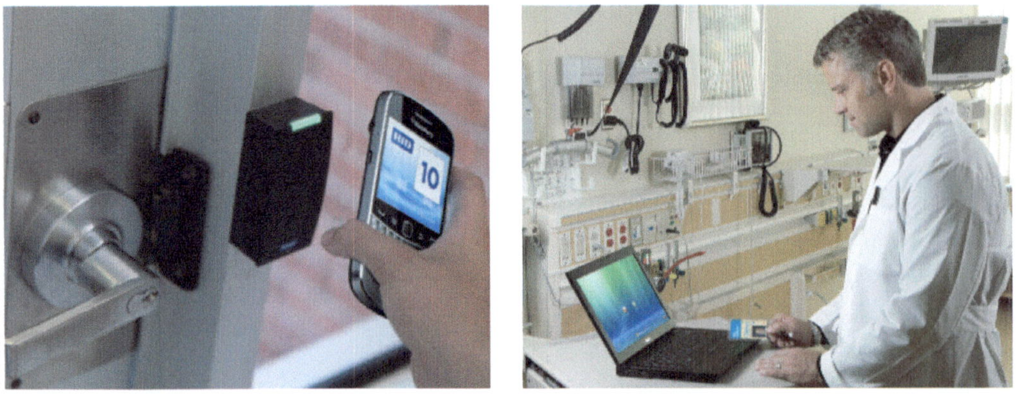

PHYSICAL ACCESS
The object (in this case a mobile phone containing an appropriate microSD card) is read by a reader to provide access to a facility.

LOGICAL ACCESS
The object (in this case a smart card employee badge) is read by a reader (this reader is integrated into the computer) to provide access to that computer system.

FIGURE 4-6
Possessed objects.
Can grant access to both facilities and computer resources (including computers, networks, and Web sites).

Biometric Access Systems

Biometrics is the study of identifying individuals using measurable, unique physiological or behavioral characteristics. **Biometric access systems** typically identify users by a particular unique biological characteristic (such as a fingerprint, a hand, a face, veins, or an iris), although personal traits are used in some systems. For instance, some systems today use *keystroke dynamics* to recognize an individual's unique typing pattern to authenticate the user as he or she types in his or her username and password; other systems identify an individual via his or her voice, signature, or gait. Because the means of access (usually a part of the body) cannot typically be used by anyone other than the authorized individual, biometric access systems can perform both identification and authentication. Biometric access systems are used for both physical and logical access (see Figure 4-7).

To identify and authenticate an individual, biometric access systems typically use a biometric reader (such as a *fingerprint reader*, *finger* or *palm vein reader*, or a *hand geometry reader*) to identify an individual based on his or her fingerprint, veins, or hand image, or a digital camera to identify an individual based on his or her face or iris, in conjunction with software and a database. The system matches the supplied biometric data with the biometric data that was stored in the database when the individual was enrolled in the system and authenticates the individual if the data matches. To speed up the process, many biometric access systems require users to identify themselves first (such as by entering a username or swiping a smart card), and then the system uses that identifying information to verify that the supplied biometric data matches the identified person.

TIP

Cuts or other changes to a finger may prevent access via a fingerprint reader. To avoid this problem, be sure to enroll more than one finger, if possible, whenever you are being set up in a system that uses a fingerprint reader—any of the registered fingers may be used for access.

>**Biometric access system.** An access control system that uses one unique physical characteristic of an individual (such as a fingerprint, a face, veins, or a voice) to authenticate that individual.

Biometric access systems are used to control access to secure facilities (such as corporate headquarters and prisons); to log users on to computers, networks, and secure Web sites (by using an external reader or camera or one built into the computer); to punch employees in and out of work; and to confirm consumers' identities at ATM machines and check-cashing services. Biometric readers are also increasingly being built into smartphones, external hard drives, USB flash drives, and other hardware to prevent unauthorized use of those devices.

In addition to being used to control access to computers, networks, and other resources, biometrics are an important part of the systems used by law enforcement agencies and the military to identify individuals. For instance, the border control systems in many countries use biometrics to identify citizens, travelers, criminal suspects, and potential terrorists, and biometric identification systems are used extensively by law enforcement agencies and the military in areas of conflict. For example, the Egyptian Hospital at Bagram Airfield in Afghanistan uses biometrics (fingerprints and iris scans—see Figure 4-7) to identify and track the records of incoming patients. In addition, *face recognition systems* (biometric systems that use cameras and a database of photos to attempt to identify individuals as they walk by the cameras) are used in many airports and other public locations to help identify known terrorists and criminal suspects.

FINGERPRINT READERS
Typically used to protect access to work facilities or computers, to log on to secure Web sites, for law enforcement identification, and to pay for products or services.

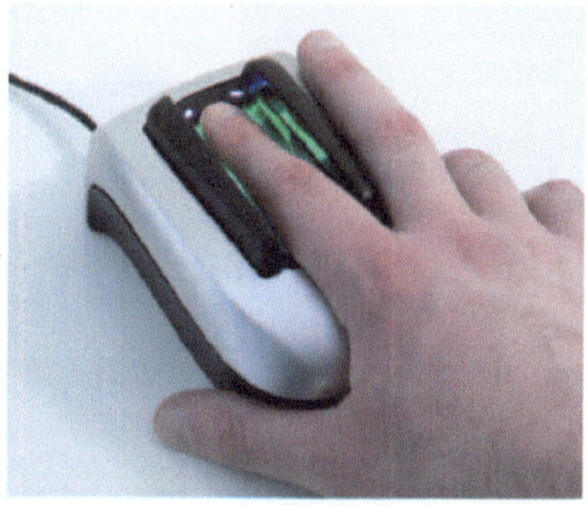

VEIN READERS
Beginning to replace hand geometry readers to control access to facilities (such as government offices, prisons, and military facilities) and to punch in and out of work.

FACE RECOGNITION SYSTEMS
Typically used to control access to highly secure areas, to identify individuals for law enforcement purposes, and to log on to devices or apps, as shown here.

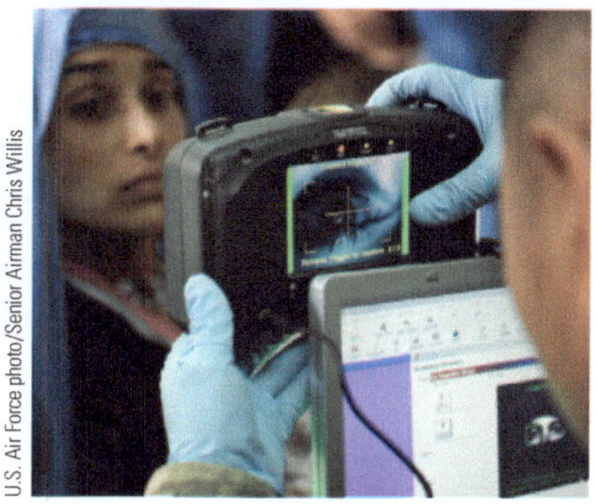

IRIS RECOGNITION SYSTEMS
Typically used to control access to highly secure areas and by the military, such as to identify Afghan patients as shown here.

FIGURE 4-7
Types of biometric access and identification systems.

Biometric access systems are very accurate. In fact, the odds of two different individuals having identical irises is 1 in 10^{78} and the statistical probability of two different irises being declared a match are 1 in 1.2 million—even identical twins (who have the same DNA structure) have different fingerprints and irises. Systems based on biological characteristics (such as a person's iris, hand geometry, face, or fingerprint) tend to be more accurate than those based on a personal trait (such as a person's voice or written signature) because biological traits do not change, but physical traits might change (such as an individual's voice, which might be affected by a cold, or a written signature, which might be affected by a broken wrist). In addition, biometric characteristics cannot be lost (like an access card), cannot be forgotten (like a password), and do not have to be pulled out of a briefcase or pocket (like an access card or other type of possessed object).

The primary disadvantages of biometric access systems are that much of the necessary hardware and software is expensive, and the data used for authentication (such as a fingerprint or an iris image) cannot be reset if it is compromised. In addition, fingerprint and hand geometry systems typically require contact with the reader device (which some users might object to)—vein systems (that use infrared LED light in conjunction with a digital camera to identify individuals based on the veins in their fingers or palms) can be contactless systems.

TIP

Fingerprint biometrics is an integral part of Windows 8.1, supporting both *touch* and *swipe fingerprint readers* for a variety of authentication functions.

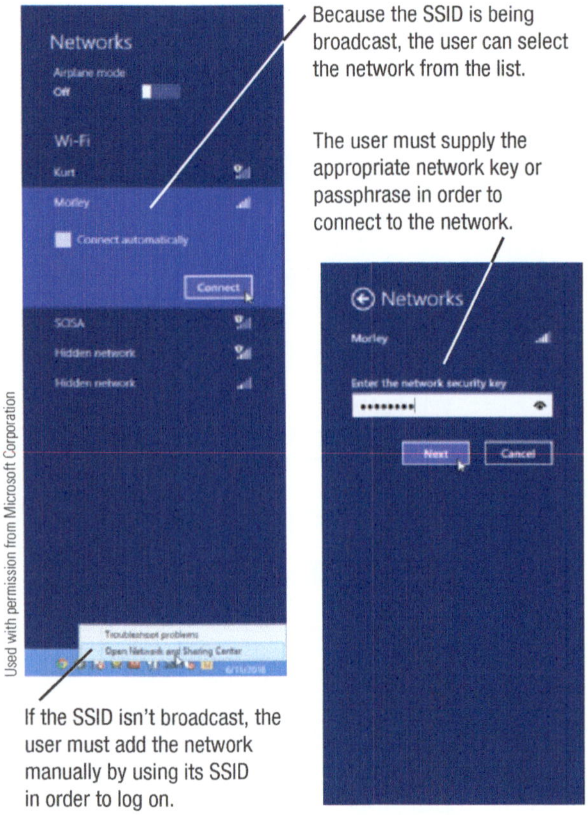

FIGURE 4-8

Accessing a Wi-Fi network. To access a secure network, the appropriate passphrase must be supplied.

Controlling Access to Wireless Networks

As already discussed, wireless networks—such as Wi-Fi networks—are less secure, in general, than wired networks. There are Wi-Fi security procedures, however, that can be used to protect against unauthorized use of a wireless network and to *encrypt* data sent over the network so that it is unreadable if it is intercepted. The original Wi-Fi security standard was *WEP* (*Wired Equivalent Privacy*). WEP is now considered insecure and has been replaced with the more secure *WPA* (*Wi-Fi Protected Access*) and the even more secure *WPA2* standards. However, Wi-Fi security features only work if they are enabled. Most Wi-Fi hardware today is shipped with the security features either switched off or enabled with a *default password* that is public knowledge; many network owners never change the default settings, leaving those networks unsecured.

To protect against unauthorized access, Wi-Fi network owners should secure their networks by changing the router or access point settings to enable one of the encryption standards and to assign a *network key* or *passphrase* (essentially a password) that must be supplied in order to access the secured network. In addition, the name of the network (called the *SSID*) can be hidden from view by switching off the SSID broadcast feature. While hiding the network name will not deter serious hackers, it may reduce the number of casual war drivers or neighbors accessing the network. Once a network is secured, users who want to connect to that network need to either select or supply the network SSID name (depending on whether or not the SSID is being broadcast) and then enter the network key assigned to that network (see Figure 4-8). For an overview of how you can secure your wireless home router, see the How It Works box.

Firewalls, Encryption, and Virtual Private Networks (VPNs)

In addition to the access control systems just discussed, there are a number of other tools that can be used to prevent access to an individual computer or to prevent data from being intercepted in an understandable form during transit. These tools are discussed next.

Firewalls

A **firewall** is a security system that essentially creates a barrier between a computer or a network and the Internet in order to protect against unauthorized access. Firewalls are typically two-way, so they check all incoming (from the Internet) and outgoing (to the Internet) traffic and allow only authorized traffic to pass through the firewall. *Personal firewalls* are software programs designed to protect home computers from hackers attempting to access those computers through their Internet connections. All computers with direct Internet connections (such as DSL, cable, satellite, or fixed wireless Internet access) should use a firewall (computers using dial-up Internet access only are relatively safe from hackers). Personal firewalls can be stand-alone programs (such as the free *ZoneAlarm* program or the free *Comodo Firewall* program shown in Figure 4-9); they are also built into many operating systems (such as the *Windows Firewall* program). Many routers, modems, and other pieces of networking hardware also include built-in firewall capabilities to help secure the networks these devices are used with. Firewalls designed to protect business networks may be software-based, hardware-based, or a combination of the two. They can typically be used both to prevent network access by hackers and other outsiders, as well as to control employee Internet access.

TIP

If a legitimate application installed on your computer needs to access the Internet but cannot, check your firewall settings—you may need to unblock that program.

>**Firewall.** A collection of hardware and/or software intended to protect a computer or computer network from unauthorized access.

HOW IT WORKS

Securing a Wireless Home Router

If you have a home wireless network, it is important to secure it properly so it cannot be used by unauthorized individuals. To open your router's configuration screen to check or modify the security settings, type the IP address assigned to that device (such as 192.168.0.1—check your router's documentation for its default IP address and username) in your browser's Address bar. Use the default password to log on the first time, and then change the password using the configuration screen to prevent unauthorized individuals from changing your router settings. To secure the router, enter the network name (SSID) you want to have associated with the router, select the appropriate security mode (such as WPA or WPA2) to be used, and then type a secure passphrase to be used in order to log on to the network.

For additional security, *MAC (Media Access Control) address filtering* can be used to allow only the devices whose network adapter MAC addresses you enter into your router's settings access to the network. While MAC address filtering should not be considered an alternative to using WPA or WPA2 encryption, it does add another layer of protection. Other precautions include designating specific times (such as when you are away from home) that the router will deny access to any device, and reducing the strength of the wireless signal if its current strength reaches farther than you need.

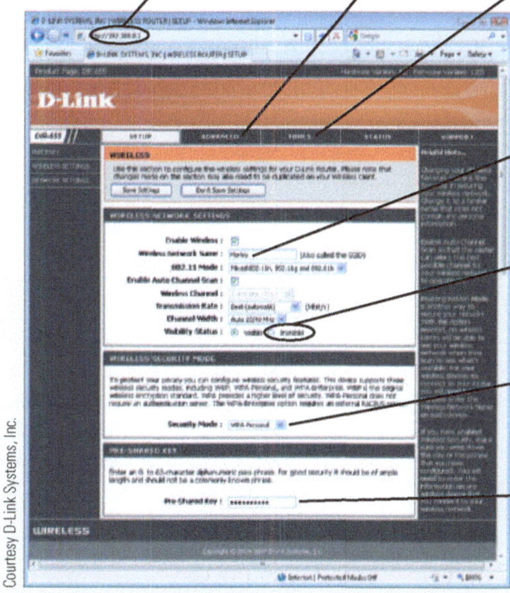

Courtesy D-Link Systems, Inc.

Configuring a home router.

Firewalls work by closing down all external *communications port addresses* (the electronic connections that allow a computer to communicate with other computers) to unauthorized computers and programs. While business firewalls are set up by the network administrator and those settings typically cannot be changed by end users, individuals may choose to change the settings for their personal firewall. For example, the user can choose to be notified when any application program on the computer is trying to access the Internet, to specify the programs that are allowed to access the Internet, or to block all incoming connections temporarily. In addition to protecting your computer from outside access, firewall programs also protect against any spyware, computer viruses, or other malicious programs located on your computer that are designed to send data from your computer

FIGURE 4-9
A personal firewall.

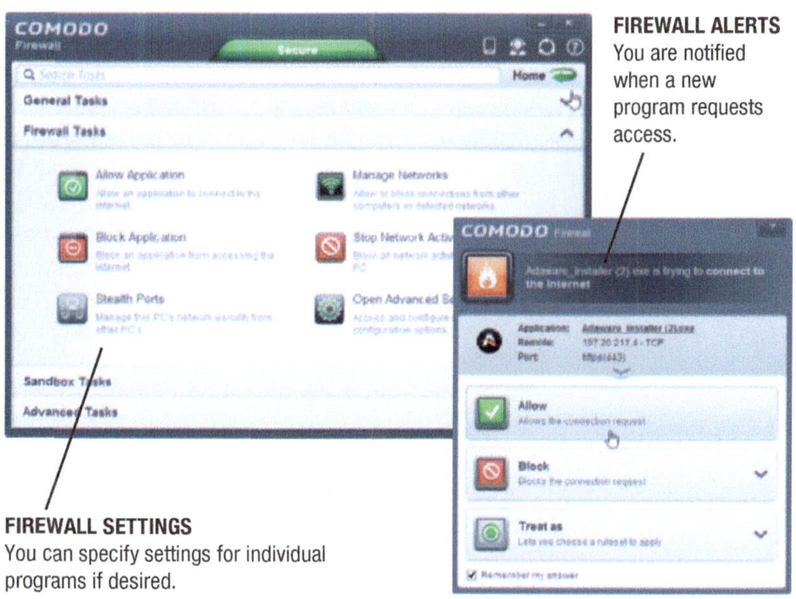

Courtesy Comodo Group, Inc.

(such as credit card numbers, Web site passwords, and other sensitive data stored on your hard drive) to a hacker at the hacker's request.

A related type of security system increasingly being used by businesses today and included in many security suites is an *intrusion prevention system* (*IPS*). Whereas a firewall tries to block unauthorized traffic, an IPS continuously monitors and analyzes the traffic allowed by the firewall to try to detect possible attacks as they are occurring. If an attack is in progress, IPS software can immediately block it.

After installing and setting up a firewall (and an IPS if needed), individuals and businesses should test their systems to determine if vulnerabilities still exist. Individuals can use online security tests—such as the *Symantec Security Check* shown in Figure 4-10 or the tests at Gibson Research's *ShieldsUP!* site—to check their computers; businesses may want to hire an outside consultant to perform a comprehensive security assessment.

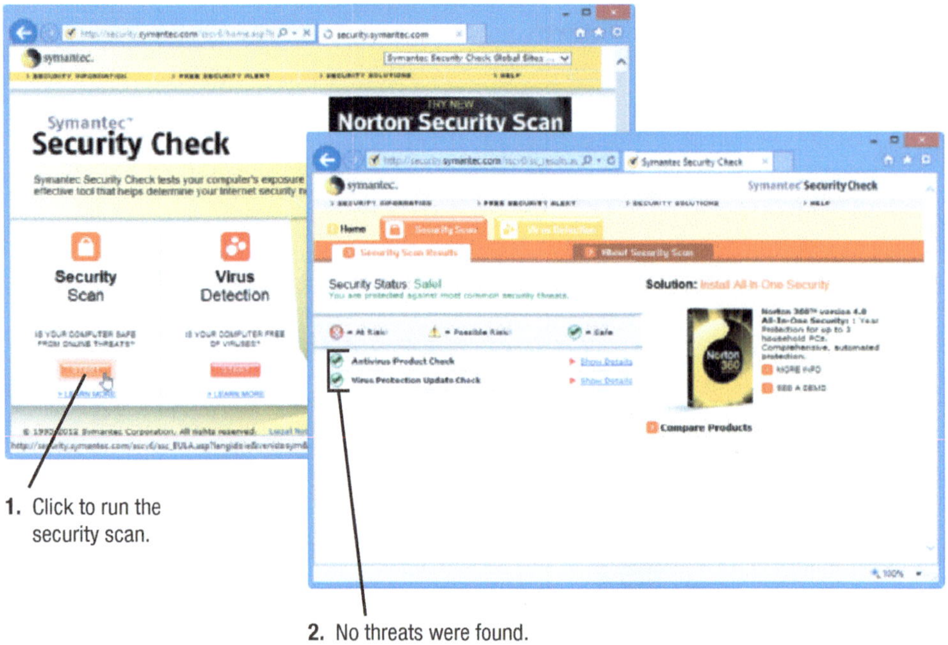

Courtesy Symantec

FIGURE 4-10
Online security scans can check your system for vulnerabilities.

Encryption

Encryption is a way of temporarily converting data into a form, known as a *cipher*, which is unreadable until it is *decrypted* (unscrambled) in order to protect that data from being viewed by unauthorized individuals. As previously discussed, secure Wi-Fi networks use encryption to secure data that is transferred over the network. **Secure Web pages** use encryption so that sensitive data (such as credit card numbers) sent via the Web page is protected as it travels over the Internet. The most common security protocols used with secure Web pages are *Secure Sockets Layer* (*SSL*) and *Extended Validation Secure Sockets Layer* (*EV SSL*). The URL for Web pages using either form of SSL begins with *https:* instead of *http:*.

Some Internet services, such as *Skype* (for VoIP calls) and *Hushmail* (for Web-based e-mails), use built-in encryption. Encryption can also be added manually to a file or an e-mail message before it is sent over the Internet to ensure that the content is unreadable if the file or message is intercepted during transit. In addition to securing files during transit, encryption can be used to protect the files stored on a hard drive so they will be unreadable if opened by an unauthorized person (such as if a hacker accesses a file containing sensitive data or if a computer containing sensitive files is lost or stolen). Increasingly, computers and storage devices (particularly those used with portable computers) are *self-encrypting*; that is, encrypting all data automatically and invisibly to the user, as discussed in Chapter 5. Windows, Mac OS, and other current operating systems support encryption and businesses are increasingly turning to encryption to prevent data loss if a data breach should occur.

TIP

An emerging encryption standard that may eventually replace SSL is *Transport Layer Security* (*TLS*).

TIP

Sensitive information (such as credit card numbers, account numbers, and Web site passwords) should only be entered on secure Web pages to prevent that data from being intercepted by a criminal.

>**Encryption.** A method of scrambling the contents of an e-mail message or a file to make it unreadable if an unauthorized user intercepts it.

>**Secure Web page.** A Web page that uses encryption to protect information transmitted via that Web page.

The two most common types of encryption in use today are *public key encryption* (often used with content being transmitted over the Internet, such as secure Web pages and encrypted e-mail) and *private key encryption* (most often used to encrypt files or the content of a hard drive or other device). **Private key encryption**, also called *symmetric key encryption*, uses a single secret *private key* (essentially a password) to both encrypt and decrypt the file or message. It is often used to encrypt files stored on an individual's computer because the individual who selects the private key is likely the only one who will need to access those files. Private key encryption can also be used to send files securely to others, provided both the sender and recipient agree on the private key that will be used to access the file. Private key encryption capabilities are incorporated into a variety of programs today, including Microsoft Office, the WinZip file compression program, and Adobe Acrobat (the program used to create PDF files). To encrypt a document in Microsoft Word 2013, for instance, you select *Info* on the FILE tab, click *Protect Document* and select *Encrypt with Password*, type the desired password (private key) when prompted, and then save the file. To open that document again (or any copies of the file, such as those sent via e-mail), the password assigned to that file must be entered correctly.

Public key encryption, also called *asymmetric key encryption*, utilizes two encryption keys to encrypt and decrypt documents. Specifically, public key encryption uses a pair of keys (a private key and a *public key*) that are related mathematically to each other and have been assigned to a particular individual. An individual's public key is not secret and is available for anyone to use, but the corresponding private key is secret and is used only by the individual to whom it was assigned. Documents or messages encrypted with a public key can only be decrypted with the matching private key.

Public/private key pairs are generated by the program being used to perform the encryption or they are obtained via the Internet through a *Certificate Authority*, such as VeriSign or Thawte. Once obtained, encryption keys are stored in your browser, e-mail program, and any other program with which they will be used—this is typically done automatically for you when you obtain your key pairs. Obtaining a business public/private key pair usually requires a fee, but free key pairs for personal use are available through some Certificate Authorities. If a third-party encryption program is used (such as *Pretty Good Privacy* or *PGP*), the program typically takes care of obtaining and managing your keys for you.

To send someone an encrypted e-mail message or file using public key encryption, you need his or her public key. If that person has previously sent you his or her public key (such as via an e-mail message), it was likely stored by your e-mail program in your address book or contacts list, or by your encryption program in a central key directory used by that program. In either case, that public key is available whenever you want to send that person an encrypted document. If you do not already have the public key belonging to the individual to whom you want to send an encrypted e-mail or file, you will need to request it from that individual. Once the recipient's public key has been used to encrypt the file or e-mail message and that document is received, the recipient uses his or her private key to decrypt the encrypted contents (see Figure 4-11).

To avoid the need to obtain the recipient's public key before sending that person an encrypted e-mail, *Web-based encrypted e-mail* can be used. Web-based encrypted e-mail works similarly to regular Web-based e-mail (in which e-mail is composed and viewed on a Web page belonging to a Web-based e-mail provider), but Web-based encrypted e-mail systems use secure Web servers to host the Web pages that are used to compose and read e-mail messages. Some Web-based encrypted e-mail systems—such as the popular free *Hushmail* service that automatically encrypts all e-mail sent through the

TIP

Both Facebook and Twitter allow you to encrypt your connections—enable this option when you are using a public Wi-Fi hotspot to protect your account from hackers.

>**Private key encryption.** A type of encryption that uses a single key to encrypt and decrypt the file or message. >**Public key encryption.** A type of encryption that uses key pairs to encrypt and decrypt the file or message.

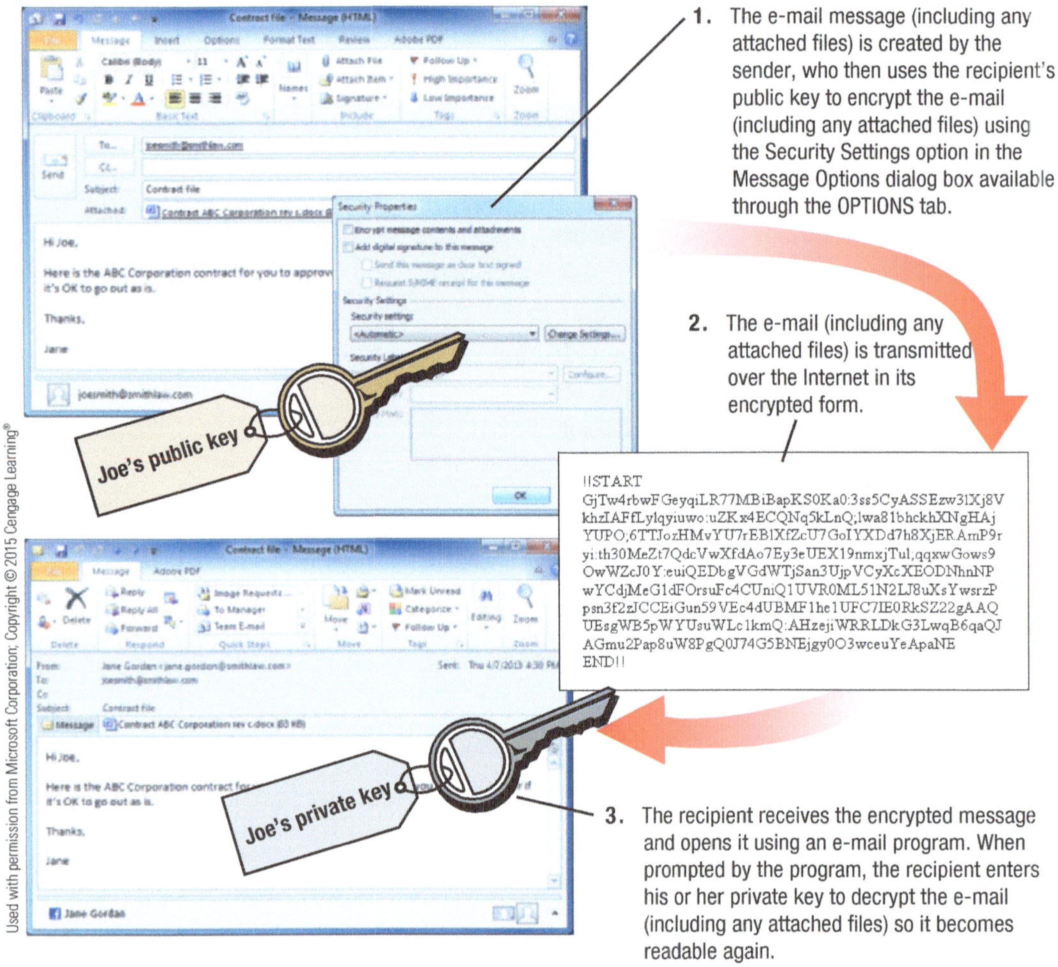

FIGURE 4-11
Using public key encryption to secure an e-mail message in Microsoft Outlook.

service—require both the sender and recipient to have accounts. Others require only the sender to have an account and the recipient is sent an e-mail containing instructions regarding how to view the message on a secure Web page.

There are various strengths of encryption available; the stronger the encryption, the more difficult it is to crack. Older 40-bit encryption (which can only use keys that are 40 bits or 5 characters long) is considered *weak encryption* and is no longer supported by Windows. Stronger encryption includes *strong 128-bit encryption* (which uses 16-character keys) and *military-strength 2,048-bit encryption* (which uses 256-character keys), although not without some objections from law enforcement agencies and the government because they state that terrorists routinely use encryption methods to communicate.

Virtual Private Networks (VPNs)

While e-mail and file encryption can be used to transfer individual messages and files securely over the Internet, a **virtual private network (VPN)** is designed to be used when a continuous secure channel over the Internet is needed. A VPN provides a secure private tunnel from the user's computer through the Internet to another destination and is most often used to provide remote employees with secure access to a company network. VPNs use encryption and other security mechanisms to ensure that only authorized users can access the remote network and that the data cannot be intercepted during transit. Because it uses the Internet instead of an expensive private physical network, a VPN can provide a secure environment over a large geographical area at a manageable cost. Once a VPN is set up, the user just needs to log on (such as with a username/password combination or a security token) in order to use the VPN.

VPNs are often used by both businesses and individuals at public Wi-Fi hotspots to prevent data interception when connecting to the Internet via the hotspot. While businesspeople will typically use a VPN set up by their companies, individuals can create *personal VPNs* using software designed for that purpose. This software automatically encrypts all inbound and outbound Internet traffic, including Web pages, e-mail messages, IMs, VoIP calls, and

TIP

Unless it is absolutely necessary and you are using a VPN, do not perform sensitive transactions (such as shopping or banking) at a public hotspot.

>**Virtual private network (VPN).** A private, secure path over the Internet that provides authorized users a secure means of accessing a private network via the Internet.

so forth, and also acts as a personal firewall. Using a personal VPN at a public hotspot can help individuals from becoming the victim of a hacker or an *evil twin*—a fake Wi-Fi hotspot set up to look like a legitimate hotspot.

Additional Public Hotspot Precautions

The precautions already discussed (such as using firewall software, secure Web pages, VPNs, and encryption) are a good start for protecting against unauthorized access and unauthorized use at a public Wi-Fi hotspot. However, there are additional precautions individuals can use to avoid data (both that which is on their devices and that which is being sent over the Internet) from being compromised. These precautions are listed in Figure 4-12.

PUBLIC HOTSPOT PRECAUTIONS

- Turn off automatic connections and pay attention to the list of available hotspots to make sure you connect to a legitimate access point (not an evil twin).
- Use a personal firewall to control the traffic going to and coming from your device and temporarily use it to block all incoming connections.
- Use a virtual private network (VPN) to secure all activity between your device and the Internet.
- Only enter passwords, credit card numbers, and other data on secure Web pages using a VPN.
- If you're not using a VPN, encrypt all sensitive files before transferring or e-mailing them.
- If you're not using a VPN, avoid online shopping, banking, and other sensitive transactions.
- Turn off file sharing so others can't access the files on your hard drive.
- Turn off Bluetooth and Wi-Fi when you are not using them.
- Disable *ad hoc* capabilities to prevent another device from connecting to your device directly without using an access point.
- Use antivirus software and make sure your operating system and browser are up to date.

FIGURE 4-12
Sensible precautions for public Wi-Fi hotspot users.

Sensible Employee Precautions

While only about 20% of business security breaches are committed by insiders (according to a recent Data Breach Investigations Report), they are responsible for the majority (66.7%) of exposed records. In addition, these breaches are typically malicious in nature, with an employee deliberately performing the act (though other times the breach occurs because the employee makes a mistake, such as losing a portable computer or removable storage medium, or inadvertently providing access to sensitive data). In either case, employers should be cautious. Some suggestions to avoid security breaches by employees are listed next.

Screen Potential New Hires Carefully

Employers should carefully investigate the background of all potential employees. Some people falsify résumés to get jobs. Others may have criminal records or currently be charged with a crime. One embarrassing mistake made by Rutgers University was to hire David Smith, the author of the *Melissa* computer virus, as a computer technician when he was out on bail following the arrest for that crime.

Watch for Disgruntled Employees and Ex-Employees

The type of employee who is most likely to commit a computer crime is one who has recently been terminated or passed over for a promotion, or one who has some reason to want to "get even" with the organization. Limiting access for each employee to only the resources needed for his or her job (referred to as the *Principle of Least Privilege*) and monitoring any attempts to access off-limit resources can help prevent some types of problems, such as unauthorized access of sensitive files, unintentional damage like deleting or changing files inadvertently, or sabotage like deleting or changing company files intentionally. In addition, it is vital that whenever an employee leaves the company for any reason, all access to the system for that individual (username, password, e-mail address, and so forth) should be removed immediately. For employees with high levels of system access, simultaneously removing access while the termination is taking place is even better. Waiting even a few minutes can be too late because just-fired employees have been known to barricade themselves in their office immediately after being terminated in order to change passwords, sabotage records, and perform other malicious acts. For example, on the day he was fired, one computer programmer at Fannie Mae embedded malicious code into a routine program on his company laptop before turning it in. The code, designed to destroy all data (including financial, securities, and mortgage information), was transmitted to nearly 5,000 Fannie Mae servers. The code was discovered before it was executed and the man was sentenced to more than three years in prison for computer intrusion.

INSIDE THE INDUSTRY

Securing BYOD

One growing trend today is *BYOD* or *Bring Your Own Device* (where students or employees bring their own smartphones, media tablets, or other devices to use instead of using issued devices—see the accompanying photo). Some businesses view BYOD as a cost-effective way of supplying employees with the devices they want to use; many IT departments view BYOD as a potential security nightmare. But it's here and not going away—research firm Gartner predicts that about half the world's companies will no longer provide computing devices to their employees by 2017.

BYOD is also changing the way many individuals perceive their work—no longer as a place, but as an activity that is independent of both location and specific technology. Consequently, it makes sense (and is more convenient) for individuals to carry with them at all times the devices that allow them to perform both work and personal functions as needed. For businesses, however, that brings the challenge of managing those devices. Disadvantages of BYOD from a company perspective include the risk of a *malware* infection via a BYOD device, as well as the potential exposure of company data via unsecured or lost personal devices or personal cloud storage systems (sometimes referred to as *Bring Your Own Cloud* or *BYOC*). Potential disadvantages from the employee perspective include having company-mandated restrictions on their personal devices (such as not using certain applications or cloud services and agreeing to allow the company to erase or reset the device remotely if it is lost or stolen), as well as the employer having access to personal data or activities performed via the phone. In addition, space on the device may be tied up for company data or apps that are used only for work.

While some companies use mobile device management (MDM) software to control the use of personal devices with corporate networks, one emerging solution is to completely separate the business and personal use of the device. For instance, software that supports *sandboxing* or *containerization* can create an isolated virtual environment on the user's device within which corporate data and applications can safely reside. With this method, the company would mandate control policies for just that portion of the device. An option for Windows 8 Enterprise companies is to use the *Windows To Go* feature, which uses a bootable USB flash drive to create a complete, managed Windows 8 environment on whatever device the USB flash drive is plugged into. Consequently, employees can use the Windows To Go environment on their personal devices at work, and then shut down the Windows To Go environment after work to use their devices as solely personal devices.

Develop Policies and Controls

All companies should develop policies and controls regarding security matters. As already mentioned, employees should be granted the least amount of access to the company network that they need to perform their job. Employees should be educated about the seriousness and consequences of hacking, data theft, and other computer crimes, and they should be taught what to do when they suspect a computer crime has been committed. Employees should also be instructed about proper device usage policies—such as whether or not downloading software on company devices is allowed, whether or not employees are responsible for updating their devices, and the types of removable storage media that may be used with company devices—in order to avoid inadvertently creating a security problem. Policies for removing computers and storage media containing sensitive data from the premises should also be implemented, enforced, and updated as needed, and sensitive documents should be shredded when they are no longer needed.

Employees who work from home or otherwise access the company network via the Internet also need to be educated about security policies for remote access and the proper precautions that need to be taken. These precautions include keeping their operating system and security software up to date and using only encrypted storage devices (such as self-encrypting USB flash drives) when transporting documents between work and home.

In addition, telecommuting workers and outside contractors should not be allowed to have peer-to-peer (P2P) software on computers containing company documents because data is increasingly being exposed through the use of P2P networks. For instance, classified data about the U.S. presidential helicopter discovered on a computer in Iran was traced back to a P2P network and the computer of a military contractor in Maryland; and the Social Security numbers and other personal data belonging to about 17,000 current and former Pfizer workers were once leaked onto a P2P network after an employee installed unauthorized P2P software on a company notebook computer provided for use at her home.

Use Software to Manage Employee Devices and Prevent Data Leaks

As employees are increasingly bringing portable devices (such as smartphones and USB flash drives) that can interact with business networks to the office, the challenge of securing these *BYOD* (*Bring Your Own Device*) devices (and the company network) has grown. While some companies prohibit all portable devices and others allow only company-issued portable devices so they can ensure appropriate security measures (such as encryption, password protection, and the ability to wipe the device clean remotely if it is lost or stolen) are implemented, the use of BYOD is growing, as discussed in the Inside the Industry box.

TIP

Deploying a centrally managed security solution to all endpoints (all user devices connected to the company network) is referred to as *endpoint security*.

To protect against employees copying or sending confidential data to others either intentionally or accidentally, *data-leakage* (also called *data-loss*) *prevention systems* can be used. Data-leakage prevention systems are available as software and/or hardware systems, and have a range of capabilities, but the overall goal is to prevent sensitive data from exposure. For instance, some systems control which devices (such as USB flash drives and smartphones) can be connected to an employee's computer in order to prevent sensitive data from being taken home inadvertently or intentionally. *Mobile device management* (*MDM*) *software* (see Figure 4-13) goes one step further by including other protections, such as specifying what apps and Web sites can be used with the device, protecting against unauthorized access and *malware*, facilitating remote access (to update software or erase a lost device, for instance), and locating a lost or stolen device. Other data-leakage prevention systems—sometimes also called *outbound-content monitoring systems*—scan all outgoing communications (e-mail, transferred files, and so forth) for documents containing Social Security numbers, intellectual property, and other confidential information and block them if they might contain prohibited content. Some can also continually scan network devices to locate documents containing sensitive data to ensure that sensitive files are not on the computer of an employee who should not have access to them. For even stronger protection of confidential company documents, *enterprise rights-management software*, which encrypts confidential documents and limits functions such as printing, editing, and copying the data to only authorized users with the appropriate password, can be used.

FIGURE 4-13
Mobile device management (MDM) software. Secures and manages the mobile devices used in an organization.

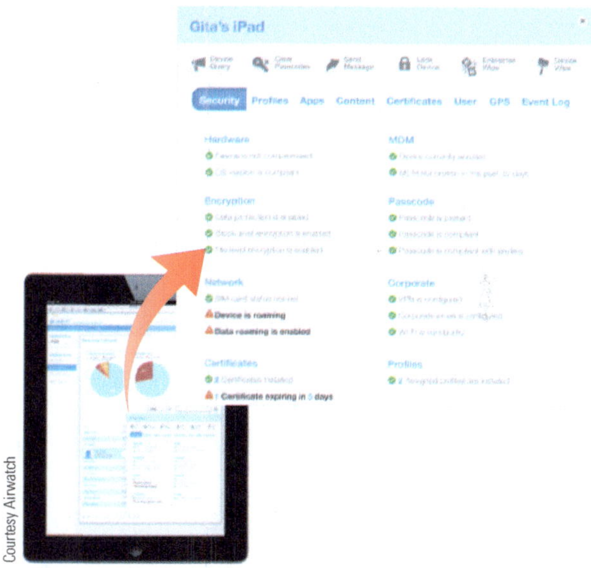

Courtesy Airwatch

Ask Business Partners to Review Their Security

In this networked economy, many organizations provide some access to internal resources for business partners. If those external companies are lax with their security measures, however, attacks through the business partners' computers (such as via an employee or hacker) are possible. Consequently, businesses should make sure that their business partners maintain adequate security policies and controls. Regulations increasingly require businesses to ensure that adequate controls are in place to protect stored data. This impacts outside companies—such as business partners and *outsourcing companies* (outside vendors for specific business tasks)—if they have access to sensitive corporate data. Companies that utilize cloud computing also need to ensure that the cloud vendor's security and privacy policies match the company's requirements.

COMPUTER SABOTAGE

Computer sabotage—acts of malicious destruction to a computer or computer resource—is another common type of computer crime today. Computer sabotage can take several forms, including launching a *computer virus* or a *denial of service (DoS) attack*, altering the content of a Web site, or changing data or programs located on a computer. A common tool used to perform computer sabotage is a *botnet*, discussed next. Computer sabotage is illegal in the United States, and acts of sabotage are estimated to cost individuals and organizations billions of dollars per year, primarily for labor costs related to correcting the problems caused by the sabotage, lost productivity, and lost sales.

> **TIP**
>
> A group of major U.S. ISPs recently committed to work together to combat three major cybersecurity threats, including bots; the FCC predicts this effort will have a significant positive effect on Internet security.

Botnets

A computer that is controlled by a hacker or other computer criminal is referred to as a **bot** or *zombie computer*; a group of bots that are controlled by one individual and can work together in a coordinated fashion is called a **botnet**. Millions of U.S. computers are part of a botnet—in 2013, one operation alone (*Operation b54*) performed by Microsoft working with the FBI cut the communications among 1,462 *Citadel* botnets (one of the largest botnets in existence and responsible for about half a billion dollars in losses) and their 5 million or more infected computers. Criminals (called *botherders*) are increasingly creating botnets to use for computer sabotage, such as to spread *malware* and to launch *denial of service (DoS) attacks*, discussed shortly. Botherders also often sell their botnet services to send spam and launch Internet attacks on their clients' behalf, as well as to steal identity information, credit card numbers, passwords, corporate secrets, and other sensitive data, which are then sold to other criminals or otherwise used in an illegal manner. Bots are also used to perform *click fraud*—automatically clicking on Internet ads to increase the fees that a company must pay.

Computer Viruses and Other Types of Malware

Malware is a generic term that refers to any type of malicious software. Malware programs are intentionally written to perform destructive acts, such as damaging programs, deleting files, erasing an entire hard drive, or slowing down the performance of a computer. This damage can take place immediately after a computer is *infected* (that is, the malware software is installed) or it can begin when a particular condition is met. A malware program that activates when it detects a certain condition, such as when a particular keystroke is pressed or an employee's name is deleted from an employee file, is called a *logic bomb*. A logic bomb that is triggered by a particular date or time is called a *time bomb*.

Writing a computer virus or other type of malware or even posting the malware code on the Internet is not illegal, but it is considered highly unethical and irresponsible behavior. Distributing malware, on the other hand, is illegal, and virus writers who release their malware are being vigorously prosecuted. Malware can be very costly in terms of the labor costs associated with removing the viruses and correcting any resulting damage, as well as the cost of lost productivity of employees. One type of malware often used by computer

> **ASK THE EXPERT**
>
> Courtesy Symantec
>
> Norton by Symantec **Marian Merritt,** Internet Safety Advocate, Symantec Corporation
>
> **Does a smartphone need virus protection?**
>
> Yes, it is increasingly important to secure your smartphone. Begin with a screen lock passcode to protect against snooping. Tape a recovery phone number to the back of the phone so a finder can contact you. Install or enable tracking software to enable you to locate or lock a lost or stolen phone. And get mobile security software to keep you from installing bad apps or clicking on a dangerous link.

>**Computer sabotage.** An act of malicious destruction to a computer or computer resource. >**Bot.** A computer that is controlled by a hacker or other computer criminal. >**Botnet.** A group of bots that are controlled by one individual. >**Malware.** Any type of malicious software.

criminals to send sensitive data secretly from infected computers to the criminal—spyware—was discussed in Chapter 3. The most common other types of malware are discussed next.

> **TIP**
>
> It is common practice for all types of malware to be referred to generically as "viruses," even though some may not technically be computer viruses.

Computer Viruses

One type of malware is the **computer virus**—a software program that is installed without the permission or knowledge of the computer user, that is designed to alter the way a computer operates, and that can replicate itself to infect any new media it has access to. Computer viruses are often embedded into program or data files (often games, videos, and music files downloaded from Web pages or shared via a P2P service). They are spread whenever the infected file is downloaded, is transferred to a new computer via an infected removable storage medium, or is e-mailed to another computer (see Figure 4-14). Viruses can also be installed when a recipient clicks a link in an e-mail message (often in an unsolicited e-mail message that resembles a legitimate e-mail message that normally contains a link, such as an electronic greeting card e-mail that contains a link to view the card); runs a Web app that either contains a virus or exploits a vulnerability in Java, Flash, or another common Web technology; or clicks a link in a message posted on a social networking site like Facebook. Viruses have also been found embedded in photos of bogus Craigslist items sent to potential buyers. Regardless of how it is obtained, once a copy of the infected file reaches a new computer it typically embeds itself into program, data, or system files on the new computer and remains there, affecting that computer according to its programmed instructions, until it is discovered and removed.

FIGURE 4-14
How a computer virus or other type of malicious software might spread.

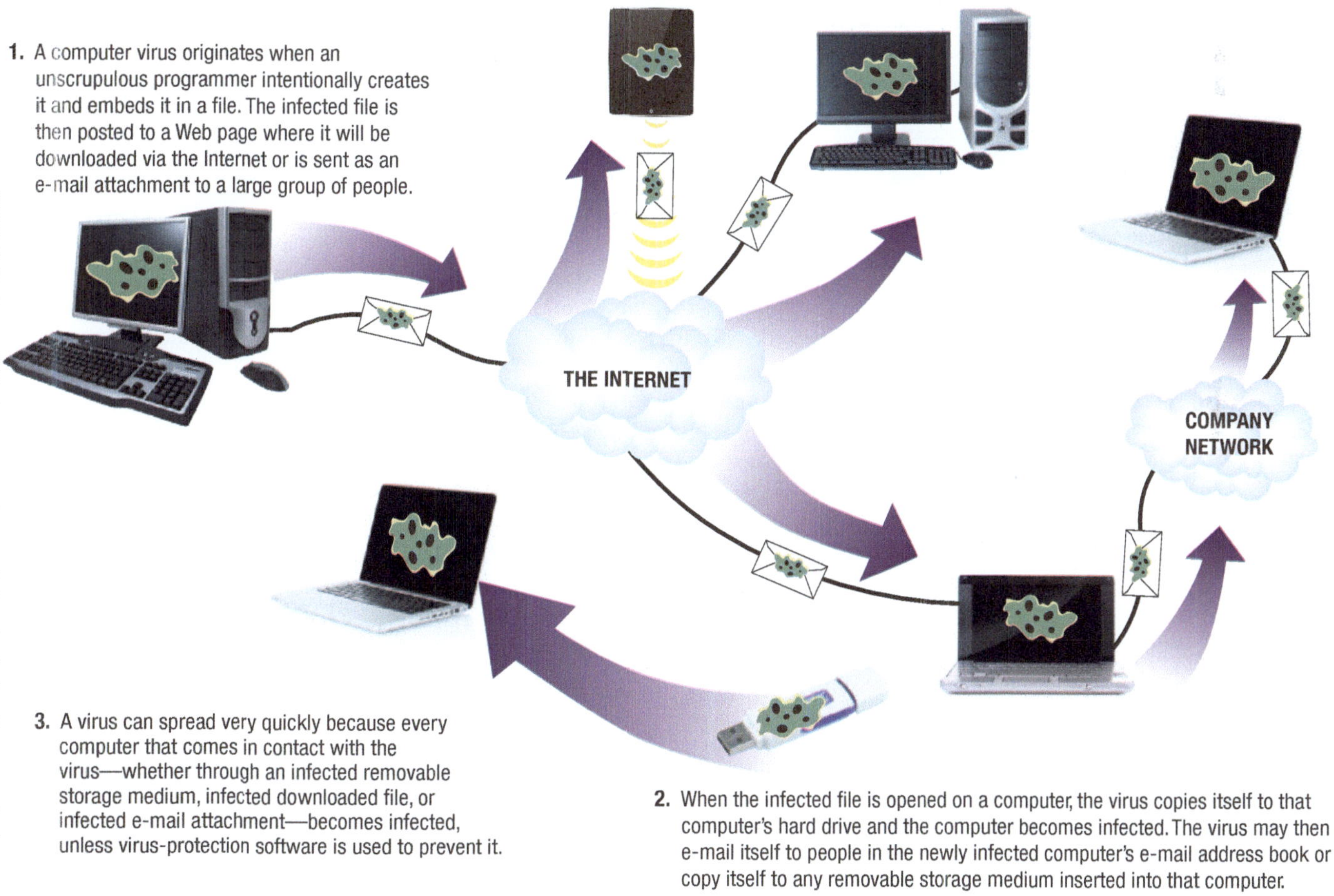

>**Computer virus.** A software program installed without the user's knowledge and designed to alter the way a computer operates or to cause harm to the computer system.

TIP

The *Stuxnet* worm, detected in 2010 and widely believed to have been created by the United States and Israel, reportedly destroyed 1,000 centrifuges in nuclear facilities located in Iran—the first instance of malware being used to cause physical damage to a facility.

Computer Worms

Another common form of malware is the **computer worm**. Like a computer virus, a computer worm is a malicious program that is typically designed to cause damage. Unlike a computer virus, however, a computer worm does not infect other computer files on the infected computer in order to replicate itself; instead, it spreads by creating copies of its code and sending those copies to other computers via a network. Often, the worm is sent to other computers as an e-mail attachment. Usually after the infected e-mail attachment is opened by an individual, the worm inflicts its damage and then automatically sends copies of itself to other computers via the Internet or a private network, typically using addresses in the e-mail address book located on the newly infected computer. When those e-mail messages and their attachments are opened, the new computers become infected and the cycle continues. Because of its distribution method, a worm can spread very rapidly. For instance, the *Mydoom* worm (which was released in 2004 and is considered one of the fastest spreading worms ever) spread so rapidly that, at one point, one out of every 10 e-mails contained the worm, and the persistent *Conficker* worm has infected a total of more than 12 million computers since it was released in 2008 and it is still active today.

Typically, worms do not require any action by the users (such as opening an e-mail attachment) to infect their computers. Instead, a worm scans the Internet looking for computers that are vulnerable to that particular worm and sends a copy of itself to those computers to infect them. Other worms just require the user to view an infected e-mail message or insert an infected removable storage medium (such as a USB flash drive) into the computer in order to infect the computer. Still other worms are specifically written to take advantage of newly discovered *security holes* (vulnerabilities) in operating systems and e-mail programs. Worms and other types of malware that are designed to take advantage of a security hole and are released at a time when no security patch to correct the problem is available are referred to as *zero-day attacks*. Unfortunately, as malware writing tools become more sophisticated, zero-day attacks are becoming more common.

FIGURE 4-15

Rogue anti-malware apps. These programs try to trick victims into purchasing subscriptions to remove nonexistent malware supposedly installed on their devices.

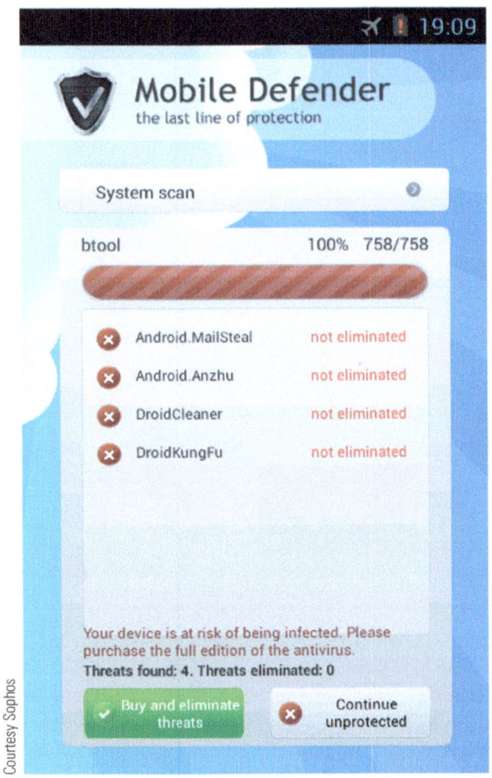

Courtesy Sophos

Trojan Horses

A **Trojan horse** is a type of malware that masquerades as something else—usually an application program (such as what appears to be a game or utility program). When the seemingly legitimate program is downloaded or installed, the malware part of the Trojan horse infects the computer. Many recent Trojan horses masquerade as normal ongoing activities (such as the Windows Update service or an *anti-malware program* telling you to download a file containing program updates) when they are installed to try to trick unsuspecting users into downloading another malware program or buying a useless program. For instance, after a *rogue anti-malware app* like the one shown in Figure 4-15 is installed (usually without the user's direct knowledge or permission), the malware takes over the device displaying bogus warning messages or scan results (see Figure 4-15) indicating the device is infected with malware. The rogue program (an example of *scareware*) typically prompts the user to buy a fake anti-malware program to get rid of the "malware." Usually the only malware on the device is the rogue program, but it is often very intrusive (such as displaying constant messages on the infected device while hiding the options needed to change the hijacked settings back to normal), it often blocks access to any Web sites other than its own, and it is extremely hard to remove. An emerging related type of Trojan is *ransomware*, which freezes up the infected device and displays a message that the device has been used for illegal activity and the user must pay a fine (which then goes to the criminal) in order to unlock the device, though

>**Computer worm.** A malicious program designed to spread rapidly to a large number of computers by sending copies of itself to other computers.
>**Trojan horse.** A malicious program that masquerades as something else.

paying the fine doesn't necessarily result in the device being returned to a usable state. Other *rogue apps* are spreading through social networks like Facebook and Twitter, primarily in the form of fake offers (such as for a free iPad) that request access to your social network information when you click the link—if granted, the scammer can then post that and additional scams (and collect information about others) via your account.

Unlike viruses and worms, Trojan horses cannot replicate themselves. Trojan horses are usually spread by being downloaded from the Internet, though they may also be sent as an e-mail attachment, either from the Trojan horse author or from individuals who forward it, not realizing the program is a Trojan horse. Some Trojan horses today act as spyware and are designed to find sensitive information about an individual (such as a Social Security number or a bank account number) or about a company (such as corporate intellectual property like mechanical designs, electronic schematics, and other valuable proprietary information) located on infected computers and then send that information to the malware creator to be used in illegal activities. One emerging type of Trojan horse is called a *RAT* (*Remote-Access Trojan*). RATs are typically installed via small files obtained from an Internet download, such as free software, games, or electronic greeting cards. Once installed, RATs are designed to record every keystroke made on the infected computer and then send the sensitive information they recorded (such as account numbers and passwords) to criminals.

TIP

About 94% of mobile malware today is written for Android phones (though Apple devices are still vulnerable).

Mobile Malware

In addition to computers, malware also can infect smartphones, media tablets, printers, and other devices that contain computing hardware and software. While more than 90% of today's mobile malware (according to a recent report) is spread via malicious links, smartphones with Bluetooth capabilities can also be infected just by being within range of an infected device. Some *mobile malware* is designed to be a nuisance by changing icons or otherwise making the device more difficult to use, but most (including half of mobile malware created in 2012) is designed to steal information or track the movement or activities of the user. Still other malware is money-oriented, such as malware that is designed to steal credit card data located on a smartphone and malware that places calls or sends text messages to premium rate numbers owned by the thief (for which the owner of the device is charged)—sometimes called *chargeware*. According to IBM, more malware will continue to be directed to smartphones and other devices—such as cars—that contain embedded computers as those devices continue to incorporate more software components and, consequently, become more vulnerable to malware. And mobile malware is getting more sophisticated—in 2013, Kaspersky Lab discovered the first ever Android malware app designed to infect any PCs or other devices the phone connects to. While the app was removed from Google Play, several thousand users had already downloaded it.

Denial of Service (DoS) Attacks

TIP

The 2013 DDoS attacks on The Spamhaus Project created a staggering 300 Gbps of traffic.

A **denial of service (DoS) attack** is an act of sabotage that attempts to flood a network server or Web server with so many requests for action that it shuts down or simply cannot handle legitimate requests any longer, causing legitimate users to be denied service. For example, a hacker might set up one or more computers to request nonexistent information continually or to *ping* (contact) a server continually with a request to send a responding ping back to a false return address. If enough useless traffic is generated, the server has no resources left to deal with legitimate requests (see Figure 4-16). An emerging trend is DoS attacks aimed at mobile wireless networks. These attacks typically involve repeatedly establishing and releasing connections with the goal of overloading the network to disrupt service.

>**Denial of service (DoS) attack.** An act of sabotage that attempts to flood a network server or a Web server with so much activity that it is unable to function.

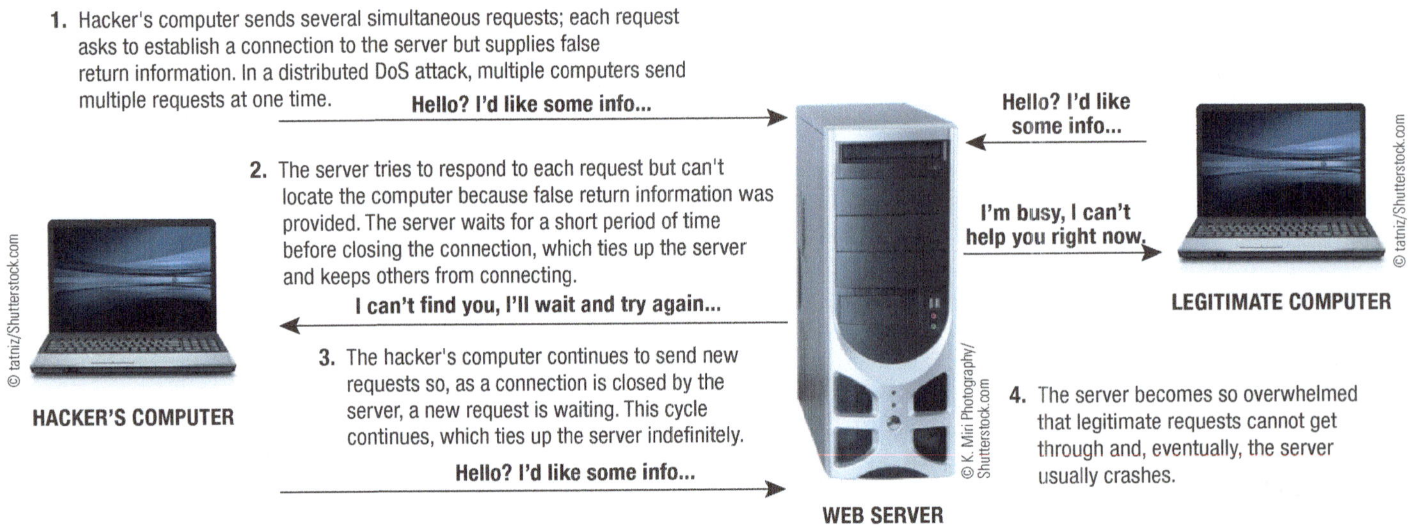

FIGURE 4-16
How a denial of service (DoS) attack might work.

DoS attacks today are often directed toward popular or controversial sites and typically are carried out via multiple computers (referred to as a *distributed denial of service attack* or *DDoS attack*). DDoS attacks are typically performed by botnets created by hackers; the computers in the botnet participate in the attacks without the owners' knowledge. Because home devices today typically use direct Internet connections but tend to be less protected than school and business computers, hackers are increasingly targeting home devices for botnets used in DDoS attacks and other forms of computer sabotage.

Denial of service attacks can be very costly in terms of business lost (such as when an e-commerce site is shut down), as well as the time and expense required to bring the site back online. Networks that use VoIP are particularly vulnerable to DoS attacks since the real-time nature of VoIP calls means their quality is immediately affected when a DoS attack slows down the network.

Data, Program, or Web Site Alteration

Another type of computer sabotage occurs when a hacker breaches a computer system in order to delete data, change data, modify programs, or otherwise alter the data and programs located there. For example, a student might try to hack into the school database to change his or her grade; a hacker might change a program located on a company server in order to steal money or information; or a disgruntled or former employee might perform a vengeful act, such as altering programs so they work incorrectly, deleting customer records or other critical data, or randomly changing data in a company's database. Like other forms of computer sabotage, data and program alteration is illegal.

Data on Web sites can also be altered by hackers. For instance, social media accounts are being increasingly targeted by hackers. In 2013, for instance, the Associated Press Twitter account was hacked and used to tweet that the president had been injured by explosions at the White House—the stock market tumbled in response. It is also becoming more common for hackers to compromise legitimate Web sites and then use those sites to perform malware attacks. Typically, a hacker alters a legitimate site to display an official-looking message that informs the user that a particular software program must be downloaded, or the hacker posts a rogue banner ad on a legitimate site that redirects the user to a malware site instead of the site for the product featured in the banner ad. According to a report by security company Websense, more than half of the Web sites classified as malicious are actually legitimate Web sites that have been compromised.

PROTECTING AGAINST COMPUTER SABOTAGE

One of the most important protections against computer sabotage is using *security software*, and ensuring that it is kept current.

Security Software

To protect against becoming infected with a computer virus or other type of malware, all computers and other devices used to access the Internet or a company network in both homes and offices should have **security software** installed. Security software typically includes a variety of security features, including a firewall, protection against spyware and bots, and protection against some types of *online fraud*, discussed shortly. Some also include a spam filter, parental controls, password managers, diagnostic software, and backup features; mobile security software also often includes *antitheft software*, discussed in more detail in Chapter 5. One of the most important components of security software is **antivirus software**, which protects against computer viruses and other types of malware.

Like most security software components, antivirus software typically runs continuously whenever the computer is on to perform real-time monitoring of the computer and incoming e-mail messages, instant messages, Web page content, and downloaded files, in order to prevent malicious software and other threats from executing. Many antivirus programs also automatically scan any devices as soon as they are connected to a USB port in order to guard against infections from a USB flash drive, a portable digital media player, or other USB device. Antivirus software helps prevent malware from being installed on your devices because it deletes or *quarantines* (safely isolates) any suspicious content (such as potentially infected e-mail attachments, downloaded files, or apps) as they arrive; regular full system scans can detect and remove any viruses or worms that find their way onto your computer (see Figure 4-17).

According to a recent Panda Security report, there are approximately 125 million malware threats in existence, and about 27 million new malware strains were discovered in 2012 alone. Consequently, it is vital that you keep your security software up to date. Security software is usually set up to download new *threat definitions* automatically from its associated Web site on a regular basis, as often as several times per day—a very important precaution. Most fee-based security

TIP

To ensure you have the latest security updates for your antivirus program, enable *automatic updates*.

TIP

According to a recent Harris Interactive survey, less than one-third of users have security software installed on their mobile devices, compared to 91% on their laptops.

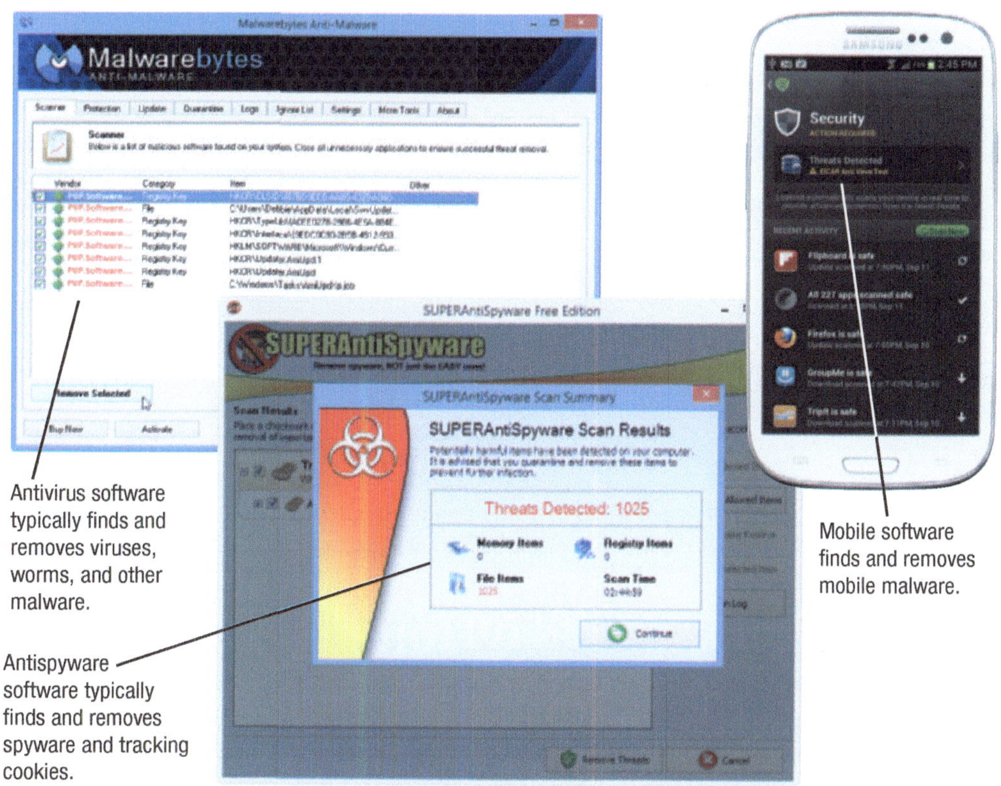

FIGURE 4-17
Security software. Different security programs will typically find different types of malware.

Courtesy Malwarebytes; Courtesy Lookout; Courtesy SUPERAntiSpyware

>Security software. Software, typically a suite of programs, used to protect your computer against a variety of threats. **>Antivirus software.** Software used to detect and eliminate computer viruses and other types of malware.

VIRUS-PREVENTION STRATEGIES

Use antivirus software to check incoming e-mail messages and files, and download updated virus definitions on a regular basis.

Limit the sharing of flash memory cards, USB flash drives, and other removable storage media with others.

Only download files from reputable sites.

Only open e-mail attachments that come from people you know and that do not have an executable file extension (such as .exe, .com, .bat, or .vbs); double-check with the sender before opening an unexpected, but seemingly legitimate, attachment.

For any downloaded file you are unsure of, upload it to a Web site (such as VirusTotal.com) that tests files for viruses before you open them.

Keep the preview window of your e-mail program closed so you will not view messages until you determine that they are safe to view.

Regularly download and install the latest security patches available for your operating system, browser, Java and other plug-ins, and e-mail programs.

Avoid downloading files from P2P sites.

FIGURE 4-18
Sensible precautions can help protect against computer virus infections.

TIP

If you suspect your computer is infected with a malware program that your regular antivirus software cannot detect or remove, try a software program that specializes in removing hard-to-remove malware, such as the free *Malwarebytes Anti-Malware* program shown in Figure 4-17.

software comes with a year of access to free updates; users should purchase additional years after that to continue to be protected or they should switch to a free antivirus program, such as *AVG Free*, that can be updated regularly at no cost. Schools and businesses should also ensure that students and employees connecting to the campus or company network with personal devices are using up-to-date antivirus software so they will not infect the network with malware inadvertently. Some colleges now require new students to go through a *quarantine process*, in which students are not granted access to the college network until they complete a security process that checks their computers for security threats, updates their operating systems, and installs antivirus software. Some additional virus-prevention strategies are listed in Figure 4-18.

Many ISPs and Web mail providers today also offer some malware protection to their subscribers. Typically, antivirus software scans all incoming e-mail messages at the mail server level to filter out messages containing a virus. If a message containing a virus is detected, it is usually deleted and the recipient is notified that the message contained a virus and was deleted. App stores can help remove a contaminated app when one is identified (by removing the app from the store and remotely wiping the app from phones), though that won't undo any damage already done to the phone by the malware.

Other Security Precautions

Individuals and businesses can protect against some types of computer sabotage (such as program, data, or Web site alteration) by controlling access to their computers and networks, as discussed earlier in this chapter. Intrusion protection systems can help businesses detect and protect against denial of service (DoS) attacks; some personal security software includes intrusion protection as well. For additional protection against spyware, rogue antivirus programs, and other specialized malware, specialized security programs (such as the *SUPERAntispyware* program shown in Figure 4-17) can be used. In addition, most Web browsers have security settings that can be used to help prevent programs from being installed on a computer without the user's permission, such as prompting the user for permission whenever a download is initiated. Enabling these security settings is a wise additional precaution.

ONLINE THEFT, ONLINE FRAUD, AND OTHER DOT CONS

A booming area of computer crime involves online fraud, theft, scams, and related activities designed to steal money or other resources from individuals or businesses—these are collectively referred to as **dot cons**. According to a report by the *Internet Crime Complaint Center (IC3)*, a joint venture of the FBI and the National White Collar Crime Center that receives cybercrime complaints from consumers and reports them to the appropriate law enforcement agency, IC3 received and processed more than 24,000 complaints per month in 2012 with reported losses more than 8% higher than in 2011. Some of the most common types of dot cons are discussed next.

>**Dot con.** A fraud or scam carried out through the Internet.

TREND

Beyond Fingerprint Readers—Digital Tattoos and More

Think passwords—even the newer types of passwords that use pictures or patterns instead of characters—are ho-hum? Well, you're in luck. A number of new alternatives that can be used to protect access to your device or log on to your Web sites are about to become available.

One option that Google is developing uses *facial gestures*, such as unlocking your phone by smiling or winking at it. Instead of using a static image (as with face recognition, which has been circumvented on phone unlocking systems by using a photograph of the authorized user), this new technology includes a "Liveness Check" where the user has to prove that he or she is alive and not a photo by blinking. In addition, the system requires a match of a facial landmark (such as an eye, mouth, or nose) in two different but related facial gestures (such as smiling and not smiling).

Two other more unusual alternatives recently demonstrated by Motorola are *electronic tattoos* and *authentication pills*. The tattoos (called *Biostamps* and originally developed for remote medical monitoring of patients) contain flexible electronic circuits that are attached to the wearer's skin (see the accompanying photo) using a rubber stamp and which then can be covered with a spray-on bandage for additional waterproofing if needed. The pills (called the *Proteus Digital Health pill* and already approved by the U.S. FDA for medication monitoring) are swallowed and then send signals from the stomach. Both devices already work with smartphones and researchers propose that both technologies could be adapted to become authentication systems, automatically logging individuals on to their phones or computers and to secure Web sites. The downside is that both systems are temporary and would have to be replaced on a regular basis, which could lead to hackers stealing additional tattoos and pills not yet used and circumventing whatever activation system is in place or even kidnapping individuals to use their bodies to log in to secure systems.

Next up? *Thought-based authentication* where you can automatically log on to your wearable devices using only your brainwaves.

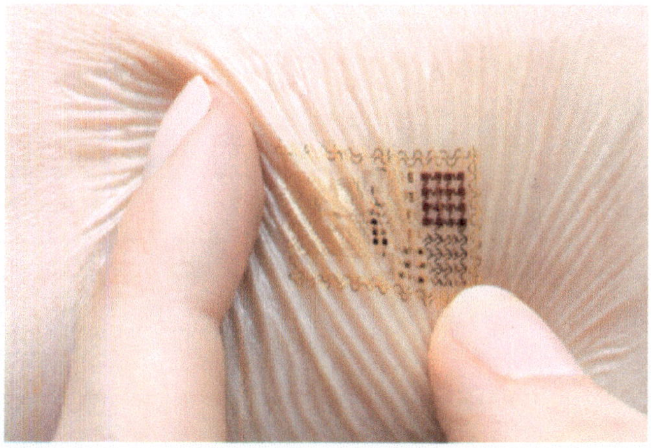

Courtesy MC10 Inc.

Theft of Data, Information, and Other Resources

Data theft or *information theft* is the theft of data or information located on or being sent from a computer. It can be committed by stealing an actual computer (as discussed in more detail in Chapter 5); it can also take place over the Internet or a network by an individual gaining unauthorized access to that data by hacking into the computer or by intercepting the data in transit. (For a look at some emerging biometric systems that may soon be used to help protect access to your PC and your Web sites, see the Trend box.) Common types of data and information stolen via the Internet or another network include customer data (such as Web site passwords or credit card information) and proprietary corporate information. As previously discussed, data breaches today frequently result in stolen customer and credit card data. Stolen consumer data is often used in fraudulent activities, such as *identity theft*, as discussed shortly.

Money is another resource that can be stolen via a computer. Company insiders sometimes steal money by altering company programs to transfer small amounts of money—for example, a few cents' worth of bank account interest—from a very large number of transactions to an account controlled by the thieves. This type of crime is sometimes called *salami shaving*. Victims of salami-shaving schemes generally are unaware that their funds have been accessed because the amount taken from each individual is very small. However, added together, the amounts can be substantial. Another example of monetary theft performed via computers involves hackers electronically transferring money illegally from online bank accounts, traditional bank accounts, credit card accounts, or accounts at online payment services (such as *PayPal*).

Identity Theft, Phishing, Social Media Hacks, and Pharming

A growing dot con trend is obtaining enough information about an individual to perform fraudulent financial transactions. Often, this is carried out in conjunction with *identity theft*; techniques frequently used to obtain the necessary personal information to commit identity theft are *phishing*, *spear phishing*, *social media hacking*, and *pharming*.

> **TIP**
>
> To help prevent identity theft, do not include your Social Security number on your résumé or any other document posted online.

> **TIP**
>
> At an estimated $388 billion per year, identity theft is approaching the illegal drug business in revenue.

Identity Theft

Identity theft occurs when someone obtains enough information about a person to be able to masquerade as that person—usually to buy products or services in that person's name (see Figure 4-19). Typically, identity theft begins when a thief obtains a person's name, address, and Social Security number, often from a discarded or stolen document (such as a preapproved credit card application that was sent in the mail), from information obtained via the Internet (such as from a résumé posted online), or from information located on a computer (such as on a stolen computer or hacked server, or information sent from a computer via a computer virus or spyware program installed on that computer). The thief may then order a copy of the individual's birth certificate, obtain a "replacement" driver's license, make purchases and charge them to the victim, and/or open credit or bank accounts in the victim's name.

Assuming the thief requests a change of address for these new accounts after they are opened, it may take quite some time—often until a company or collections agency contacts the victim about overdue bills—for the victim to become aware that his or her identity has been stolen. Although identity theft often takes place via a computer today, information used in identity theft can also be gathered from trash dumpsters, mailboxes, and other locations. Other commonly used techniques are *skimming* and *social engineering*. Skimming involves stealing credit card or debit card numbers by using an illegal device attached to a credit card reader or an ATM machine that reads and stores the card numbers (and used in conjunction with a hidden camera to capture ATM PIN numbers) to be retrieved by the thief at a later time. Social engineering involves pretending—typically via phone or e-mail—to be a bank officer, potential employer, or other trusted individual in order to get the potential victim to supply personal information. Today, social engineering schemes often use social media to obtain the needed information and gain the trust of a victim. Because of this, *social engineering tests* are often included when a company runs a security evaluation of its company and employees, as discussed in Chapter 5.

FIGURE 4-19
How identity theft works.

1. The thief obtains information about an individual from discarded mail, employee records, credit card transactions, Web server files, or some other method.
2. The thief makes purchases, opens new credit card accounts, and more in the victim's name. Often, the thief changes the address on the account to delay discovery.
3. The victim usually finds out by being denied credit or by being contacted about overdue bills generated by the thief. Clearing one's name after identity theft is time consuming and can be very difficult and frustrating for the victim.

>**Identity theft.** Using someone else's identity to purchase goods or services, obtain new credit cards or bank loans, or otherwise illegally masquerade as that individual.

Unfortunately, identity theft is a very real danger to individuals today. According to the Federal Trade Commission (FTC), millions of Americans have their identity stolen each year and identity theft has topped the list of consumer complaints for 13 straight years. Identity theft can be extremely distressing for victims, can take years to straighten out, and can be very expensive. Some identity theft victims, such as Michelle Brown, believe that they will always be dealing with their "alter reality" to some extent. For a year and a half, an identity thief used Brown's identity to obtain over $50,000 in goods and services, to rent properties—even to engage in drug trafficking. Although the culprit was eventually arrested and convicted for other criminal acts, she continued to use Brown's identity and was even booked into jail using Brown's stolen identity. As a final insult after the culprit was in prison, U.S. customs agents detained the real Michelle Brown when she was returning from a trip to Mexico because of the criminal record of the identity thief. Brown states that she has not traveled out of the country since, fearing an arrest or some other serious problem resulting from the theft of her identity, and estimates she has spent over 500 hours trying to correct all the problems related to the identity theft.

ASK THE EXPERT

Courtesy Symantec

Marian Merritt, Internet Safety Advocate, Symantec Corporation

What is the single most important thing computer users should do to protect themselves from online threats?

The single most important step to protect computer users from online threats is to make sure their Internet security solution is current and up to date. There are several all-in-one security solutions available, such as Symantec's Norton 360, which combine PC security, antiphishing capabilities, backup, and tuneup technologies.

It's also pivotal to maintain a healthy wariness when receiving online communications. Do not click on links in suspicious e-mails or instant messages (IMs). These links will often direct you to sites that will ask you to reveal passwords, PINs, or other confidential data. Genuine organizations or institutions do not send such e-mails, nor do they ask for confidential data (like your Social Security number) for ordinary business transactions. If you're unsure whether or not an e-mail is legitimate, type the URL directly in your browser or call the institution to confirm they sent you that e-mail. Finally, do not open attachments in e-mails of questionable origin because they may contain viruses.

Phishing and Spear Phishing

Phishing (pronounced "fishing") is the use of a *spoofed* communications (typically an e-mail message, such as one appearing to come from eBay, PayPal, Google, Bank of America, or another well-known legitimate organization, but is actually sent from a phisher) to trick the recipient into revealing sensitive personal information (such as Web site logon information or credit card numbers). Once obtained, this information is used in identity theft and other fraudulent activities. A phishing e-mail typically looks legitimate and it contains links in the e-mail that appear to go to the Web site of the legitimate business, but these links go to the phisher's Web site that is set up to look like the legitimate site instead—an act called *Web site spoofing*. Phishing e-mails are typically sent to a wide group of individuals and usually include an urgent message stating that the individual's credit card or account information needs to be updated and instructing the recipient of the e-mail to click the link provided in the e-mail in order to keep the account active. If the victim clicks the link and supplies the requested information via the spoofed site, the criminal gains access to all information provided by the victim, such as account numbers, credit card numbers, and Web site passwords. Phishing attempts can occur today via IM, text messages (called *smishing*), fake messages sent via eBay or Facebook, Twitter tweets, pop-up security alert windows, and phone calls, in addition to e-mail. Phishers also frequently utilize spyware; typically

>**Phishing.** The use of spoofed communications (typically e-mail messages) to gain credit card numbers and other personal data to be used for fraudulent purposes.

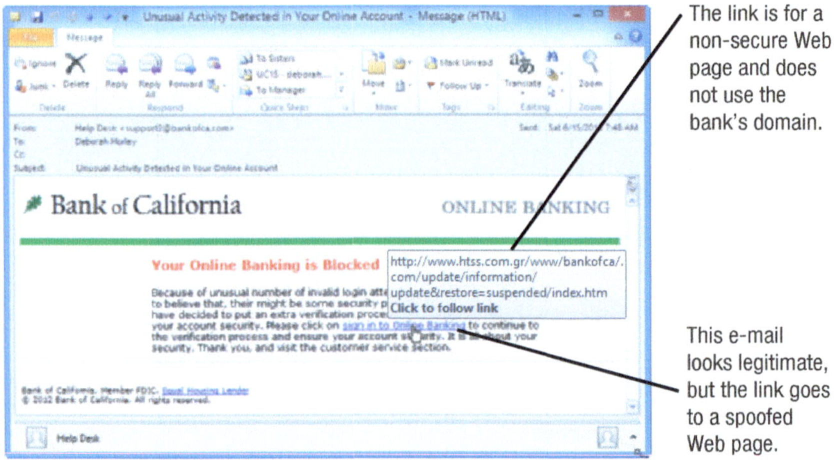

FIGURE 4-20

Phishing. Phishing schemes typically use legitimate-looking e-mails to trick users into providing private information.

clicking the link in the phishing e-mail installs the spyware on the victim's computer, and it will remain there (transmitting passwords and other sensitive data to a phisher) until it is detected and removed.

To fool victims into using the spoofed Web site, phishing e-mails and the spoofed Web sites often look legitimate (see Figure 4-20). To accomplish this, phishers typically use copies of the spoofed organization's logo and other Web site content from the legitimate Web site. For spoofed banking Web pages and other pages where the victim would expect to see a secure Web page, some criminals use a secure connection between the victim and the criminal's server so the Web page looks secure with an *https:* in the Address bar. The domain name of the legitimate company (such as *ebay* for an eBay phishing page) is also often used as part of the URL of the phishing link (such as a URL starting with the text *ebay* even though the URL's domain is not ebay.com) to make it appear more legitimate. Other phishing schemes use a technique called *typosquatting*, which is setting up spoofed Web sites with addresses slightly different from legitimate sites. For example, a spoofed Web site using the URL www.amazom.com might be used to catch shoppers intending to reach the Amazon.com Web site located at www.amazon.com in hopes that customers making this error when typing the URL will not notice it and will supply logon information via the spoofed site when they arrive.

Another recent trend is the use of more targeted, personalized phishing schemes, known as **spear phishing**. Spear phishing e-mails are directly targeted to a specific individual and typically appear to come from an organization or a person that the targeted individual has an association with. They also often include personalized information (such as the potential victim's name, employer, and other information frequently found on social networking sites and other public resources) to make the spear phishing e-mails seem even more legitimate. Some attacks use spoofed logon pages for social networking sites to obtain an individual's logon information and password. Because many individuals use the same logon information for a variety of sites, once a scammer has a valid username/password combination, he or she can try it on a variety of common e-commerce sites, such as shopping sites, online banking sites, and online payment services like PayPal.

Spear phishers also target employees of selected organizations by posing as someone within the company, such as a human resource or technical support employee. These spear phishing e-mails often request confidential information (such as logon IDs and passwords) or direct the employee to click a link to supposedly reset his or her password. The goal for corporate spear phishing attacks is usually to steal intellectual property, such as software source code, design documents, or schematics. It can also be used to steal money. For instance, in one recent case, a grocery store chain received fraudulent e-mails that appeared to come from two approved suppliers. The e-mails instructed the grocery store chain to send future payments to new bank accounts listed in the e-mail—the grocery store chain deposited more than $10 million into two fraudulent bank accounts before the scam was discovered.

> **TIP**
>
> Spear phishing attacks are expected to increase as a result of the Epsilon data breach, which exposed names and e-mail addresses of individuals along with businesses that they patronize, such as banks, hotels, and stores.

Social Media Hacks

The use of phishing e-mails declined dramatically in 2012, as thieves appeared to shift to other online communications, such as social networks, according to a recent Symantec

>**Spear phishing.** A personalized phishing scheme targeted at an individual.

Internet Security Threat Report. In addition to obtaining information from social networks that can be used in phishing schemes, **social media hacks** can provide phishers with social media logon information that can be used by the phishers to log on to the victim's account and then *hijack* it—posting comments or sending messages containing phishing links (posing as the victim) to the victim's friends, who are much more likely to click on the links because they appear to come from a friend. In addition to individuals' social networking accounts being hacked, business accounts have been recent targets as well. For example, the Twitter accounts of several businesses (including Burger King and Jeep) were hacked in 2013 and erroneous information posted (Burger King being purchased by McDonald's was one tweet made by the hackers). While hacking into a business's social media account and hijacking it temporarily is often a public embarrassment, sometimes (like when the stock market dipped after the recent AP Twitter hack that there was an explosion at the White House), the consequences of business social media hacking are more severe.

Pharming and Drive-By Pharming

Pharming is another type of scam that uses spoofing—specifically spoofed domain names used to obtain personal information for use in fraudulent activities. With pharming, the criminal reroutes traffic intended for a commonly used Web site to a spoofed Web site set up by the pharmer. Sometimes pharming takes place via malicious code sent to a computer via an e-mail message or other distribution method. More often, however, it takes place via changes made to a *DNS server*—a computer that translates URLs into the appropriate IP addresses needed to display the Web page corresponding to a URL. This type of pharming can take place at one of the 13 *root DNS servers* (the DNS servers used in conjunction with the Internet), but it more often takes place at a *company DNS server* (the DNS server for that company used to route Web page requests received via company Web site URLs to the appropriate company server). After hacking into a company DNS server (typically for a company with a commonly used Web site), the pharmer changes the IP addresses used in conjunction with a particular company URL (called *DNS poisoning*) so any Web page requests made via the legitimate company URL is routed (via the company's poisoned DNS server) to a phony spoofed Web page located on the pharmer's Web server. So, even though a user types the proper URL to display the legitimate company Web page in his or her browser, the spoofed page is displayed instead.

Because spoofed sites are set up to look like the legitimate sites, the user typically does not notice any difference, and any information sent via that site is captured by the pharmer. To avoid suspicion, some pharming schemes capture the user's account name and password as it is entered the first time on the spoofed site, and then display a password error message. The spoofed site then redirects the user back to the legitimate site where he or she is able to log on to the legitimate site, leaving the user to think that he or she must have just mistyped the password the first time. But, by then, the pharmer has already captured the victim's username and password and can use that information to gain access to the victim's account.

A recent variation of pharming is *drive-by pharming*. The goal is still to redirect victims to spoofed sites; however, the pharmer accomplishes this by changing the victim's designated DNS server (which often belongs to the individual's ISP and is specified in the victim's router settings) to the pharmer's DNS server in order to direct the victim to spoofed versions of legitimate Web sites when the victim enters the URLs for those sites. Typically, the pharmer uses malicious JavaScript code placed on a Web page to changes the victim's DNS settings to use the pharmer's DNS server; this change can only occur on a router in which the default administrator password was not changed.

TIP

In 2013, the Department of Homeland Security began recommending disabling Java on Web browsers due to security flaws; while not possible for all users, try it—if your Web sites function fine without it, leave it disabled.

>**Social media hack.** The act of accessing someone else's social media account to make changes to the content or to perform an activity as that individual. >**Pharming.** The use of spoofed domain names to obtain personal information in order to use that information in fraudulent activities.

Online Auction Fraud

Online auction fraud (sometimes called *Internet auction fraud*) occurs when an online auction buyer pays for merchandise that is never delivered, or that is delivered but it is not as represented. It can also occur when an online buyer receives the proper items but falsely claims that they never arrived. Like other types of fraud, online auction fraud is illegal, but similar to many types of Internet cons, prosecution is difficult for online auction fraud because multiple jurisdictions are usually involved. Although most online auction sites have policies that suspend sellers with a certain number of complaints lodged against them, it is very easy for those sellers to come back using a new e-mail address and identity.

Other Internet Scams

There is a wide range of other scams that can occur via Web sites or unsolicited e-mails. The anonymity of the Internet makes it very easy for con artists to appear to be anyone they want to be, including a charitable organization or a reputable-looking business. Common types of scams include loan scams, work-at-home cons, pyramid schemes, bogus credit card offers and prize promotions, and fraudulent business opportunities and franchises. These offers typically try to sell potential victims nonexistent services or worthless information, or they try to convince potential victims to voluntarily supply their credit card details and other personal information. Some scammers hack into a system to obtain e-mail addresses to use as targets for a scam that is based on something those indviduals have in common in order to increase the odds of a potential victim falling for the scam. Others send messages to a potential victim impersonating a distant friend or old classmate (typically found via a social networking site) and requesting money (such as by saying they are traveling out of the country and were just robbed).

One ongoing Internet scam is the *Nigerian letter fraud* scheme. This scheme involves an e-mail message that appears to come from the Nigerian government and that promises the potential victim a share of a substantial amount of money in exchange for the use of the victim's bank account. Supposedly the victim's bank account information is needed to facilitate a wire transfer (but the victim's account is emptied instead) and/or up-front cash is needed to pay for nonexistent fees (but that is kept by the con artist). The scams often change to fit current events, such as the war in Iraq or a recent natural disaster. However, the scams always involve a so-called fortune that is inaccessible to the con artist without the potential victims' help (see Figure 4-21) and the victims always lose any money they provide.

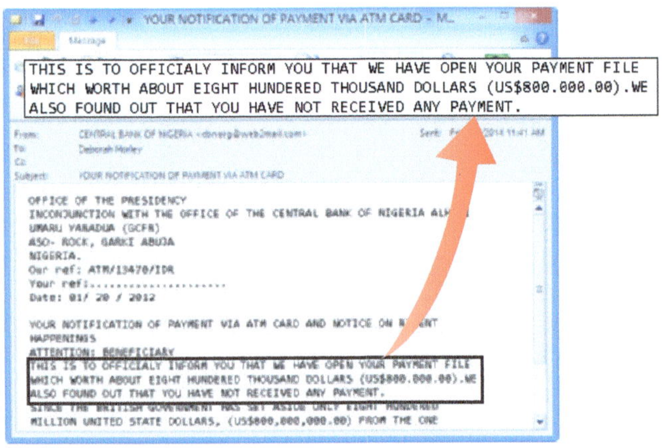

FIGURE 4-21
A Nigerian letter fraud e-mail.

Other schemes involve con artists who solicit donations for charitable organizations after disasters and other tragic events, but who keep the donations instead. Another common scam involves setting up a pornographic site that requires a valid credit card, supposedly to prove that the visitor is an adult, but which is then used for credit card fraud. A relatively new type of scam involves posting fake job listings on job search sites to elicit personal information (such as Social Security numbers) from job seekers. An even more recent twist is to hire individuals through online job sites for seemingly legitimate positions involving money handling (such as bookkeeping or accounting positions), but then use those individuals—often without their knowledge—to facilitate Internet auction scams and other monetary scams.

>**Online auction fraud.** When an item purchased through an online auction is never delivered after payment, or the item is not as specified by the seller.

PROTECTING AGAINST ONLINE THEFT, ONLINE FRAUD, AND OTHER DOT CONS

In a nutshell, the best protection against many dot cons is protecting your identity; that is, protecting any identifying information about you that could be used in fraudulent activities. There are also specific precautions that can help protect against online theft, identity theft, online auction fraud, and other types of dot cons, as discussed next. With any dot con, it is important to act quickly if you think you have been a victim. For instance, you should work with your local law enforcement agency, credit card companies, and the three major consumer credit bureaus (*Equifax*, *Experian*, and *TransUnion*) to close any accessed or fraudulent accounts, place fraud alerts on your credit report, and take other actions to prevent additional fraudulent activity while the fraud is being investigated.

Arrests and prosecutions by law enforcement agencies may also help cut down on cybercrimes. Prosecution of online scammers has been increasing and sentences are not light. For instance, two Romanian citizens were recently sentenced for their involvement in a phishing scheme (the first time the United States has sentenced a foreigner for phishing)—one received 80 months in federal prison; the other received 27 months.

Protecting Against Data and Information Theft

Businesses and individuals can both help to prevent some types of data and information theft. For instance, businesses should use good security measures to protect the data stored on their computers. Individuals should be vigilant about protecting their private information by sending sensitive information via secure Web servers only and not disclosing personal information—especially a Social Security number or a mother's maiden name—unless it is absolutely necessary and they know how the information will be used and that it will not be shared with others. In addition, individuals should never give out sensitive personal information to anyone who requests it over the phone or by e-mail—businesses that legitimately need bank account information, passwords, or credit card numbers will not request that information via phone or e-mail. Encrypting computers and other hardware containing sensitive information, so it will not be readable if the hardware is lost or stolen, is another important precaution.

TIP

When using a public computer, always log out of your accounts at the end of your session to make sure the next user won't have access to them.

Protecting Against Identity Theft, Phishing, Social Media Hacks, and Pharming

Some precautions already discussed (such as disclosing your personal information only when necessary and only via secure Web pages) can help reduce your risk of identity theft. So can using security software (and keeping it up to date) to guard against malware that can send information from your computer or about your activities (the Web site passwords that you type, for example) to a criminal. In addition, to prevent someone from using the preapproved credit card offers and other documents containing personal information that are mailed to you, shred them before throwing them in the trash. To prevent the theft of outgoing mail containing sensitive information, don't place it in your mailbox—mail it at the post office or in a USPS drop box.

To avoid phishing schemes, never click a link in an e-mail message to go to a secure Web site—always type the URL for that site in your browser (not necessarily the URL shown in the e-mail message) instead. Phishing e-mails typically sound urgent and often contain spelling and grammatical errors—see Figure 4-22 for some tips to help

FIGURE 4-22
Tips for identifying phishing e-mail messages.

A PHISHING E-MAIL OFTEN . . .

Tries to scare you into responding by sounding urgent, including a warning that your account will be cancelled if you do not respond, or telling you that you have been a victim of fraud.

Asks you to provide personal information, such as your bank account number, an account password, credit card number, PIN number, mother's maiden name, or Social Security number.

Contains links that do not go where the link text says it will go (point to a hyperlink in the e-mail message to view the URL for that link to see the actual domain being used—a phisher would have to use a URL like microsoft.phisher.com, not microsoft.com).

Uses legitimate logos from the company the phisher is posing as.

Appears to come from a known organization, but one you may not have an association with.

Appears to be text or text and images but is actually a single image; it has been created that way to avoid being caught in a spam filter (a program that sorts e-mail based on legitimate e-mail and suspected spam) because spam filters cannot read text that is part of an image in an e-mail message.

Contains spelling or grammatical errors.

TIPS FOR AVOIDING IDENTITY THEFT

- Protect your Social Security number—give it out only when necessary.
- Be careful with your physical mail and trash—shred all documents containing sensitive data.
- Secure your computer—update your operating system and use up-to-date security (antivirus, antispyware, firewall, etc.) software.
- Be cautious—never click on a link in an e-mail message or respond to a too-good-to-be-true offer.
- Use strong passwords for your computer and online accounts.
- Verify sources before sharing sensitive information—never respond to e-mail or phone requests for sensitive information.
- Be vigilant while on the go—safeguard your wallet, smartphone, and portable computer.
- Watch your bills and monitor your credit reports—react immediately if you suspect fraudulent activity.
- Use security software or browser features that warn you if you try to view a known phishing site.

FIGURE 4-23
Tips to reduce your risk of identity theft.

you recognize phishing e-mails. Remember that spear phishing schemes may include personalized information (such as your name)—do not let that fool you into thinking the phishing e-mail is legitimate. If you think an unsolicited e-mail message requesting information from you may be legitimate (for instance, if the credit card you use to make an automatic payment for an ongoing service is about to expire and you receive an e-mail message asking you to update your credit card information), type the URL for that site in your browser to load the legitimate site and then update your account information. To prevent a drive-by pharming attack, all businesses and individuals should change the administrator password for routers, access points, and other networking hardware from the default password to a strong password. Individuals can also change the DNS server for their router to one (such as *OpenDNS*) that uses filtering to block malicious sites and protect against pharming attempts.

Keeping a close eye on your credit card bills and credit history is also important to make sure you catch any fraudulent charges or accounts opened by an identity thief as soon as possible. Make sure your bills come in every month (some thieves will change your mailing address to delay detection), and read credit card statements carefully to look for unauthorized charges. Be sure to follow up on any calls you get from creditors, instead of assuming it is just a mistake. Most security experts also recommend ordering a full credit history on yourself a few times a year to check for accounts listed in your name that you did not open and any other problems. The *Fair and Accurate Credit Transactions Act* (*FACTA*) enables all Americans to get a free copy of their credit report, upon request, each year from the three major consumer credit bureaus. Ideally, you should request a report from one of these bureaus every four months to monitor your credit on a regular basis. These reports contain information about inquiries related to new accounts requested in your name, as well as any delinquent balances or other negative reports. For another tool that you can use to help detect identity theft—*online financial alerts*—see the Technology and You box. You can also use browser-based *antiphishing* tools and *digital certificates* to help guard against identity theft and the phishing and pharming schemes used in conjunction with identity theft, as discussed next. Some additional tips for minimizing your risk of identity theft are listed in Figure 4-23.

TIP

You can order your free credit reports online quickly and easily via Web sites like *AnnualCreditReport.com.*

Antiphishing Tools

Antiphishing tools are built into many e-mail programs and Web browsers to help notify users of possible phishing Web sites. For instance, some e-mail programs will disable links in e-mail messages identified as questionable, unless the user overrides them; most recent browsers warn users when a Web page associated with a possible phishing URL is requested (see Figure 4-24); and antiphishing capabilities are included in many recent security suites.

In addition, some secure Web sites are adding additional layers in security to protect against identity thieves. For example, some online banking sites analyze users' habits to look for patterns that vary from the norm, such as accessing accounts online at an hour unusual for that individual or a higher than normal level of online purchases. If a bank suspects the account may be compromised, it contacts the owner for verification. Bank of America and some other financial institutions have also added an additional step in their logon process—displaying an image or word preselected by the user and stored on the bank's server—to prove

FIGURE 4-24
Unsafe Web site alerts.

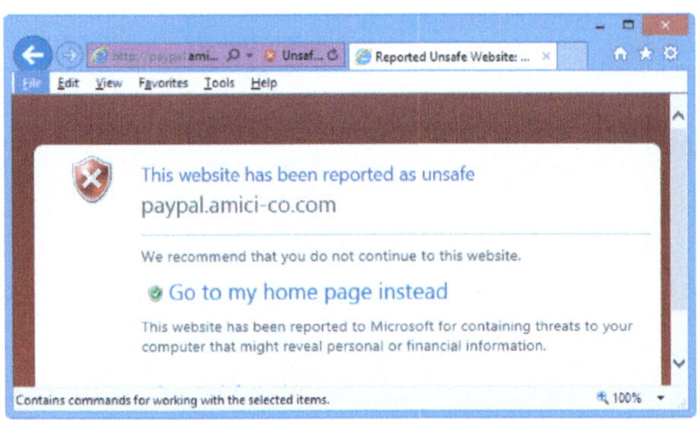

TECHNOLOGY AND YOU

Online Financial Alerts

Want to know ASAP when a transaction that might be fraudulent is charged to your credit card or deducted from your checking account? Well, *online financial alerts* might be the answer.

Many online banking services today allow users to set up e-mail alerts for credit card and bank account activity over a certain amount, low balances, and so forth. For individuals wishing to monitor multiple accounts, however, online money management aggregator services (such as *Mint.com*) make it easier. Once you have set up a free Mint.com account with your financial accounts (including credit cards and checking, savings, and PayPal accounts) and their respective passwords, you can see the status of all your accounts through the Mint.com interface. You can also set up alerts for any of the accounts based on your desired criteria, such as any fee charged or an unusual transaction (see the accompanying photo). The alerts are sent to you via e-mail or text message, depending on your preference, to help notify you as soon as possible if a suspicious activity occurs. And timeliness is of the essence, because the sooner identity theft is discovered, the less time the thief has to make additional fraudulent transactions. For security purposes, Mint.com doesn't store online banking usernames and passwords; instead, a secure online financial services provider is used to connect Mint.com to the appropriate financial institutions to update your activity. In addition, the Mint.com Web site cannot be used to move money out of or between financial accounts—it can be used only to view information.

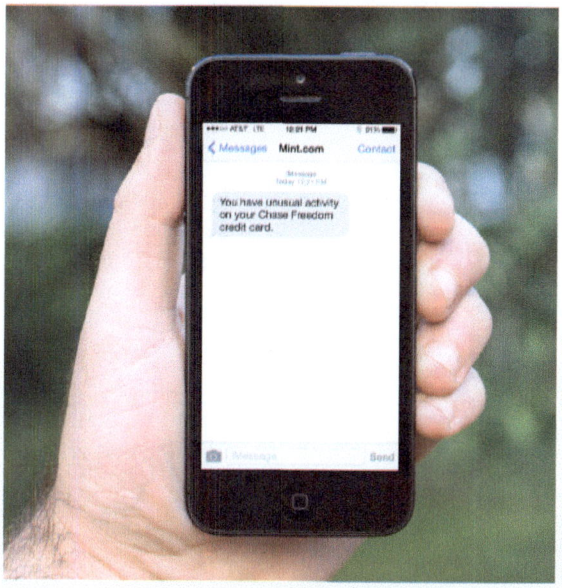

© franckreporter/iStockphoto; Courtesy Mint.com

to the user that the site being viewed is the legitimate (not a phishing) site. In addition, if the system does not recognize the computer that the user is using to log on to the system, the user is required to go through an authentication process (typically by correctly answering cognitive authentication questions) before being allowed to access the system via that computer. The questions used are specifically designed to be "out of wallet" questions—easy for the individual to answer but difficult for hackers to guess the correct answer or find in a stolen wallet. Bank of America is also one bank offering customers the option of adding the use of one-time passwords (autogenerated by a security token sent via text message to the individual's mobile phone, as in Figure 4-5) to their online banking logon procedure.

TIP

Facebook, Google, Microsoft, and other major technology companies are in the process of developing a new *DMARC* (*Domain-based Message Authentication, Report, and Conformance*) specification expected to make it easier to detect phishing e-mails using spoofed domains.

Digital Certificates and Digital Signatures

The purpose of a **digital certificate** (also called a **digital ID**) is to authenticate the identity of an individual or organization. Digital certificates are granted by Certificate Authorities and typically contain the name of the person, organization, or Web site being certified along with a certificate serial number and an expiration date. Digital certificates also include a public/private key pair. In addition to being used by the certificate holder to encrypt files and e-mail messages (as discussed earlier in this chapter), these keys and the digital certificate are used with secure Web pages to guarantee the Web pages are secure and actually belong to the stated organization (so users can know for sure who their credit

>**Digital certificate.** A group of electronic data that can be used to verify the identity of a person or organization; includes a key pair that can be used for encryption and digital signatures (also called a **digital ID**).

card number or other sensitive data is really being sent to in order to protect against some online scams).

Secure Web sites can obtain either a normal *SSL digital certificate* or a newer *Extended Validation (EV) SSL digital certificate* that was developed to provide consumers with a higher level of trust while online. While both digital certificates require an application process, the verification process to obtain an EV SSL digital certificate is more thorough, requiring the use of reputable third-party sources to verify that the company has the right to use the Web site domain name in question and that the business requesting the certificate is authorized to do so. With both types of certificates, individuals can click the secure Web page icon in their browser window to view that site's digital certificate in order to ensure that the certificate is valid and issued to the company associated with the Web site being viewed. If an EV SSL certificate is used, however, additional information is displayed when the Web site is viewed in an EV-compliant browser, such as recoloring the Address bar green to indicate a site using a valid EV SSL certificate and displaying certificate information in the *Security Status bar* to the right of the Address bar, as shown in Figure 4-25.

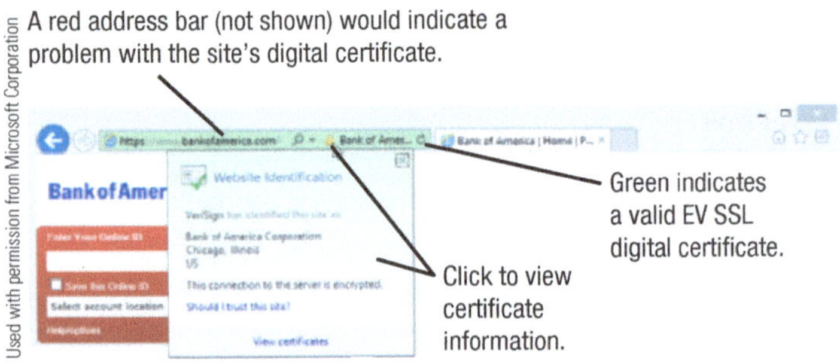

FIGURE 4-25
EV SSL certificates. The browser's Address bar reflects information about the digital certificate being used.

The keys included in a digital certificate can also be used to authenticate the identity of a person sending an e-mail message or other document via a **digital signature**. To digitally sign an e-mail message or other document, the sender's private key is used and that key, along with the contents of the document, generates a unique digital signature; consequently, a digital signature is different with each signed document. When a digitally signed document is received, the recipient's computer uses the sender's public key to verify the digital signature. Because the document is signed with the sender's private key (that only the sender should know) and the digital signature will be deemed invalid if even one character of the document is changed after it is signed, digital signatures guarantee that the document was sent by a specific individual and that it was not tampered with after it was signed.

Individuals can obtain a free digital certificate for personal use from several Certificate Authorities (such as *Comodo*). Once you obtain one, you will need to install it on your computer (Windows users can use the *Certificates* option on the Content tab in the Internet Properties dialog box available through the Control Panel), and then you can use the digital signature option in your e-mail program (such as Microsoft Outlook, see Figure 4-26) to sign all or just selected messages. At this time, most Web mail programs (such as Gmail and Outlook.com) do not support the use of digital signatures.

FIGURE 4-26
Digitally signing an e-mail message in Microsoft Outlook.

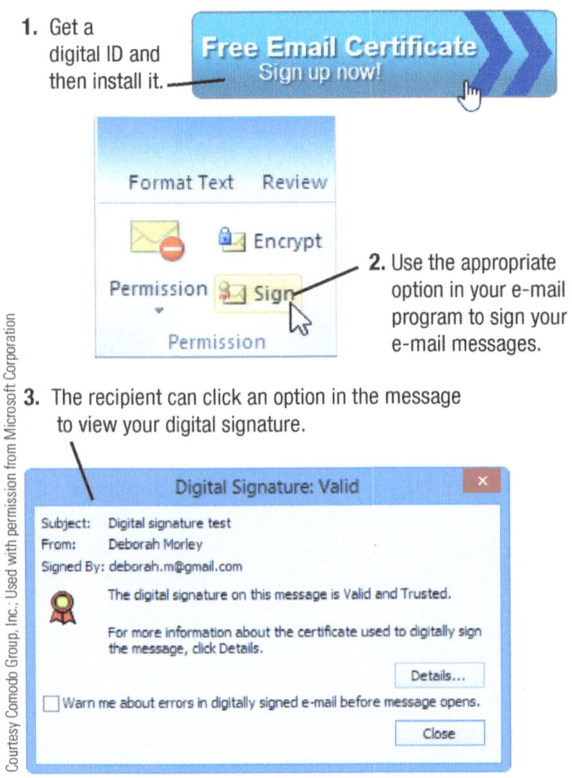

Protecting Against Online Auction Fraud and Other Internet Scams

The best protection against many dot cons is common sense. Be extremely cautious of any unsolicited e-mail messages you receive and realize that if an offer sounds too good to be true, it probably is. You should also be cautious when dealing with individuals online through auctions and other person-to-person activities. Before bidding on an auction item, check out the feedback rating of the seller to see comments written by other auction sellers and buyers as well as the sellers' return policy. Always pay for auctions and other online purchases using a credit card or an online payment service (such as PayPal) that accepts credit card payments so you can dispute the

>**Digital signature.** A unique digital code that can be attached to a file or an e-mail message to verify the identity of the sender and guarantee the file or message has not been changed since it was signed.

transaction through your credit card company, if needed. Using an online payment service that bills the charge to your credit card, instead of allowing the seller to charge your credit card, has the extra advantage of keeping your credit card information private. In addition, some auction sites and online payment services offer free buyer protection against undelivered items or auction items that are significantly different from their description. For instance, most eBay purchases paid for via PayPal have at least $200 of buyer protection coverage at no additional cost. For expensive items, consider using a reputable *escrow service*, which allows you to ensure that the merchandise is as specified before your payment is released to the seller.

PERSONAL SAFETY ISSUES

In addition to being expensive and inconvenient, cybercrime can also be physically dangerous. Although most of us may not ordinarily view using the Internet as a potentially dangerous activity, cases of physical harm due to Internet activity do happen. For example, children and teenagers have become the victims of pedophiles who arranged face-to-face meetings by using information gathered via e-mail, online games, social networking sites, or other online sources. There are also a growing number of incidents in which children are threatened by classmates via e-mail, social media posts, or text messages. Adults have fallen victim to unscrupulous or dangerous individuals who misrepresent themselves online, and the availability of personal information online has made it more difficult for individuals to hide from people who may want to do them harm, such as abused women trying to hide from their abusive husbands. Two of the most common ways individuals are harassed online—*cyberbullying* and *cyberstalking*—are discussed next.

Cyberbullying and Cyberstalking

Children and teenagers bullying other children or teenagers via the Internet—such as through e-mail, a text message, a social networking site, a blog, or other online communications method—is referred to as **cyberbullying**. Unfortunately, cyberbullying is common today—it affects more than one-half of all U.S. teenagers, according to a recent report. Cyberbullying can take place via direct online communications (such as with an e-mail or a text message), as well as via more subtle means. For instance, there have been cases of students posting videos on YouTube of other students being bullied or shown in compromising situations, as well as cases of individuals hacking into a student's social networking account and changing the content on the student's pages to harass that student. Unfortunately, there are also several instances where teenagers have committed suicide because of cyberbullying, which have prompted many states and schools to look at harassment statutes and bullying policies. Several antibullying campaigns have been initiated by school districts and government organizations (see Figure 4-27) and most states have implemented new laws or amended existing harassment laws to address electronic harassment. And Web sites (along with the individuals or companies responsible for them) that provide the means for the harassment may also be at risk for prosecution. In Italy, three Google executives were given suspended jail terms for ignoring a parent's request to remove a video of a boy being bullied, and at the time of this writing, Italian prosecutors were investigating whether to sue Facebook for not removing harrassing messages that led to a teenage girl's suicide.

While incidents of online harrassment between adults can be referred to as *cyberharassment*, repeated threats or other malicious behavior that poses a credible threat of harm carried out online between adults is referred to as **cyberstalking**. Cyberstalkers sometimes find their victims online; for instance, someone who makes a comment on a

Courtesy National Crime Prevention Council

FIGURE 4-27
An anti-cyberbullying Web banner.

>**Cyberbullying.** Children or teenagers bullying other children or teenagers via the Internet. >**Cyberstalking.** Repeated threats or harassing behavior between adults carried out via e-mail or another Internet communications method.

social networking site that the cyberstalker does not like, or bloggers who are harassed and threatened because of their blogging activities. Other times, the attack is more personal, such as employers who are stalked online by ex-employees who were fired or otherwise left their position under adverse conditions, and celebrities who are stalked online by fans.

Cyberstalking typically begins with online harassment—such as sending harassing or threatening e-mail messages or unwanted files to the victim, posing as the victim in order to sign the victim up for pornographic or otherwise offensive e-mail newsletters, publicizing the victim's home address and telephone number, or hacking into the victim's social networking pages to alter the content. Cyberstalking can also lead to offline stalking and possibly physical harm to, and sometimes even the death of, the victim. While there are as yet no specific federal laws against cyberstalking, all states have made it illegal (and it is being increasingly prosecuted), and some federal laws do apply if the online actions include computer fraud or another type of computer crime, suggest a threat of personal injury, or involve sending obscene e-mail messages. Many cyberstalkers are not caught, however, due in part to the anonymity of the Internet, which assists cyberstalkers in concealing their true identities.

Online Pornography

A variety of controversial and potentially objectionable material is available on the Internet. Although there have been attempts to ban this type of material from the Internet, they have not been successful. For example, the *Communications Decency Act*, signed into law in 1996—which made it a criminal offense to distribute patently indecent or offensive material online—was ruled unconstitutional in 1997 by the U.S. Supreme Court. However, like its printed counterpart, online pornography involving minors is illegal. Because of the strong link they believe exists between child pornography and child molestation, many experts are very concerned about the amount of child pornography that can be found and distributed via the Internet. They also believe that the Internet makes it easier for sexual predators to act out, such as by striking up "friendships" with children online and convincing these children to meet them in real life. And this can have devastating consequences, as it did for a 13-year-old girl from Connecticut who was strangled to death in 2002 by a 25-year-old man she met originally online and eventually in person.

PROTECTING AGAINST CYBERBULLYING, CYBERSTALKING, AND OTHER PERSONAL SAFETY CONCERNS

The growing increase in attention to cyberbullying and cyberstalking is leading to more efforts to improve safeguards for children. For instance, social networking sites have privacy features that can be used to protect the private information of their members. In addition, numerous states in the United States have implemented cyberbullying and cyberstalking laws. While there is no surefire way to protect against cyberbullying, cyberstalking, and other online dangers completely, some common-sense precautions can reduce the chance of a serious personal safety problem occurring due to online activities.

> **TIP**
>
> Search for yourself using search sites and online telephone books to see what personal information is available about you on the Internet.

Safety Tips for Adults

It is wise to be cautious and discreet online—especially in online profiles, Twitter tweets, forums, and other online locations where individuals communicate with strangers. To protect yourself against cyberstalking and other types of online harassment, use gender-neutral, nonprovocative identifying names, such as *jsmith*, instead of *janesmith* or *iamcute*. Be careful about the types of photos you post of yourself online and do not reveal personal information—such as your real name, address, or telephone number—to people you meet online. In addition, do not respond to any insults or other harassing comments you may receive online. You may also want to request that your personal information be removed from online directories—especially those associated with your e-mail address or other online identifiers.

> **TIP**
>
> Both adults and children should avoid including personal information on their social networking pages that could be used by an online stalker.

Safety Tips for Children and Teens

Most experts agree that the best way to protect children from online dangers is to stay in close touch with them as they explore the Internet. Parents should monitor their children's computer and mobile phone activities, and children and teenagers should be told which activities are allowed, which types of Web sites are off-limits, and why. In addition, it should be made clear that they are never to reveal personal information about themselves online without a parent's permission. They should also be instructed to tell a parent (or teacher if at school) if an individual ever requests personal information or a personal meeting, or threatens or otherwise harasses the child, via any type of online communications medium. Older children should also be cautioned about sending compromising photos of themselves or sexually explicit messages to others—a growing practice referred to as *sexting*. Part of the problem is that many young people don't realize they lose control of photos and other compromising content once that information has been sent to others. The issue is also complicated by *sextortion*—where someone who sees a teen's explicit photo in a text message or on the Internet threatens to expose the teen's behavior unless the teen sends more explicit photos. Sexting can result in child pornography charges being filed against teens, though some states are passing legislation to make it illegal but have lesser charges for a minor's first offense.

TIP

One controversial bill under consideration is *CISPA* (*Cyber Intelligence Sharing and Protection Act*), which would allow for voluntary information sharing between private companies and the government in the event of a cyber attack.

NETWORK AND INTERNET SECURITY LEGISLATION

Although new legislation is introduced frequently to address new types of computer crimes, it is rarely passed due to differences in opinion regarding the balance of protection vs. civil liberties. In addition, there are both domestic and international jurisdictional issues because many computer crimes affect businesses and individuals located in geographic areas other than the one in which the computer criminal is located, and hackers can make it appear that activity is coming from a different location than it really is. Nevertheless, computer crime legislation continues to be proposed and computer crimes are being prosecuted. A list of selected federal laws concerning network and Internet security is shown in Figure 4-28.

FIGURE 4-28
Computer network and Internet security legislation.

DATE	LAW AND DESCRIPTION
2004	**Identity Theft Penalty Enhancement Act** Adds extra years to prison sentences for criminals who use identity theft (including the use of stolen credit card numbers) to commit other crimes.
2003	**CAN-SPAM Act** Implements regulations for unsolicited e-mail messages.
2003	**Fair and Accurate Credit Transactions Act (FACTA)** Amends the Fair Credit Reporting Act (FCRA) to require that the three nationwide consumer reporting agencies (Equifax, Experian, and TransUnion) provide consumers, upon request, a free copy of their credit report once every 12 months.
2003	**PROTECT Act** Includes provisions to prohibit virtual child pornography.
2003	**Health Insurance Portability and Accountability Act (HIPAA)** Includes a Security Rule that sets minimum security standards to protect health information stored electronically.
2002	**Homeland Security Act** Includes provisions to combat cyberterrorism, including protecting ISPs against lawsuits from customers for revealing private information to law enforcement agencies.
2002	**Sarbanes-Oxley Act** Requires archiving a variety of electronic records and protecting the integrity of corporate financial data.
2001	**USA PATRIOT Act** Grants federal authorities expanded surveillance and intelligence-gathering powers, such as broadening the ability of federal agents to obtain the real identity of Internet users, intercept e-mail and other types of Internet communications, follow online activity of suspects, expand their wiretapping authority, and more.
1998	**Identity Theft and Assumption Deterrence Act of 1998** Makes it a federal crime to knowingly use someone else's means of identification, such as name, Social Security number, or credit card, to commit any unlawful activity.
1997	**No Electronic Theft (NET) Act** Expands computer piracy laws to include online distribution of copyrighted materials.
1996	**National Information Infrastructure Protection Act** Amends the Computer Fraud and Abuse Act of 1984 to punish information theft crossing state lines and to crack down on network trespassing.
1984	**Computer Fraud and Abuse Act of 1984** Makes it a crime to break into computers owned by the federal government. This act has been regularly amended over the years as technology has changed.

SUMMARY

WHY BE CONCERNED ABOUT NETWORK AND INTERNET SECURITY?

Chapter Objective 1:
Explain why computer users should be concerned about network and Internet security.

There are a number of important security concerns related to computers and the Internet. Many of these are **computer crimes**. Because computers and networks are so widespread and many opportunities for criminals exist, all computer users should be aware of the risks of using networks and the Internet so they can take appropriate precautions.

UNAUTHORIZED ACCESS AND UNAUTHORIZED USE

Chapter Objective 2:
List several examples of unauthorized access and unauthorized use.

Two risks related to networks and the Internet are **unauthorized access** and **unauthorized use**. **Hacking** is using a computer to break into a computer. **War driving** and **Wi-Fi piggybacking** refer to the unauthorized use of an unsecured Wi-Fi network. Data can be intercepted as it is transmitted over the Internet or a wireless network.

PROTECTING AGAINST UNAUTHORIZED ACCESS AND UNAUTHORIZED USE

Chapter Objective 3:
Explain several ways to protect against unauthorized access and unauthorized use, including access control systems, firewalls, and encryption.

Access control systems are used to control access to a computer, network, or other resource. These include **possessed knowledge access systems** that use **passwords** or other types of possessed knowledge; **possessed object access systems** that use physical objects; and **biometric access systems** that identify users by a particular unique biological characteristic, such as a fingerprint. Passwords should be *strong passwords*; **two-factor authentication** systems that use multiple factors are more effective than single-factor systems.

To protect wireless networks, they should be secured; **firewalls** protect against unauthorized access. Sensitive transactions should be performed only on **secure Web pages**; sensitive files and e-mails should be secured with **encryption. Public key encryption** uses a private key and matching public key; **private key encryption** uses only a private key. A **virtual private network (VPN)** can be used to provide a secure remote connection to a company network, as well as to protect individuals at public Wi-Fi hotspots. Employers should take appropriate precautions with current and former employees to limit the risk of unauthorized access and use, as well as accidental exposure of sensitive information.

COMPUTER SABOTAGE

Chapter Objective 4:
Provide several examples of computer sabotage.

Computer sabotage includes **malware** (**computer viruses**, **computer worms**, and **Trojan horses** designed to cause harm to computer systems), **denial of service (DoS) attacks** (designed to shut down a Web server), and data and program alteration. Computer sabotage is often performed via the Internet, increasingly by the **bots** in a **botnet**.

PROTECTING AGAINST COMPUTER SABOTAGE

Chapter Objective 5:
List how individuals and businesses can protect against computer sabotage.

Protection against computer sabotage includes using appropriate access control systems to keep unauthorized individuals from accessing computers and networks, as well as using **security software**. In particular, **antivirus software** protects against computer viruses and other types of malware. It is important to keep your security software up to date.

ONLINE THEFT, ONLINE FRAUD, AND OTHER DOT CONS

There are a variety of types of theft, fraud, and scams related to the Internet—collectively referred to as **dot cons**—that all Internet users should be aware of. Data, information, or money can be stolen from individuals and businesses. A common crime today is **identity theft**, in which an individual poses as another individual—typically to steal money or make purchases posing as the victim. The information used in identity theft is often gathered via **phishing**, **spear phishing**, **social media hacking**, and **pharming**. **Online auction fraud** is another common dot con.

Chapter Objective 6:
Discuss online theft, identity theft, spoofing, phishing, and other types of dot cons.

PROTECTING AGAINST ONLINE THEFT, ONLINE FRAUD, AND OTHER DOT CONS

To protect against identity theft, individuals should guard their personal information carefully. To check for identity theft, watch your bills and credit history. When interacting with other individuals online or buying from an online auction, it is wise to be conservative and use a credit card whenever possible. To avoid other types of dot cons, be very wary of responding to unsolicited offers and e-mails, and steer clear of offers that seem too good to be true. Never click a link in an e-mail message to update your personal information. To verify a Web site, a **digital certificate** (also called a **digital ID**) can be used. To verify the sender of a document, a **digital signature** can be used. Digital certificates include key pairs that can be used to both digitally sign documents and to encrypt files.

Chapter Objective 7:
Detail steps an individual can take to protect against online theft, identity theft, spoofing, phishing, and other types of dot cons.

PERSONAL SAFETY ISSUES

There are also personal safety risks for both adults and children stemming from Internet use. **Cyberbullying** and **cyberstalking**—online harassment that frightens or threatens the victim—is more common in recent years, even though most states have passed laws against it. Cyberbully is a growing risk for children, as are the risks of potential exposure to online pornography and other materials inappropriate for children, as well as the growing *sexting* and *sextortion* trends.

Chapter Objective 8:
Identify personal safety risks associated with Internet use.

PROTECTING AGAINST CYBERBULLING, CYBERSTALKING, AND OTHER PERSONAL SAFETY CONCERNS

To protect their personal safety, adults and children should be cautious in online communications. They should be wary of revealing any personal information or meeting online acquaintances in person. To protect children, parents should keep a close watch on their children's online activities, and children should be taught never to reveal personal information to others online without a parent's consent.

Chapter Objective 9:
List steps individuals can take to safeguard their personal safety when using the Internet.

NETWORK AND INTERNET SECURITY LEGISLATION

The rapid growth of the Internet and jurisdictional issues have contributed to the lack of network and Internet security legislation. However, computer crime legislation continues to be proposed and computer crimes are actively prosecuted.

Chapter Objective 10:
Discuss the current state of network and Internet security legislation.

REVIEW ACTIVITIES

KEY TERM MATCHING

a. computer virus

b. denial of service (DoS) attack

c. dot con

d. encryption

e. firewall

f. hacking

g. identity theft

h. password

i. phishing

j. Trojan horse

Instructions: Match each key term on the left with the definition on the right that best describes it.

1. ________ A collection of hardware and/or software intended to protect a computer or computer network from unauthorized access.

2. ________ A fraud or scam carried out through the Internet.

3. ________ A malicious program that masquerades as something else.

4. ________ A method of scrambling the contents of an e-mail message or a file to make it unreadable if it is intercepted by an unauthorized user.

5. ________ A secret combination of characters used to gain access to a computer, computer network, or other resource.

6. ________ A software program installed without the user's knowledge and designed to alter the way a computer operates or to cause harm to the computer system.

7. ________ An act of sabotage that attempts to flood a network server or a Web server with so much activity that it is unable to function.

8. ________ The use of spoofed communications (typically e-mail messages) to gain credit card numbers and other personal data to be used for fraudulent purposes.

9. ________ Using a computer to break into another computer system.

10. ________ Using someone else's identity to purchase goods or services, obtain new credit cards or bank loans, or otherwise illegally masquerade as that individual.

SELF-QUIZ

Instructions: Circle **T** if the statement is true, **F** if the statement is false, or write the best answer in the space provided. **Answers for the self-quiz are located in the References and Resources Guide at the end of the book.**

1. T F A computer virus can only be transferred to another computer via a storage medium.

2. T F An access control system that uses passwords is a possessed knowledge access system.

3. T F Using a password that is two characters long is an example of two-factor authentication.

4. T F Secure Web pages use encryption to securely transfer data sent via those pages.

5. T F Cyberstalking is the use of spoofed e-mail messages to gain credit card numbers and other personal data to be used for fraudulent purposes.

6. Driving around looking for a Wi-Fi network to access is referred to as ________.

7. ________ access control systems use some type of unique physical characteristic of a person to authenticate that individual.

8. A(n) ________ can be used at a Wi-Fi hotspot to create a secure path over the Internet.

9. A(n) ________ can be added to a file or an e-mail message to verify the identity of the sender and guarantee the file or message has not been changed.

10. Match each computer crime to its description, and write the corresponding number in the blank to the left of the description.

   a. ________ A person working for the Motor Vehicle Division deletes a friend's speeding ticket from a database.

   b. ________ An individual does not like someone's comment on a message board and begins to send that individual harassing e-mail messages.

   c. ________ An individual sells the same item to 10 individuals via an online auction site.

   d. ________ A person accesses a computer belonging to the IRS without authorization.

   1. Online auction fraud
   2. Hacking
   3. Data or program alteration
   4. Cyberstalking

EXERCISES

1. Write the appropriate letter in the blank to the left of each term to indicate whether it is related to unauthorized access (U) or computer sabotage (C).

   a. ________ Time bomb   c. ________ Malware   e. ________ War driving

   b. ________ DoS attack   d. ________ Wi-Fi piggybacking

2. Is the password *john1* a good password? Why or why not? If not, suggest a better password.

3. Supply the missing words to complete the following statements regarding public/private key pairs.

   a. With an encrypted e-mail message, the recipient's ________ key is used to encrypt the message, and the recipient's ________ key is used to decrypt the message.

   b. With a digital signature, the sender's ________ key is used to sign the document, and the sender's ________ key is used to validate the signature.

4. To secure files on your computer so they are unreadable to a hacker who might gain access to your computer, what type of encryption (public key or private key) would be the most appropriate? Explain.

5. List two precautions you can take to protect against someone hacking your social media accounts.

DISCUSSION QUESTIONS

1. The term *hacktivism* is sometimes used to refer to the act of hacking into a computer system for a politically or socially motivated purpose. While some view hacktivists no differently than they view other hackers, hacktivists contend that they break into systems in order to bring attention to political or social causes. Is hacktivism a valid method of bringing attention to specific causes? Why or why not? Should hacktivists be treated differently from other types of hackers when caught?

2. According to security experts, several worms released in past years contain more than just the virus code—they contain code to remove competing malware from the computers they infect and messages taunting other virus writers. The goal seems to be not only to gain control of an increasing number of infected machines—a type of "bot war" to build the biggest botnet—but also to one-up rivals. If this trend continues, do you think it will affect how hackers and other computer criminals will be viewed? Will they become cult heroes or be viewed as dangerous criminals? Will continuing to increase prosecution of these individuals help or hurt the situation?

PROJECTS

HOT TOPICS

1. **Wi-Fi Hotspot Safety** As mentioned in the chapter, it is possible to inadvertently connect to an evil twin instead of the legitimate Wi-Fi hotspot you intended to connect to and, even if you are connected to a legitimate hotspot, any data you send unsecured via the hotspot can be intercepted by a criminal. In either case, if a thief intercepts your credit card number, Web site passwords, or other sensitive data, it can be used for identity theft and other criminal activities.

   For this project, research these and any other possible risks you can think of related to using a Wi-Fi hotspot. For each risk, identify a possible precaution that can be taken to guard against that risk. If you have ever used a Wi-Fi hotspot, were you at risk? Knowing what you do now, would you take any different precautions the next time you use one? Is it possible to surf safely using a Wi-Fi hotspot? What about activity performed via your smartphone wireless provider—is that safe? At the conclusion of your research, prepare a one-page summary of your findings and opinions and submit it to your instructor.

SHORT ANSWER/ RESEARCH

2. **New Viruses** Unfortunately, new computer viruses and other types of malware are released all the time. In addition to malware targeted toward computers, there is also mobile malware targeted to smartphones, media tablets, and other Internet-enabled devices.

   For this project, identify a current virus or worm (most security companies, such as Symantec and McAfee, list the most recent security threats on their Web sites) and answer the following questions: When was it introduced? What does it do? How is it spread? Is it targeted to computers or mobile devices? How many devices have been affected so far? Is there an estimated cost associated with it? Is it still in existence? At the conclusion of your research, prepare a one-page summary of your findings and submit it to your instructor.

HANDS ON

3. **Virus Check** There are several Web sites that include a free virus check, as well as other types of diagnostic software.

   For this project, locate a free virus check (such as one available from Microsoft or from a company that makes antivirus software) and run the free virus check. NOTE: If you are on a school computer, only run online checks, not downloaded programs. If the check takes more than 10 minutes and there is an option to limit the check to a particular drive and folder, redo the check but scan only part of the hard drive (such as the Documents folder) to save time. After the virus scan is completed, print the page displaying the result. Did the program find any viruses or other security threats? At the conclusion of this task, submit your printout with any additional comments about your experience to your instructor.

ETHICS IN ACTION

4. **Teaching Computer Viruses** Some college computer classes include instruction on writing computer viruses. At one university, precautions for containing code created during this course include allowing only fourth-year students to take the course, not having a network connection in the classroom, and prohibiting the removal of storage media from the classroom. Do you think these precautions are sufficient? Should writing virus code be allowed as part of a computer degree curriculum? Some believe that students need to know how viruses work in order to be able to develop antivirus software; however, the antivirus industry disagrees, and most antivirus professionals were never virus writers. Is it ethical for colleges to teach computer virus writing? Is it ethical for students to take such a course? Will teaching illegal and unethical acts (such as writing virus code) in college classes help to legitimize the behavior in society? Would you feel comfortable taking such a course? Why or why not?

   For this project, form an opinion about the ethical implications of writing virus code in college classes and be prepared to discuss your position (in class, via an online class discussion group, in a class chat room, or via a class blog, depending on your instructor's directions). You may also be asked to write a short paper expressing your opinion.

PRESENTATION/ DEMONSTRATION

5. **Virus Hoaxes** In addition to the valid reports about new viruses found in the news and on antivirus software Web sites, reports of viruses that turn out to be hoaxes abound on the Internet. In addition to being an annoyance, virus hoaxes waste time and computing resources. In addition, they may eventually lead some users to routinely ignore all virus warning messages, leaving them vulnerable to a genuine, destructive virus.

   For this project, visit at least two Web sites that identify virus hoaxes, such as the Symantec or McAfee Web sites and Snopes.com. Explore the sites to find information about recent virus hoaxes, as well as general guidelines for identifying virus hoaxes and other types of online hoaxes. Share your findings with the class in the form of a short presentation. The presentation should not exceed 10 minutes and should make use of one or more presentation aids, such as a whiteboard, handouts, or a computer-based slide presentation (your instructor may provide additional requirements). You may also be asked to submit a summary of the presentation to your instructor.

BALANCING ACT

6. **Is Mobile Banking More Secure than Online Banking?** You may have used your smartphone to pay a bill or deposit a check. While becoming common today, it is still newer than traditional online banking performed via a computer and so does not have as long of a track record. While banks are continually upgrading their security systems in response to new threats and technologies, is the security of online and mobile banking equal? Some consider traditional online banking safer because it has been tested longer, is used with computers that may have better security software installed, and is performed via home computers that are not as likely to be lost or misplaced as mobile devices. Others view mobile banking as safer because individuals tend to have their phones with them at all times and so can be notified more quickly of security breaches, GPS information can be used to identify transactions that occur in a different physical location from the registered location of the phone (and therefore might be fraudulent), and mobile banking accounts are often associated with a single phone. Mobile banking can be performed via a Web app, mobile Web site, or text messaging. Is one method safer than the other? How do the risks associated with mobile banking compare with the risks associated wtih traditional online banking? Would you feel safer using one or the other? Why?

   Pick a side on this issue, form an opinion and gather supporting evidence, and be prepared to discuss and defend your position in a classroom debate or in a 1–2 page paper, depending on your instructor's directions.

expert insight on...

Networks and the Internet

Courtesy McAfee

McAfee
An Intel Company

Greg Hampton is the Vice President of Product Management for the Network Security team at McAfee. Before joining McAfee, Hampton served as the Vice President of Marketing at Clearswift Corporation, an e-mail and Web security company based in the UK. He was also a founder and the CEO of a Silicon Valley start up for delivering network management solutions. Greg has a Bachelor of Arts degree in Economics and brings a broad range of enterprise software experience to the company.

A conversation with GREG HAMPTON

Vice President, Product Management, McAfee

“. . . protect your identity and your online reputation—it will keep you and your data safe and will improve your career prospects.”

My Background . . .

I am the Vice President of Product Management for Network Security at McAfee. In product management, our role is to ensure that our product roadmap is forward looking, and to help connect users with engineers so that we can build outstanding products that meet user needs. I became involved with product management when I was a general manager for a high tech company overseeing its Canadian and Latin American operations and I was asked to oversee a newly acquired company. In the process, I was exposed to the role of product management and developed an interest in it. I have found my experiences in sales management and marketing roles at high tech companies directly applicable and useful to my current position. In addition, pursuing my Bachelor of Arts degree was invaluable. It helped me develop an interest in and the skills needed to be able to learn new ideas in new areas, which is essential for individuals who work in the world of high tech.

It's Important to Know . . .

How the Internet and other networks work. Because the Internet is so integrated into our society today, it is important for people to understand the basic functions of the Internet—how it connects devices and resources, how people access it, how data is stored, and what the cloud is—so that they may understand how best to use and secure this resource in both their personal and professional lives.

That it is essential to protect your identity. Online theft, identity theft, and other privacy and security risks impact what we call our “identity.” Protecting identities is a unique area of security that is important because it touches each of us personally—as employees, as students, and as individuals. In the digital world, you are your digital identity. What is associated with your digital identity becomes associated with you—and that could impact your finances, your legal standing, and your career.

Passwords alone are not an adequate security control. Today, most of our digital identities are protected by passwords. Unfortunately, a simple username and password is easy to break. What's worse, many of us use the same username and password over and over again so once one account—say, an online e-mail account—is breached, all other accounts (such as your bank account) using that same combination are then directly accessible. To make matters worse, the password policies often implemented to help prevent this (such as using a unique strong password for every account, changing them every few months, and telling people not to save them anywhere) increases these habits. Implementing better controls, such as two-factor and biometric authentication (e.g. voice and facial recognition used with our LiveSafe cloud storage product), is both safer and easier to use!

How I Use this Technology . . .

Because my job involves collecting requirements for Internet Security software and appliances, I use this knowledge and these solutions daily in my professional life. But I also use them in my personal life. For example, I use antivirus protection for all of my devices and I use two-factor or strong authentication to protect my financial and personal e-mail accounts.

What the Future Holds . . .

Today in our connected society, our identity is our most valuable and our most vulnerable link. And our society will continue to become more connected. The Internet of Things (IoT) is moving beyond mobile devices and networked cars to wearable devices, household items, medical devices, and other items we use in our daily lives. In the near future, we will be connected in ways we're just beginning to imagine. As this happens, it will become increasingly important that we—as individuals, students, and a business community—continue to watch the trends around identity protection; how trust relationships are established between people, systems, data and applications; and the laws and governance for personal privacy.

"... a simple username and password is easy to break"

Already, the most vulnerable link in our networks today is our identity, and it will become more vulnerable in the even more connected future. And, as the consumerization of IT increases the pressure to move business tools and applications to the cloud, businesses will be more challenged than ever to securely grant remote, mobile, and highly social business users and their identities easy access while not compromising their security—especially as the lines between the personal and professional continue to blur. To address these challenges, McAfee, Intel, and other companies are actively developing solutions like McAfee One Time Password and McAfee LiveSafe for businesses and consumers that use technologies like multi-factor authentication, which combines passwords with other methods like biometrics, smartphones, chips in our devices like Intel Identity Protection Technology (IPT), or other physical objects.

In the future, we can expect to see accelerated movement toward these solutions and technologies as we leave our weak and difficult-to-keep-track-of passwords behind.

My Advice to Students . . .

Protect yourself by implementing multi-factor authentication and strong passwords—today. And all of us, particularly students, should be careful of what we publish in social media. You can expose yourself to risk by sharing too much data about where you live, who you know, and what you are doing. If you share too much information, it can also impact your online reputation. Employers are increasing their scrutiny of social presence when considering job applicants and you don't want something you say or post online to hurt your job prospects in the future.

So, protect your identity and your online reputation—it will keep you and your data safe, and will improve your career prospects.

Discussion Question

Greg Hampton stresses the importance of protecting your digital identity. Think about the systems that contain personal data about you. How would you feel if those systems were breached and your information was stolen? Does your viewpoint change if the information was monetary (such as credit card information) versus private information (such as grades or health information)? What security precautions, if any, do you think should be imposed by laws? Are organizations that hold your personal data morally responsible for going beyond the minimum requirements? Be prepared to discuss your position (in class, via an online class discussion group, in a class chat room, or via a class blog, depending on your instructor's directions). You may also be asked to write a short paper expressing your opinion.

>For more information about McAfee, visit www.mcafee.com. For information about specific security issues and solutions, visit www.mcafee.com/identity and blogs.mcafee.com.

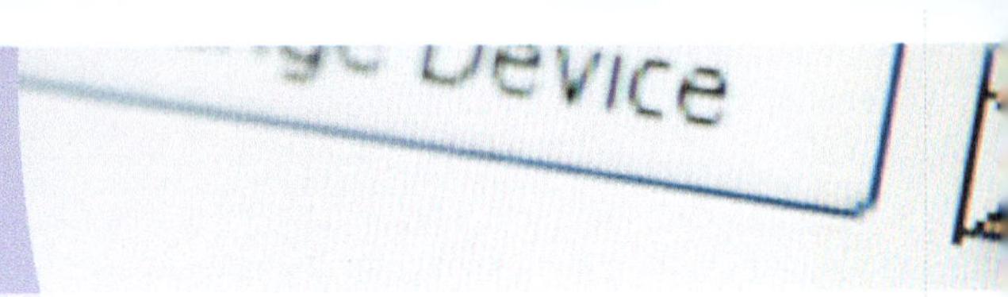

chapter 5

Computer Security and Privacy

After completing this chapter, you will be able to do the following:

1. Explain why all computer users should be concerned about computer security.
2. List some risks associated with hardware loss, hardware damage, and system failure, and understand ways to safeguard a computer against these risks.
3. Define software piracy and digital counterfeiting, and explain how they can be prevented.
4. Explain what information privacy is and why computer users should be concerned about it.
5. Describe some privacy concerns regarding databases, electronic profiling, spam, and telemarketing, and identify ways individuals can protect their privacy.
6. Discuss several types of electronic surveillance and monitoring, and list ways individuals can protect their privacy.
7. Discuss the status of computer security and privacy legislation.

outline

Overview

Why Be Concerned About Computer Security?

Hardware Loss, Hardware Damage, and System Failure
- Hardware Loss
- Hardware Damage
- System Failure and Other Disasters
- Protecting Against Hardware Loss, Hardware Damage, and System Failure

Software Piracy and Digital Counterfeiting
- Software Piracy
- Digital Counterfeiting
- Protecting Against Software Piracy and Digital Counterfeiting

Why Be Concerned About Information Privacy?

Databases, Electronic Profiling, Spam, and Other Marketing Activities
- Databases and Electronic Profiling
- Spam and Other Marketing Activities
- Protecting the Privacy of Personal Information

Electronic Surveillance and Monitoring
- Computer Monitoring Software
- Video Surveillance
- Employee Monitoring
- Presence Technology
- Protecting Personal and Workplace Privacy

Computer Security and Privacy Legislation

OVERVIEW

The increasing use of computers in our society today has many advantages. It also, however, opens up new possibilities for problems (such as data loss due to a system malfunction or a disaster), as well as new opportunities for computer crime (such as hardware theft, software piracy, and digital counterfeiting). In addition, our networked society has raised a number of privacy concerns. Although we can appreciate that sometimes selected people or organizations have a legitimate need for some types of personal information, whenever information is provided to others there is the danger that the information will be misused. For instance, facts may be taken out of context and used to draw distorted conclusions, or private information may end up being distributed to others without one's consent or knowledge. And, with the vast amount of sensitive information stored in databases accessible via the Internet today, privacy is an enormous concern for both individuals and businesses.

Chapter 4 discussed security risks related to network and Internet use. This chapter looks at other types of computer-related security concerns, as well as the computer-related privacy concerns facing us today. First, we explore hardware loss, hardware damage, and system failure, and the safeguards that can help reduce the risk of a problem occurring due to these security concerns. Next, software piracy and digital counterfeiting are discussed, along with the steps that are being taken to prevent these computer crimes. We then turn to privacy topics, including possible risks to personal privacy and precautions that can be taken to safeguard one's privacy. The chapter closes with a summary of legislation related to computer security and privacy. ■

WHY BE CONCERNED ABOUT COMPUTER SECURITY?

Today, there are a number of security concerns surrounding computers and related technology that all individuals should be concerned about, including having your computer stolen, losing a term paper because the storage medium your paper was stored on becomes unreadable, losing your smartphone containing your entire contact list and calendar, or running the risk of buying pirated or digitally counterfeited products. The most common security risks and computer crimes (including hacking, computer viruses, identity theft, and cyberbullying) that take place via networks and the Internet were discussed in Chapter 4, along with their respective precautions. While these concerns are extremely important today, there are additional computer security issues that are not related specifically to networks and the Internet. These computer security concerns, along with some precautions that users can take to reduce the risks of problems occurring due to these security concerns, are discussed in the next few sections.

TIP

New security risks are revealed all the time. For instance, it was recently discovered that data from some unencrypted smart meters can be accessed from nearly 1,000 feet away, enabling would-be burglars to monitor homes to see if they are occupied based on electricity usage within the homes.

HARDWARE LOSS, HARDWARE DAMAGE, AND SYSTEM FAILURE

Hardware loss can occur when a personal computer, USB flash drive, mobile device, or other piece of hardware is stolen or is lost by the owner. Hardware loss, as well as other security issues, can also result from *hardware damage* (both intentional and accidental) and *system failure*.

> **TIP**
>
> According to Norton research, 35% of people worldwide have lost a smartphone and the person who finds a lost phone will more often than not look through the photos and private information stored on a found phone, even when they intend to return it.

Hardware Loss

One of the most obvious types of hardware loss is **hardware theft**, which occurs when hardware is stolen from an individual or from a business, school, or other organization. Computers, printers, mobile phones, and other hardware can be stolen during a break-in; portable computers and mobile devices are also frequently stolen from cars, as well as from restaurants, airports, hotels, and other public locations. Although security experts stress that the vast majority of hardware theft is done for the value of the hardware itself, corporate executives and government employees may be targeted for computer theft for the information contained on their computers. In fact, *C-level attacks* (attacks aimed at C-level executives, such as CEOs and CIOs) are rapidly growing as executives are increasingly using e-mail and storing documents on their computers and mobile devices, as well as traveling more with these devices. And even if the data on a device is not the primary reason for a theft, any unencrypted sensitive data stored on the stolen device is at risk of being exposed or used for fraudulent purposes, and this is happening at unprecedented levels today.

Hardware loss also occurs when hardware is being transported in luggage or in a package that is lost by an airline or shipping company or when hardware is stolen during transit (for example, two thieves recently used forklifts to steal two pallets containing 3,600 iPads from a JFK cargo building); it can also occur when an individual misplaces or otherwise loses a piece of hardware. With the vast number of portable devices that individuals carry with them today (such as portable computers, media tablets, mobile phones, and USB flash drives), this latter type of hardware loss is a growing concern—by one estimate, 70 million mobile phones are lost annually in the United States alone. While lost hardware may be covered by insurance and the data stored on a lost or stolen device may not be used in a fraudulent manner, having to replace the hardware and restore the data—or, worse yet, losing the data entirely if it was not backed up—is still a huge inconvenience. If any sensitive data (such as Social Security numbers, Web site passwords, or credit card data) was contained on the lost hardware, individuals risk identity theft; in fact, one study revealed that 80% of users store information that could be used for identity theft on their mobile phones. Businesses hosting sensitive data that is breached have to deal with the numerous issues and potential consequences of that loss, such as notifying customers that their personal information was exposed (as required by nearly all of the states in the United States), responding to potential lawsuits, and trying to repair damage to the company's reputation.

> **TIP**
>
> According to one recent study, data breaches cost U.S. companies nearly $200 per compromised personal record.

Hardware Damage

Computer hardware often consists of relatively delicate components that can be damaged easily by power fluctuations, heat, dust, static electricity, water, and abuse. For instance, fans clogged by dust can cause a computer to overheat, dropping a device will often break it, and spilling a drink on a keyboard or leaving a mobile phone in the pocket of your jeans while they go through the wash will likely damage or ruin it. In addition to accidental damage, computers and other hardware can also be intentionally damaged by burglars, vandals, disgruntled employees, and other individuals who have access to the hardware.

> **TIP**
>
> To avoid future problems, some damaged landline telephone lines (such as those on the East Coast damaged by Hurricane Sandy) are being replaced with fixed wireless systems, such as Verizon's *Voice Link* system.

System Failure and Other Disasters

Although many of us may prefer not to think about it, **system failure**—the complete malfunction of a computer system—and other types of computer-related disasters do happen. From accidentally deleting a file to having your computer just stop working, computer problems can be a huge inconvenience, as well as cost you a great deal of time and money. When the system contains your personal documents and data, it is a problem; when it

>**Hardware theft.** The theft of computer hardware. >**System failure.** The complete malfunction of a computer system.

contains the only copy of your company records or controls a vital system—such as a nuclear power plant—it can be a disaster.

System failure can occur because of a hardware problem, software problem, or computer virus. It can also occur because of a natural disaster (such as a tornado, fire, flood, or hurricane), sabotage, or a terrorist attack. The terrorist attack on the New York City World Trade Center Twin Towers on September 11, 2001, illustrated this all too clearly. When the Twin Towers collapsed, nearly 3,000 people were killed and hundreds of offices—over 13 million square feet of office space—were completely destroyed; another 7 million square feet of office space was damaged (see Figure 5-1). In addition to the devastating human loss, the offices located in the WTC lost their computer systems—including all the equipment, records, and data stored at that location. The ramifications of these system failures and the corresponding data loss were felt around the world by all the businesses and people connected directly or indirectly to these organizations.

Courtesy of Verizon Communications

FIGURE 5-1
System destruction. The 9/11 attacks killed nearly 3,000 people and destroyed hundreds of business offices, including critical cables located in this Verizon office adjacent to Ground Zero.

Protecting Against Hardware Loss, Hardware Damage, and System Failure

To protect against hardware loss, hardware damage, and system failure, a number of precautions can be taken, as discussed next.

Door and Computer Equipment Locks

Locked doors and equipment can be simple deterrents to computer theft. For instance, doors to facilities should be secured with door locks, alarm systems, and whatever other access control methods (such as the possessed object and biometric access systems discussed in Chapter 4) are needed to make it difficult to gain access to hardware that might be stolen. In addition, employees should be trained regarding the proper procedures for ensuring visitors only have access to the parts of the facility that they are authorized to access. To evaluate their employees and security procedures, some companies use *social engineering tests*, also known as *vulnerability assessments*. For instance, these tests check whether or not employees will click a phishing e-mail message or give out sensitive information in response to a phishing telephone call, will grant a potential thief physical access to the facility, or will plug a USB flash drive found in the office or parking lot (and potentially containing malware planted by a hacker) into their computers. To perform a social engineering test, one company (TraceSecurity) has engineers that typically impersonate pest control workers or fire inspectors in order to gain entry to server rooms and other locations where they can then access sensitive data and equipment. They sometimes precede their visit with a spoofed internal e-mail to office employees, such as announcing an upcoming pest inspection and requesting employees grant the pest control workers full access to check for infestation. Once at the office, TraceSecurity personnel attempt to talk their way into the building and into a room that allows access to the company network. As proof of access, they tag equipment with TraceSecurity stickers (see Figure 5-2), take photographs of the documents and data they were able to access, and sometimes even remove hardware from the building (assuming the business requests this and has granted the appropriate permission). The business then receives a report detailing which tests employees passed and failed, as well as recommendations for precautions that should be taken.

To secure computers and other hardware to a table or other object that is difficult to move, *cable locks* can be used. Cable locks are frequently used to secure computers, media tablets, monitors, external hard drives, and other hardware found in schools and

FIGURE 5-2
Social engineering tests. The red and white stickers mark equipment accessed during a TraceSecurity test.

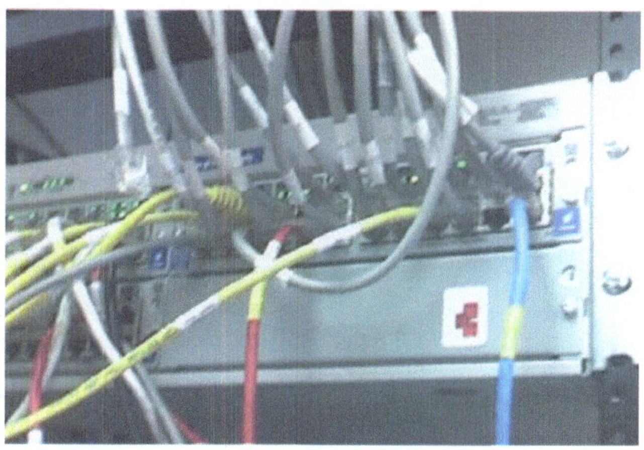

Courtesy TraceSecurity

TREND

Self-Healing Devices

Imagine being able to drop your phone or laptop without worrying about permanently damaging it. Or not having to worry about getting scratches on a touch screen. Well, you may be in luck in the near future. While protective cases and screen protectors have been available for quite some time, researchers are now going a step further by working on ways for your device to heal itself when damaged. For example, researchers at the University of Southern Mississippi in Hattiesburg recently announced a new type of plastic that mimics our skin's ability to repair itself. When the plastic is scratched or cracked, it breaks the tiny molecular links in the material, which results in that area turning red. When the plastic is exposed to light or temperature changes, it reforms—or "repairs"—itself.

Another example is the *Scratch Shield* iPhone case developed by Nissan and shown in the accompanying photograph. This case uses a special paint that can slowly return to its original state after being damaged, such as when the case receives scratches or even deep cuts. Small scratches can heal in as little as an hour; deeper scratches can take up to a week. While the paint was developed initially for use with Nissan and Infiniti cars, this iPhone case is currently being tested and may be available in the near future.

Courtesy Nissan

This Scratch Shield case from Nissan can repair itself when scratched.

TIP

iPad security cases are increasingly being used with iPads in retail environments so they can be securely used by employees and/or customers.

businesses. They are also used by college students, business travelers, and other individuals while on the go to temporarily secure their portable devices when they are not being used. To facilitate using a computer lock, most computers today come with a *security slot*—a small opening built into the system unit case designed for computer locks (see Figure 5-3). If a security slot is not available, *cable anchors* (which attach to a piece of hardware using industrial strength adhesive and which contain a connector through which the cable lock can be passed) or special *security cases* (which enclose a device and attach to a cable lock—refer again to Figure 5-3) can be used. Computer locks are available in key and number or letter combination versions.

As an additional precaution with portable computers, *laptop alarm software* that emits a very loud alarm noise if the computer is unplugged, if USB devices are removed, or if the computer is shut down without the owner's permission can be used. In addition to physically securing computers, it is also extremely important for businesses to ensure that employees follow security protocols related to portable storage media such as signing in and out portable hard drives, USB flash drives, and other storage media if required, and keeping those devices locked up when they are not in use. An emerging option for protecting mobile devices from physical damage—*self-healing devices*—is discussed in the Trend box.

FIGURE 5-3
Cable locks secure computers and other hardware.

Courtesy of Kensington Computer Products Group

NOTEBOOK LOCKS
This combination cable lock connects to the security slot built into the notebook computer.

SECURITY CASES
This iPad security case/stand encloses the iPad and secures it via a keyed cable lock.

Encryption and Self-Encrypting Hard Drives

As discussed in Chapter 4, encryption can be used to prevent a file from being readable if it is intercepted or viewed by an unauthorized individual. To protect the data on an entire computer in case it is lost or stolen, **full disk encryption (FDE)** can be used. FDE systems encrypt everything stored on the drive (the operating system, application programs, data, temporary files, and so forth) automatically without any user interaction, so users don't have to remember to encrypt sensitive documents and the encryption is always enabled. To access a hard drive that uses FDE (often referred to as a **self-encrypting hard drive**), a username and password, biometric characteristic, or other authentication control is needed.

While self-encrypting hard drives are used most often with portable computers (in fact, the U.S. federal government is in the process of implementing FDE on all government-owned portable computers and mobile devices), they are also used with desktop computers and servers. Because FDE requires no user input to enable it and all files are encrypted automatically, these systems provide an easy way to ensure all data is protected, provided strong passwords are used in conjunction with the encryption system so the system cannot be easily hacked. Devices using *hardware encryption* with *hardware authentication*, where both the encryption and authentication systems are built into hardware (such as the device itself or a microSD card) instead of using software, are even more secure against hackers. Encrypted devices are used today by individuals, as well as businesses. In addition, businesses, such as law firms, are beginning to use encryption systems with their mobile phones in order to protect client-related voice calls and text messages.

Encryption can also be used to protect the data stored on removable media, such as flash memory cards and USB flash drives; a strong password, a biometric feature, or a PIN number (such as is used with the device shown in Figure 5-4) provides access to the data on the drive. Many encrypted devices allow multiple users to be registered as authorized users (by assigning each individual a password or registering his or her fingerprint image, for instance); some allow a portion of the device to be designated as unencrypted for nonsensitive documents, if desired. Many businesses today are requiring that all desktop computers, portable computers, portable storage devices, and mobile phones issued to employees be encrypted in order to protect against a data breach.

ASK THE EXPERT

Courtesy SONIC

Craig Miller, Chief Information Officer, Sonic, America's Drive-In

If the computers or software supporting the order entry system in one of your restaurants fails, can the restaurant still process orders?

Even in this age of dependency on technology, SONIC drive-in locations can continue to run should our point-of-sales (POS) system not function. Each drive-in is equipped with a crash kit that includes guest tickets for order taking, menus for pricing reference, and a "tax chart" so that crew members can manually take orders. SONIC crew members also have specific steps that our Operations team has set out for them to follow. Our main focus is to ensure guest satisfaction remains high, even if our system goes down.

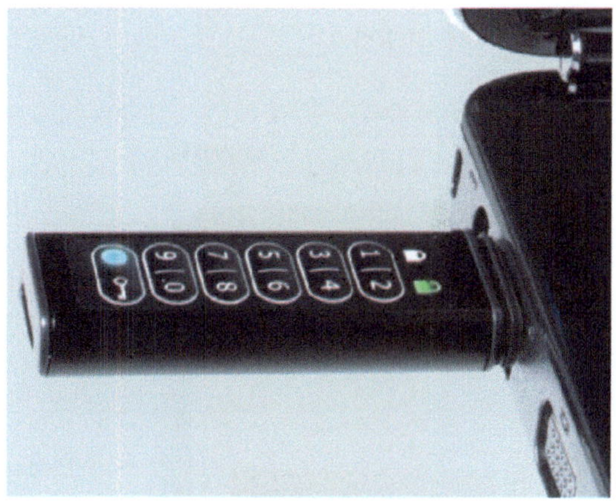

LOK-IT Secure Flash Drive ®

FIGURE 5-4
Encrypted devices. The data on this encrypted USB flash drive cannot be accessed until the user enters the appropriate PIN.

Device Tracking Software and Antitheft Tools

Some software tools are not designed to prevent hardware from being stolen; instead, they are designed to aid in its recovery. This can be beneficial because, according to FBI statistics, 1 in 10 newly-purchased laptops will be stolen within 12 months and only 3% will be recovered. One software tool that can be used to help increase the chances of a stolen or lost device being recovered is *device tracking software*. When a device with tracking

>**Full disk encryption (FDE).** A technology that encrypts everything stored on a storage medium automatically, without any user interaction.
>**Self-encrypting hard drive.** A hard drive that uses full disk encryption (FDE).

HOW IT WORKS

Self-Destructing Devices

When a business or an individual is less concerned about recovering a stolen device than about ensuring the data located on the device is not compromised, devices that self-destruct upon command are a viable option. Available as part of some device tracking apps, as well as stand-alone utilities, *kill switch* capabilities destroy the data on a device (typically by overwriting preselected files multiple times, rendering them unreadable) when instructed—see the example in the accompanying illustration. Kill switches built into device tracking systems are typically activated by the customer or by the tracking company upon customer request when the device is determined to be lost or stolen. Once the kill switch is activated, all data on the device is erased the next time it connects to the Internet or when another predesignated remote trigger is activated (such as a certain number of unsuccessful logon attempts). Users of some cloud services can also use those services to remotely wipe their mobile devices when needed.

Kill switch technology is also beginning to be built into some USB flash drives and hard drives. For example, some encrypted hard drives automatically delete the encryption key (which leaves the data unaccessible) after a specific number of unsuccessful password entry attempts. Not quite *Mission Impossible*, but when hardware containing sensitive data is stolen (which could impact an individual's personal privacy or a business's legal liability, reputation, and bottom line), kill switch technology could save the day.

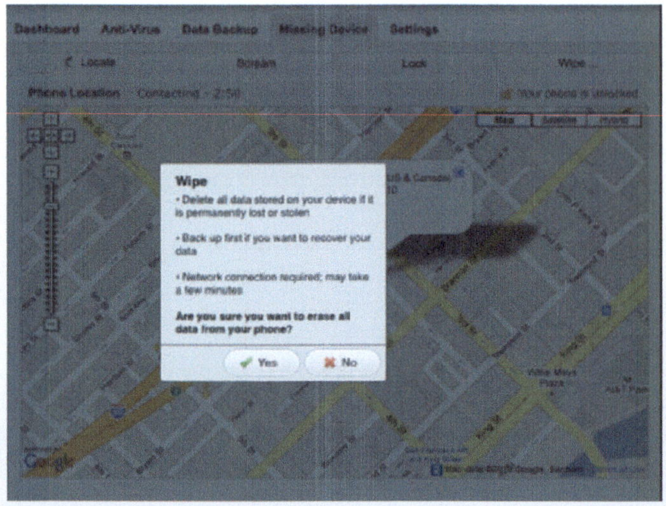

Courtesy of Lookout Mobile Security

FIGURE 5-5
Device tracking software.

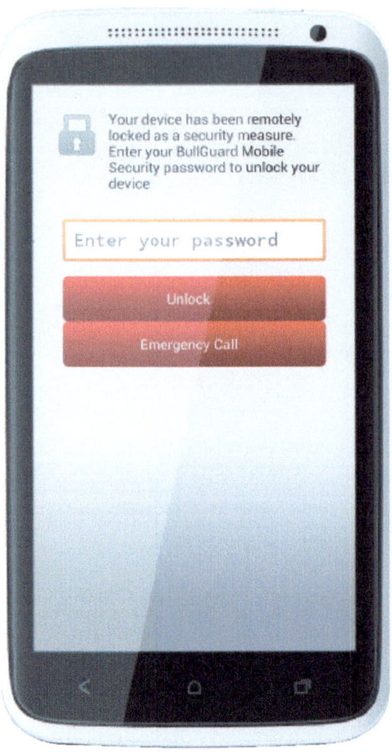

Courtesy Bullguard

software installed is reported lost or stolen, the tracking software sends information about the location of the device, typically determined by GPS or the nearest Wi-Fi network, to the tracking software company on a regular basis when the device is connected to the Internet so that information can be provided to law enforcement agencies to help them recover the device. Some tracking software can even take video or photos of the person using the stolen device (via the device's video camera) to help identify and prosecute the thief.

Most tracking software is available on a subscription basis; to protect itself, most tracking software can also survive operating system reinstallations and hard drive reformats. Some can also display a message on the screen when the device is lost or stolen. This message might be a plea to return the device for a reward or simply a message like "THIS DEVICE IS STOLEN" in a big bright banner on the desktop or lock screen to call attention to the fact that the device is stolen. Another common option is the ability to *remotely lock* the device and display a message that the device is locked and won't function without the appropriate password (see one example in Figure 5-5). A feature included in many device tracking programs is a *kill switch*—a technology that causes the device to self-destruct, as discussed in the How It Works box. A different type of kill switch that federal prosecutors are urging smartphone manufacturers to implement as part of the 2013 *Secure Our Smartphones (SOS) Initiative* is technology that would make all stolen smartphones inoperable, on any network, anywhere in the world, even if the SIM card is removed. This push is due to growing crime—including murder—related to smartphone theft. In fact, one in every three robberies nationwide involves a stolen mobile phone.

Another antitheft tool is the use of *asset tags* on hardware and other expensive assets. These labels usually identify the owner of the asset and are designed to be permanently attached to the asset. Some tags are designed to be indestructible; others are *tamper evident labels* that change their appearance if someone (such as a thief) tries to remove them. For instance, some labels have a printed message hidden underneath the label that is etched into the surface of the device and is exposed when the label is removed. Both of these features alert a potential buyer to the fact that the item is likely stolen.

Additional Precautions for Mobile Users

With the increased use of smartphones and other mobile devices today, securing these devices against theft and unauthorized use is becoming increasingly more important. Businesses today often utilize *mobile device management* (*MDM*) software to manage the various mobile devices used by their employees. For instance, MDM software can control the apps installed or available on a device, or disable the camera while on the premises if cameras are not allowed. In addition, the software typically includes device tracking software to remotely lock down or wipe a lost or stolen phone, display a message on the phone containing instructions for returning the device, display the current location of the device on a map (using GPS coordinates), and/or overrule volume settings to play a loud sound to help the owner locate the phone if it is nearby. Another option is a *wireless tether* system that ties your phone to a key fob in order to sound an alarm and lock the phone if the phone and key fob become further away than the specified allowable distance. However, to avoid losing the device in the first place or to prevent someone from accessing the data stored on the device, other precautions should be used.

MOBILE COMPUTING PRECAUTIONS

- Install and use encryption, antivirus, antispyware, and firewall software.
- Secure computers with boot passwords; set your mobile phone to autolock the screen after a short period of time and require a passcode to unlock it.
- Use only secure Wi-Fi connections and disable Wi-Fi and Bluetooth when they are not needed.
- Never leave usernames, passwords, or other data attached to your computer or inside its carrying case.
- Use a plain carrying case to make a portable computer less conspicuous.
- Keep an eye on your devices at all times, especially when going through airport security.
- Avoid setting your devices on the floor or leaving them in your hotel room; use a cable lock to secure the device to a desk or other object whenever this is unavoidable.
- Back up the data stored on the device regularly, but don't carry the backup media with your device and don't store unencrypted sensitive data on your device.
- Consider installing tracking or kill switch software.

FIGURE 5-6 Common-sense precautions for portable computer and mobile device users.

While on the go, the best antitheft measure is common sense. For example, you should never leave a portable computer or mobile device unattended in a public location (keep it in your line of sight or in physical contact at all times so it cannot be stolen without you noticing). When staying in a hotel, take your computer with you, use a cable lock to secure it to a piece of furniture, or lock it in a hotel safe (many hotel rooms today have room safes large enough to hold a portable computer) when you leave your hotel room for the day. Other sensible precautions include using a plain carrying case to make a portable computer less conspicuous and labeling your portable computer (and other portable devices and hardware that you take with you on the go) with your contact information so a lost or stolen device can be returned to you when it is recovered. One additional possibility for protecting data while on the road is using cloud services to store all data online or on the company server instead of on your device—if no data is stored on the device, then there is no data that can be directly compromised if the device is lost or stolen. In addition, mobile users should disable wireless connections when they are not needed and enable password protection for accessing the device. These precautions are summarized in Figure 5-6.

Proper Hardware Care

Proper care of hardware can help to prevent serious damage to a computer system. The most obvious precaution is to not harm your hardware physically, such as by dropping a device, knocking a piece of hardware off a desk, or jostling a desktop computer's system unit. *Protective cases* (see Figure 5-7) can be used

MOBILE PHONES

MEDIA TABLETS

FIGURE 5-7 Protective cases.

RUGGED LAPTOPS

RUGGED TABLETS

RUGGED PHONES

FIGURE 5-8
Ruggedized devices.

> **TIP**
> Some devices today look conventional but have some rugged features, such as the Sony *Xperia Tablet Z* media tablet and the Kyocera *Hydro* smartphone that can withstand being under 1 meter (about 3 feet) of water for up to 30 minutes.

to help protect portable devices against minor abuse. These cases are usually padded or made from protective material to prevent damage due to occasional bumps and bangs; they typically also have a thin protective layer over the device's display to protect against scratches. Some protective cases are water resistant to protect the device from rain or dust damage. There are also neoprene *laptop sleeves* available to protect portable computers from scratches and other damage when they are carried in a conventional briefcase or bag.

For users who need more protection than a protective case can provide, **ruggedized devices** are available (see Figure 5-8). These devices are designed to withstand much more physical abuse than conventional devices and range from *semirugged* to *ultrarugged*. For instance, semirugged devices typically have a more durable case and are spill-resistant. Rugged and ultrarugged devices go a few steps further—they are designed to withstand falls from three feet or more onto concrete, extreme temperature ranges, wet conditions, and use while being bounced around over rough terrain in a vehicle. Many rugged devices are also cooled without fans to avoid bringing dust into the circuitry; some are designed to be used in bright sunlight and while wearing gloves. Ruggedized devices are used most often by individuals who work out of the office, such as field workers, construction workers, outdoor technicians, military personnel, police officers, and firefighters.

To protect hardware from damage due to power fluctuations, it is important for all users to use a **surge suppressor** (see Figure 5-9); the surge suppressor should be used to connect a computer and other hardware whenever they are plugged into a power outlet. When electrical power spikes occur, the surge suppressor prevents them from harming your devices. For the best protection, surge suppressors should be used with all the powered components that have a wired connection to the computer (such as a monitor or printer). There are small surge suppressors designed for use while on the go, and others designed for business and industrial use.

Users who want their desktop computers to remain powered up when the electricity goes off should use an **uninterruptible power supply (UPS)**, which contains a built-in battery (see Figure 5-9). The length of time that a UPS can power a system depends on the type and

FIGURE 5-9
Surge suppressors and uninterruptible power supplies (UPSs).

SURGE SUPPRESSOR

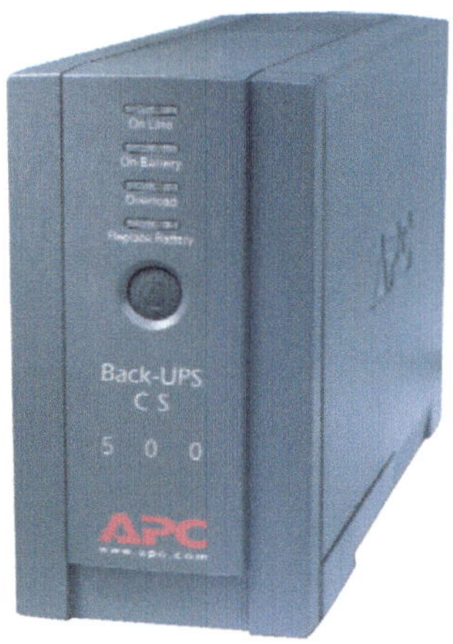

UPS

>**Ruggedized device.** A device (such as a portable computer or mobile phone) that is designed to withstand much more physical abuse than its conventional counterpart. >**Surge suppressor.** A device that protects hardware from damage due to electrical fluctuations. >**Uninterruptible power supply (UPS).** A device containing a built-in battery that provides continuous power to a computer and other connected components when the electricity goes out.

number of devices connected to the UPS, the power capacity of the UPS device (typically measured in watts), and the age of the battery (most UPS batteries last only 3 to 5 years before they need to be replaced). Most UPS devices also protect against power fluctuations. UPSs designed for use by individuals usually provide power for a few minutes to keep the system powered up during short power blips, as well as to allow the user to save open documents and shut down the computer properly in case the electricity remains off. Industrial-level UPSs typically run for a significantly longer amount of time (such as a few hours), but not long enough to power a facility during an extended power outage such as those that happen periodically in some parts of the United States due to winter storms, summer rotating blackouts, and other factors. To provide longer-term power during extended power outages, as well as to provide continuous power to facilities (such as hospitals, nuclear power plants, and business data centers) that cannot afford to be without power for any period of time, *generators* can be used.

TIP

Use surge suppressors to protect all of your sensitive electronics, such as televisions and gaming consoles in addition to computers, from electrical fluctuations.

Dust, heat, static electricity, and moisture can also be dangerous to hardware, so be sure not to place your devices in direct sunlight or in a dusty area. Small handheld vacuums made for electrical equipment can be used periodically to remove the dust from the keyboard and from inside the system unit of a computer, but be very careful when vacuuming inside the system unit. Also, be sure the system unit has plenty of ventilation, especially around the fan vents. To help reduce the amount of dust that is drawn into the fan vents, raise your desktop computer several inches off the floor. You should also avoid placing a portable computer on a soft surface, such as a couch or blanket, to help prevent overheating (*notebook cooling stands* can be used to provide air circulation when a soft surface must be used). To prevent static electricity from damaging the inside of your computer when installing a new expansion card, RAM, or other internal device, turn off the power to the computer and unplug the power cord from the computer before removing the cover from the system unit. Wearing an antistatic wristband is an additional good precaution. Unless your computer is ruggedized (like the one shown in Figure 5-10), do not get it wet or otherwise expose it to adverse conditions. Be especially careful with mobile phones and other mobile devices when you are near water (such as a swimming pool, lake, or large puddle) so you do not drop them into the water (more than 50% of the phones received by one data recovery firm are water damaged).

FIGURE 5-10

Proper hardware care. Unless your computer is ruggedized (such as the one shown here), keep it out of the heat, cold, rain, water, and other adverse conditions.

Courtesy General Dynamics Itronix

Both internal and external magnetic hard drives also need to be protected against jostling or other excess motion that can result in a *head crash*, which occurs when a hard drive's read/write heads actually touch the surface of a hard disk. Unless your portable computer contains a solid-state drive instead of a magnetic hard drive, it is a good idea to turn off the computer, hibernate it, or put it into standby mode before moving it because magnetic hard drives are more vulnerable to damage while they are spinning. In addition, storage media—such as flash memory cards, hard drives, CDs, and DVDs—are all sensitive storage media that work well over time, as long as appropriate care is used. Don't remove a USB storage device (such as a USB flash drive or USB hard drive) when it is being accessed—use the *Safely Remove Hardware and Eject Media* icon in the system tray on a Windows computer to stop the device before unplugging it to avoid data loss and damage to the device. Keep CDs and DVDs in their protective *jewel cases* and handle them carefully to prevent fingerprints and scratches on the data sides of the discs (usually the bottom, unprinted side on a single-sided disc). A *screen protector* (a thin plastic film that covers the display screen of a smartphone or other mobile device) can be used to protect the displays of pen-based and touch devices.

For more tips on how to protect your desktop or portable computer, see the Technology and You box. Many of these tips apply to smartphones, media tablets, and other mobile devices as well.

TECHNOLOGY AND YOU

Protecting Your PC

All computer users should take specific actions to protect their computers. In this world of viruses, worms, hackers, spyware, and "buggy" (error-prone) software, it pays to be cautious. Although safeguards have been covered in detail throughout this book, some specific precautionary steps all computer users should follow are summarized in this box.

Step 1: Protect your hardware.
Be sure to plug all components of your computer system (such as the system unit, monitor, printer, and scanner) into a surge suppressor. Be careful not to bump or move the computer when it is on. Don't spill food or drink onto the keyboard or any other piece of hardware. Store your flash memory cards and CDs properly. If you need to work inside the system unit, turn off the computer and unplug it before touching any component inside the system unit. When taking a portable computer on the road, never leave it unattended, and be careful not to drop or lose it.

Step 2: Install and use security software.
Install a good security program and set it up to scan your system on a continual basis, including checking all files and e-mail messages before they are downloaded to your computer. To detect the newest viruses and types of malware, keep your security program up to date (have it automatically check for and install updates) and use a personal two-way firewall program to protect your computer from unauthorized access via the Internet, as well as to detect any attempts by spyware to send data from your computer to another party. For additional protection, enable file sharing only for files and folders that really need to be accessed by other users. Run an antispyware program—such as Ad-Aware or Spybot Search & Destroy—on a regular basis to detect and remove spyware.

Step 3: Back up regularly.
Once you have a new computer set up with all programs installed and the menus and other settings the way you like them, create a full backup so the computer can be restored to that configuration in case of a major problem with your computer or hard drive. Be sure also to back up your data files on a regular basis. Depending on how important your documents are, you may want to back up all of your data every night, or copy each document to a removable storage medium after each major revision. If you use local (instead of Web-based) e-mail, periodically back up the folder containing your e-mail, such as the *Outlook.pst* file used to store Microsoft Outlook mail. To facilitate data backup, keep your data organized using folders (such as storing all data files in a main folder called "Data"). For an even higher level of security, use *continuous data protection* (*CDP*) in conjunction with an external hard drive or an online backup service (see the iDrive CDP program in the accompanying illustration)—if your main hard drive ever becomes unstable and needs to be reformatted or replaced, you can restore your computer using the backup. If an online backup service is not used, backup media should be stored in a location that is different from the location where your computer is stored, such as in a different building or in a fire-resistant safe.

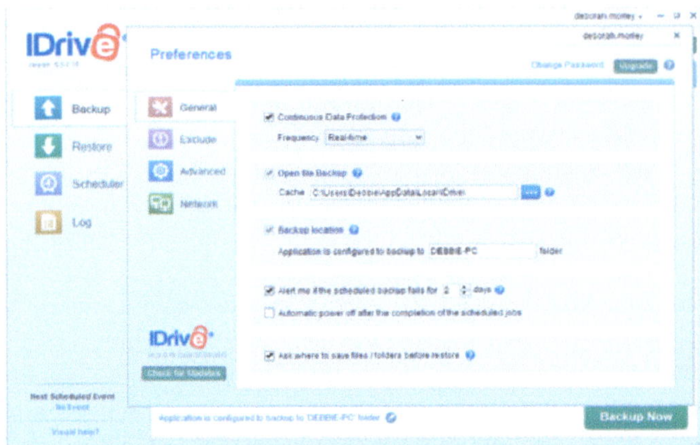

Continuous data protection (CDP) protects your data on an ongoing basis.

Step 4: Update your operating system, browser, and e-mail program regularly.
Most companies that produce operating systems, Web browsers, or e-mail programs regularly post updates and patches—small programs that take care of software-specific problems or bugs, such as security holes—on their Web sites regularly. Some programs include an option within the program to check online for updates; for other programs, you will need to go to each manufacturer's Web site directly to check for any critical or recommended updates. For any programs—such as Windows and most antivirus and firewall programs—that have the option to check for updates automatically, enable that option.

Step 5: Test your system for vulnerabilities.
There are several free tests available through Web sites to see if your computer's ports are accessible to hackers or if your computer is infected with a virus or spyware. These tests, such as the one on the Symantec Web site shown in Figure 4-10 in Chapter 4 or the ShieldsUP! test available on the Gibson Research Web site, should be run to check for any remaining vulnerabilities once you believe your antivirus software, firewall, and any other protective components you are using are set up correctly.

Backups and Disaster Recovery Plans

As mentioned in Chapter 1, creating a *backup* means making a duplicate copy of important files so that when a problem occurs (such as a hard drive failure or a stolen computer), you can restore those files using the backup copy. Data to be backed up includes company files, personal documents, photos, e-mail messages, and any other files that are important and the owner of the files would miss if they were lost. Backups can be performed for personal computers, servers, mobile phones, and other devices that contain important data. Backing up a smartphone often involves syncing the data to a cloud account or a computer.

Businesses should make backups of at least all new data on a regular basis (at least once per day) and include data located on both company computers and employer-issued smartphones. Individuals should make backups of important documents as they are created and back up the rest of their data periodically. Businesses and individuals that utilize cloud computing should also back up important data stored online.

After a backup is performed, the backup media used needs to be secured so that it will be intact when it is needed. If backup media is stored in-house, it should be placed in a fire-resistant safe; however, it is even better to store backup media in a different physical location or in the cloud. For instance, many businesses today use *online backup services* or *data storage companies* that store their backup media at a secure remote location; businesses can request their backups stored at a data storage facility be returned whenever they are needed. To secure the data on the backup media while it is in transit and being stored, as well as data stored in the cloud, the data should be encrypted.

For an even higher level of security than a scheduled backup, *continuous data protection* (*CDP*) can be used. A CDP backup system backs up data in real time as it changes so that data can be recovered from any point in time (even just a few minutes ago) with no data loss, and recovery can be as fast as five minutes after a failure. Although expensive when used with large quantities of data, it is one of the best ways to ensure that company data is protected. In addition to business data, CDP is beginning to be used by individuals to safeguard their data (one online CDP backup service is shown in the Technology and You box). For extra protection against data loss due to a natural disaster or other geographic-specific risk, businesses should use cloud providers that are in a physical location that is different from the company's location.

To supplement backup procedures, businesses and other organizations should have a **disaster recovery plan** (also called a *business continuity* plan)—a plan that spells out what

ASK THE EXPERT

Courtesy of DriveSavers Data Recovery www.drivesavers.com

Mike Cobb, Director of Engineering, DriveSavers Data Recovery

Of the hard drives sent to you for recovery, what is the most common type of problem you see and is there a way that problem can be prevented?

We often receive hard drives that have severe media damage. That means that the read/write heads have come in contact with the platters and scraped off portions of the surface and data. This often occurs because the hard drive was left powered on after the problem occurred. The platters inside a drive spin at high speed, so a great deal of damage can occur in a very short period of time as the heads bounce around and create more debris. Eventually the damage becomes too great for even a professional data recovery company to overcome.

The best rule of thumb to prevent the loss of critical data is to back up religiously and to verify that the backup is really backing up the critical files. In addition, if a hard drive exhibits any sign of failure including unusual noises (such as repetitive clicking or grinding) and if the data is irreplaceable and has not been backed up recently, the best solution is to immediately shut down the computer and then seek the assistance of a professional data recovery company like DriveSavers.

TIP

Be sure backup generators and servers are located in an appropriate location; for example, they should not be in a basement or in any locations prone to flooding. As an extra precaution, consider moving primary servers or installing remote backup servers in regions of the country that don't have the same risk factors as the company's location.

>**Disaster recovery plan.** A written plan that describes the steps a company will take following the occurrence of a disaster.

TIP

Be sure to also back up important nonelectronic documents in your life, such as birth certificates, tax returns, passports, and so forth, by making copies of them and storing the copies in a safe place.

TIP

If you use Web mail and don't automatically download new messages to your computer, be sure to back up your Web mail frequently (such as by using *Gmail Backup* if you are a Gmail user) to avoid losing your mail if the Web mail service is disrupted.

the organization will do to prepare for and recover from a disruptive event, such as a fire, natural disaster, terrorist attack, power outage, or computer failure. Disaster recovery plans should include information about who will be in charge immediately after the disaster has occurred, what alternate facilities and equipment (including computers and mobile devices) can be used, where backup media is located, the priority of getting each operation back online, disaster insurance coverage information, emergency communications methods, and so forth. If a *hot site*—an alternate location equipped with the computers, cabling, desks, and other equipment necessary to keep a business's operations going—is to be used following a major disaster, it should be set up ahead of time, and information about the hot site should be included in the disaster recovery plan. Businesses that host their e-mail on site should also consider making arrangements with an *emergency mail system provider* to act as a temporary mail server if the company mail server is not functioning. Copies of the disaster recovery plan should be located off site, such as at an appropriate employee's house or at the office of an associated organization located in a different city.

It is important to realize that disaster recovery planning isn't just for large businesses. In fact, disasters such as a fire or computer malfunction can cause a small company to go out of business if its data is not backed up. Measures as straightforward as backing up data daily and storing the backups in a fire-resistant safe at the owner's house with a plan regarding how that data can be quickly reinstated on a new system or otherwise used for business continuity can go a long way in protecting a small business. Companies that are evaluating cloud computing services should find out what types of outages are to be expected (such as for regular maintenance) and what type of advance notice will be sent regarding these outages, as well as what types of disaster recovery services (such as switching to alternate servers if the main servers go down) are available.

The importance of a good disaster recovery plan was made obvious following the collapse of the World Trade Center Twin Towers in 2001. Minutes after the first airplane hit the towers, corporate executives, disaster recovery firms, and backup storage companies began arranging for employees and backup data to be moved to alternate sites. Employees at the data storage company Recall Corporation spent the day of the attack gathering backup tapes belonging to clients located in and near the attacks, using barcode readers to locate the needed 30,000 tapes out of the 2 million in their secure storage facility. Bond trader Cantor Fitzgerald, which lost 700 employees and all the equipment and data located in its WTC offices, relocated to a prearranged hot site where employees received backup tapes the day after the attack, and it was able to begin trading the next morning. Although Cantor Fitzgerald—like the other organizations and businesses located in the WTC—suffered enormous human loss, good disaster recovery planning enabled Cantor Fitzgerald to restore the records containing client accounts and portfolios completely, avoiding an additional economic disaster related to this tragedy.

SOFTWARE PIRACY AND DIGITAL COUNTERFEITING

TIP

The piracy of and ethical use of digital music and movies are discussed in detail in Chapter 6.

Instead of stealing an existing computer program, object, or other valuable that belongs to someone else, *software piracy* and *digital counterfeiting* involve creating duplicates of these items, and then selling them or using them as authentic items.

Software Piracy

Software piracy, the unauthorized copying of a computer program, is illegal in the United States and many other—but not all—countries. Because of the ease with which computers can create exact copies of a software program, software piracy is a widespread problem.

>**Software piracy.** The unauthorized copying of a computer program.

According to a recent study by research firm IDC, at least one-third of all software is counterfeit. In addition, 78% of pirated software has spyware attached to it and consumers visiting Web sites to obtain (typically stolen) activation keys for counterfeit software have a 36% chance of being infected with malware in the process. The study also estimates that the total annual cost to businesses of dealing with malware from counterfeit software exceeds $110 billion, and consumers worldwide will waste 1.5 billion hours each year dealing with the malware resulting from countefeit software.

Software piracy can take many forms, including individuals making illegal copies of programs to give to friends, businesses installing software on more computers than permitted in the program's *end-user license agreement* or *EULA* (see Figure 5-11), computer retailers installing unlicensed copies of software on computers sold to consumers, and large-scale operations in which the software and its packaging are illegally duplicated and then sold as supposedly legitimate products. Pirated software—as well as pirated music CDs and movie DVDs—are commonly offered for sale at online auctions; they can also be downloaded from some Web sites and peer-to-peer file sharing services. Creating and distributing pirated copies of any type of *intellectual property* (such as software, music, e-books, and movies) is illegal. Intellectual property is discussed in more detail in Chapter 6.

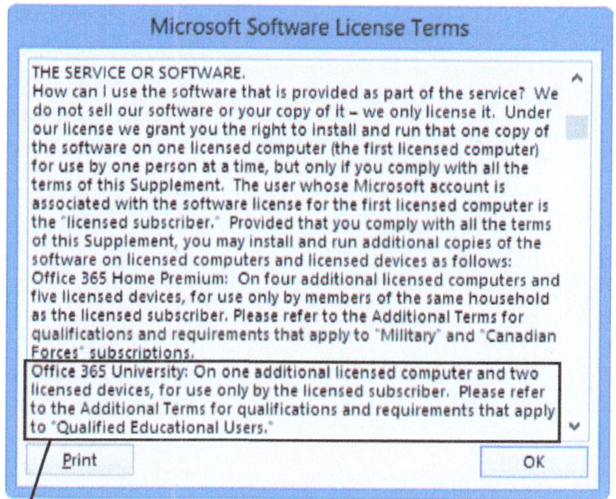

This software can be installed on one primary computer, one additional computer, and two additional devices to be used by a single user.

FIGURE 5-11
An end-user license agreement (EULA). Specifies the number of computers on which the software can be installed and other restrictions for use.

Digital Counterfeiting

The availability of high-quality, full-color imaging products (such as scanners, color printers, and color copiers) has made **digital counterfeiting**—creating counterfeit copies of items (such as currency and other printed resources) using computers and other types of digital equipment—easier and less costly than in the recent past. The U.S. Secret Service estimates that more than 60% of all counterfeit money today is produced digitally—up from 1% in 1996.

With digital counterfeiting, the bill (or other item to be counterfeited) is either color-copied or it is scanned into a computer and then printed. In addition to counterfeiting currency, other items that are digitally counterfeited include fake business checks, credit cards, printed collectibles (such as baseball cards or celebrity autographs), and fake identification papers (such as corporate IDs, driver's licenses, passports, and visas)—see Figure 5-12.

Counterfeiting is illegal in the United States and is taken very seriously. For creating or knowingly circulating counterfeit currency, for instance, offenders can face up to 15 years in prison for each offense. In spite of the risk of prosecution, counterfeiting of U.S. currency and other documents is a growing problem both in the United States and in other countries. Although the majority of counterfeit currency is produced by serious criminals (such as organized crime, gangs, and terrorist organizations), the Secret Service has seen an increase in counterfeiting among high school and college students. This is attributed primarily to the ease of creating counterfeit bills—although not necessarily high-quality counterfeit bills—using digital technology. Because the paper used with real U.S. bills is very expensive and cannot legally be made by paper mills for any other purpose and because U.S. bills contain a number of other characteristics that are difficult to reproduce accurately, as discussed in more

FIGURE 5-12
Digitally counterfeited documents.

>**Digital counterfeiting.** The use of computers or other types of digital equipment to make illegal copies of currency, checks, collectibles, and other items.

detail shortly, the majority of the counterfeit money made by amateurs is easily detectable. However, counterfeit bills made by bleaching genuine small denomination bills and printing higher denominations on them that don't include special security features are harder to detect because the paper used is authentic.

Protecting Against Software Piracy and Digital Counterfeiting

Software piracy and digital counterfeiting affect individuals, as well as businesses and the government. For instance, some software companies charge higher prices and have less money available for research and development because of the losses from software pirates, which ultimately hurts law-abiding consumers. In addition, individuals and businesses that unknowingly accept counterfeit currency lose the face value of that currency if it is identified as counterfeit while it is in their possession, and they risk legal issues if they knowingly pass the counterfeit bills on to others. Some tools currently being used to curb software piracy and digital counterfeiting are discussed next.

Software Antipiracy Tools

One tool the software industry is using in an attempt to prevent software piracy is education. By educating businesses and consumers about the legal use of software and the possible negative consequences associated with breaking antipiracy laws, the industry hopes to reduce the use of illegal software. To counteract piracy performed because of time or convenience issues, many software companies offer consumers the option of downloading software and, therefore, giving them a legal option for obtaining software that is as fast and convenient as downloading a pirated version. Some software manufacturers have launched extensive public relations campaigns—such as including information on their Web sites, in product information, and in ads—to inform consumers what software piracy is, and why they should not commit it or buy pirated software.

Another antipiracy tool is requiring a unique activation code (often called a *registration code*, an *activation key*, or a *product key*) before the software can be installed (for commercial software) or before certain key features of a program are unlocked (for shareware or demo software). Typically the activation code is included in the product packaging (for software purchased on CD or DVD) or is displayed on the screen or sent to the user via e-mail once payment is made (for downloaded software). A related tool is checking the validity of a software installation before upgrades or other resources related to the program can be accessed. For instance, Microsoft checks a user's Windows installation before the user is allowed to download software from Microsoft's Web site (such as templates or updates for Microsoft Office)—if their operating system is identified as invalid, users cannot download the resources. The goal of these techniques is to make pirated software unusable enough so that individuals will buy the licensed software.

Other antipiracy techniques used by software companies include watching online auction sites and requesting the removal of suspicious items, as well as buying pirated copies of software via Web sites and then filing lawsuits against the sellers. The increase in actions against individuals who illegally sell or share software (and other types of digital content, such as music and movies) may also help reduce piracy and encourage individuals to obtain legal copies of these products. The inclusion of malware in counterfeit software may also help with detection. For example, Microsoft recently settled 3,265 software piracy cases worldwide—the majority of the cases were reported to Microsoft by customers unhappy with the included malware or because the software didn't work correctly. In addition, Microsoft continually finds and requests the removal of URLs that are related to the distribution of pirated software from search sites.

One new option for software vendors is incorporating code into their programs that is designed to inform the vendor when pirated copies of its software are being used or when its software is being used in another manner that violates the terms of the software license. For instance, commercial software that contains the newest version of V.i Labs *CodeArmor Intelligence* software is designed to detect and report products in use that have been tampered with (such as products whose licensing features have been disabled and then resold as legitimate products), as well as products that are being used with more computers than allowed by the software license. Once piracy is detected, information about the infringement is sent to the software vendor's piracy dashboard. This information includes identifying data about the user of the pirated software (such as the business's domain name or IP address and a link to its location on Google Maps—see Figure 5-13) that can be used to help the vendor contact the business to give them the opportunity to come into license compliance before pursuing any legal actions. It also provides the vendor with useful data about the overall state of piracy of their products in order to help the company make appropriate business decisions regarding the distribution channels and the safeguards used with its products.

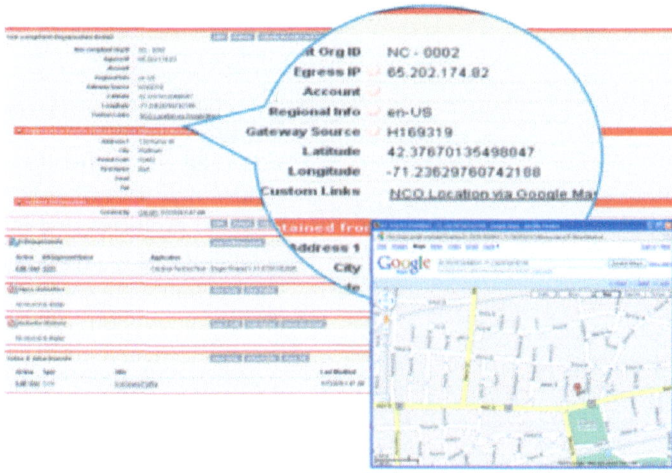

Courtesy Vi Labs; Google screenshot © Google Inc. and used with permission.

FIGURE 5-13
Antipiracy software.

Digital Counterfeiting Prevention

To prevent the counterfeiting of U.S. currency, the Treasury Department releases new currency designs every 7 to 10 years. These new designs (such as the new $100 bill released in 2013 and shown in Figure 5-14) contain features (such as *microprinting, watermarks*, a *security thread*, a *security ribbon, color-shifting ink,* and *raised printing*) that make the new currency much more difficult to duplicate than older currency. Because the watermarks, security thread, and security ribbon are embedded in the paper, counterfeiters are unable to duplicate those features when creating counterfeit bills either from scratch or by bleaching the ink out of existing lower-denomination bills and reprinting them with higher denominations. Consequently, counterfeit copies of bills using the new designs are easy to detect just by holding them up to the light and looking for the proper watermark, security thread, or security ribbon, or by feeling for the raised printing. In addition, hardware and software companies that have adopted the *counterfeit deterrence system* (*CDS*) developed by the *Central Bank Counterfeit Deterrence Group* (*CBCDG*) help to deter the use of digital counterfeiting of currency. For instance, some hardware and software will not allow images of currency to be printed and many color copiers print invisible codes on copied documents, making counterfeit money copied on those machines traceable.

Prevention measures for the counterfeiting of other types of documents—such as checks and identification cards—include using RFID tags, *digital watermarks*, and other difficult-to-reproduce content. As discussed in more detail in Chapter 6, a digital watermark is a subtle alteration that is not noticeable when the work is viewed or played but that can be read using special software to authenticate or identify the owner of the item. Finally, educating consumers about how the appearance of fake products differs from that of authentic products is a vital step in the ongoing battle against counterfeiting.

TIP

The new $100 bill also includes a large gold *100* on the back to help visually-impaired individuals identify the denomination.

Photo courtesy of U.S. Department of the Treasury

FIGURE 5-14
Anticounterfeiting measures used with U.S. currency.

WHY BE CONCERNED ABOUT INFORMATION PRIVACY?

Privacy is usually defined as the state of being concealed or free from unauthorized intrusion. The term **information privacy** refers to the rights of individuals and companies to control how information about them is collected and used. The problem of how to protect personal privacy—that is, how to keep personal information private—existed long before computers entered the picture. For example, sealing wax and unique signet rings were used centuries ago to seal letters, wills, and other personal documents to guard against their content being revealed to unauthorized individuals, as well as to alert the recipient if such an intrusion occurred while the document was in transit. But today's computers, with their ability to store, duplicate, and manipulate large quantities of data—combined with the fact that databases containing our personal information can be accessed and shared via the Internet—have added a new twist to the issue of personal privacy. Another new twist is the increased ability of *electronic surveillance* tools used by some government and law enforcement agencies.

As discussed in Chapters 3 and 4, one concern of many individuals is the privacy of their Web site activities and e-mail messages. Cookies and spyware are possible privacy risks, and e-mail and other documents can be read if intercepted by another individual during transit unless they are encrypted. For businesses and employees, there is the additional issue of whether or not Web activities, e-mail, and instant messages sent through a company network are private. In addition, businesses need to make sure they comply with privacy laws regarding the protection and the security of the private information they store on their servers. Recently, there has been an unprecedented number of high-profile data breaches—some via hacking and other network intrusions discussed in Chapter 4, and others due to lost or stolen hardware, or carelessness with papers or storage media containing Social Security numbers or other sensitive data. Because every data breach occurring today is a risk to information privacy, protecting the data stored in databases today is an important concern for everyone. Other privacy concerns are *spam* and other marketing activities, electronic surveillance, and *electronic monitoring*. These concerns, along with precautions that can be taken to safeguard information privacy, are discussed throughout the remainder of this chapter.

ASK THE EXPERT

Courtesy of EFF

Jillian York, Director for International Freedom of Expression, Electronic Frontier Foundation (EFF)

What are the biggest Internet-related privacy risks for individuals today?

With Internet use on the rise globally, the latest threats to privacy come both from companies looking to capitalize on user data and from governments seeking to track citizens' conversations and movements. But although Internet users have good reason to be concerned about the privacy practices of corporations like Google, I believe the biggest threat facing them today is surveillance by government agencies, such as the United States' National Security Agency (NSA). The mass surveillance conducted by such agencies means that all of us are being spied on, whether or not we're suspected of committing a crime. It is all too easy for governments to abuse this type of power. Even if you think you have nothing to hide, your privacy is being invaded on a daily basis by governments and by big business. To try to protect yourself, minimize the amount of personal data stored on your devices, encrypt your data and use secure passwords, and use privacy-enhancing browsing tools and settings.

>**Privacy.** The state of being concealed or free from unauthorized intrusion. >**Information privacy.** The rights of individuals and companies to control how information about them is collected and used.

DATABASES, ELECTRONIC PROFILING, SPAM, AND OTHER MARKETING ACTIVITIES

There are marketing activities that can be considered privacy risks or, at least, a potential invasion of privacy. These include *databases, electronic profiling*, and *spam*.

Databases and Electronic Profiling

Information about individuals can be located in many different databases. For example, most educational institutions have databases containing student information, most organizations use an employee database to hold employee information, and most physicians and health insurance providers maintain databases containing individuals' medical information. If these databases are adequately protected from hackers and other unauthorized individuals and if the data is not transported on a portable computer or other device that may be vulnerable to loss or theft, then these databases do not pose a significant privacy concern to consumers because the information can rarely be shared without the individuals' permission. However, the data stored in these types of databases is not always sufficiently protected and has been breached quite often in the past. Consequently, these databases, along with two other types of databases—*marketing databases* and *government databases*—that are typically associated with a higher risk of personal privacy violations and are discussed next, are of growing concern to privacy advocates.

Marketing databases contain marketing and demographic data about people, such as where they live and what products they buy. This information is used for marketing purposes, such as sending advertisements that fit each individual's interests (via regular mail or e-mail) or trying to sign people up over the phone for some type of service. Virtually anytime you provide information about yourself online or offline—for example, when you subscribe to a magazine, fill out a sweepstakes entry or product registration card, or buy a product or service using a credit card—there is a good chance that the information will find its way into a marketing database.

> **TIP**
> Judges and police investigators made 37,196 requests to Microsoft for end-user data in the first half of 2013 alone.

Marketing databases are also used in conjunction with Web activities, such as social media activity and searches performed via some personalized search services. For instance, the data stored on Facebook, MySpace, Google+, and other social networking sites can be gathered and used for advertising purposes by marketing companies, and the activities of users of personalized search services (where users log in to use the service) can be tracked and that data can be used for marketing purposes. And Google, with its vast array of services that collect enormous amounts of data about individuals, worries many privacy advocates. For instance, Google may have data stored about your search history (Google search site), browsing history (Google Chrome), e-mail (Gmail), appointments (Google Calendar), telephone calls (Google Voice), photos (Picasa Web Albums), shopping history (Google Checkout), and friends and activities (Google+). While Google allows users to *opt out* of collecting some data (such as by not signing into a service) and states that the data stored on separate servers is not combined, the vast amount of collected data is a concern to some.

> **TIP**
> To download a copy of your data stored within Google products, use the *Google Takeout* service.

Other emerging privacy concerns center on location-based services and reward apps. Location-based services, such as Foursquare, use the GPS information from your smartphone to provide services such as enabling you to meet up with friends who are close to your current location or allowing you to *check in* to the businesses that you frequent to share your location with others or participate in marketing activities. For example, reward apps, such as shopkick, offer you rewards or discounts for checking into participating businesses. While

>**Marketing database.** A collection of data about people that is stored in a large database and used for marketing purposes.

popular with many individuals, there is concern about location information being used inappropriately (such as by stalkers and home burglars), as well as if and for how long location data is stored. In addition, some of these apps (such as Foursquare) can tie into other social networks, such as Facebook or Twitter, so your friends on those social networks can access your location information even if they are not your friend on the location app.

Information about individuals is also available in **government databases**. Some information, such as Social Security earnings and income tax returns, is confidential and can legally be seen only by authorized individuals. Other information—such as birth records, marriage certificates, and divorce information, as well as property purchases, assessments, liens, and tax values—is available to the public, including to the marketing companies that specialize in creating marketing databases. One emerging government database application is the creation of a *national ID system* that links driver's license databases across the country. Although controversial, this system is mandated by the *Real ID Act* that was passed in 2005, which also requires states to meet new federal standards for driver's licenses and other identification cards (such as the inclusion of a barcode or other machine-readable technology that can be used in conjunction with the ID database). The emerging *Federal Services Data Hub* database that will be used to connect healthcare insurance exchanges with numerous federal databases containing Social Security, IRS, and other personal data of Americans in order to share data has also been controversial due to security and privacy concerns.

In the past, the data about any one individual was stored in a variety of separate locations, such as at different government agencies, individual retail stores, the person's bank and credit card companies, and so forth. Because it would be extremely time consuming to locate all the information about one person from all these different places, there was a fairly high level of information privacy. Today, however, most of an individual's data is stored on computers that can communicate with each other, and some *database search services* are available online for free or for a fee (see some examples in Figure 5-15). Although often

FIGURE 5-15

A variety of searchable databases are available via the Internet.

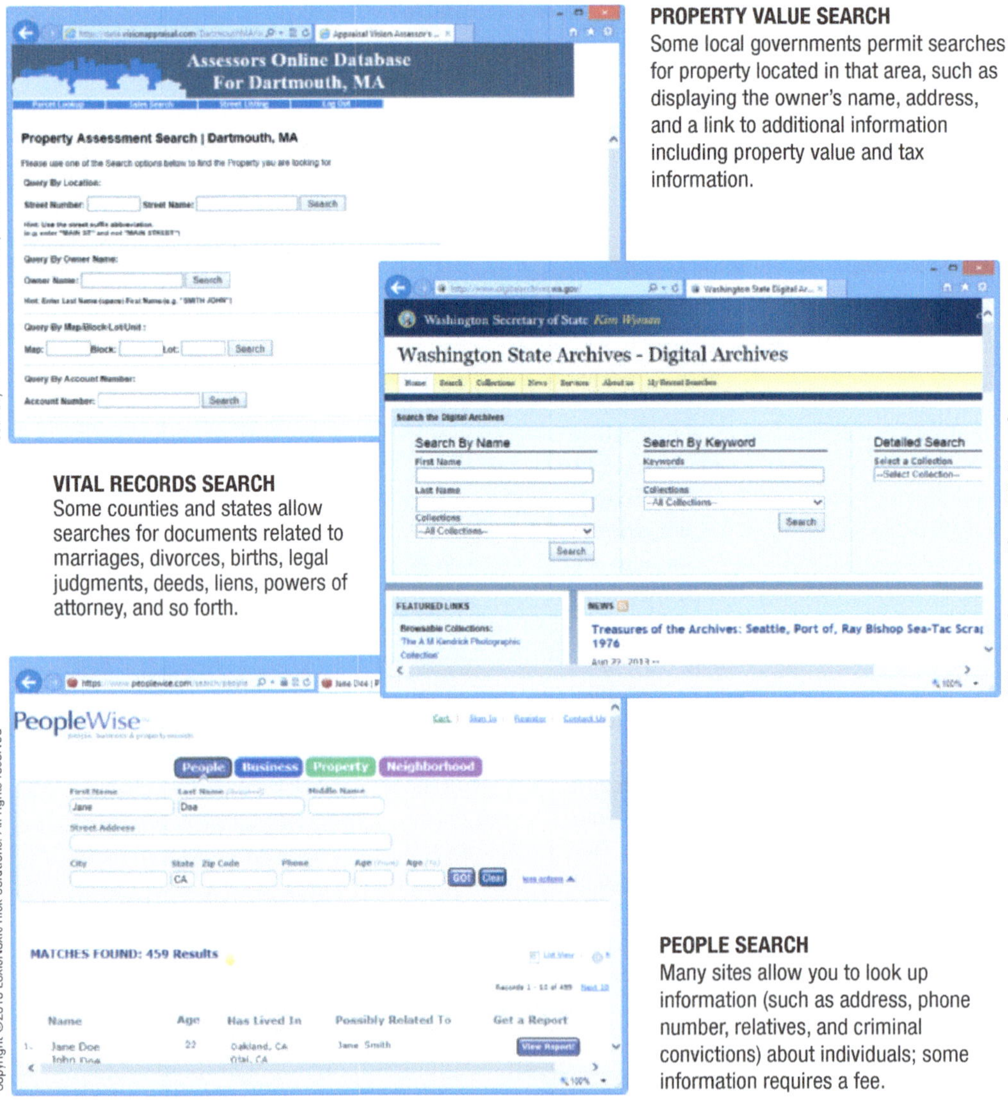

PROPERTY VALUE SEARCH
Some local governments permit searches for property located in that area, such as displaying the owner's name, address, and a link to additional information including property value and tax information.

VITAL RECORDS SEARCH
Some counties and states allow searches for documents related to marriages, divorces, births, legal judgments, deeds, liens, powers of attorney, and so forth.

PEOPLE SEARCH
Many sites allow you to look up information (such as address, phone number, relatives, and criminal convictions) about individuals; some information requires a fee.

>**Government database.** A collection of data about people that is collected and maintained by the government.

When you make an electronic transaction, information about who you are and what you buy is recorded, usually in a database.

Databases containing the identities of people and what they buy are sold to marketing companies.

The marketing companies add the new data to their marketing databases; they can then reorganize the data in ways that might be valuable to other companies.

The marketing companies create lists of individuals matching the specific needs of companies; the companies buy the lists for their own marketing purposes.

FIGURE 5-16
How electronic profiling might work.

this ability to search online databases is an advantage—such as checking the background of a potential employee or looking up a misplaced phone number—it does raise privacy concerns. In response to the increased occurrence of identity theft (discussed in detail in Chapter 4), some local governments have removed birth and death information from their available online database records.

Collecting in-depth information about an individual is known as **electronic profiling**. Marketing companies often use data acquired from a variety of sources—such as from product and service purchases that are tied to personally identifiable information, as well as from public information like property values, vehicle registrations, births, marriages, and deaths—to create electronic profiles of individuals for marketing purposes. Electronic profiles are generally designed to provide specific information and can include an individual's name, current and previous addresses, telephone number, marital status, number and age of children, spending habits, and product preferences. The information retrieved from electronic profiles is then sold to companies upon request to be used for marketing purposes (see Figure 5-16). For example, one company might request a list of all individuals in a particular state whose street addresses are considered to be in an affluent area and who buy baby products. Another company might request a list of all SUV owners in a particular city who have not purchased a car in five years. Still another company may want a list of business travelers who fly to the East Coast frequently.

Most businesses and Web sites that collect personal information have a **privacy policy** (see the Facebook privacy policy in Figure 5-17) that discloses how the personal information you provide will be used. As long as their actions do not violate their privacy policy, it is legal for businesses to sell the personal data that they collect. There are some

FIGURE 5-17
Privacy policies. Web site privacy policies explain how your personal information might be used.

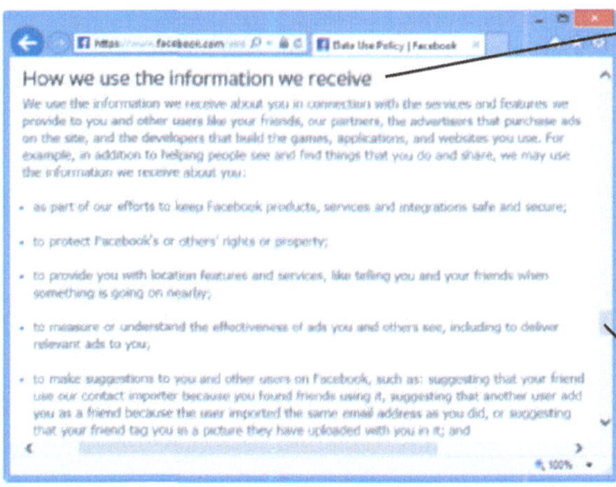

>**Electronic profiling.** Using electronic means to collect a variety of in-depth information about an individual, such as name, address, income, and buying habits. >**Privacy policy.** A policy, commonly posted on a company's Web site, that explains how personal information provided to that company will be used.

problems with privacy policies, however, such as the fact that they are sometimes difficult to decipher and the reality that most people do not take the time to read them before using a site. In addition, many businesses periodically change their privacy policies without warning, requiring consumers to reread privacy policies frequently or risk their personal information being used in a manner that they did not agree to when the information was initially provided. Some companies notify customers by e-mail when their privacy policies change but, more commonly, they expect customers to check the current policy periodically and notify the business if any new actions are objectionable.

Spam and Other Marketing Activities

Spam refers to unsolicited e-mail sent to a large group of individuals at one time. The electronic equivalent of junk mail (see Figure 5-18), spam is most often used to sell products or services to individuals. Spam is also used in phishing schemes and other dot cons and is sent frequently via botnets, as discussed in Chapter 4 (the text message spam shown in Figure 5-18 is an example of a phishing spam message). A great deal of spam involves health-related products (such as medicine or weight loss systems), counterfeit products (such as watches and medicine), pornography, and new—and often fraudulent—business opportunities and stock deals. Spam can also be generated by individuals forwarding e-mail messages they receive (such as jokes, recipes, or notices of possible new privacy or health concerns) to everyone in their address books. In addition to spam, most individuals receive marketing e-mails either from companies they directly provided with their e-mail addresses or from other companies that acquired their e-mail addresses from a third party to whom that information was provided (such as from a partner site or via a purchased mailing list). While these latter types of marketing e-mail messages do not technically fit the definition of spam because they were permission-based, many individuals consider them to be spam. Spam can also be sent via IM (called *spim*); via text message (called *mobile phone spam* or *SMS spam*); to Facebook, MySpace, Google+, and Twitter pages and via other social networking communications methods; via phone calls; and to fax machines.

FIGURE 5-18
Examples of spam.

E-MAIL SPAM

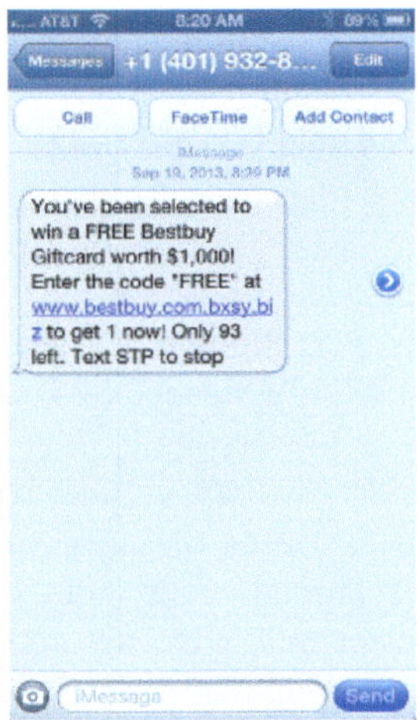

TEXT MESSAGE SPAM

While e-mail spam is decreasing as a result of better *spam filters* and other protections (discussed shortly), it is still a problem (Kasperkey Labs recently estimated that more about 72% of all e-mail messages are now spam). At best, spam is an annoyance to recipients and can slow down a mail server's delivery of important messages. At worst, spam can disable a mail network completely, or it can cause recipients to miss or lose important e-mail messages because those messages have been caught in a spam filter or were accidentally deleted by the recipient while he or she was deleting a large number of spam e-mail messages. Most Internet users spend several minutes each day dealing with spam, making spam very expensive for businesses in terms of lost productivity, consumption of communications bandwidth, and drain of technical support. Spam sent to a mobile phone (either via text message or e-mail) is also expensive for end users that have a limited data or text message allowance.

TIP

According to the Pew Internet & American Life Project, 69% of individuals who use text messaging on their mobile phones receive spam—25% said they face problems with spam texts at least weekly.

>**Spam.** Unsolicited, bulk e-mail sent over the Internet.

One of the most common ways of getting on a spam mailing list is by having your e-mail address entered into a marketing database, which can happen when you sign up for a free online service or use your e-mail address to register a product or make an online purchase. Spammers also use software to gather e-mail addresses from Web pages, online posts, and social networking sites. Many individuals view spam as an invasion of privacy because it arrives on computers without permission and costs them time and other resources (bandwidth, mailbox space, and hard drive space, for instance).

Most spam is legal, but there are requirements that must be adhered to in order for it to be legal. For instance, the *CAN-SPAM Act of 2003* established requirements (such as using truthful subject lines and honoring remove requests) for commercial e-mailers, as well as specified penalties for companies and individuals that break the law. While the *CAN-SPAM Act* has not reduced the amount of spam circulated today, it has increased the number of spammers prosecuted for sending spam. In fact, several spammers have been convicted in recent years. They have either been fined or sent to prison, and more are awaiting trial. For instance, one spammer was ordered to pay $230 million to MySpace for spamming MySpace users and another was ordered to pay Facebook a record $873 million for spamming its members.

TIP

When posting your e-mail address online, write it so individuals can read it, but spiders and other automated programs cannot, such as writing *johndoe at xyz.com* instead of *johndoe@xyz.com*. To send you an e-mail, individuals will just need to substitute the @ sign for the word "at" and the spaces surrounding it.

Protecting the Privacy of Personal Information

There are a number of precautions that can be taken to protect the privacy of personal information. Safeguarding your e-mail address and other personal information is a good start. You can also surf anonymously, *opt out* of some marketing activities, and use filters and other tools to limit your exposure to spam. Businesses also need to take adequate measures to protect the privacy of information stored on their servers and storage media. These precautions are discussed next.

Safeguard Your E-Mail Address

Protecting your e-mail address is one of the best ways to avoid spam. One way to accomplish this is to use one private e-mail address for family, friends, colleagues, and other trusted sources, and use a *disposable* or **throw-away e-mail address**—such as a second address obtained from your ISP or a free e-mail address from Yahoo! Mail, AOL Mail, Outlook.com, or Gmail (see Figure 5-19)—for online shopping, signing up for free offers, forums, product registration, and other activities that typically lead to junk e-mail. Although you will want to check your alternate e-mail address periodically (to check for online shopping receipts or shipping notifications, for instance), this precaution can prevent a great deal of spam from getting to your regular e-mail account.

Another advantage of using a throw-away e-mail address for only noncritical applications is that you can quit using it and obtain a new one if spam begins to get overwhelming or too annoying. To help with this, some ISPs (such as EarthLink) provide disposable anonymous e-mail addresses to their subscribers—e-mail messages sent to a subscriber's anonymous address are forwarded to the subscriber's account until the disposable address is deleted by the subscriber. Consequently, individuals can easily change disposable addresses when they

FIGURE 5-19
Free e-mail accounts. Can be used for throw-away e-mail addresses.

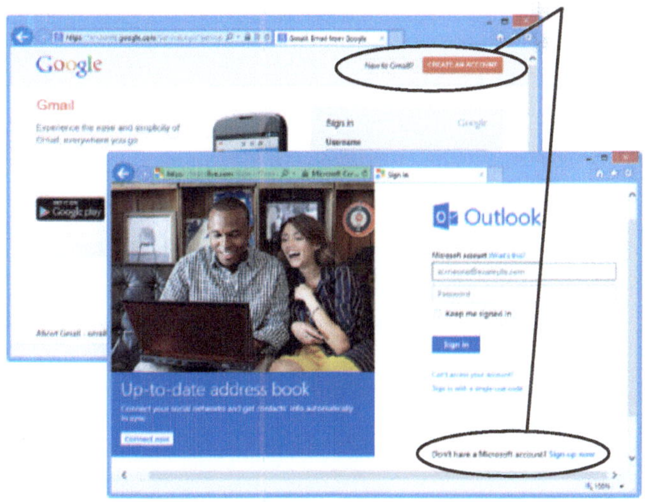

>**Throw-away e-mail address.** An e-mail address used only for nonessential purposes and activities that may result in spam; the address can be disposed of and replaced if spam becomes a problem; also called a *disposable e-mail address.*

TIP

If you only need an e-mail address for a very short period of time (such as to receive a confirmation for registering for a free online service), use a *temporary disposable e-mail address*, such as the ones available through *10 Minute Mail* that are valid for only 10 minutes.

begin to receive too much spam or when the disposable address is no longer needed. There are also *anonymous e-mail services* (such as the one provided by *Anonymous Speech*) that allow users to route e-mail messages (and other Web activities if desired) using an anonymous domain. These services typically range from free to about $75 per year.

To comply with truth-in-advertising laws, an *unsubscribe e-mail address* included in an unsolicited e-mail must be a working address. If you receive a marketing e-mail from a reputable source, you may be able to unsubscribe by clicking the supplied link or otherwise following the unsubscribe instructions. Because spam from less-legitimate sources often has unsubscribe links that do not work or that are present only to verify that your e-mail address is genuine—a very valuable piece of information for future use—many privacy experts recommend never replying to or trying to unsubscribe from any spam.

Be Cautious of Revealing Personal Information

In addition to protecting your real e-mail address, protecting your personal information is a critical step toward safeguarding your privacy. Consequently, it makes sense to be cautious about revealing your private information to anyone. Privacy tips for safeguarding personal information include the following:

TIP

Don't forget that once you post content on a Web site or send it via e-mail, you cannot control how long it will "live" in digital form. Be very careful about the personal information you post and send to avoid the possibility of that information creating problems for you in the future.

- Read a Web site's privacy policy (if one exists) before providing any personal information. If the Web site reserves the right to share your information unless you specifically notify them otherwise, it is best to assume that any information you provide will eventually be shared with others—do not use the site if that is unacceptable to you.
- Avoid putting too many personal details on your Web site or on a social networking site. Although complete anonymity would defeat the purpose of using a social network, it is a good idea to be careful about what content you post and who can view it. If you would like to post photos or other personal documents on a Web site for friends and family members to see, use a photo sharing site that allows you to restrict access to your photos (such as *Flickr*, *Snapfish*, or *Fotki*). Avoid using location-based services that share your location information with strangers. For more tips related to how to protect your privacy on social networking sites, see Figure 5-20.
- When you sign up for free trials or other services that may result in spam, use your throw-away e-mail address.
- Consider using privacy software, such as *Privacy Guardian*, to hide your personal information as you browse the Web so it is not revealed and your activities cannot be tracked by marketers. Also check the privacy settings of the cloud services that you use to see what control you have over what personal data is collected and shared. For instance, Google users can use the *Google Dashboard* to control the privacy settings of Google services.
- Just because a Web site or registration form asks for personal information, that does not mean you have to give it. Supply only the required information and if you are asked for more personal information than you are comfortable providing, look for an alternate Web site for the product or information you are seeking. As a rule of thumb, do not provide an e-mail address (or else use a throw-away address) if you do not want to receive offers or other e-mail from that company.

FIGURE 5-20 Social media privacy tips.

Facebook (use Privacy Settings)	Limit who can see your posts to *Friends* only.
	Limit who can look you up to *Friends* or *Friends of Friends* only.
	Disable search engines linking to your timeline.
	If you allow friends to post on your timeline, enable the settings to review the posts first.
	On your profile's *About* page, click each section and limit viewing to *Friends* only.
Google+ (use Profile Settings)	Organize your contacts into *circles* based on the content you will share with them (such as work, friends, and family) and then post or share content only with the appropriate circle.
	On your profile's *About* page, click each section and limit viewing to *Your circles* only.
Twitter (use Account Settings)	Enable *Tweet privacy* so only those who you approve will receive your tweets.
	Keep location information disabled so your location won't be added to your tweets.

- If you are using a public computer (such as at a school, a library, or an Internet café), be sure to remove any personal information and settings stored on the computer during your session. You can use browser options to delete this data manually from the computer before you leave (use the *Browsing history* option on the General tab of the Internet Options dialog box in Internet Explorer to delete this data). To prevent the deleted data from being recovered, run the Windows Disk Cleanup program on the hard drive, making sure that the options for Temporary Internet Files and the Recycle Bin are selected during the Disk Cleanup process. An easier option is using the *private browsing* mode offered by some browsers, such as Internet Explorer's *InPrivate* or Chrome's *Incognito* modes (see Figure 5-21), that allow you to browse the Web without leaving any history (such as browsing history, temporary Internet files, form data, cookies, usernames, and passwords) on the computer you are using. In either case, be sure to log out of any Web sites you were using before leaving the computer.

Indicates private browsing mode is enabled.

Use this button to enable private browsing.

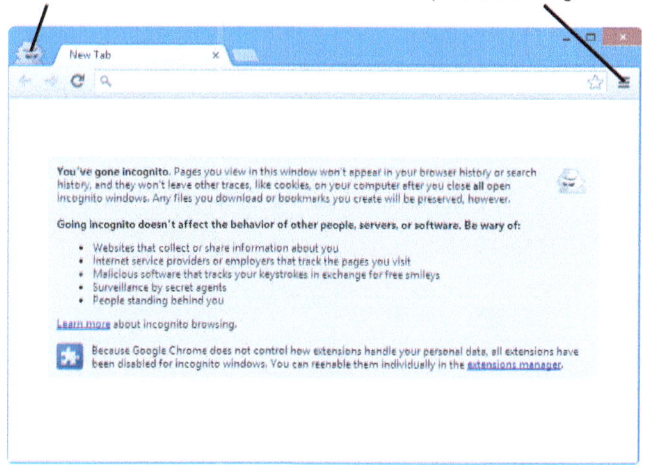

FIGURE 5-21
Private browsing can protect your Web-surfing privacy at public computers.

Use Filters and Opt Out

While keeping your personal information as private as possible can help to reduce spam and other direct marketing activities, *filtering* can also be helpful. Some ISPs automatically block all e-mail messages originating from known or suspected spammers so those e-mail messages never reach the individuals' mailboxes; other ISPs flag suspicious e-mail messages as possible spam, based on their content or subject lines, to warn individuals that those messages may contain spam. To deal with spam that makes it to your computer, you can use an **e-mail filter**—a tool for automatically sorting your incoming e-mail messages. E-mail filters used to capture spam are called **spam filters**. Many e-mail programs have built-in spam filters that identify possible spam and either flag it or move it to a Spam or Junk E-mail folder. Individuals can typically change the spam settings used in their e-mail program to indicate the actions that should be taken with suspected spam. In addition, they can create e-mail filters in their e-mail program, or they can use third-party filtering software to customize their spam filtering further. Many spam filters can also "learn" what each user views as spam based on the user identifying e-mail messages that were classified incorrectly (either spam messages placed in the Inbox or legitimate messages placed in the Spam folder) by the spam filter. The user typically provides this information by clicking a button such as *Report Spam* or *Not Spam* when the message is selected; the spam filter uses this input to classify messages from that sender correctly in the future. Businesses can set up spam filters in-house, but they are increasingly turning to dedicated *antispam appliances* to filter out spam without increasing the load on the company e-mail server.

Custom e-mail filters are used to route messages automatically to particular folders based on stated criteria. For example, you can specify that e-mail messages with keywords frequently used in spam subject lines (such as *free, porn, opportunity, last chance, weight, pharmacy*, and similar terms) be routed into a folder named *Possible Spam*, and you can specify that all e-mail messages from your boss's e-mail address be routed into an *Urgent*

TIP

To perform Web searches anonymously, without being tracked for advertising purposes, try the *DuckDuckGo* search site.

>**E-mail filter.** A tool that automatically sorts your incoming e-mail messages based on specific criteria. >**Spam filter.** An e-mail filter used to redirect spam from a user's Inbox.

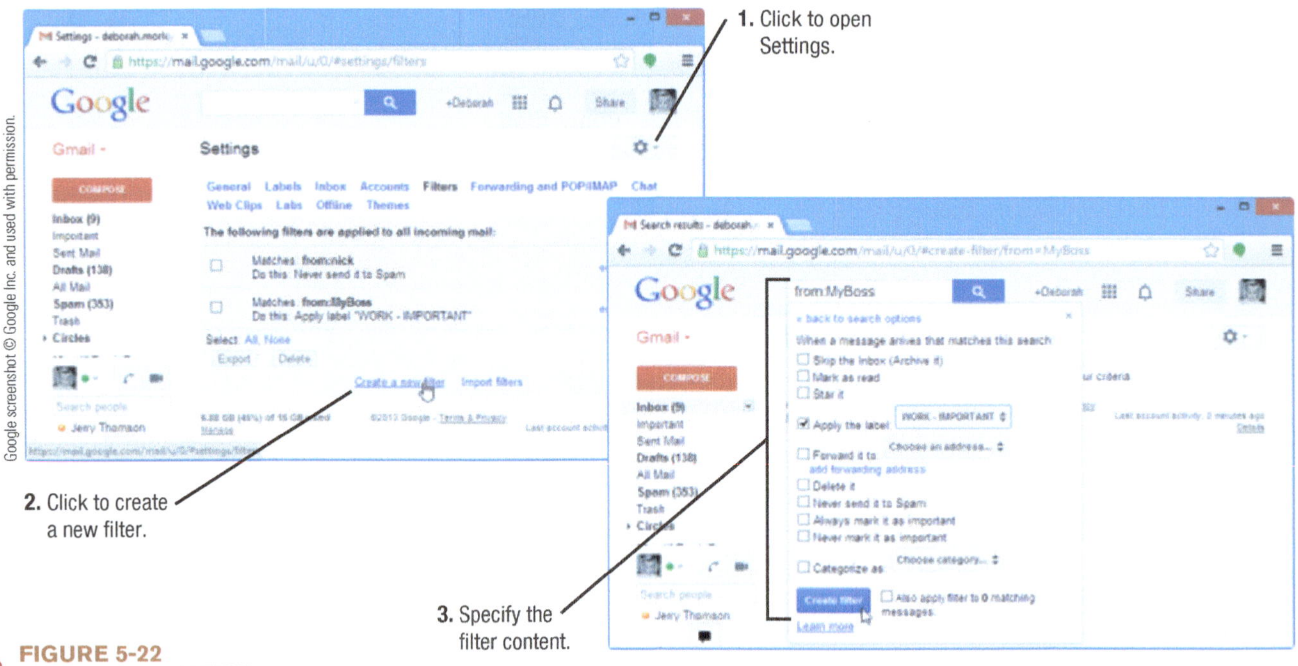

FIGURE 5-22
Creating a Gmail filter.

FIGURE 5-23
Mobile spam filtering. Can detect both spam texts and spam calls.

folder. Filtering can help you find important messages in your Inbox by preventing it from becoming cluttered with spam. However, you need to be sure to check your Possible Spam or Junk E-mail folder periodically to locate any e-mail messages mistakenly filed there—especially before you permanently delete those messages. Creating a new e-mail filter in Gmail is shown in Figure 5-22.

Mobile users who receive Web-based e-mail via smartphones can use the filters available via their Web mail provider to filter out spam. There are also some *mobile spam apps* available to detect or block spam sent via text message or voice calls (see one example in Figure 5-23).

Another alternative for reducing the amount of spam you receive is to **opt out**. *Opting out* refers to following a predesignated procedure to remove yourself from marketing lists, or otherwise preventing your personal information from being obtained by or shared with others. By opting out, you instruct companies you do business with (such as your bank, insurance company, investment company, or an online store) not to share your personal information with third parties. You can also opt out of being contacted by direct and online marketing companies.

To opt out from a particular company or direct marketing association, you can contact them directly—many organizations include opt-out instructions in the privacy policies posted on their Web sites. For Web sites that use registered accounts for repeat visitors, opt-out options are sometimes included in your personal settings and can be activated by modifying your personal settings for that site. Opt-out instructions for financial institutions and credit card companies are often included in the disclosure statements that are periodically mailed to customers; they can also often be found on the company's Web site.

To assist consumers with the opt-out process, there are a number of Web sites, such as the *Center for Democracy and Technology* and the *PrivacyRightsNow!* Web sites, which provide opt-out tools for consumers. For example, some sites help visitors

>**Opt out.** To request that you be removed from marketing activities or that your information not be shared with other companies.

create opt-out letters that can be sent to the companies in order to opt out. For online marketing activities, organizations—such as the *Network Advertising Initiative* (*NAI*)—have tools on their Web sites to help consumers opt out of online targeted ads. Typically, this process replaces an advertiser's marketing cookie with an *opt-out cookie*. The opt-out cookie prevents any more marketing cookies belonging to that particular advertiser from being placed on the user's hard drive as long as the opt-out cookie is present (usually until the user deletes the opt-out cookie file, either intentionally or unintentionally). You can also use the *tracking protection* options available with some browsers; for example, the Internet Explorer tracking protection is enabled using the *Safety* settings. Once enabled (see Figure 5-24), it will send a "do not track" indicator to Web sites, which will then display generic ads instead of targeted ads. This process may become easier and more automatic in the future if proposed *Do Not Track* legislation becomes a reality.

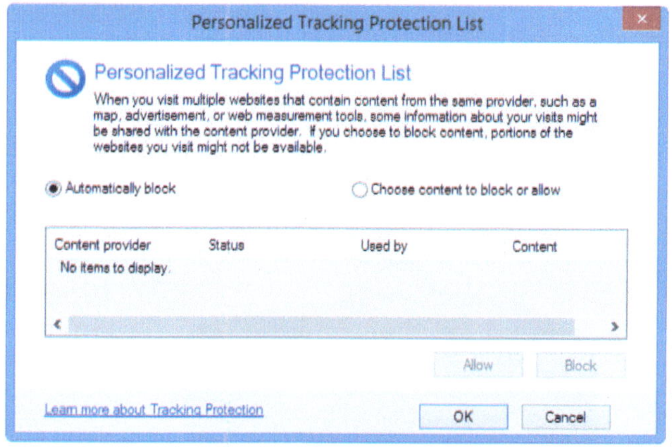

FIGURE 5-24
Enabling tracking protection in Internet Explorer.

At the present time, opting-out procedures are confusing and time consuming, and they do not always work well. Consequently, some privacy groups are pushing to change to an *opt-in* process, in which individuals would need to **opt in** (request participation in) to a particular marketing activity before companies can collect or share any personal data (as is the case in the European Union). In fact, Walmart recently changed its privacy policy to share information with third parties only if customers opt in. However, the general practice in the U.S. business community today is to use your information as allowed for by each privacy policy unless you specifically opt out.

TIP

Google recently paid $22.5 million to settle a lawsuit regarding its alleged circumventing of Do Not Track technologies connected to the Safari Web browser.

Secure Servers and Otherwise Protect Personal Information

Any business that stores personal information about employees, customers, or other individuals must take adequate security measures to protect the privacy of that information. As discussed in Chapter 4, secure servers and encryption can protect the data stored on a server; firewalls and access systems can protect against unauthorized access. To prevent personal information from being sent intentionally or inadvertently via e-mail, organizations can use e-mail encryption systems that automatically encrypt or block e-mail messages containing certain keywords. For instance, some hospitals use encryption systems that scan all outgoing e-mail messages and attachments and then automatically encrypt or block all messages that appear to contain patient-identifiable information, such as a Social Security number, medical record number, patient name, or medical term like "cancer." The recipient of an encrypted e-mail message typically receives a link to a secure Web site to log in and view the encrypted e-mail message. Similar systems are used by banks and other businesses. Businesses also need to be very careful with papers, portable hard drives, and other media that contain personal data. For instance, many recent data breaches have occurred because of carelessness, such as papers containing personal information being found in dumpsters, lost in transit, or faxed to the wrong individual.

TIP

Register both your landline and mobile phone numbers with the *National Do Not Call Registry* by going to www.donotcall.gov to prevent telemarketing calls from companies you do not have a business relationship with.

Ensuring that the private data stored by a business is adequately protected is increasingly the responsibility of a *chief privacy officer* (*CPO*)—a rapidly growing new position in business today. Typically, CPOs are responsible for ensuring privacy laws are complied with, identifying the data in a company that needs to be protected, developing policies to

>**Opt in.** To request that you be included in marketing activities or that your information be shared with other companies.

protect that data, and responding to any incidents that occur. Another issue that must be dealt with by CPOs is the changing definition of what information is regarded as personal and, therefore, needs to be safeguarded. For instance, some privacy advocates view the IP address of computers and the location information of mobile phones to be personal data. As protecting new types of information becomes integrated into privacy laws, these laws impact companies that store or utilize that information.

Courtesy Fellowes, Inc

FIGURE 5-25
Media disposal.
When disposing of CDs, DVDs, and other storage media, the media should be shredded to ensure the information on the media is destroyed.

Properly Dispose of Hardware Containing Data

A final consideration for protecting the privacy of personal information for both individuals and businesses is protecting the information located on paper documents and hardware (such as old backup media, used CDs, obsolete computers, and old mobile phones) that are to be disposed of. Papers, CDs, DVDs, and other media containing sensitive data should be shredded (see Figure 5-25), and the hard drives of computers to be disposed of should be *wiped*—overwritten several times using special *disk-wiping* or *disk-erasing* software—before they are sold or recycled. Unlike the data on a drive that has merely been erased or even reformatted (which can still be recovered), data on a properly wiped drive is very difficult or impossible to recover.

Wiping is typically viewed as an acceptable precaution for deleting sensitive data (such as Web site passwords and tax returns) from hard drives and other storage media belonging to individuals, as well as for storage media to be reused within an organization. However, before disposing of storage media containing sensitive data, businesses should consider physically destroying the media, such as by shredding or melting the hardware. To help with this process, *data destruction services* can be used, as discussed in the Inside the Industry box. To ensure that all hardware containing business data is properly disposed of, it is important for all businesses today to develop and implement a policy (often called a *media sanitization* or *data destruction policy*) for destroying data that is no longer needed.

TIP

Be sure to remove personal data from any device containing a hard drive before disposing of it, including gaming consoles, portable digital media players, and cars with entertainment system hard drives.

CAUTION CAUTION CAUTION CAUTION CAUTION CAUTION CAUT

When upgrading your mobile phone, be careful not to expose the personal data stored on your old phone to others. Before disposing of or recycling it, be sure to reset your mobile phone to its factory settings to clear all personal data from the phone.

ELECTRONIC SURVEILLANCE AND MONITORING

There are many ways electronic tools can be used to watch individuals, listen in on their conversations, or monitor their activities. Some of these tools—such as devices used by individuals to eavesdrop on wireless telephone conversations—are not legal for individuals to use. Other products and technologies, such as the GPS devices that are built into some cars so they can be located if they are stolen or the monitoring ankle bracelets used for offenders sentenced to house arrest, are used solely for law enforcement purposes. GPS technology can also be used by law enforcement agencies to track criminal suspects but, according to a 2012 U.S. Supreme Court ruling, only with a search warrant. Still other electronic tools, such as *computer monitoring software*, *video surveillance* equipment, and *presence technology*, discussed next, can often be used legally by individuals, by businesses in conjunction with *employee monitoring*, and by law enforcement agencies.

INSIDE THE INDUSTRY

Data Killers

With the vast amount of sensitive and classified data stored on personal and business devices today, disposing of those devices or removing the data from those devices so they can be reused is an important issue. In particular, business computers tend to contain a wide variety of sensitive data that needs to be removed if the hard drive containing that data needs to be disposed of or will be reused by another employee. *Data destruction services* are designed for this purpose.

Data destruction ranges from purging the data (such as wiping a magnetic hard drive clean or *degaussing* (demagnetizing) the drive so the data cannot be restored) to destroying the drive physically. The level of destruction needed depends on the type of drive (SSDs cannot be as reliably erased as magnetic hard drives), the type of data being deleted, and where the hardware will go next. For instance, purging might be appropriate for personal hard drives being sold and for business hard drives that will be reused within the company, but all business hard drives that will no longer be used within the company and that contain sensitive data should be physically destroyed.

While data destruction can be performed by in-house personnel, there are also external data destruction services (such as *Data Killers*) designed for this purpose. Such services typically can purge, degauss, or shred hard drives and other media, depending on the customer's preference. Once a hard drive has been shredded (see the accompanying photo), it is virtually impossible for any data to be recovered from the pieces. However, for extra security, magnetic drives containing extremely sensitive data can be degaussed and then shredded. To ensure drives are not lost or compromised in transit, most data destruction companies offer secure transportation to the destruction facility using tamper-proof locked cases, and will provide signed and dated Certificates of Purging or Certificates of Destruction, when requested. Some even offer destruction on site, if the customer desires. Purged hard drives are returned to the customer; shredded hard drives are typically recycled.

Courtesy of Data Killers

Hard drive before (left) and after (right) shredding.

Computer Monitoring Software

Computer monitoring software is used specifically for the purpose of recording keystrokes, logging the programs or Web sites accessed, or otherwise monitoring someone's computer activity; some programs also have apps that can be used to monitor media tablet and smartphone activity. These programs are typically marketed toward parents (to check on their children's online activities), spouses (to determine if a spouse is having an affair, viewing pornography, or participating in other activities that are unacceptable to the other spouse), law enforcement agencies (to collect evidence against suspected criminals), or employers (to ensure employees are using company computers and time only for work-related or otherwise approved activities). Computer monitoring programs can keep a log of all computer keystrokes performed on a computer, record the activities taking place (such as the amount of time spent on and tasks performed via the Web or installed software), take screenshots of the screen at specified intervals, and more (see Figure 5-26). Computer monitoring software designed for businesses also typically provides a summary of the

>**Computer monitoring software.** Software that can be used to record an individual's computer usage, such as capturing images of the screen, recording the actual keystrokes used, or creating a summary of Web sites and programs accessed.

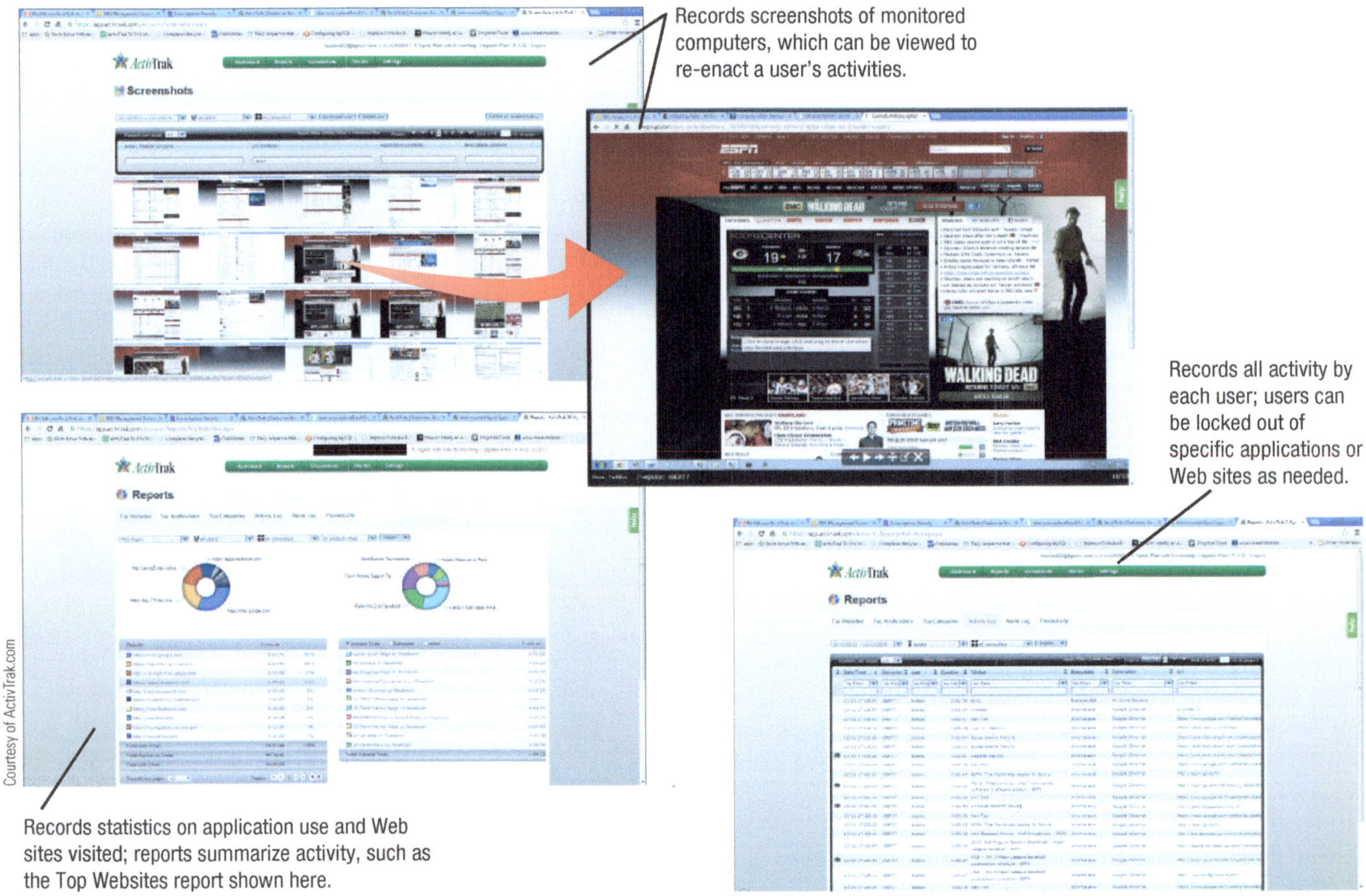

Courtesy of ActivTrak.com

FIGURE 5-26
Computer monitoring software. Can be used to monitor employee computer activity, as shown here.

activities (such as the programs used or the Web sites visited) performed on all company computers (refer again to Figure 5-26). In addition, some computer monitoring software can block specific Web sites, as well as notify a designated party (such as the parent or computer administrator) if the individual using the computer being monitored uses specified keywords (such as inappropriate language for children or terms referring to company secrets for employees) or visits a Web site deemed inappropriate.

Although it is legal to use computer monitoring software on your own computer or on the computers of your employees, installing it on other computers without the owners' knowledge to monitor their computer activity is usually illegal. A growing illegal use of computer monitoring software is the use of a *keystroke logging system* by hackers. A keystroke logging system is typically software-based, but it can also be implemented via a small device that is installed between the system unit and the keyboard of a computer. In either case, it is used to record all keystrokes performed on the computer in order to capture usernames, passwords, and other sensitive data entered into the computer via the keyboard. Keystroke logging software can be installed on an individual's computer via malware, or it can be installed on public computers in person if the proper precautions are not taken. For instance, in 2008, a Colombian man pled guilty to installing keystroke logging software on computers located in hotel business centers and Internet cafés around the world; the software collected the personal information he needed to access the bank, payroll, brokerage, and other financial accounts of over 600 individuals. He was sentenced in mid-2009 to nine years in prison and ordered to pay $347,000 in restitution.

In addition to computer monitoring products designed for individuals and businesses, there are also computer monitoring programs available for use only by law enforcement and other government agencies. Like wiretapping, electronic monitoring of computer activity requires a court order or similar authorization to be legal (although the *USA PATRIOT Act* does allow the FBI to conduct a limited form of Internet surveillance first, such as to capture e-mail addresses or IP addresses used with traffic going to or coming from a suspect's computer). With proper authorization and cooperation from a suspect's ISP, law enforcement agencies can use computer monitoring software to intercept files and e-mail messages sent to or from a suspect's computer. If the documents are encrypted, keystroke logging software can be used to record e-mail messages and documents before they are encrypted, as well as to record the private keys used to encrypt messages and files. As recent disclosures have revealed, the U.S. *National Security Agency* (*NSA*) routinely accesses and monitors Web activity (including e-mail messages, Skype calls, cloud documents, browsing activity, and other Web-related communications). In fact, the *Wall Street Journal* recently reported that the NSA has the capacity to reach about 75% of all U.S. Internet communications and NSA officials recently announced that this surveillance has helped to stop more than 50 terrorist plots since 9/11. One tool supposedly used to collect this data is referred to as *PRISM*; the huge new data center being built to house this data is referred to as the *Utah Data Center*.

Video Surveillance

The idea of **video surveillance** is nothing new. Many retail stores, banks, office buildings, and other privately owned facilities that are open to the public routinely use closed-circuit security cameras to monitor activities taking place at those facilities for security purposes. In recent years, however, video surveillance has been expanded to a number of additional public locations (such as streets, parks, airports, sporting arenas, subway systems, and so forth) in many cities in the United States and other countries for law enforcement purposes (worldwide, two of the most monitored cities are London and New York City). These cameras are typically located outside and attached to or built into fixtures, such as lamp posts (see Figure 5-27), or attached to buildings. Video surveillance cameras are also commonly installed in schools in the United States and other countries to enable administrators to monitor both teacher and student activities and to have a record of incidents as they occur. A snapshot of a live video feed from a camera installed at a university in Oregon is shown in Figure 5-27.

Public video surveillance systems are often used in conjunction with face recognition technology to try to identify known terrorists and other criminals, to identify criminals when their crimes are caught on tape, and to prevent crimes from occurring. Video surveillance data is proving to be valuable to police for catching terrorists and other types of criminals, and it is routinely used to identify the individuals and cars used in attacks; this benefit is expected to increase as video

FIGURE 5-27
Examples of public video surveillance.

Image source EPIC.org project Observing Surveillance

OUTDOOR SURVEILLANCE
Many cameras placed in public locations are designed to blend into their surroundings to be less intrusive, such as the camera inside this light fixture on a Washington, D.C., street.

INDOOR SURVEILLANCE
Many cameras are placed inside businesses, schools, and other locations; a snapshot from a video camera located at a university in Oregon is shown here.

Courtesy University of Oregon

>Video surveillance. The use of video cameras to monitor activities of individuals, such as employees or individuals in public locations, for work-related or crime-prevention purposes.

surveillance moves to high definition. For example, video surveillance systems helped police identify six of the attackers in the deadly 2013 Westgate Mall attack in Kenya. Some public video surveillance systems are also beginning to be used in conjunction with software to try to identify suspicious behavior (such as an unattended bag or a truck circling a skyscraper) and alert authorities to these possible threats before they do any damage.

Many privacy advocates object to the use of video surveillance and face recognition technology in public locations; their concerns are primarily based on how the video captured by these systems will be used. Privacy advocates also have doubts about the usefulness of these systems in protecting citizens against terrorism. They also object to the fact that, unlike private security video that is typically viewed only after a crime has occurred, the images from many public video cameras are watched all the time. In addition, networks of police video cameras that feed into a central operations center allow the observation of innocent people and activities on a massive scale. Some privacy advocates also fear being under perpetual police surveillance and the eventual expansion of these security surveillance systems, such as using them to look for "deadbeat dads" or for other applications not vital for national security. However, law enforcement agencies contend that face recognition systems and public video surveillance are no different from the many private video surveillance systems in place today in a wide variety of public locations, such as in retail stores and banks. They view this technology as just one more tool to be used to protect the public, similar to scanning luggage at the airport.

An emerging privacy issue related to public video cameras is their use with the display screens used to project advertisements in public places, such as a mall, health club, or retail store. This marketing technique uses tiny video cameras embedded in or on the edge of the screen, in conjunction with software, to identify characteristics of the individual looking at the screen (such as gender and approximate age) in order to display advertising content targeted to each viewer. The video cameras can also be used to determine if the displayed ads are reaching the intended demographic. Similar technology is used with some in-store mannequins to analyze shopper characteristics to help stores adjust in-store displays accordingly. While still in the infancy stage, this advertising tool is expected to be more prominent in the near future. To alleviate privacy concerns, developers state that no images are ever stored and individuals are not personally identified—only their characteristics. However, the idea of targeted advertisements based on physical appearance is a concern for some privacy advocates.

A related privacy concern is the inclusion of imaging capabilities in many mobile devices today, such as mobile phones (see Figure 5-28), media tablets, and Google Glass. Although digital cameras in mobile devices are increasingly being used to help law enforcement (such as being used by citizens to take photos of crimes as they are being committed) and camera functions are included for personal enjoyment and convenience, some fear that the ubiquitous nature of mobile phones will lead to increased privacy violations. In fact, some athletic clubs have banned mobile phones entirely to protect the privacy of their members while working out and in the dressing rooms. Many YMCAs, city parks and recreation departments, and other recreational facilities have banned camera phone use in locker rooms and restrooms to protect the privacy of both children and adults. Camera phones are also being banned by some schools to prevent cheating, by many courthouses to prevent witness or jury intimidation, and by many research and production facilities to prevent corporate espionage. Google Glass has the additional issue of the user being able to take photos and record videos in an even more subtle manner than with a mobile phone. Legally speaking, people typically have few rights to privacy in public places, but many believe that new technology—such as camera phones and Google Glass—will require the law to reconsider and redefine what is considered to be a public place and where citizens can expect to retain particular aspects of personal privacy.

FIGURE 5-28
Camera phones are ubiquitous today.

Employee Monitoring

Employee monitoring refers to companies recording or observing the actions of employees while on the job. With today's technology, employee monitoring is very easy to perform, and much of it can be done through the use of computers. Common employee monitoring activities include screening telephone calls, reviewing e-mail, and tracking computer and Internet usage; with the growing inclusion of video cameras in computers and monitors today, employee monitoring via webcams may become more prominent in the near future. Although many employees feel that being watched at work is an invasion of their personal privacy, it is legal and very common in the United States. According to the American Management Association (AMA), the vast majority of all U.S. companies use some type of electronic surveillance with their employees, and it is common for employers to discipline employees for misuse of e-mail or the Internet at work. Typically, the primary reason is to monitor Internet usage for legal liability, but monitoring employee productivity is another motivating factor. Many employers are finding that some employees waste large amounts of time on social networking sites and other Web activities. While access to these sites is frequently blocked by employers, many believe a better alternative is identifying employees who abuse their Internet access and then dealing with those employees directly. This can be accomplished using the computer monitoring software discussed in a previous section.

For monitoring the physical locations of employees, video cameras (such as video surveillance cameras or webcams) can be used, but another possibility is the use of smart or RFID-enabled ID cards (sometimes called *proximity cards*). While these cards are most often used for access control—such as to facilitate access to a building or computer network, to automatically lock an employee's computer when he or she gets a certain distance away from it (to eliminate the problem of nosy coworkers), and to automatically unlock the computer when the employee returns (to eliminate the need for passwords)—they can also be used to track the physical location of employees. There are also *proximity apps* that use the Bluetooth connection on your smartphone, media tablet, or other Bluetooth-enabled mobile device to lock or unlock your computer based on the phone's physical location (your phone needs to be within Bluetooth range of the computer in order for the computer to be unlocked)—see the *Keycard app* in Figure 5-29. Other types of employee monitoring systems designed for tracking an employee's location are location-based systems, such as those systems that track an employee via his or her smartphone or those that notify the employer if the employee's company vehicle exits a prescribed work area. GPS monitoring systems are discussed in more detail in Chapter 8.

FIGURE 5-29
Proximity apps. This app locks and unlocks your computer automatically as your iPhone moves in and out of range.

Although some employees may view workplace monitoring as an invasion of their personal privacy, employers have several valid reasons for monitoring employee activities, such as security concerns, productivity measurement, legal compliance, and legal liability. For example, management has a responsibility to the company (and to its stockholders, for publicly held corporations) to make sure employees do the jobs that they are being paid to do. If any employees are spending too much time away from their desks chatting with other employees, answering their personal e-mail, or placing bids at online auctions, the company has the right to know and the responsibility to stop that misuse of company time and resources. For example, there have been many instances of employees viewing

>**Employee monitoring.** Observing or reviewing employees' actions while they are on the job.

pornography, downloading pirated movies or music, watching live sports video feeds—even running their own businesses—on company time and computers. In addition, the company needs to protect itself against lost business (due to employee incompetence or poor client skills, for example) and lawsuits (such as from employees when offensive e-mail messages are circulated within the office or when an employee includes statements that defame another business or reveal private information in a company blog). In addition, government regulations—such as the *Sarbanes-Oxley Act*, which requires publicly traded companies to keep track of which employees look at sensitive documents—may require it. However, some employees object to being monitored and some privacy advocates feel that some types of employee monitoring cross the line between valid employee monitoring and an invasion of privacy.

Comprehensive employee monitoring systems can be expensive; however, many companies view the cost as insignificant compared with the risk of a potential multimillion-dollar lawsuit. It is becoming increasingly common for U.S. firms to face sexual harassment and/or racial discrimination claims stemming from employee e-mail and Internet use and lawsuits can be costly—Chevron was once ordered to pay female employees $2.2 million to settle a sexual harassment lawsuit stemming from inappropriate e-mails sent by male employees.

To reduce cost and objections from employees, some businesses have found employee training and education to be an effective and cost-efficient alternative to continuous monitoring. Others use statistical-analysis software to detect unusual patterns in data collected about employee computer usage, and then use the reports to investigate only the employees and situations indicated as possible problems. Regardless of the techniques used, it is wise for businesses to inform employees about their monitoring practices (including what activities may be monitored and how long records of that monitoring will be archived), although they are not required by law in the United States at the current time to do so. However, bills have been introduced in several states in the United States that would prohibit employee monitoring without employee notification and some countries—such as in the European Union—are much more limiting with respect to the types of employee monitoring that can be performed without active notification. In addition, legislation has been implemented or is being considered in several states to prevent employers from implanting employees with RFID chips without the employee's consent in order to prevent employers from requiring that chips be implanted into employees for monitoring purposes, security access, or other work-related functions.

Presence Technology

Presence technology refers to the ability of one computing device (a desktop computer, portable computer, or smartphone, for example) on a network (such as the Internet or a mobile phone network) to identify another device on the same network and determine its status. It can be used to tell when someone on the network is using his or her computer or mobile device, as well as the individual's availability for communications; that is, whether or not the individual is able and willing to take a voice or video call or respond to an IM at the present time. For example, when an employee at a company utilizing presence technology (sometimes called *presence management* in a business context) has a question that needs answering, he or she can check the directory displayed on his or her computer or mobile device to see which team members are available, regardless of where those team members are physically located. The employee can then call an available team member or send an instant message. Presence technology is expected to be used eventually

TIP

The ability of a device to share status information (including presence and location information) across a network is a form of *context-aware computing*.

>**Presence technology.** Technology that enables one computing device (such as a computer or mobile device) to locate and identify the current status of another device on the same network.

on company Web pages so that visitors—usually potential or current customers—can see which salespeople, service representatives, or other contacts are currently available. Another possible application is including dynamic presence buttons in e-mail messages—the presence button would display one message (such as "I'm online") if the sender is online at the time the e-mail message is read, and a different message (such as "I'm offline") if the sender is not online at that time.

Presence technology today can be implemented via software, as well as by GPS, RFID, or other technology. For instance, IM software indicates the current status of each buddy on an individual's contact list (based on each buddy's signed-in status) and chat tools (such as in Facebook) reveal which of your contacts are currently online. In addition, the presence technology built into many mobile devices today enables individuals to see when a contact is available (see Figure 5-30). The GPS capabilities integrated in many smartphones today also allow you to keep track of your friends' physical locations, such as by using the Buddy Beacon or GyPSii application to view their current locations on a map. The GPS capabilities built into smartphones can also be used by law enforcement to determine the location of a phone (such as one belonging to a missing individual or a criminal) when needed.

FIGURE 5-30
Presence technology. Presence icons indicate the status of individual contacts.

While some aspects of presence technology are useful and intriguing, such as being able to tell that a loved one's flight arrived safely when you notice that his or her smartphone is on again, knowing if a friend or colleague is available for a phone call before dialing the number, or identifying the location of your children at any point in time, privacy advocates are concerned about the use of this technology. They are concerned about presence technology being used to target ads and information to individuals based on their current physical location (such as close to a particular restaurant at lunchtime) and other activities that they view as potential privacy violations. In addition, there are concerns about location data being archived and how that archived data may be used.

Protecting Personal and Workplace Privacy

There are not many options for protecting yourself against computer monitoring by your employer or the government, or against video surveillance systems. However, businesses should take the necessary security measures (such as protecting the company network from hackers, monitoring for intrusions, and using security software) to ensure that employee activities are not being monitored by a hacker or other unauthorized individual. Individuals should also secure their home computers to protect against keystroke logging or other computer monitoring software that may be inadvertently installed via an electronic greeting card, game, or other downloaded file, and that is designed to provide a hacker with account numbers, passwords, and other sensitive data that could be used in identity theft or other fraudulent activities. *Antispyware software*, such as the programs discussed in Chapter 4, can be used to detect and remove some types of illegal computer monitoring and spyware software. To prevent location data associated with your smartphone from being available to strangers, change the privacy settings of the services you use to limit location data to specific friends, if that option is available. If you don't use location-based services frequently, turn off the GPS feature on your phone until you need it, if possible.

The Employer's Responsibilities

To protect the personal privacy of their employees and customers, businesses and organizations have a responsibility to keep private information about their employees, the company, and their customers safe. Strong security measures, such as firewalls and access-prevention methods for both computer data and facilities, can help to protect against unauthorized access by hackers. Businesses and organizations should take precautions against both intentional and accidental breaches of privacy by employees. Finally, businesses and organizations have the responsibility to monitor their employees' activities to ensure workers are productive. In general, businesses must maintain a safe and productive workplace environment and protect the privacy of their customers and employees, while at the same time ensure the company is not vulnerable to lawsuits.

All businesses should have an *employee policy* that informs employees about what personal activities (if any) are allowed during company time or on company equipment, as well as about what company communications (such as e-mail messages and blog postings) and what employee activities (such as Web surfing, e-mail, telephone calls, and downloading files to an office computer) may be monitored. Employee policies are usually included in an employee handbook or posted on the company intranet.

The Employees' Responsibilities

Employees have the responsibility to read a company's employee policy when initially hired and to review it periodically to ensure that they understand the policy and do not violate any company rules while working for that organization. In addition, because at-work activities may legally be monitored by an employer, it is wise—from a privacy standpoint—to avoid personal activities at work. From reading the organization's employee policy, an employee can determine if any personal activities are allowed at all (such as checking personal e-mail during the lunch hour), but it is safer to perform personal activities at home, regardless. Be especially careful with any activity, such as sending a joke via e-mail to a coworker, that might be interpreted as harassment. For personal phone calls, employees should use their mobile phones during their lunch hour or a rest break.

COMPUTER SECURITY AND PRIVACY LEGISLATION

The high level of concern regarding computer security and personal privacy has led state and federal legislators to pass a variety of laws since the 1970s. Internet privacy is viewed as one of the top policy issues facing Congress today, and numerous bills have been proposed in the last several years regarding spam, telemarketing, spyware, online profiling, and other very important privacy issues (such as the *Do-Not-Track Online Act of 2013* recently introduced in the U.S. Congress and the *Consumer Privacy Bill of Rights* unveiled recently by the Obama Administration). However, despite a renewed interest in privacy legislation, due at least in part to the recent leak of NSA surveillance operations, Congress has had difficulty passing new legislation. There are several reasons for this, including that it is difficult for the legal system to keep pace with the rate at which technology changes, and there are jurisdictional issues because many computer crimes affect businesses and individuals located in geographic areas other than the one in which the computer criminal is located. In addition, privacy is difficult to define and there is a struggle to balance freedom of speech with the right to privacy.

Another issue is weighing the need to implement legislation versus the use of voluntary methods to protect computer security and personal privacy. For instance, the *Child Online Protection Act* (*COPA*) has been controversial since it was passed in 1998, and, in fact, it has never been implemented. This legislation prohibited making pornography or any other content deemed harmful to minors available to minors via the Internet. This law was blocked by the U.S. Supreme Court several times, based on the likelihood that it violates the First Amendment and that less-restrictive alternatives (such as Internet filtering) can be used instead to prevent the access of inappropriate materials by minors. A list of selected federal laws related to computer security and privacy are shown in Figure 5-31.

DATE	LAW AND DESCRIPTION
2009	**American Recovery and Reinvestment Act** Requires HIPAA covered entities to notify patients and/or customers when protected health information has been compromised.
2006	**U.S. SAFE WEB Act of 2006** Grants additional authority to the FTC to help protect consumers from spam, spyware, and Internet fraud and deception.
2005	**Real ID Act** Establishes national standards for state-issued driver's licenses and identification cards.
2005	**Junk Fax Prevention Act** Requires unsolicited faxes to have a highly visible opt-out notice.
2003	**CAN-SPAM Act** Implements regulations for unsolicited e-mail messages and lays the groundwork for a federal Do Not E-Mail Registry.
2003	**Do Not Call Implementation Act** Amends the Telephone Consumer Protection Act to implement the National Do Not Call Registry.
2003	**Health Insurance Portability and Accountability Act (HIPAA)** Includes a Security Rule that sets minimum security standards to protect health information stored electronically.
2002	**Sarbanes-Oxley Act** Requires archiving a variety of electronic records and protecting the integrity of corporate financial data.
2001	**USA PATRIOT Act** Grants federal authorities expanded surveillance and intelligence-gathering powers, such as broadening the ability of federal agents to obtain the real identity of Internet users and to intercept e-mail and other types of Internet communications.
1999	**Financial Modernization (Gramm-Leach-Bliley) Act** Extends the ability of banks, securities firms, and insurance companies to share consumers' non-public personal information, but requires them to notify consumers and give them the opportunity to opt out before disclosing any information.
1998	**Child Online Protection Act (COPA)** Prohibits online pornography and other content deemed harmful to minors; has been blocked by the Supreme Court.
1998	**Children's Online Privacy Protection Act (COPPA)** Regulates how Web sites can collect information from minors and communicate with them.
1998	**Telephone Anti-Spamming Amendments Act** Applies restrictions to unsolicited, bulk commercial e-mail.
1991	**Telephone Consumer Protection Act** Requires telemarketing companies to respect the rights of people who do not want to be called.
1988	**Computer Matching and Privacy Protection Act** Limits the use of government data in determining federal-benefit recipients.
1988	**Video Privacy Protection Act** Limits disclosure of customer information by video-rental companies.
1986	**Electronic Communications Privacy Act** Extends traditional privacy protections governing postal delivery and telephone services to include e-mail, mobile phones, and voice mail.
1984	**Cable Communications Policy Act** Limits disclosure of customer records by cable TV companies; extended in 1992 to include companies that sell wireless services.
1974	**Education Privacy Act** Stipulates that, in both public and private schools that receive any federal funding, individuals have the right to keep the schools from releasing information such as grades and evaluations of behavior.
1974	**Privacy Act** Stipulates that the collection of data by federal agencies must have a legitimate purpose.
1970	**Fair Credit Reporting Act** Prevents private organizations from unfairly denying credit and provides individuals the right to inspect their credit records.
1970	**Freedom of Information Act** Gives individuals the right to inspect data concerning them that is stored by the federal government.

FIGURE 5-31
Federal legislation related to computer security and privacy.

SUMMARY

WHY BE CONCERNED ABOUT COMPUTER SECURITY?

Chapter Objective 1: Explain why all computer users should be concerned about computer security.

There are a number of important security concerns related to computers, such as having your computer stolen, losing data, and running the risk of buying pirated or digitally counterfeited products online. All computer users should be aware of possible security risks and the safeguards they can implement to prevent security problems because these problems can cost them time and money, as well as be an inconvenience.

HARDWARE LOSS, HARDWARE DAMAGE, AND SYSTEM FAILURE

Chapter Objective 2: List some risks associated with hardware loss, hardware damage, and system failure, and understand ways to safeguard a computer against these risks.

Hardware loss (perhaps as a result of **hardware theft** or lost hardware), hardware damage (both intentional and unintentional), and **system failure** are important concerns. System failure can occur because of a hardware problem, or it can be the result of a natural or man-made disaster. To protect against hardware theft, door and equipment locks can be used. To protect against accidental hardware damage, **surge suppressors**, **uninterruptible power supplies** (**UPSs**), proper storage media care, and precautions against excess dust, heat, and static electricity are important. **Ruggedized devices** can be used when necessary. To protect against data loss, backups are essential for both individuals and businesses—most businesses should also develop a **disaster recovery plan** for natural and man-made disasters. Encryption can be used to protect individual files and the content of data stored on a storage medium. **Full disk encryption** (**FDE**) and **self-encrypting hard drives** can be used to encrypt all the content located on a hard drive automatically.

SOFTWARE PIRACY AND DIGITAL COUNTERFEITING

Chapter Objective 3: Define software piracy and digital counterfeiting, and explain how they can be prevented.

Software piracy (the unauthorized copying of a computer program) and **digital counterfeiting** (creating fake copies of currency and other resources) are illegal in the United States. They cost manufacturers billions of dollars each year, and some of these costs are passed on to law-abiding consumers. Various tools, such as consumer education, holograms, and software activation procedures, can be used to prevent software piracy. Many businesses are also aggressively pursuing software pirates in court in an attempt to reduce piracy. The government has various methods in place to prevent digital counterfeiting of currency, such as using difficult-to-reproduce materials and features like *security threads* and *watermarks*.

WHY BE CONCERNED ABOUT INFORMATION PRIVACY?

Chapter Objective 4: Explain what information privacy is and why computer users should be concerned about it.

Privacy issues affect the lives of everyone. A number of important **privacy** concerns are related to computers and the Internet. For instance, **information privacy** refers to the rights of individuals and companies to control how information about them is collected and used. Other common concerns include the privacy of Web site activities and e-mail messages, as well as the high number of security breaches on systems that contain personal information. Businesses need to be concerned with protecting the privacy of the personal information they store because data breaches violate the privacy of their customers. In addition, data breaches are costly, and they can result in lawsuits and damaged reputations.

DATABASES, ELECTRONIC PROFILING, SPAM, AND OTHER MARKETING ACTIVITIES

The extensive use of **marketing databases** and **government databases** is of concern to many privacy organizations and individuals. Information in marketing databases is frequently sold to companies and other organizations; information in some government databases is available to the public. Some public information can be retrieved from databases via the Web. **Electronic profiling** is the collection of diverse information about an individual. An organization's **privacy policy** addresses how any personal information submitted to that company will be used. Another privacy issue that individuals need to be concerned about centers on the vast amount of **spam** (unsolicited bulk e-mail) that occurs today.

Chapter Objective 5:
Describe some privacy concerns regarding databases, electronic profiling, spam, and telemarketing, and identify ways individuals can protect their privacy.

Protecting your e-mail address is one of the best ways to avoid spam. A **throw-away e-mail address** can be used for any activities that may result in spam; your permanent personal e-mail address can then be reserved for communications that should not result in spam. Before providing any personal information via a Web page, it is a good idea to review the Web site's privacy policy to see if the information will be shared with other organizations. Consider whether or not the Web site is requesting too much personal information, and only provide the required data. Do not provide personal details in chat rooms and personal Web sites. Unless you do not mind spam or are using a throw-away e-mail address, avoid completing online forms, such as those used to enter sweepstakes.

E-mail filters can be used to manage an individual's e-mail; **spam filters** are used to identify possible spam. To reduce the amount of spam, junk mail, online ads, and telemarketing calls received, an individual can **opt out** of marketing activities. It's possible that future marketing activities will require individuals to **opt in** in order to participate.

Individuals and businesses should be cautious when disposing of old hardware, such as hard drives and CDs, that contain sensitive data. Minimally, hard drives to be reused should be *wiped* clean; CDs, DVDs, and other media to be disposed of should be shredded.

ELECTRONIC SURVEILLANCE AND MONITORING

Computer monitoring software that can record an individual's computer use is viewed as a privacy violation by some, as is the increased use of **video surveillance** in public locations. Although it is allowed by law, some employees view **employee monitoring** (such as monitoring computer use, telephone calls, and an individual's location using a smart ID card or video surveillance) as an invasion of their privacy. **Presence technology**—the ability of one device on a network to know the status of another device on that network—allows users of computers, mobile phones, and other communications devices to determine the availability of other individuals before contacting them.

Chapter Objective 6:
Discuss several types of electronic surveillance and monitoring, and list ways individuals can protect their privacy.

To protect the privacy of employees and customers, businesses have a responsibility to keep private information about their employees, the company, and their customers safe. Firewalls, password-protected files, and encryption can help secure this information. Businesses have the responsibility to monitor employee activities in order to ensure that employees are performing the jobs they are being paid to do, are not causing lost business, and are not leaving the company open to lawsuits. To inform employees of allowable activities, an *employee policy* or code of conduct should be developed and distributed to employees. For the highest level of privacy while at the workplace, employees should perform only work-related activities on the job.

COMPUTER SECURITY AND PRIVACY LEGISLATION

Although computer security and privacy are viewed as extremely important issues, legislating these issues is difficult due to ongoing changes in technology, jurisdictional issues, and varying opinions. Some legislation related to computer security has been enacted; new legislation is being considered on a regular basis.

Chapter Objective 7:
Discuss the status of computer security and privacy legislation.

REVIEW ACTIVITIES

KEY TERM MATCHING

a. digital counterfeiting

b. disaster recovery plan

c. full disk encryption (FDE)

d. information privacy

e. presence technology

f. software piracy

g. spam

h. surge suppressor

i. system failure

j. uninterruptible power supply (UPS)

Instructions: Match each key term on the left with the definition on the right that best describes it.

1. ________ A device containing a built-in battery that provides continuous power to a computer and other connected components when the electricity goes out.

2. ________ A device that protects hardware from damage due to electrical fluctuations.

3. ________ A written plan that describes the steps a company will take following the occurrence of a disaster.

4. ________ Technology that enables one computing device (such as a computer or mobile device) to locate and identify the current status of another device on the same network.

5. ________ The complete malfunction of a computer system.

6. ________ The rights of individuals and companies to control how information about them is collected and used.

7. ________ A technology that encrypts everything stored on a storage medium automatically, without any user interaction.

8. ________ The unauthorized copying of a computer program.

9. ________ The use of computers or other types of digital equipment to make illegal copies of currency, checks, collectibles, and other items.

10. ________ Unsolicited, bulk e-mail sent over the Internet.

SELF-QUIZ

Instructions: Circle **T** if the statement is true, **F** if the statement is false, or write the best answer in the space provided. **Answers for the self-quiz are located in the References and Resources Guide at the end of the book.**

1. **T F** As long as a business owns one legal copy of a software program, it can install that program on as many computers as desired without fear of retribution.

2. **T F** Electronic profiling is the act of using electronic means to collect a variety of in-depth information about an individual, such as name, address, income, and buying habits.

3. **T F** Encryption can be used for privacy purposes, in addition to security purposes.

4. **T F** One way of safeguarding your e-mail address is to use a single e-mail address for all online activity, including personal e-mail and online shopping.

5. **T F** Very few major U.S. companies monitor the online activities of their employees.

6. A(n) ________ plan can help a business get operational again following a fire, an act of sabotage, or a similar disaster.

7. Color copying money is an example of ________.

8. An e-mail ________ can be used to route suspected spam automatically into an e-mail folder.

9. If you ________, you are requesting that you be removed from marketing activities or that your information not be shared with other companies; if you ________, you are requesting to participate.

10. Match each precaution with the security risk it is designed to protect against, and write the corresponding number in the blank to the left of each security risk.

a. ________ Digital counterfeiting		**1.** Encryption
b. ________ Hardware theft		**2.** Surge suppressor
c. ________ Privacy breach		**3.** Security thread
d. ________ System damage		**4.** Proximity app
e. ________ Unauthorized computer access		**5.** Cable lock

EXERCISES

1. Match each privacy risk with its related phrase, and write the corresponding number in the blank to the left of each phrase.

a. ________ Throw-away e-mail address	**1.** Employee monitoring
b. ________ Computer monitoring software	**2.** Video surveillance
c. ________ Riding public transportation	**3.** Spam

2. Supply the missing words to complete the following statements.
   a. ________ refers to all content on a storage medium being encrypted automatically.
   b. ________ refers to the ability to locate the current status of an individual via a network.
3. List two precautions that can be taken while traveling with a portable computer to guard against its theft.
4. Explain the purpose of an uninterruptible power supply (UPS) and how it differs in function from a surge suppressor.
5. Think of one computer-related security or privacy risk you have encountered recently. Describe the risk and list at least one precaution that could be taken to minimize that risk.

DISCUSSION QUESTIONS

1. Some privacy controversies stem from the fact that individuals are automatically included instead of having to opt in. For instance, with several new Facebook features over the past few years members were automatically enrolled when the feature was introduced until the member opted out. Should all online marketing activities be on an opt-in basis? How would you feel if your online activities (such as your online purchases) were shared with others without your consent? Does it make a difference if the activities are linked to your identity or anonymous? Facebook was once ordered to pay $9.5 million ($6.5 million of which was used to fund a privacy foundation) in response to a lawsuit related to its Beacon advertising program that was eventually abandoned due to user privacy complaints—is this justified?
2. Spam is increasingly being filtered by ISPs and e-mail programs, and pop-up blockers can block many Web page advertisements. If this trend continues and these activities are no longer viable marketing activities, what will the long-term effect be? Will free Web content begin to disappear? Is paying Internet users to receive spam or view Web ads a viable option? Just as with television, some amount of advertising is typically necessary in order to support free content. What do you think is the optimal balance for the Web?

PROJECTS

HOT TOPICS

1. **Electronic Health Records (EHRs)** The use of electronic health records (EHRs) is growing rapidly. Proponents view EHRs as a means to deliver better care more efficiently. However, some privacy advocates are concerned about the possible security breaches of servers containing digital private medical information.

   For this project, research the current use of EHRs. What are the benefits? Are EHRs widely used? Are you concerned about your medical history being stored on a computer that, potentially, could be accessed by a hacker or other unauthorized individual? Do you think the risk of a privacy breach is higher with EHRs as compared with the records contained in conventional paper file folders? At the conclusion of your research, prepare a one-page summary of your findings and opinions and submit it to your instructor.

SHORT ANSWER/ RESEARCH

2. **E-Voting** E-voting—casting ballots online or via an electronic e-voting machine—has been surrounded by controversy. Concerns include the accuracy and security of e-voting machines, the ability of online voting systems to prevent someone from voting as another individual and to protect the privacy of votes cast electronically, and the ability to perform an accurate recount.

   For this project, research the current status of e-voting. Have universal standards been developed for all e-voting machines used in the United States or is that decision made on a state-by-state basis? What security measures are being used with e-voting and online voting systems to ensure they cannot be hacked and that only the registered voter is permitted to cast his or her vote? Form an opinion about the use of e-voting machines and online voting. Would you be comfortable casting your vote via an e-voting machine? How about online? At some point, do you think online voting will become the norm? If so, how would you suggest handling individuals who have no Internet access available to them on Election Day? At the conclusion of your research, submit your findings and opinions to your instructor in the form of a short paper, no more than two pages in length.

HANDS ON

3. **Browser Privacy Settings** There are a variety of settings in a Web browser that pertain to privacy, such as cookie, cache, and history settings.

   For this project, find a computer (either your own or one in a school computer lab or at your local public library) on which you are permitted to change the Internet options (ask permission first if you are not sure if these actions are allowed) and perform the following tasks:

   a. Open Internet Explorer and use the *Internet Options* option on the Tools menu or button to check the current settings on the General and Privacy tabs. Using the General tab, delete your browsing history (temporary files, history, cookies, saved passwords, and Web form information).

   b. Visit at least five different Web sites to build a history and cookie list. You may want to go to an e-commerce site and add items to your shopping cart (but don't check out) or personalize a portal page, such as MSNBC.com or My Yahoo!.

   c. Display your history list. Are the Web sites you visited listed? Use the Browsing history Settings button on the Internet Options dialog box to view the temporary files, including your cookie files. Were new cookies added during your session? If so, are they all from the Web sites you visited, or are any of them third-party cookies?

   d. Delete all temporary Internet files, sign out of any personalized pages, and close the browser window. Prepare a short summary of your work to submit to your instructor.

ETHICS IN ACTION

4. **Security Camera Networks** As discussed in the chapter, live surveillance cameras are being used at an increasing number of public locations. Some view this as a valid crime prevention tool; others think it is an invasion of privacy. Is it ethical for businesses to use video cameras to record customers' activities? If so, for what purposes? Does the government have the responsibility to use every means possible to protect the country and its citizens? Or do citizens have the right not to be watched in public? One objection stated about these systems is "It's not the same as a cop on the corner. This is a cop on every corner." What if it were a live police officer at each public video camera location instead of a camera? Would that be more acceptable from a privacy standpoint? If people do not plan to commit criminal acts in public, should they be concerned that law enforcement personnel may see them? Does the risk of being recorded deter some illegal or unethical acts?

    For this project, form an opinion about the ethical ramifications of public video surveillance and be prepared to discuss your position (in class, via an online class discussion group, in a class chat room, or via a class blog, depending on your instructor's directions). You may also be asked to write a short paper expressing your opinion.

PRESENTATION/ DEMONSTRATION

5. **Privacy Policy Flip-Flops** Although a company's privacy policy may look acceptable when you read it before submitting personal information to that company, there is no guarantee that the policy will not be changed.

    For this project, locate three different privacy policies on Web sites, analyze them, and compare them. Do the policies specify what personal information might be shared and with whom? Do the organizations reserve the right to change their policies at a later time without notice? If so, will they try to notify consumers? Do any of the policies allow for any sharing of data to third-party organizations? If so, is the data personally identifiable, and can customers opt out? Form an opinion regarding a company's right to change its privacy policy and the impact such a change may have on customer loyalty. Share your findings with the class in the form of a short presentation. The presentation should not exceed 10 minutes and should make use of one or more presentation aids, such as a whiteboard, handouts, or a computer-based slide presentation (your instructor may provide additional requirements). You may also be asked to submit a summary of the presentation to your instructor.

BALANCING ACT

6. **Should the Government Be Allowed to Prevent Web Site Tracking?** The proposed *Do-Not-Track Online Act of 2013* has rekindled the debate surrounding tracking Web site activity for advertising purposes. Though the law, if enacted, wouldn't prohibit tracking, it would require the FTC to establish standardized mechanisms that people could use to have their Web browser tell Web sites and other online entities if they agree to tracking activities. Advocates of do-not-track provisions argue that they just want to protect privacy. Companies with Web sites (particularly small- and medium-sized businesses) state they depend on ad networks and other online resources to connect with potential customers and do-not-track provisions may create a hardship. If tracking provisions are enabled, should consumers be required to opt in to marketing activities or to opt out of them? Who should make the regulations—technology companies? Consumers? The government? Are you concerned that some Web sites track your browsing activities to display relevant ads and offers or do you like the customization provided by the tracking? Is voluntary compliance with standards developed by the industry sufficient or does this issue require legislation? If you use social media, how does Web site tracking compare with the information you share via your social networking sites in terms of loss of privacy? If tracking were illegal unless a consumer opts in, would you? Why or why not?

    Pick a side on this issue, form an opinion and gather supporting evidence, and be prepared to discuss and defend your position in a classroom debate or in a 1–2 page paper, depending on your instructor's directions.

expert insight on...

Web-Based Multimedia and E-Commerce

Jim Griffith, aka "Griff," is the Dean of eBay Education, a roving eBay ambassador, an eBay spokesperson, the host of eBay Radio, and the author of *The Official eBay Bible*. An enthusiastic eBay buyer and seller since 1996, Griff spends nearly all his waking hours teaching others how to use eBay effectively, safely, and profitably, and spreading the word about eBay across print, radio, and TV. Griff has worked for eBay for 17 years.

A Conversation with JIM GRIFFITH

Dean of eBay Education, eBay

> *". . . the most valuable asset for any business, online or offline, is the customer."*

My Background . . .

Although I have many roles at eBay, my most public role—Dean of eBay Education—is unique, slightly unorthodox, and best understood in the context of my history with the company. I was originally a user on eBay in the very early days (1996) and spent a lot of time assisting other buyers and sellers on eBay's one chat board. My posts came to the attention of eBay founder Pierre Omidyar who offered me a job as eBay's first customer support rep. I continued to be an active member of the eBay community along with my new duties at the time, which included assisting and teaching buyers, sellers, and eBay employees how to use eBay. Over time, I also became an eBay spokesperson, lead instructor of our eBay University program, author of *The Official eBay Bible* (now in its third edition), and host of eBay Radio.

In addition to the obvious knowledge of the eBay Web site, our policies, and the basics of business, the skills that proved to be most critical during my seventeen-year tenure at eBay (and I should say I am still refining them) would be diplomacy, empathy, civility, and a strong sense of self-deprecating humor.

It's Important to Know . . .

The basic principles behind successful e-commerce are no different than those behind traditional offline commerce. For example, the most valuable asset for any business, online or offline, is the customer. This is especially true for e-commerce where the competition for customers is fierce. Although the technologies and transaction experience for the Web and for traditional retail are markedly different, the standard, tried-and-true business basics (such as business planning, inventory procurement and management, customer acquisition and management, and marketing) are as crucial to e-commerce as they are to traditional business.

The importance of an easy-to-use, well-designed, and appealing Web site. All of the inventory in the world is for naught if the buyer cannot search through it and purchase it with ease.

Online commerce technologies are constantly changing. What is cutting edge today will soon be passé. Anyone who makes his or her living online absolutely must stay on top of all online marketplace technology advances and adopt and implement them as necessary. As an example, the recent explosion in the popularity and adoption of social networking sites like Twitter and Facebook have created an entire new field of online business called "Social Commerce." Consumers in general—and online consumers in particular—are much more business and technology savvy than they were a mere 5 years ago. Demanding consumers will have little or no patience for online businesses that do not provide the best possible shopping experience.

How I Use this Technology . . .

Besides working for eBay, I am an avid consumer and seller online. I make at least one online purchase a day and I always have a selection of items up for sale (on eBay). My online e-commerce activity along with my job of instructing and assisting buyers and sellers to navigate and utilize eBay and PayPal requires an extensive working knowledge of and familiarity with our own Web sites (eBay and PayPal).

"Anyone who makes his or her living online absolutely must stay on top of all online marketplace technology advances . . ."

What the Future Holds . . .

The Internet revolution has in many ways changed the nature of human commerce forever. The most important impact of the Internet revolution has been the empowerment of the consumer. Never before has the buyer had so much control over the direction of the marketplace. This will only increase as time goes on, and the businesses that acknowledge this new reality and plan accordingly are the ones that will survive and thrive.

In the future, more brick-and-mortar business owners will adopt the Internet as a primary or secondary channel for their businesses. In addition, more small businesses will start up solely on the Internet as the cost of entry into the online marketplace continues to drop and the gap in the costs of starting an online and offline business continues to grow. This will lead to even more choices for the online consumer, who will continue to exert increasing service demands and pricing pressure on online sellers.

However, as the Internet becomes more a part of our day-to-day lives, the idea of the Internet as a unique environment will start to disappear, especially as access to the Internet becomes cheaper and more widespread (for example, embedded in appliances, cell phones, media devices, and even the walls of our homes!). Just like technologies before it (such as telegraph, telephone, radio, and television), we will soon take the Internet for granted as it matures and eventually becomes completely entwined within the matrix of our daily lives.

My Advice to Students . . .

Unless you're interested in pursuing a career in computer science, engineering, or programming, an academic study of the inner workings of the Internet or computers will not be a requirement for a career in an Internet-based industry. However, Internet companies will have an ever-increasing demand for inventive product marketing personnel, product designers, and intellectual property attorneys.

That said, whatever career you pursue, never forget that the direction of online commerce (and the world in general) is toward more control in the hands of the individual. Adjust your career path accordingly!

Discussion Question

Jim Griffith views the online buyer as an extremely influential part of the e-commerce marketplace. Think of online purchases you have made. How did your buying decision differ from shopping locally? What factors influenced your final decision? How does the increased number of online sources for products impact the online marketplace? Do consumers have more influence over online stores than over brick-and-mortar stores? Why or why not? If you were starting a business, would you have an e-commerce presence? A brick-and-mortar presence? Both? Be prepared to discuss your position (in class, via an online class discussion group, in a class chat room, or via a class blog, depending on your instructor's directions). You may also be asked to write a short paper expressing your opinion.

>For more information on eBay, visit www.ebay.com. For more information about e-commerce, read *FutureShop* by Daniel Nissanoff, and for more information about effective, safe, and successful buying or selling on eBay, refer to *The Official eBay Bible* by Jim "Griff" Griffith.

chapter 8

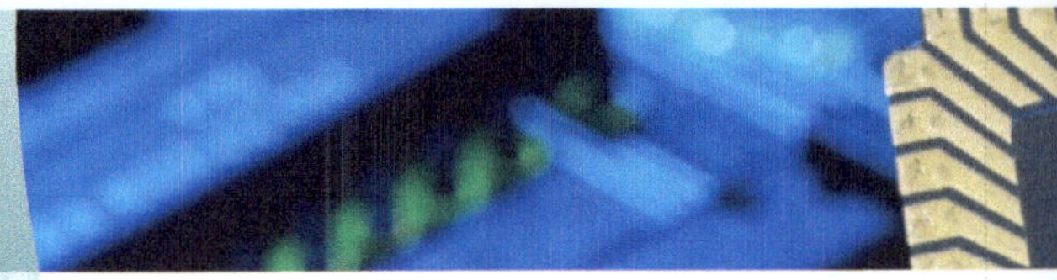

Emerging Technologies

After completing this chapter, you will be able to do the following:

1. Describe what the computer of the future might look like, including some examples of emerging types of hardware.
2. Understand the effect that emerging computer technologies, such as nanotechnology, quantum computers, and optical computers, may have on the computer of the future.
3. Name some emerging wired and wireless networking technologies.
4. Explain what is meant by the term *artificial intelligence* (AI) and list some AI applications.
5. List some new and upcoming technological advances in medicine.
6. Name some new and upcoming technological advances in the military.
7. Discuss potential societal implications of emerging technologies.

outline

© Stockbyte/ Getty Images

OVERVIEW

No study of computers would be complete without a look to the future. The rapid technological advancements that we've seen in the last few decades have been extraordinary, but some believe the best is yet to come. New advances are being made all the time in areas such as computer hardware, Internet applications, and networking technologies. In general, technology is continuing to become more user-friendly and more integrated into our daily lives, and that trend is expected to continue. For instance, imagine the following scenario: You walk up to your locked front door and gain access simply by touching the doorknob or speaking your name. When you enter a room, the lights, stereo system, and digital artwork on the walls change automatically to reflect your preferences. Your refrigerator and pantry keep up-to-the-moment inventories of their contents, and your closet automatically selects outfits for you based on the weather and your schedule for the day. Sounds like something out of a science fiction movie, doesn't it? Yet, all the technologies just mentioned are either already available or in development.

Many of us are excited to see what new applications and technological improvements the future will bring, as well as how computers, the Internet, and other technologies will evolve. However, our enthusiasm for this progress should be balanced with the understanding that some future applications may not turn out the way we expect or may actually have a negative impact on society. One of the biggest challenges in an era of rapidly changing technologies is evaluating the potential impact of new technology and trying to ensure that new products and services do not adversely affect our security, privacy, and safety.

This chapter focuses on some of the emerging technologies that are already beginning to impact our lives. Topics include the computer of the future, emerging networking technologies, artificial intelligence (AI), and technological advances in medicine and in the military. The chapter closes with a discussion of the societal implications of emerging technologies. ■

THE COMPUTER OF THE FUTURE

While the exact makeup of future computers is anyone's guess, it is expected that they will keep getting smaller, faster, more powerful, and more user-friendly, and that they will eventually use voice, touch, gestures, and other alternative input methods more than keyboards and mice. Portable computers and mobile devices will continue to be used as primary computing devices at home and work, as well as while on the go. Tomorrow's home and business computers will likely not even look like today's computers—instead they may be built into walls, desks, appliances, and perhaps even jewelry and clothing. In addition to their changing appearance, computers are expected to keep converging with other devices and to continue to take on multiple roles to serve our personal needs, as well as to control our household or office environment. Computers in the future may also be able to offer multisensory output—enabling users to see, hear, feel, taste, and smell output—and they will likely become even more environmentally friendly.

Some examples of emerging new hardware are discussed next, followed by a discussion of some technologies that may change the overall makeup of computers in the future—namely, *nanotechnology*, *quantum computers*, and *optical computers*.

TIP

Google's new *Handwrite* feature allows you to use your finger to write out search queries on the device's screen in order to perform a mobile search more quickly than using an on-screen keyboard, and it is likely more accurate than using voice input. To use the Handwrite feature, just write your search terms anywhere on the Google home page displayed on your smartphone or tablet screen.

ASK THE EXPERT

Courtesy TabletKiosk

Martin Smekal, President and Founder, TabletKiosk

What do you expect to be the optimal input device of the future?

The launch of Apple's iPad has brought unprecedented awareness of the tablet form factor and created wider market acceptance of touch screen technology. As a result, we've seen a sharp rise in companies looking to incorporate touch technology into their business solutions. The optimal device, in our opinion, will offer a range of input options for total flexibility—multiple touch input options, digital inking for handwriting recognition, voice recognition, and, soon, even gesture recognition will be the norm.

Emerging Hardware

The overall size and appearance of computers seem to change on a continual basis. We now have fully functioning personal computers that are small enough to fit in a pocket or be worn on the body. Technologies are continuing to be developed to make computers and computer components smaller, faster, and more capable. Some of the exciting emerging input, processing, output, and storage hardware and technologies are discussed next.

Emerging Input Devices

Because of the increasing amount of data entered into mobile devices today, these devices often have a keyboard or can be inserted into a *keyboard dock* or *keyboard folio* (see Figure 8-1) when a keyboard is needed. New input methods for mobile devices include tiny keyboards (such as on smart watches) that automatically zoom in on the part of the keyboard you touch to allow you to touch a larger key for your final selection, and the *Swype* app used with on-screen keyboards to supply input by continuously dragging through the letters in a word to spell that word (refer again to Figure 8-1). In addition, voice input and speech recognition capabilities are increasingly being incorporated into computers, smartphones, car navigation systems, and other devices to enable hands-free input. Specialty speech recognition systems are frequently used to control robots and other electronic equipment, such as those used by surgeons during surgical procedures. Touch, pen, and *gesture* input is beginning to be used with personal computers and is becoming the norm for mobile devices. The use of gesture input started with motion-sensitive gaming controllers, such as the *Wii Remote* and the *Xbox Kinect*. Today, gesture input is also used to detect gestures made in conjunction with large screen interactive advertising displays and it may soon be incorporated into computers of the future (see the Trend box).

One new trend in the area of touch input is the *table PC*—a large screen computer either built into a table or designed to be used on a table (such as the 27-inch table PC shown in Figure 8-1) and that allows multi-touch input from multiple users. Table PCs can be used by several individuals at once to play games together, work together on a project, participate in an interactive museum display together, and so forth.

FIGURE 8-1
Examples of emerging input devices.

Courtesy Logitech · Courtesy Nuance · Courtesy Lenovo

KEYBOARD FOLIOS **SWIPE APP** **TABLE PCS**

TREND

Perceptual Computing

In the 2002 futuristic movie *Minority Report*, Tom Cruise changes the images on his display by gesturing with his hands. While it was fiction in the movie, it is now just about a reality. Enter the trend of *perceptual computing* where users control their devices with three dimensional (3D) gestures, voice commands, and facial expressions instead of with traditional input devices like the keyboard and mouse.

Gesture input itself isn't new—it's been used in various forms for several years with devices such as the Nintendo Wii, Xbox Kinect, and the Apple iPhone and in large screen consumer gaming and advertising applications; it is also an important component of the Windows 8 operating system. But the gesture-input systems of the future are expected to be much more sophisticated and combined with other types of input to allow users to more naturally control their computers and to allow the devices to adapt to each individual's need. For example, a computer or phone could offer to make a game easier if a player appears frustrated or could offer to turn the page on a tablet displaying a recipe if the hands of the person cooking are covered with flour.

One recent step in this direction is the *Leap 3D System* shown in the accompanying photograph. It is an iPod-sized box that connects to a computer via a USB port and creates an eight-cubic-foot 3D interactive space inside which users can swipe, grab, pinch (refer again to the photo), and move objects around as if they were using a touch screen, except that they are not actually touching the screen. And noncontact systems such as this have additional advantages, such as being able to use 3D gestures instead of just 2D gestures, avoiding the fingerprint and germ issues related to public keyboard and touch screen use, allowing for full body input, and enabling input to be performed from a slight distance (such as from a nearby chair or through a glass storefront window).

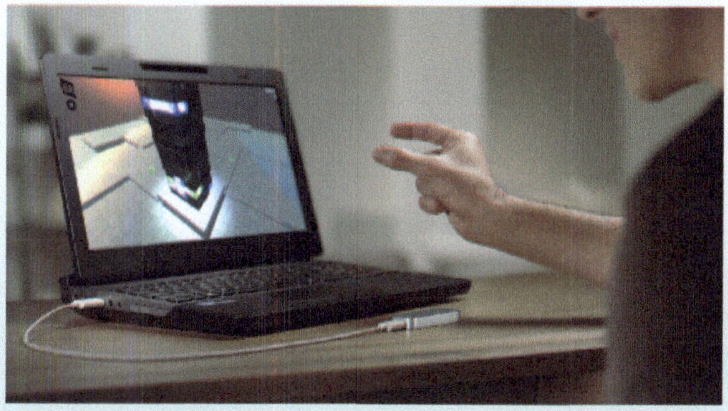

Courtesy Leap Motion

The digital camera capabilities built into most smartphones today allow for several types of emerging input applications. For instance, they allow gesture input, as well as the use of *two-dimensional (2D) barcodes* and *augmented reality applications* to retrieve and display useful information. **Two-dimensional (2D) barcodes**—such as the *QR (Quick Response) code* that represents data with a matrix of small squares—store information both horizontally and vertically and so can hold significantly more data than conventional one-dimensional barcodes. Most 2D barcodes today are designed to be used by consumers with smartphones. For instance, capturing the image of a QR barcode located on a magazine or newspaper ad, poster, or billboard with a smartphone's camera could enable the consumer's smartphone to load a Web page, dial a phone number or send a text message (to enter a contest, for example), display a video clip or photo (stored either in the code or online), download a coupon or ticket, or Like a Facebook page (see Figure 8-2). QR codes can also be used to transfer contact information to a phone or add an event to an online calendar. **Augmented reality** is another emerging smartphone application. With augmented reality, computer-generated images are overlayed on top of real-time images. Today, Web-based content is typically displayed over the images seen through a smartphone's camera and displayed on the smartphone. The content is

FIGURE 8-2
Most smartphones can read 2D barcodes.

Courtesy SPARQCode

>Two-dimensional (2D) barcode. A barcode that represents data with a matrix of small squares and stores information both horizontally and vertically so it can hold significantly more data than a conventional one-dimensional barcode. **>Augmented reality.** When computer generated images are overlayed on top of real-time images, such as to overlay information over the photo or video displayed on a smartphone.

typically based on the user's location (determined by the smartphone's GPS), the video feed from the smartphone's camera, a digital compass, and other data obtained from the smartphone. Displaying this information requires a *mobile AR browser* or an appropriate *mobile AR app*. Some initial mobile augmented reality apps include overlaying home listing information over the video images displayed as a phone is pointing at houses in a neighborhood, displaying stats and player information as a phone is pointing at a sporting event, and displaying activity opportunities (such as restaurant, movie, museum, or shopping information) as a phone is pointing at a business district.

For making electronic payments while on the go, use of *Near Field Communication* (*NFC*) technology is expected to grow in the near future. NFC uses RFID technology to facilitate communication between devices, including transferring payment information, receipts, boarding passes, and other information wirelessly between payment terminals and smartphones. Worldwide, vending machines are also increasingly going cashless, supporting only NFC, credit cards, and other electronic payment methods, instead of cash.

FIGURE 8-3
Flexible electronics.

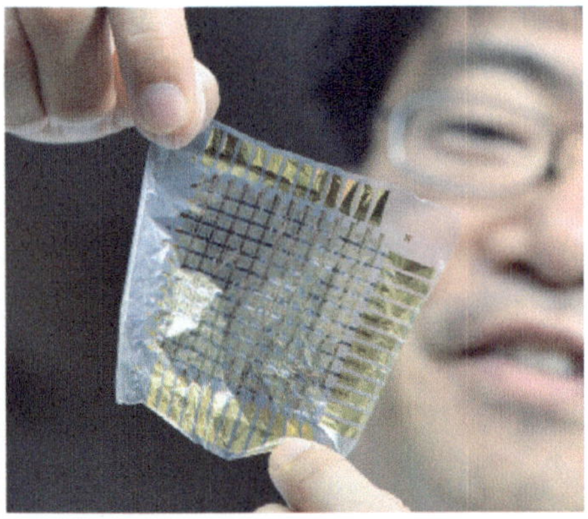

Emerging Processing Technologies

Computers and CPU manufacturers are continually working to develop ways to make computers work better, faster, more reliably, and more efficiently. For example, new designs for motherboards and CPUs are always under development, computer components are continually being built smaller so more power and capabilities can be contained in the same size package, new materials are being used, and new technologies are being developed on a continual basis. For instance, the new *USB 3.0* standard allows peripheral devices to communicate with a computer at more than 10 times the speed of USB 2.0. And, for integrating CPUs and other computer components into clothing and other flexible materials, as well as for creating flexible devices (such as the flexible smartphone screens that are expected to be available soon), *flexible electronic components* (see Figure 8-3) are needed and are currently being developed. In addition to the ability to be bent without damaging the circuitry, flexible circuits will be thinner, lighter, generate little heat, and consume significantly less energy than conventional processors.

For packing an increasing number of components onto small chips, the *three-dimensional* (*3D*) *chip* is one emerging technology. Typically, 3D chips are created by layering individual silicon wafers on top of one another, which cuts down on the surface area required. 3D chips are now being used with memory, flash memory, and CPUs. For example, recent Intel CPUs (such as third-generation Core processors) include a 3D transistor called *Tri-Gate* (see the illustration in Figure 8-4). Tri-Gate transistors provide increased performance and low voltage, making them ideal for use in small devices, such as mobile devices. In addition, Samsung recently announced the release of the world's first mass-produced 3D flash memory chip. By using a special etching technology to drill down through the chip layers to connect them electronically, Samsung plans to eventually produce chips with 24 layers.

FIGURE 8-4
3D chips. In this 3D transistor, the electrical current (represented by the yellow dots) flows on three sides of a vertical fin.

One hurdle in 3D chip development, as well as in other means of packing an increasing amount of technology into a smaller system unit, is the amount of heat generated. Because heat can damage components and cooler chips can run faster, virtually all computers today employ *fans*, *heat sinks* (small components usually made out of aluminum with fins that help to dissipate heat), or other methods to cool the CPU and system unit. Mobile device cases today aren't designed for fans and so their cooling systems typically rely on using mobile CPUs that run cooler than desktop CPUs and on adapting the speed and power of the device's components to cool the device as needed. However, as the speed and capabilities of mobile devices continue to increase, additional cooling methods may become necessary and are currently under development. *Liquid cooling systems* consist of liquid (often a water solution) filled tubes that draw heat away from processors and other critical components, and they can be designed to cool between the layers of 3D chips, as well as to cool the inside of the system unit. An emerging possibility for cooling servers is *immersion cooling* where the hardware is actually submerged into units filled with a liquid cooling solution (refer to Figure 8-5).

As demand by consumers and businesses for online software, services, and media-rich experiences continues to increase, some experts predict that *tera-scale computing*—the ability of a computer to process one trillion floating point operations per second (*teraflops*)—will eventually be more common. While supercomputers currently reach teraflop and *petaflop* (1,000 teraflops) speeds, much of today's tera-scale research is focusing on creating multi-core processors with tens to hundreds of cores used in conjunction with multithreaded hardware and software that can execute multiple streams of instructions—*threads*—at the same time in order to achieve teraflop performance. The research also includes working on developing higher-speed communications between computers, such as between Web servers and high-performance mobile devices or computers, to help facilitate high-performance cloud computing. Intel, one of the leaders in tera-scale research, has created a *teraflop processor* that contains 80 cores to test strategies for moving terabytes of data rapidly from core to core and between cores and memory. It has also developed a 20 MB *SRAM* memory chip that is attached directly to the processor in order to speed up communication between processors and memory. This design allows thousands of interconnections, which enable data to travel at more than one *terabyte per second* (*TBps*) between memory and the processor cores. It is expected that this speed will be needed to handle the terabytes of data used by applications in the near future. In fact, *exascale computers* that perform 1 million trillion calculations per second and may have as many as 100 million CPU cores are expected to appear by 2018.

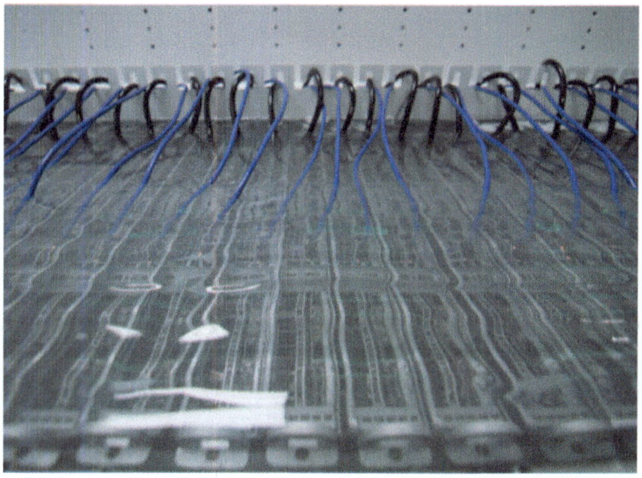

Courtesy Green Revolution Cooling

FIGURE 8-5
Immersion cooling systems. Can be used to cool servers in large data centers.

TIP

To more easily fit into the shrinking notebook and tablet PC form factor, fans the size and thickness of a credit card are in development and expected to become available before 2015.

For memory improvements, several forms of **nonvolatile RAM (NVRAM)**—that is, memory that retains its data when the power to the device is off—are either becoming available or under development. For instance, *magnetic RAM* (commonly referred to as *MRAM*) uses *magnetic polarization* rather than an electrical charge to store data, *memristor-based RAM* uses memristors (short for *memory resistors*) that change their resistance in response to current flowing through them, *NRAM* uses *carbon nanotubes* (discussed later in this chapter), and *PRAM* (*phase change random access memory*) has a special coating that changes its physical state when heat is applied (similar to the rewritable CDs and DVDs discussed in Chapter 2). The most common applications for nonvolatile RAM today include storing critical data for enterprise systems as they operate to guard against data loss and saving the data necessary to help industrial automation and robotics systems recover quickly from a power loss. Other emerging applications include "instant-on" computers and mobile devices that can be turned on and off like an electric light, without any loss of data. Another advantage of nonvolatile RAM is that it doesn't require power to retain data so, when used in mobile devices, it consumes less power, which can extend battery life. It is expected that, in the future, a form of nonvolatile RAM will replace volatile RAM, flash memory chips, and possibly even hard drives in computers. As capacities increase (Crossbar recently announced the development of a 1 TB NVRAM chip), that day may be getting closer.

>**Nonvolatile RAM (NVRAM).** Memory chips that do not lose their contents when the power to the computer is turned off.

> **TIP**
>
> Researchers at Intel Labs predict that much of the Internet will use realistic-looking 3D applications by 2020.

Emerging Output Devices

Some of the most recent improvements in display technology center on more versatile output devices and new flat-screen technologies. For instance, recent improvements in flat-panel display technology and graphics processing have led to several emerging *three-dimensional (3D) output devices*, including *3D display screens* for computers. While traditional 3D displays (and most 3D televisions today) require special 3D glasses, the newest 3D computer display products use filters, prisms, multiple lenses, and other technologies built into the display screen to create the 3D effect and, as a result, do not require 3D glasses. Some 3D displays resemble conventional monitors; others are shaped differently, such as the dome-shaped *Perspecta* 3D display that is used primarily for medical imaging. 3D consumer products are increasingly available as well, such as the *Nintendo 3DS* handheld gaming device.

Another emerging 3D output device is the *3D projector*. Some 3D projectors are designed to project 3D images that are viewed with 3D glasses, similar to 3D televisions. Others are designed to project actual 3D projections or *holograms*. For instance, holograms of individuals and objects can be projected onto a stage for a presentation, and hologram display devices can be used in retail stores, exhibitions, and other locations to showcase products or other items in 3D. Another emerging projection option that can be used to project content to a small audience while on the go is the *pico projector*. These pocket-sized projectors typically connect to a smartphone or portable computer to enable the device to project an image (such as a document, presentation, or movie) onto a wall or other flat surface from up to 12 feet away. Pico projectors are also beginning to be integrated directly into mobile devices (see the Samsung Beam *projector phone* shown in Figure 8-6).

> **TIP**
>
> NASA is preparing to launch a 3D printer into space in 2014 in order to enable astronauts to print tools, spare parts, rocket pieces, and even small satellites using spools of plastic strands.

When permanent 3D output is required, such as to print a 3D model of a new building or prototype of a new product, *3D printers* (which typically form output in layers using molten plastic during a series of passes to build a 3D version of the desired output—see Figure 8-6) can be used. 3D printers are becoming available in a variety of sizes, from personal printers for printing smartphone cases, toys, jewelry, and other personal objects to professional printers for printing working product prototypes or custom manufacturing parts. They have even begun to be used to print medical implants using FDA-approved 3D material. One issue with the increased availability of 3D printers is the risk of them being used to print dangerous or illegal items, such as working plastic guns. In fact, after a 3D-printed gun was recently demonstrated firing standard bullets, lawmakers are considering enacting legislation to ban plastic weapons created by 3D printers.

FIGURE 8-6
Some emerging output devices.

PICO PROJECTORS
Can be stand-alone or built into a mobile device; images from the mobile device (such as the smartphone shown here) are projected onto any surface.

3D PRINTERS
This printer can print objects up to the size of a standard basketball.

INTEGRATED PRINTERS
This printer uses no ink and is integrated into the digital camera to print digital photographs.

The capabilities of ink-jet printers are also expanding. For instance, ink-jet technology may eventually be used for dispensing liquid metals, aromas, computer chips and other circuitry, and even "printing" human tissue and other organic materials for medical purposes. In addition, printers are beginning to be integrated into other devices, such as the camera in Figure 8-6 that contains an integrated *ZINK printer*. Unlike conventional printers, ZINK printers use no ink; instead, they use special paper that is coated with special color dye crystals. Before printing, the embedded dye crystals are clear, so *ZINK Paper* looks like regular white photo paper. The ZINK printer uses heat to activate and colorize these dye crystals when a photo is printed, creating a full-color image.

For display screens used with computers, mobile devices, and other electronic devices, there are a number of technologies under development designed to create displays that are more visible, while at the same time using less energy. Some of these technologies are based on *organic light emitting diode* (*OLED*) technology. **Organic light emitting diode (OLED) displays** use layers of organic material, which emit a visible light when electric current is applied. While conventional flat-panel displays based on *LCD* (*liquid crystal display*) technology do not produce light and so require *backlighting*, OLEDs emit a visible light and, therefore, do not use backlighting. This characteristic makes OLEDs more energy efficient than LCDs and lengthens the battery life of portable devices using OLED displays. Other advantages of OLEDs are that they are thinner than LCDs, they have a wider viewing angle than LCDs and so displayed content is visible from virtually all directions, and their images are brighter and sharper than LCDs. Today, OLED displays are incorporated into many digital cameras, mobile phones, portable digital media players, *Google Glass*, and other consumer devices. They are also beginning to appear in television and computer displays and are expected to be more prominent in the near future.

Special types of OLEDs also support applications not possible with CRT or LCD technology. For instance, *flexible OLED* (*FOLED*) displays are built on flexible surfaces, such as plastic or metallic foil, and so they can roll up when not in use (see Figure 8-7). Flexible screens may also be used for integrating displays on military uniform sleeves, as well as allowing retractable wall-mounted large screen displays. *Transparent OLED* (*TOLED*) displays are transparent. The portion of the display that does not currently have an image displayed (and the entire display device when it is off) is nearly as transparent as glass, so the user can see through the screen. TOLEDs open up the possibility of displays on home windows, car windshields, helmet face shields, and other transparent items.

Another emerging flat-panel display technology is *interferometric modulator* (*IMOD*) *displays*. Designed

TIP

Another emerging option in display technology is the *USB monitor*, which connects to a computer via a USB port. Conventional monitors can also connect to a computer via a *USB display adapter*, enabling multiple monitors to be connected to a computer without requiring a new video card.

TIP

White OLED displays are in development for use with light bulbs.

FIGURE 8-7
Some emerging display technologies.

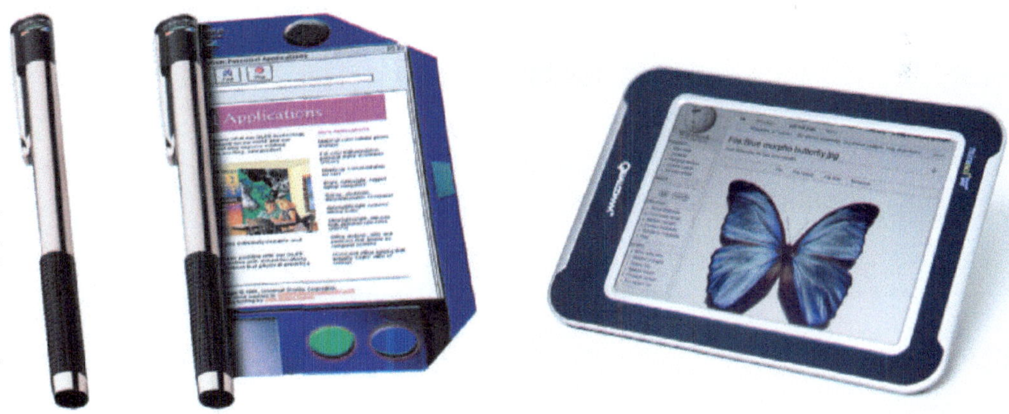

Courtesy of Universal Display Corporation

FOLEDS
Used to create flexible displays on plastic or another type of flexible material.

Courtesy of QUALCOMM MEMS Technologies, Inc.

IMODS
Display is bright and readable, even in direct sunlight.

>**Organic light emitting diode (OLED) display.** A type of flat-panel display that uses emissive organic material to display brighter and sharper images than LCDs.

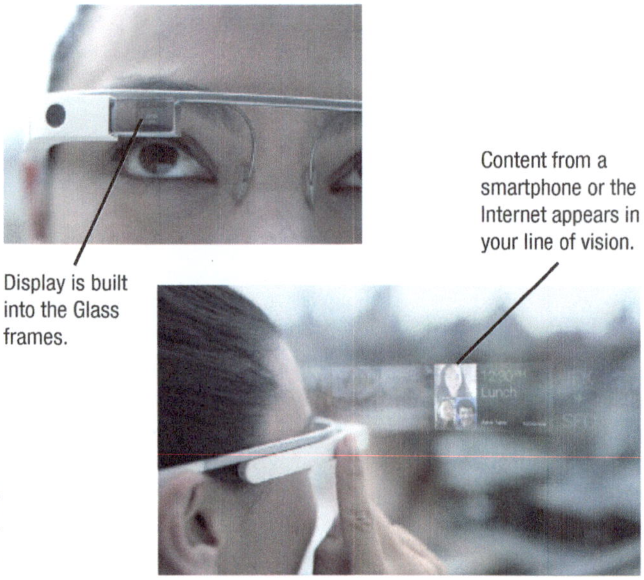

Courtesy Google

FIGURE 8-8
Google Glass.

initially for mobile phones and other portable devices, IMOD displays use external light, such as from the sun or artificial light inside a building, to display images so images are bright and clear even in direct sunlight (refer again to Figure 8-7). And, because backlighting isn't used, power consumption is much less than what is needed for LCD displays. In fact, similar to the e-paper discussed in the Chapter 7 Inside the Industry box, devices using IMOD displays use no power unless the image changes, which means they can remain on at all times without draining the device battery. Beginning to be used with mobile devices, IMODs could eventually be used for outdoor television screens, large digital signs, and other outdoor display devices that normally consume a great deal of power.

While most displays are designed to be looked at from at least several inches away, some displays are designed to be wearable. A *wearable display* usually projects the image from a mobile device (such as a smartphone or media tablet) to a display screen built into the glasses via a wireless connection. Typically, the technology allows the user to see the image as if it is on a distant large screen display, and many wearable displays overlay the projected image on top of what the user is seeing in real time to provide augmented reality. For example, the *Google Glass* eyeglasses-based display shown in Figure 8-8 has a tiny display located where the right lens would be and users can see content projected on that screen in front of what they are seeing normally. Google Glass is typically connected (via Bluetooth) to a smartphone and then content (such as text messages, maps and directions, video calls, and Web pages) is streamed from that phone to the Google Glass display. Google Glass also has a built-in Web browser and can connect directly to a Wi-Fi hotspot when needed, has a touch-sensitive pad on the right side of the frame for input, and a bone-conductive audio output system so that audio output is heard only by the user. In addition to consumer wearable displays that have entertainment and productivity applications (such as being able to access GPS directions as needed or to monitor your e-mail during a meeting), there are also wearable displays designed for soldiers and other mobile workers.

ASK THE EXPERT

Seagate

Courtesy of Seagate Technology LLC

Josh Tinker, Product Planning Manager, Seagate Technology

Should my next computer have a magnetic hard drive or an SSD?

Your storage options for a new PC include traditional hard drives (HDDs), solid-state drives (SSDs), and the newer solid-state hybrid drives (SSHDs). Selecting what is right for you is a trade-off between price, performance, and capacity.

- SSDs have maximized PC performance and very good shock resistance, but are low capacity and pricey.
- HDDs have the lowest cost and high capacity but have average performance.
- SSHDs have SSD-like performance and high capacity, but have a small price premium.

Emerging Storage Devices

Improvements in magnetic disk technology are continuing to increase the data that can be stored on hard drives. Traditionally, the magnetic particles on a hard disk have been aligned horizontally, parallel to the hard disk's surface (referred to as *longitudinal magnetic recording*). To increase capacity and reliability, most new hard drives today use *perpendicular magnetic recording* (*PMR*), in which the bits are placed upright to allow them to be closer together than is possible with a horizontal layout. For instance, PMR currently allows a recording density up to 1 *terabit per square inch* (*Tb/inch*^{2}), which results in internal hard drives with capacities up to about 4 TB of storage for a 3.5-inch hard drive, 1 TB for a 2.5-inch hard drive, and 100 GB for a 1-inch hard drive. To allow for higher capacities, new hard drive technologies are under development. For instance, *shingled magnetic recording* (*SMR*), which squeezes more data onto disks by overlapping the data tracks on them like the shingles on a roof, is expected to become available sometime in 2014 and offer increased capacities. Another option for the future is *Heat-Assisted Magnetic Recording* (*HAMR*), which uses lasers to temporarily heat the surface of the hard disks when storing data in order to pack more data onto the surface than is normally possible—it is expected to boost the storage capacity of a 3.5-inch hard drive to 60 TB by 2016.

One high-capacity storage possibility that, after many years of research and development, is just about a reality is **holographic storage**. *Holographic drives* record data onto *holographic discs* or *holographic cartridges*. To record data, the holographic drive splits the light from a blue laser beam into two beams (a *reference beam* whose angle determines the address used to store data at that particular location on the storage medium and a *signal beam* that contains the data). The signal beam passes through a device called a *spatial light modulator* (*SLM*), which translates the data's 0s and 1s into a *hologram*—a three-dimensional representation of data in the form of a checkerboard pattern of light and dark pixels. The two beams intersect within the recording medium to store the holographic image at that location (see Figure 8-9) by changing the optical density of the medium.

Data stored on a holographic medium is arranged into pages of data containing 1.5 million bits each. An entire page of data can be stored at one time in a single flash of light, so holographic storage systems are very fast. And, because the hologram goes through

TIP

Researchers recently demonstrated the ability to store data in 5D in synthetic crystals—this technology may eventually result in discs that can store 360 TB each and that are stable enough to last essentially forever.

FIGURE 8-9

Holographic storage. Holographic drives store more than one million bits of data in a single flash of light.

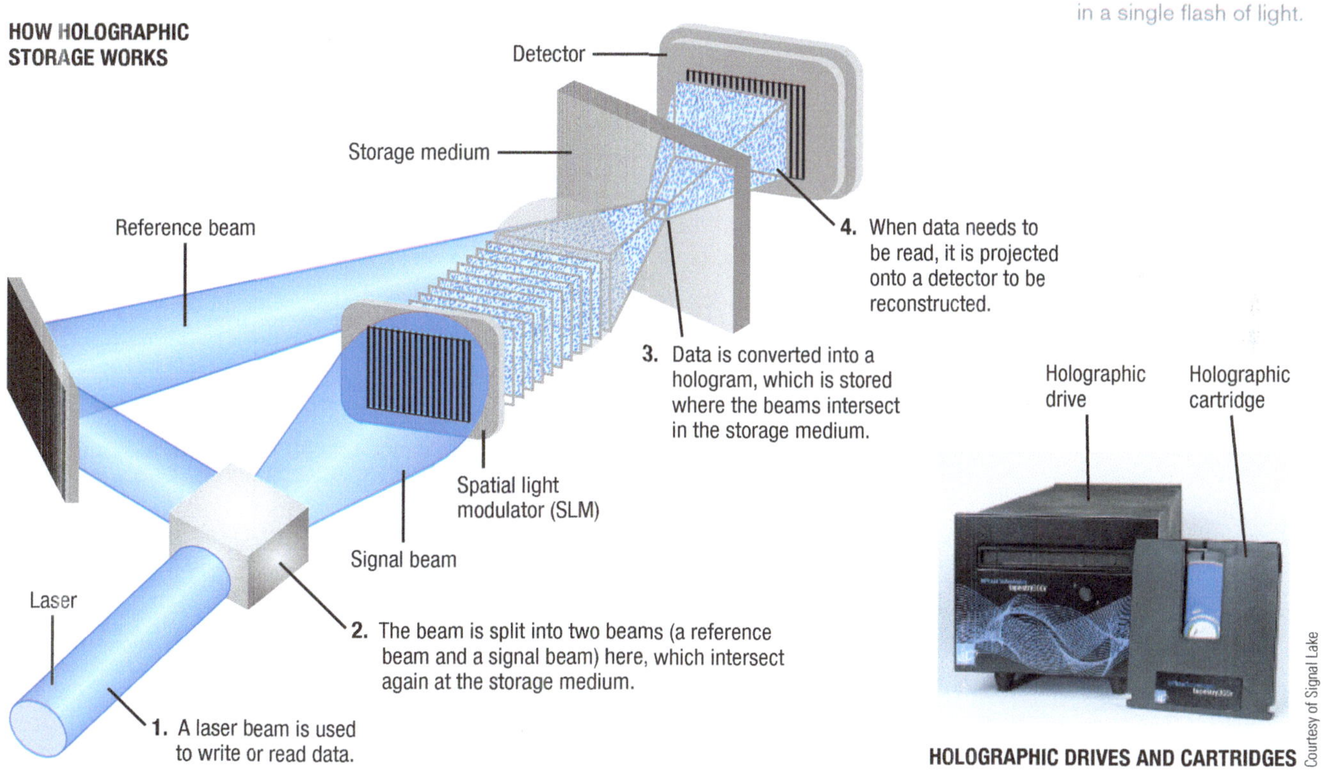

>**Holographic storage.** An emerging type of storage technology that uses multiple blue laser beams to store data in three dimensions.

the entire thickness of the medium, much more data can be stored on a holographic disc or cartridge than on a CD, DVD, or BD of the same physical size. In fact, hundreds of holograms can be stored in an overlapping manner in the same area of the medium—a different reference beam angle or position is used for each hologram so it can be uniquely stored and retrieved when needed. To read data, the reference beam projects the hologram containing the requested data onto a *detector* that reads the entire data page at one time. Holographic storage systems will initially use removable recordable holographic discs that hold 300 GB to 500 GB per disc; most systems can hold multiple discs for increased storage capacity. Holographic data storage systems are particularly suited to applications in which large amounts of data need to be stored or retrieved quickly but rarely changed, such as for business data archiving, high-speed digital video delivery, and image processing for medical, video, and military purposes.

The Impact of Nanotechnology

Although there are varying definitions, most agree that **nanotechnology** involves creating computer components, machines, and other structures that are less than 100 nanometers in size. Consequently, today's CPUs contain components that fit the definition of nanotechnology. However, some experts believe that, eventually, current technology will reach its limits. At that point, transistors and other computer components may need to be built at the atomic and molecular level; that is, starting with single atoms or molecules to construct the components. Prototypes of computer products built in this fashion include a *single atom transistor*, which is a single switch that can be turned on and off like a transistor but is made from a single organic molecule, as well as tiny nickel-based *nanodots* that would, theoretically, allow about 5 TB of data to be stored on a hard drive roughly the size of a postage stamp. In other nanotechnology developments, prototypes of tiny *nanogenerators* have been developed that can be squeezed to generate power; they are expected to eventually be able to power mobile devices with low-frequency vibrations, such as a heartbeat or a simple body movement like walking. And researchers are looking at DNA as a possible long-term high-density archiving storage option and, in fact, have already encoded a variety of data—including Shakespeare's sonnets, a JPEG photo, and an MP3 recording of Martin Luther King Jr.'s "I Have a Dream" speech—into DNA material by translating the data into binary 0s and 1s and then rewriting that data as strings of DNA's chemical bases and storing it in DNA. For a look at a recent nanotechnology development that may lead to new and improved glass on your future mobile phone, see the Technology and You box.

FIGURE 8-10

Carbon nanotubes. This light bulb is powered and held in place by two carbon nanotube fibers.

One nanotechnology development that is already being used in a variety of products available today is **carbon nanotubes** (**CNTs**), which are tiny, hollow tubes made up of carbon atoms. The wall of a single-walled carbon nanotube is only one carbon atom thick and the tube diameter is approximately 10,000 times smaller than a human hair. Carbon nanotubes have great potential for future computing products because they conduct electricity better than copper, are 100 times stronger than steel at one-sixth the weight, conduct heat better than diamonds, and transmit electronic impulses faster than silicon. One recent development is *carbon nanotube fibers* that look and act like thread but conduct heat and electricity like a metal wire (see Figure 8-10). According to the researchers, these fibers are expected to eventually be used in new products for the aerospace, automotive, medical, and smart-clothing markets.

>**Nanotechnology.** The science of creating tiny computers and components by working at the individual atomic and molecular levels. >**Carbon nanotubes (CNTs).** Tiny, hollow tubes made of carbon atoms.

TECHNOLOGY AND YOU

"Magic" Glass

A smartphone with a non-glare, self-cleaning screen? That could be the wave of the future based on a recent development by MIT researchers. By creating nano-sized conical patterns on the surface of the glass using coating and etching techniques, the researchers were able to eliminate its reflective properties, resulting in glass that resists fogging and glare (see the accompanying illustration) and is even self-cleaning.

In addition to making it easier to use mobile devices outdoors, the technology has a host of other possible applications, such as being used for eyeglasses, televisions, car windshields, and even windows in buildings. It could also be applied to solar panels, which can lose as much as 40% of their efficiency within three months due to dust and dirt accumulating on their surfaces. But, for most people, it will likely be the possibility of a tablet or smartphone with glass that eliminates reflections and cleans itself of fingerprints that gets the most attention.

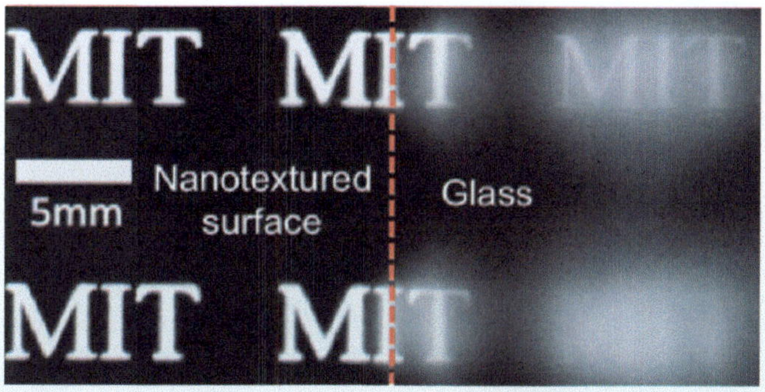

Courtesy KYOO-CHUL PARK and HYUNGRYUL CHOI

MIT GLASS NORMAL GLASS

MIT "magic" glass vs. normal glass. The normal half of this piece of glass (right) can fog up and produce glare; the MIT glass half (left) remains clear.

CNT products currently on the market include lithium ion batteries, and several nanotube-based computing products—like nanotube-based display screens and memory—are currently under development. In addition, IBM researchers are experimenting with a combination of DNA molecules and carbon nanotubes to make smaller, more powerful, and more energy-efficient computer chips. Because carbon nanotubes can transmit electricity and are transparent, they are also being used for product development in the areas of TVs, solar cells, light bulbs, and other similar noncomputing applications. In addition, because of their strength and lightness for their size, carbon nanotubes are being integrated into products that benefit from those characteristics, such as automobile panels, airplanes, tennis rackets, and racing bikes. In fact, the Army recently initiated a two-year program to develop carbon nanotube products to replace conventional copper-based wires and cables in aircraft. Carbon nanotubes are also beginning to be combined with other materials, such as plastic, to increase the durability of materials used to produce other consumer items, such as surfboards.

> **TIP**
>
> Data stored in DNA uses densities that are at least 1,000 times greater than current storage media—about 2.2 PB per gram. At that rate, if you took everything human beings have ever written (an estimated 50 PB of text) and stored it in DNA, it would weigh less than a granola bar.

Two recent developments are *nanofilters* that can remove contaminants from water sources and *nanosensors* that can detect cancer-causing toxins or cancer drugs inside single living cells. Possible future applications of nanotechnology include disposing of e-waste by rearranging dangerous components at the atomic level into inert substances, *nanosponges* that can enter the bloodstream and soak up toxins, improved military uniforms that protect against bullets and germ warfare, and computers and sensors that are small enough to be woven into the fibers of clothing or embedded into paint and other materials. Some of the devices generated by nanotechnology research may contain or be constructed out of organic material.

Quantum and Optical Computers

Computers a few decades from now will likely use technology that is very different from the silicon chips and electronic bits and bytes we are accustomed to today. In addition to being miniature—based on nanotechnology—and likely incorporated into a variety of everyday devices, computers in the future may be *quantum* or *optical computers*.

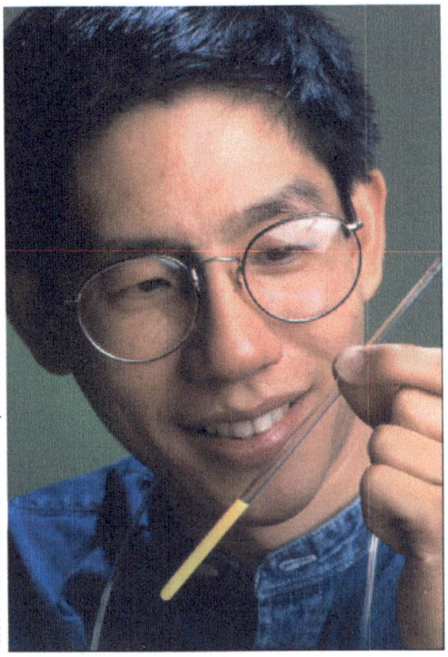

FIGURE 8-11
Quantum computers. The vial of liquid shown here contains the 7-qubit computer used by IBM researchers in 2001 to perform the most complicated computation by a quantum computer to date—factoring the number 15.

Quantum Computing

The idea of **quantum computing** emerged in the 1970s, and it has received renewed interest lately. Quantum computing applies the principles of quantum physics and quantum mechanics to computers, going beyond traditional physics to work at the subatomic level. Quantum computers differ from conventional computers in that they utilize atoms or nuclei working together as *quantum bits* or *qubits*. Qubits function simultaneously as both the computer's processor and memory, and each qubit can represent more than just the two states (one and zero) available to today's electronic bits; a qubit can even represent many states at one time. Quantum computers can perform computations on many numbers at one time, making them, theoretically, exponentially faster than conventional computers. Physically, quantum computers in the future might consist of a thimbleful of liquid whose atoms are used to perform calculations as instructed by an external device.

Even though quantum computers are still in the pioneering stage, working quantum computers do exist. For instance, in 2001 the researchers at IBM's Almaden Research Center created a 7-qubit quantum computer (see Figure 8-11) composed of the nuclei of seven atoms that can interact with each other and be programmed by radio frequency pulses. This quantum computer successfully factored the number 15—not a complicated computation for a conventional computer, but the fact that a quantum computer was able to understand the problem and compute the correct answer is viewed as a highly significant event in the area of quantum computer research. One of the obstacles to creating a fully functional quantum computer has been the inability of qubits to hold information for long periods of time. Recently, UCLA scientists developed a new technique for cooling molecules, which may be applied to future quantum computers in order to bring the molecules to the state at which they can be manipulated to store and transmit data. In addition, scientists in Australia have created a silicon quantum bit using a single atom—this development is viewed as a big step forward in the development of silicon-based quantum computers. These breakthroughs are viewed as significant steps toward the ability to create more sophisticated working quantum computers in the future.

Quantum computing is not well suited for general computing tasks but it is ideal for, and expected to be widely used in, highly data-intensive applications, such as encryption and code breaking.

Optical Computing

Optical chips, which use light waves to transmit data, are also currently in development. A possibility for the future is the **optical computer**—a computer that uses light, such as from laser beams or infrared beams, to perform digital computations. Because light beams do not interfere with each other, optical computers can be much smaller and faster than electronic computers. For instance, according to one NASA senior research scientist, an optical computer could solve a problem in one hour that would take an electronic computer 11 years to solve. While some researchers are working on developing an all-optical computer, others believe that a mix of optical and electronic components—or an *opto-electronic*

>**Quantum computing.** A technology that applies the principles of quantum physics and quantum mechanics to computers to direct atoms or nuclei to work together as quantum bits (qubits), which function simultaneously as the computer's processor and memory. >**Optical computer.** A computer that uses light, such as from laser beams or infrared beams, to perform digital computations.

computer—may be the best bet for the future. Opto-electronic technology is already being used to improve long-distance fiber-optic communications. Initial opto-electronic computer applications are expected to be applied to the area of speeding up communications between computers and other devices, as well as between computer components. In fact, IBM recently created chips that have both optical and electrical functions combined on a single silicon chip and that use standard semiconductor processes—a feat that was thought to be impossible until recently. One additional benefit of opto-electronic chips is reduced power consumption. While increased bandwidth (such as between servers, between CPU cores, or between the CPU and memory) increases power consumption using electrical connections, the impact is much less with opto-electronic chips because they move data with light instead of electricity.

FIGURE 8-12
Telepresence videoconferencing.

Courtesy Cisco Systems, Inc.

EMERGING NETWORKING TECHNOLOGIES

Improvements are being made on a continual basis to both wired and wireless networking technologies to increase speed and connectivity options for *local area networks* (*LANs*) and Internet connections, as well as to support the continued growth in Internet-based multimedia and communications applications used by computers and mobile devices that require fast, dependable connections, such as Voice over IP (VoIP), video-on-demand (VOD), video calls, mobile TV, and teleconferencing. For instance, one new improvement to videoconferencing technology to make it more closely mimic a real-time meeting environment is referred to as *telepresence videoconferencing*. Although telepresence videoconferencing setups are expensive, with travel becoming increasingly more expensive and time consuming, many businesses view videoconferencing as a viable replacement for face-to-face meetings. Telepresence videoconferencing is also used in educational settings (for instance, the system shown in Figure 8-12 is installed at the Wharton School campuses in both Philadelphia and San Francisco to hold bicoastal classes).

Monitoring Systems

Some emerging networking applications involve location information, such as the geobrowsing and geofencing applications discussed in the Chapter 3 How It Works box and monitoring systems that utilize GPS. For instance, *vehicle monitoring systems* are available that can be installed in cars by parents and employers to monitor the location and use of the vehicles (by teenagers or employees, respectively) using networking technology; *child monitoring systems* allow parents to monitor the physical locations of their children. Both types of monitoring systems typically record a location history; many also allow the location of a vehicle or child to be tracked in real time via a Web site or mobile app (see Figure 8-13). Some systems can even be used to set up a "virtual fence" for a child or a car or a maximum allowable car speed; the parent or employer is notified (usually via a text message) anytime the child or vehicle leaves the prescribed geographical area or exceeds the designated speed. Child monitoring systems often include additional features, such as the ability to have the child's location pushed to the parent's device at regular intervals, the ability to have the parent notified if the child is within 500 feet of a registered sex offender, and an "SOS" button that the child can press if he or she is lost or afraid. The child monitoring system shown in Figure 8-13 is also available

FIGURE 8-13
GPS-based child monitoring systems. Allow parents to track their children in real time.

Courtesy Amber Alert GPS; © Chardchanin/Shutterstock.com

Courtesy Nest Labs

FIGURE 8-14
Smart themostats.
This thermostat (left) contains a variety of sensors and can be controlled remotely via a mobile app (right).

as a smartphone app for teenagers. Similar GPS systems are designed to be used to track elderly parents or by individuals who are hiking or traveling so they can be located if they become lost or injured.

Other monitoring systems are designed for use in the home. For instance, *home health monitoring systems* are designed to monitor elderly or infirm individuals (such as by taking the vital signs of the individual or prompting him or her to answer questions about food or medication consumed that day) and to notify someone if a possible problem is detected. Other home monitoring systems use *sensors*—devices that respond to a stimulus (such as heat, light, or pressure) and generate an electrical signal that can be measured or interpreted. For example, *smart door locks* allow you to unlock your front door with your smartphone and the thermostat shown in Figure 8-14 contains temperature, humidity, activity, and light sensors; can be controlled via a mobile app; and can be programmed based on your activity within the home. IBM expects to see the use of sensor technology expanding to additional areas in the future, such as nano-sized sensors embedded in paint that help manage the energy use of a building or as a coating applied to plumbing systems to detect leaks and other potential problems.

> **TIP**
>
> It has been predicted that 50 billion devices (essentially anything with an on-off switch) will be connected to the Internet by 2020, creating the Internet of Things (IoT).

New Wireless and Cloud Applications

Improved networking technology has also created a host of new wireless networking applications. For instance, *wireless displays* connect to a computer or other device (such as to a smartphone, as in Figure 8-15) using a wireless networking connection. Once connected, either all content or selected content from the source device is displayed on the wireless display. Printers are also increasingly using a wireless connection and, if your printer has Internet access, you can print content from your smartphone, media tablet, or other mobile device to your home or office printer from any location with Internet access (refer again to Figure 8-15); you can also send printouts wirelessly to public printers, such as those located at airports, libraries, office stores, and shipping stores such as FedEx Office and the UPS Store.

Wired Networking Standards

Ethernet is the most widely used standard for wired networks. It was invented in the mid-1970s and has continued to evolve over the years to support faster speeds. The most common Ethernet standards for LANs today are *Fast Ethernet*, which supports data transfer rates of up to 100 Mbps; *Gigabit Ethernet*, which is even faster at 1,000 Mbps (1 Gbps); and *10 Gigabit Ethernet*, which supports data transfer rates of 10 Gbps. The

FIGURE 8-15
New wireless and cloud applications.

Courtesy HTC

Courtesy Epson America

WIRELESS DISPLAYS

CLOUD PRINTING

newer *40 Gigabit Ethernet* and *100 Gigabit Ethernet* standards were ratified in 2010. Development of the even faster *400 Gigabit Ethernet* and *Terabit Ethernet* standards are currently being explored; if ratified, they are expected to be used for connections between servers, as well as for delivering video, digital X-rays and other digital medical images, and other high-speed, bandwidth-intensive Internet applications.

A relatively new Ethernet development is **Power over Ethernet (PoE)**, which allows electrical power to be sent along the cables in an Ethernet network (often referred to as *Ethernet cables*) along with data (see Figure 8-16). Consequently, the Ethernet cable, in addition to sending data, can be used to supply power to the devices on the network. PoE is most often used in business networks with remote wired devices (such as outdoor networking hardware, security cameras, and other devices) that are not located near a power outlet. Using PoE requires special hardware and devices designed for PoE; regular Ethernet-enabled devices can be powered via PoE if a special *PoE adapter*, such as the one shown in Figure 8-16, is used.

ASK THE EXPERT

D-Link Building Networks for People

Courtesy D-Link Systems, Inc.

Daniel Kelley, Vice President, Marketing, D-Link Systems, Inc.

How will the Internet of Things (IoT) affect our daily lives?

The Internet of Things (IoT) is one of the more intriguing topics on where technology is going and how it will impact almost every aspect of our daily lives. We are already seeing technology with embedded Internet connectivity emerge in things like cars, buildings, and more in order to develop a conversation between devices, the user, and the devices around them. While most IoT applications today are focused on information and entertainment, I foresee a big advancement in safety when cars are able to not only avoid traffic but also avoid accidents by getting "smarter" and having constant dialogue with other cars and the environment around them.

For easily creating wired home networks, the *Phoneline* (also called *HomePNA*) and *Powerline* (also called *HomePlug AV*) *standards* allow computers to be networked through ordinary existing telephone jacks and power outlets, respectively. As both of these standards have emerged, their speeds have increased and now both can be used to network home entertainment devices in addition to computers. The *G.hn standard* is a new standard designed as a unified worldwide standard for creating home networks over any existing home wiring—phone lines, power lines, and/or coaxial cable. It is viewed as the next-generation standard for wired home networking and it may eventually replace the Powerline and Phoneline standards. G.hn is fast—up to 1 Gbps—and G.hn adapters and other products are expected to be available soon.

FIGURE 8-16
Power over Ethernet (PoE) powers devices through an Ethernet connection.

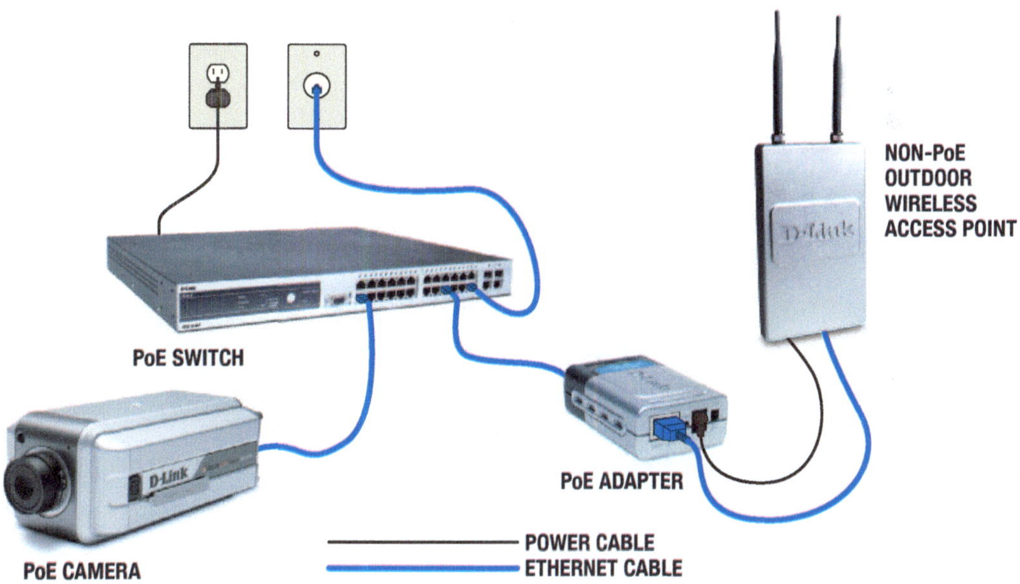

Courtesy D-Link Systems, Inc.

>**Power over Ethernet (PoE).** A wired networking standard that allows electrical power to be sent along with data over standard Ethernet cables.

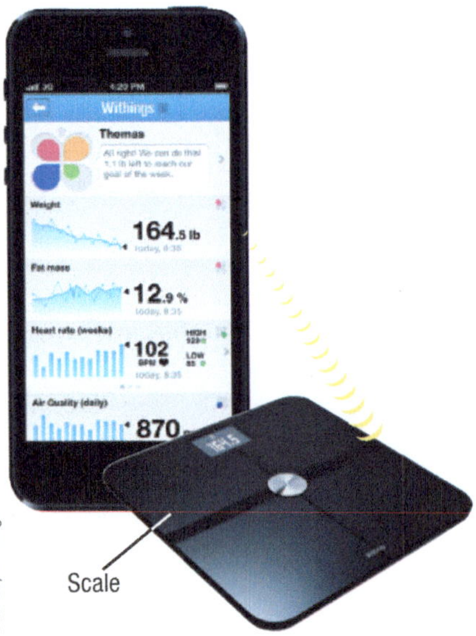

Courtesy Withings

FIGURE 8-17
Smart scales.
This scale transmits readings to a smartphone via Wi-Fi.

Wireless Networking Standards

Developed in the late 1990s, **Wi-Fi** (for *wireless fidelity*) is a family of wireless networking standards that use the IEEE standard **802.11**. Wi-Fi is the current standard for wireless networks in the home or office, as well as for public Wi-Fi hotspots. Wi-Fi capabilities are built into virtually all portable computers and mobile devices today; they are also becoming increasingly integrated into everyday products, such as printers, digital cameras, portable digital media players, external hard drives, baby monitors, gaming consoles, home audio systems, televisions—even bathroom scales (see Figure 8-17)—to allow those devices to wirelessly network with other devices or to access the Internet. Like Ethernet, the Wi-Fi standard is continually evolving to support increased speed and other capabilities. The speed of a Wi-Fi network and the area it can cover depend on a variety of factors, including the *Wi-Fi standard* and hardware being used, the number of solid objects (such as walls, trees, or buildings) between the access point and the computer or other device being used, and the amount of interference from cordless phones, baby monitors, microwave ovens, and other devices that also operate on the same radio frequency as Wi-Fi (usually 2.4 GHz). In general, Wi-Fi is designed for medium-range data transfers—typically between 100 and 300 feet indoors and 300 to 900 feet outdoors. There are a number of different versions of the 802.11 standard; the *802.11g*, *802.11n*, and *802.11ac* standards are the most widely used today. Emerging 802.11 standards under development are expected to offer increased speed, security, and other factors in the future.

While Wi-Fi is very widely used today, it does have some limitations—particularly its relatively limited range. For instance, an individual using a Wi-Fi hotspot inside a Starbucks coffeehouse will lose that Internet connection when he or she moves out of range of that network and will need to locate another hotspot at his or her next location. In addition, other wireless technologies are in development for specific purposes, such as *multimedia networking*. These emerging wireless technologies are discussed next. For a look at another emerging wireless technology—powering your hardware devices via *wireless power*—see the Inside the Industry box.

WiMAX (802.16)

WiMAX (802.16) is a series of standards designed for longer range wireless networking connections. Similar to Wi-Fi, *fixed WiMAX* (also known as *802.16a*) is designed to provide Internet access to fixed locations (sometimes called *hotzones*), but the coverage area is significantly larger (a typical hotzone radius is between 2 and 6 miles, though WiMAX can transmit data as far as 10 miles or more—see Figure 8-18). With fixed WiMAX, it is feasible to provide coverage to an entire city or other geographical area by using multiple WiMAX towers (refer again to Figure 8-18). *Mobile WiMAX* (*802.16e*) is the mobile version of the WiMAX wireless networking standard. It is designed to deliver fast wireless networking to mobile users via a mobile

FIGURE 8-18
WiMAX vs. Wi-Fi.
A WiMAX hotzone can provide service to anyone in the hotzone, including mobile users.

>**Wi-Fi (802.11).** A widely used networking standard for medium-range wireless networks. >**WiMAX (802.16).** A wireless networking standard that is faster and has a larger range than Wi-Fi.

INSIDE THE INDUSTRY

Wireless Power

Imagine recharging your notebook computer or mobile phone just by setting it down in the right place, or using your kitchen blender just by placing it on a countertop but not plugging it in. These scenarios are possible with *wireless power*. While wireless power products are now becoming available, one of the challenges has been creating a standard for wireless power so that multiple devices from different manufacturers can be charged at the same time using the same technology.

One company working toward this standard is Fulton Innovation. This company, along with the more than 100 other companies that are members of the *Wireless Power Consortium* (including Panasonic, Verizon Wireless, Sony, Energizer, Motorola Mobility, Nokia, and LG Electronics), supports wireless power technology that uses *magnetic induction* to transfer power wirelessly from a charging power supply device to a target device containing the appropriate receiving technology. Products meeting the consortium standard will be able to use the *Qi* (pronounced "chee") logo. Qi systems are compatible with one another (though not with competing charging systems that are also under development). They automatically adjust the power transmitted to each device being charged to meet the needs of that device, and they deactivate the charging process when the device is fully charged. Charging works with the device's regular battery (but the device needs an embedded receiver) and takes about the same time as a regular wired charger.

Assuming the Qi standard becomes the norm, virtually all devices in the future are expected to contain a built-in charging receiver; some Nokia, LG, and HTC mobile phones already include one. Several cars with Qi charging stations (see the accompanying photo) are already on the market. In the near future, charging bases are expected to be built into other objects, such as desks, kitchen countertops, restaurant tabletops, hotel nightstands, airline tray tables—basically anywhere you might normally place your devices—in order to power all your devices in all of the spaces that you use. Qi technology can also be used with household and kitchen appliances. Future wireless power applications could even include charging transmitters built into walls to power all of the devices located in the home on a continual basis, as well as into garage floors and parking lots to wirelessly recharge electric vehicles.

Because there is a cost associated with providing the wireless power, it is expected that businesses providing wireless charging services may eventually charge for these services or include a certain amount of recharge with a purchase, similar to when Wi-Fi hotspots first started appearing in public locations.

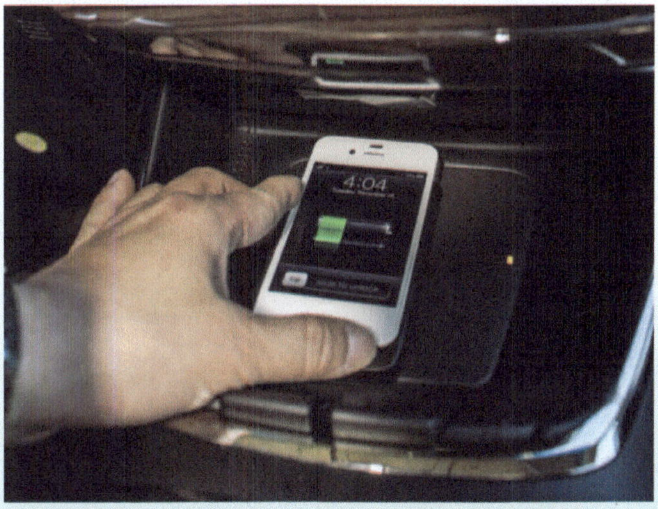

Courtesy Toyota Motor Sales, U.S.A., Inc.

Qi wireless charging stations are available in some recent cars, such as the Toyota Avalon shown here.

phone, portable computer, or other WiMAX-enabled device. Mobile WiMAX is capable of speeds of approximately 70 Mbps, but speeds of 1 to 6 Mbps are more typical. The newest version of mobile WiMAX (*802.16m* or *WiMAX Release 2*) supports speeds up to approximately 120 Mbps.

WiMAX capabilities are beginning to be built into portable computers and other devices, and WiMAX is currently being used to provide Internet access to more than 1 billion people in about 150 countries.

> **TIP**
>
> If your Internet connection slows down, try *power cycling* your modem and router: Unplug the modem and router and wait for 30 seconds, plug in the modem and wait for 30 seconds, and then plug in the router.

Cellular Standards

Cellular standards have also evolved over the years to better fulfill the demand for mobile Internet, mobile multimedia delivery, and other relatively recent mobile trends. The current standards for cellular networks today in the United States and many other countries are *3G (third generation)* and *4G (fourth generation)*. 3G and 4G networks are designed to support both data and voice. Users of both 3G and 4G smartphones and other mobile devices can access broadband Internet content (such as online maps, music, games, TV, videos, and more) at relatively fast speeds—typically, between 1 and 4 Mbps and 3 to 15 Mbps, respectively. Because 3G and 4G speeds are equivalent to the speeds many home broadband Internet users experience, Internet access via a 3G or 4G network is often referred to as *mobile broadband*. Virtually all wireless providers today have both a 3G and a 4G network, though 4G service may not be available in all areas. There are two primary standards for 4G networks today: the mobile WiMAX standard already discussed and *Long Term Evolution (LTE)*, supported by AT&T Wireless, Verizon Wireless, and T-Mobile. LTE is the fastest standard and the *Phase 2 LTE network* currently being implemented by AT&T is expected to double 4G speeds. While mobile WiMAX is not technically a cellular standard, it is being used by some companies (such as Sprint) to provide 4G wireless service to subscribers.

TIP

The SmartGlass app that enables you to have a second Xbox 360 screen via your smartphone or tablet can connect via either Wi-Fi or a 3G/4G cellular network.

TIP

NFC is also being used for new networking applications, such as the emerging *NFC ring* that can be used to automatically unlock assigned doors or smartphones within range of your ring finger.

Short-Range Wireless Standards

There are several wireless networking standards in existence or being developed that are designed for short-range wireless networking connections (for a summary of these standards and the standards already discussed, see Figure 8-19). **Bluetooth** is a wireless standard that was originally designed for very short-range (10 meters, approximately 33 feet, or less) connections, though there is no maximum range and some industrial products have a range of 300 feet. Bluetooth is designed to replace cables between devices, such as to connect a wireless keyboard or mouse to a desktop computer, to send print jobs wirelessly from a portable computer to a printer, or to connect a mobile phone to a wireless headset. The Bluetooth standard is continually evolving to be faster and to support new applications. One of the key enhancements in the newest Bluetooth specification (*Bluetooth 4.0*, also called *Bluetooth Smart*) is low energy, which enables small devices to run for years on a single button-sized battery. Consequently, Bluetooth is increasingly being used with consumer devices, such as to connect health and fitness devices to a watch or smartphone, to connect a mobile phone to a portable speaker, and to connect 3D glasses to a 3D television set.

FIGURE 8-19
Summary of common wireless networking standards.

CATEGORY	EXAMPLES	INTENDED PURPOSE	RANGE
Short range	Bluetooth Wireless USB	To connect peripheral devices to a mobile phone or computer.	33 feet–200 feet
	Ultra Wideband (UWB) WirelessHD (WiHD) TransferJet WiGig	To connect and transfer multimedia content between home consumer electronic devices (computers, TVs, DVD players, etc.).	1 inch–33 feet
Medium range	Wi-Fi (802.11)	To connect computers and other devices to a local area network.	100–300 feet indoors; 300–900 feet outdoors
	Wi-Fi Direct	To connect computers and other devices directly together.	600 feet
Long range	WiMAX Mobile WiMAX	To provide Internet access to a large geographic area for fixed and/or mobile users.	6 miles non-line of sight; 30 miles line of sight
	Cellular standards	To connect mobile phones and mobile devices to a cellular network for telephone and Internet service.	10 miles

Another standard that is designed to connect peripheral devices, similar to Bluetooth, but that transfers data more quickly is **wireless USB**. The speed of wireless USB depends on the distance between the devices being used, but it is approximately 100 Mbps at 10 meters (about 33 feet) or 480 Mbps at 3 meters (about 10 feet). While Bluetooth and wireless USB can be used for similar applications, it is possible they might coexist. For example, wireless USB might

>**Bluetooth.** A networking standard for very short-range wireless connections; the devices are automatically connected once they get within the allowable range. >**Wireless USB.** A wireless version of USB designed to connect peripheral devices.

be used to connect computer hardware in more permanent setups, while Bluetooth might be used in short-range mobile situations with portable computers and mobile devices.

A newer standard also designed to connect devices for short-range communications is **Wi-Fi Direct**. Wi-Fi Direct enables Wi-Fi devices to connect directly to each other, such as to transfer photos or documents or to *tether* devices to a Wi-Fi Direct device's Internet connection by creating a hotspot (see Figure 8-20), without needing any additional networking hardware. Wi-Fi Direct is not designed to replace traditional Wi-Fi networks, but it is considered a competitor to Bluetooth because it has the advantage of faster speeds (up to 250 Mbps) and a greater range (up to 600 feet).

For transferring multimedia content quickly between nearby devices (such as between televisions and DVD players, or between computers and mobile devices), a number of different standards are emerging. For instance, *Ultra Wideband* (*UWB*) transfers data at speeds from 100 Mbps at 10 meters (about 33 feet) to 480 Mbps at 2 meters (about 6.5 feet). Similar, but faster, standards include *WiGig*, which is being developed by the *Wi-Fi Alliance* and supports short-range data transfers of up to 7 Gbps, and *wirelessHD* (*WiHD*), which is backed by seven major electronics companies and is designed to transfer full-quality uncompressed high-definition audio, video, and data within a single room at speeds up to 28 Gbps. A wireless standard designed for fast transfers between devices that are extremely close together (essentially touching each other) is *TransferJet*. Developed by Sony, TransferJet is designed to transfer large files (such as digital photos, music, and video) quickly between devices as soon as they come in contact with each other (such as to transfer data between smartphones or between digital cameras, to download music or video from a consumer kiosk or digital signage system to a smartphone or other mobile device, or to transfer images or video from a digital camera to a TV or printer). At a maximum speed of 560 Mbps, TransferJet is slower than some of the other technologies, but it is fast enough to support the transfer of video files.

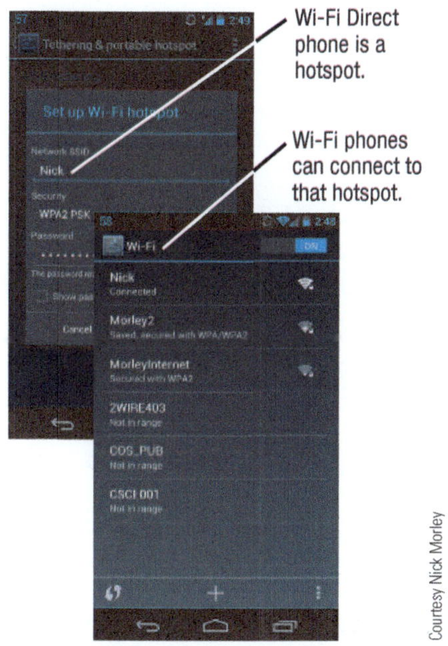

FIGURE 8-20
Wi-Fi Direct. Allows Wi-Fi devices to connect directly to one another.

ARTIFICIAL INTELLIGENCE (AI)

Although they cannot yet think completely on their own, computers and software programs have become more sophisticated, and computers are being programmed to act in an increasingly intelligent manner.

What Is Artificial Intelligence (AI)?

According to John McCarthy, who coined the term **artificial intelligence (AI)** in 1956 and is considered by many to be one of its fathers, AI is "the science and engineering of making intelligent machines." In other words, AI researchers are working to create intelligent devices controlled by intelligent software programs; in essence, machines that think and act like people and that perform in ways that would be considered intelligent if observed in human beings. In 1950, Alan Turing—one of the first AI researchers—argued that if a machine could successfully appear to be human to a knowledgeable observer, then it should be considered intelligent. To illustrate this idea, Turing developed a test—later called the *Turing Test*—in which one observer interacts electronically with both a computer and a person. During the test, the observer submits written questions electronically to both the computer and the person, evaluates the typed responses, and tries to identify which answers came from the computer and which came from the person. Turing argued that if the computer could repeatedly fool the observer into thinking it was human, then it should be viewed as intelligent.

TIP

DARPA (*Defense Advanced Research Projects Agency*) is experimenting with AI (in conjunction with computational linguistics, machine learning, and natural language technologies) to create an automated system to help analysts more efficiently evaluate and understand the connections among large volumes of text-based documents.

>**Wi-Fi Direct.** A standard for connecting Wi-Fi devices directly, without using a router or an access point. >**Artificial intelligence (AI).** When a computer performs actions that are characteristic of human intelligence.

Courtesy of Dr. Hugh Loebner

FIGURE 8-21
The Loebner Prize gold medal has yet to be awarded.

Many Turing Test contests have been held over the years, and in 1990, Dr. Hugh Loebner initiated the Loebner Prize, pledging a grand prize of $100,000 and a solid gold medal (see Figure 8-21) for the developer of the first computer whose responses to a Turing Test were indistinguishable from that of a human's responses. A contest is held every year, awarding a prize of $4,000 and a bronze medal to the developer of the most humanlike computer but, so far, the gold medal has not been awarded. However, some experts believe that a computer will pass the Turing Test within the next 20 years. Although the Turing Test is interesting and is still providing grounds for research today, many experts believe that the Turing Test provides only one possible test of computer intelligence. These experts argue that there could be different definitions of intelligence, and a machine could still be considered intelligent without knowing enough about humans to imitate one.

Some of the initial advances in AI were made in the area of game playing—namely, chess. Early chess-playing programs were easily defeated by amateur chess players. But, as computers became more powerful and AI software became more sophisticated, chess-playing programs improved significantly. In 1996, IBM's Deep Blue computer won two of six games in a chess match against then world chess champion Garry Kasparov. A landmark moment in AI history occurred in 1997 when Deep Blue beat Kasparov in a rematch, winning the match 3½ to 2½ (three of the six games ended in a draw). And in late 2006, world chess champion Vladimir Kramnik lost a match to the chess program *Deep Fritz* (see Figure 8-22)—the beginning of the end of humans being able to beat chess programs, in the opinion of some AI researchers. One reason for this is because once the human player makes a mistake, there is no hope (as there would be with a human opponent) that the computer opponent will make its own mistake at a later time to level the playing field in that game.

TIP

Self-driving cars generate 1 GB of data during each second of operation—this and other types of fast-moving data that can't easily be handled by existing data tools are referred to as *big data*.

AI Applications

Today's AI applications contain some aspect of artificial intelligence, although they tend to mimic human intelligence rather than display pure intelligence. Technological advances will undoubtedly help AI applications continue to evolve and become more intelligent and sophisticated in the future. For instance, one recent advancement is IBM's Watson supercomputer that has the ability to analyze complex questions and form answers well enough to compete with human beings on the *Jeopardy!* game show and win (see Figure 8-22)—Watson's software is now being applied to other applications, such as medical diagnosis systems and business intelligence systems. However, just as the debate about what constitutes intelligence in nonhumans will continue, so will the debate about how far we as a society should delve into the area of artificial intelligence. AI applications that exist in some form today include *intelligent agents*, *expert systems*, *neural networks*, and *robotics*. For a look at the *self-driving cars* you may be using in the future, see the How It Works box.

FIGURE 8-22
AI and game playing.

Courtesy ChessBase.com

KRAMNIK VS. DEEP FRITZ
Deep Fritz beat world champion Vladimir Kramnik 4 games to 2 in 2006.

Courtesy of IBM Corporation

WATSON VS. *JEOPARDY!* CHAMPIONS
Watson easily beat both champions in 2011.

Intelligent Agents

Intelligent agents (also called *smart assistants*) are programs that perform

>**Intelligent agent.** A program that performs specific tasks to help make a user's work environment more efficient or entertaining and that typically modifies its behavior based on the user's actions.

HOW IT WORKS

Self-Driving Cars

Did you ever wish you had a car that could drive itself? Well, you're in luck—self-driving cars are here. Google's self-driving car (shown in the accompanying photo) has already logged half a million miles during testing. And, recently, California, Florida, and Nevada passed legislation allowing self-driving cars to be tested on state roads. To plan for the future, California has directed the DMV to work with other state agencies (such as highway patrol, transportation, and insurance) to determine how *autonomous vehicles* will be allowed to be used in the state once they become available. Issues include how the cars and riders should be licensed, any limitations on use for safety (such as use in school zones or bad weather), any allowable use by blind or underage individuals, how the cars will be insured if there is no driver assigned to them, how to protect the cars against hackers, and so forth.

Google autonomous cars are essentially robotic cars. They include an onboard computer, cameras, and a roof-mounted laser range finder; the data generated by these devices is combined with GPS data to enable the cars to avoid obstacles and adhere to traffic laws. Because they are analytical, aren't capable of being distracted, don't make mistakes, and can't be impaired by alcohol, drugs, or lack of sleep, Google and other autonomous vehicle promoters propose that self-driving cars are safer, in addition to making driving more enjoyable and more efficient. In addition, these vehicles could use short-range communications technology to communicate with each other to avoid collisions—by one estimate, these cars could prevent, or reduce in severity, as many as 80% of crashes involving non-impaired drivers alone.

Currently, the use of autonomous cars is in the testing phase and requires a licensed driver to be in the car, but California plans to have regulations in place within a year to prepare for autonomous cars coming on the market in the near future, once they are deemed safe. It is expected that, initially, a licensed driver will be required to be in the car. But, who knows in the future? You may be able to send your car out for pizza or to pick up a guest arriving at the airport. Only time will tell.

Courtesy Google

specific tasks to help make a user's work environment more efficient or entertaining. Typically, the agent program runs in the background until it is time for the agent to perform a task, and it usually modifies its behavior based on the user's actions or instructions. Intelligent agents are found on Web sites, as well as incorporated into software programs and mobile operating systems. Some specific types of intelligent agents include the following:

- *Application assistants*—provide help or assistance for a particular application program. Some can detect when the user might be having trouble with the program and automatically offer appropriate advice. Others add speech capabilities to common programs, such as instant messaging programs.
- *Shopping bots*—search online stores to find the best prices for specified products.
- *Entertainment bots*—provide entertainment, such as a virtual pet to take care of or an animated character to play games with.
- *Chatterbots*—carry on written "conversations" with people in a *natural language* (such as English, Spanish, French, or Japanese). Chatterbots typically respond both verbally and with appropriate facial expressions to create the illusion that the exchange is taking place between two thinking, living entities (see Figure 8-23).

Intelligent agents are expected to be an important part of the *Semantic Web*—a predicted evolution of the current Web in which all Web content is stored in formats

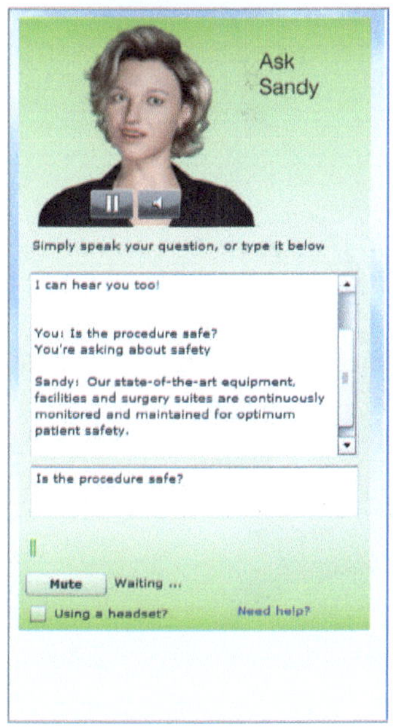

Courtesy of Humanity Online

FIGURE 8-23
A Web page chatterbot.

that are more easily read by software applications and intelligent agents so those tools can perform an increasing number of tasks. To accomplish this, the *semantics* (structure) of the data is defined in a standard manner (using tags and other identifying data). Whether or not the Semantic Web—viewed as part of the next generation *Web 3.0* by some—actually arrives, and arrives in the format in which it is now envisioned, remains to be seen.

Expert Systems

Expert systems are software programs that can make decisions and draw conclusions, similar to a human expert. Expert systems (see Figure 8-24) have two main components: a *knowledge base* (a database that contains facts provided by a human expert and rules that the expert system should use to make decisions based on those facts) and an *inference engine* (a software program that applies the rules to the data stored in the knowledge base in order to reach decisions). For instance, as shown in Figure 8-24, an expert system used to authorize credit for credit card customers would have a knowledge base with facts about customers and rules about credit authorization, such as "Do not automatically authorize purchase if the customer has exceeded his or her credit limit."

Expert systems are widely used for tasks such as diagnosing illnesses, making financial forecasts, scheduling routes for delivery vehicles, diagnosing mechanical problems, and performing credit authorizations. Some expert systems are designed to take the place of human experts, while others are designed to assist them. For instance, medical expert systems are often used to assist physicians with patient diagnoses, suggesting possible diagnoses based on the patient's symptoms and other data supplied to the expert system. Because it has access to an extensive knowledge base, the expert system may provide more possible diagnoses to the attending physician than he or she may have thought of otherwise.

When using an expert system, it is important to realize that its conclusions are based on the data and rules stored in its knowledge base, as well as the information provided by the users. If the expert knowledge is correct, the inference engine program is written correctly, and the user supplies accurate information in response to the questions posed by the expert system, the system will draw correct conclusions; if the knowledge base is wrong, the inference engine is faulty, or the user provides inaccurate input, the system will not work correctly.

FIGURE 8-24
An expert system at work.

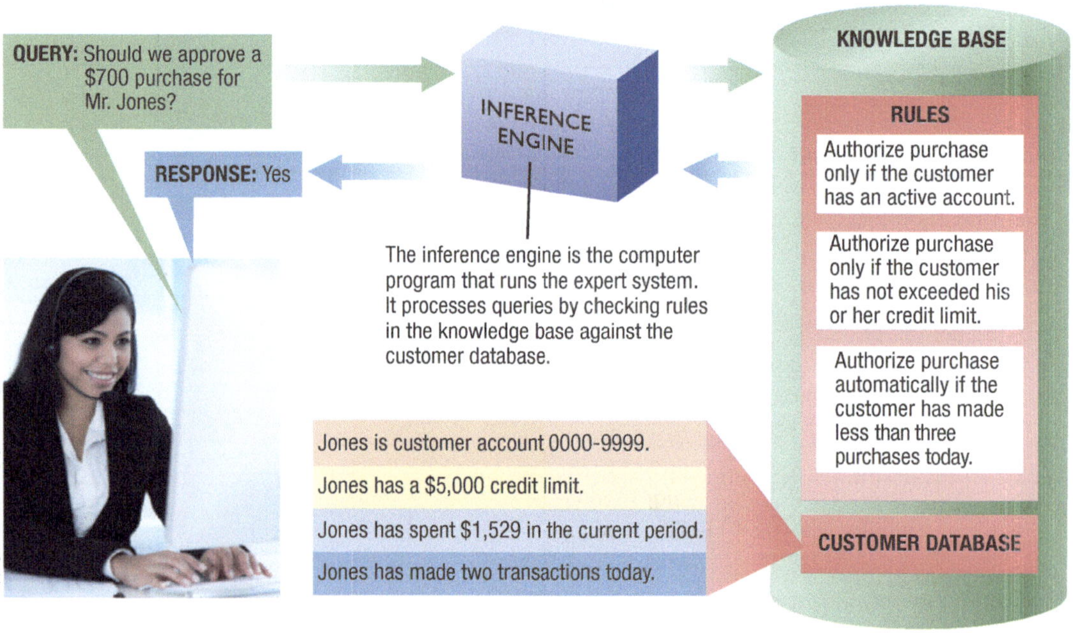

Neural Networks

Artificial intelligence systems that attempt to imitate the way a human brain works are called **neural networks**. Neural networks (also called *neural nets*) are networks of processors that are connected together in a manner similar to the way the neurons in a human brain are connected. They are designed to emulate the brain's pattern-recognition process in order to recognize patterns in data and make more progressive leaps in associations and predictions than conventional computer systems. Neural networks are used in areas such as handwriting, speech, and image recognition; medical imaging; crime analysis; biometric identification (see Figure 8-25); and *vision systems* that use cameras to inspect objects and make determinations—for example, the systems that check products for defects at manufacturing plants or that recognize stamps during postal processing.

Courtesy of Crossmatch

FIGURE 8-25
Neural network systems. Often used in biometric identification systems, such as to analyze fingerprints.

Robotics

Robotics is the field devoted to the study of **robots**—devices, controlled by a person or a computer, that can move and react to sensory input. Robots are widely used by the military and businesses to perform high-precision but monotonous jobs, as well as to perform tasks that are dangerous or impossible for people to perform. There are also robots designed to perform personal tasks for individuals. The appearance of robots varies depending on their purpose, such as robot arms permanently connected to an assembly line, robots built on sturdy mobile platforms designed to travel over rough terrain, robots with fins for water tasks, robots shaped like animals (such as snakes or spiders) for special climbing abilities, and robots that resemble pets or human beings for consumer applications. Robots used for medical and military applications are discussed shortly; robots used for business and consumer applications are discussed next.

Robots are used in business for a variety of purposes, such as for looking for intruders, gas leaks, and other hazards, as well as working on factory assembly lines and other monotonous tasks (see Figure 8-26). Robots are also used for mining coal, repairing oil rigs, locating survivors in collapsed mines and buildings, and other dangerous tasks. They are also used to facilitate videoconferencing and other *remote presence* applications by sitting in for a remote participant and relaying video and audio images to and from that participant. For instance, the videoconferencing robot shown in Figure 8-26 enables remote individuals to more actively participate in meetings and other face-to-face encounters from their current location. In addition, robots are used for service tasks such as search and rescue missions and fighting fires.

There are also a number of *personal robots* available or in development to assist with personal tasks. Some are primarily entertainment robots and are designed to interact with people (such as by reciting phrases, delivering messages, taking photos or video, or singing and dancing). Others, such as the toy robot shown in Figure 8-26, are designed to be toys or companions for children. Still other personal robots are designed for household tasks, such as to mow the lawn (see Figure 8-26) or clean the pool.

Household robots that can assist individuals with more complex tasks, such as putting away the dishes or picking up toys before vacuuming the living room, are a little further in the future—after robot technology improves to allow for better navigation and improved physical manipulation and after prices come down. Expected to have a more *humanoid* form than the household robots currently on the market, these future robots could be used to assist the elderly and wheelchair-bound individuals, in addition to

TIP

Some personal robots can act autonomously once they are assigned a program; others are designed to be controlled remotely—increasingly via smartphones.

>**Neural network.** An expert system in which the human brain's pattern-recognition process is emulated by the computer system.
>**Robotics.** The study of robot technology. >**Robot.** A device, controlled by a human operator or a computer, that can move and react to sensory input.

FIGURE 8-26 Business and personal robots.

helping with household tasks. In fact, it has been reported that the South Korean government expects to have at least one robot in every South Korean household by 2020.

Many would agree that the use of robots has numerous benefits to society—such as adding convenience to our lives, replacing human beings for dangerous tasks, and, potentially, monitoring and assisting the disabled and the elderly. But some individuals are concerned that, as true artificial intelligence becomes closer to reality, a class of robots with the potential for great harm could be created. In response, several organizations—including the South Korean government and the European Robotics Research Network (EURON)—are developing standards for robots, users, and manufacturers concerning the appropriate use and development of robots. The U.S. military is also studying ways to ensure robotic soldiers can be programmed to recognize and obey international laws of war and the U.S. military's rules of engagement in order to prevent them from performing acts such as firing on a hospital or crowd of civilians, even if enemy forces are nearby. Regardless of the progress made in implementing controls on robots, the roles robots should take in our society are likely to be debated for quite some time.

TIP

You can download new apps for your personal robots at the *Robot App Store*.

CAUTION CAUTION CAUTION CAUTION CAUTION CAUTION CAUT

While some robots are designed to be durable and used in adverse conditions, remember that robotic devices are electronic. To avoid the risk of electric shock and damage to robotic devices, do not use them in the water or in other adverse conditions unless the instructions specifically state that the action is safe.

TECHNOLOGICAL ADVANCES IN MEDICINE

Technological advances in the area of medicine in the past several years include computers that can analyze test results to identify precancerous cells too small for a person to see, implanted devices that enhance the functions of a current organ (such as cochlear implants that can restore hearing), electronic monitors that detect potentially dangerous medical conditions, and digital cameras the size of a pill that are swallowed to photograph the patient's digestive tract. Other topics in the forefront of medical technology research include *brain-to-computer interfacing* (*BCI*), *telemedicine*, and *telesurgery*.

Brain-to-Computer Interfacing (BCI)

Brain-to-computer interfacing (BCI) is the process of connecting the brain with a computer, such as implanting electrodes directly into the brain or using a headset that wirelessly reads and interprets brainwaves. Medical applications of BCI—such as using it to restore lost functionality to or facilitate the communications of severely disabled individuals—are under development. For instance, after training, a severely paralyzed individual can use BCI to move a mouse, click it to type text, and perform other computer-related tasks using only his or her thoughts—raising the possibility that paralyzed individuals will someday be able to control robot assistants with their thoughts. A recent experiment went one step further—human *brain-to-brain interfacing*. In this experiment, two University of Washington researchers were located in separate labs across campus and each wore a special cap (one to read electrical brain activity and one to stimulate the motor cortex). As the first researcher played a simple video game, using only his mind to visualize his right hand hitting the "fire" button, the second researcher involuntarily moved his right hand to push the spacebar on the keyboard in front of him, as if to hit the "fire" button.

Despite the potential benefits of brain interfacing, there is the concern that this technology could be misused. Medical ethicists are currently working on setting up standards and criteria to ensure that brain implant devices allow, according to medical ethicist Joseph Fins of Cornell University, ". . . patients to have control, not be under control." While the focus of brain interfacing and thought-controlled computers is bringing communications capabilities to the severely disabled, gaming applications are also under development and some researchers foresee the technology someday becoming mainstream—viewing brainwave input as the next step in the evolution of the human-computer input interface.

Telemedicine and Telesurgery

Telemedicine is the use of networking technology to provide medical information and services. At its simplest level, it includes Web sites that patients can access to contact their physicians, make appointments, view lab results, and more. However, more complex telemedicine systems (such as the examples shown in Figure 8-27) are often used to provide care to individuals who may not otherwise have access to that care, such

FIGURE 8-27
Examples of telemedicine applications.

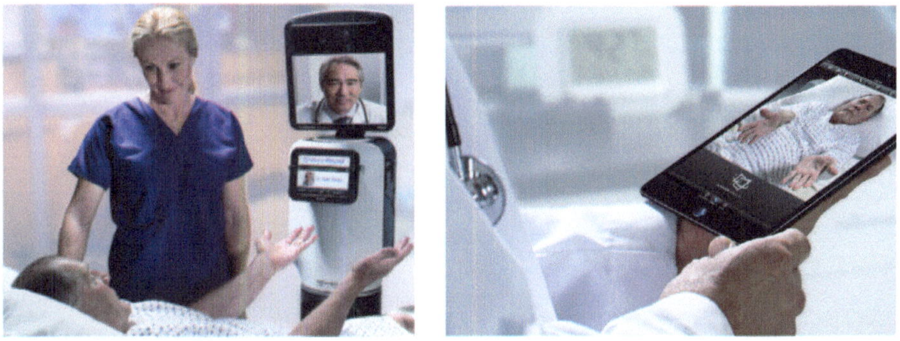

Courtesy InTouch Health, Inc.

Courtesy InTouch Health, Inc.

REMOTE CONSULTATIONS
Using remote-controlled teleconferencing robots, physicians can "virtually" consult with patients or other physicians in a different physical location; the robot (left photo) transmits video images and audio to and from the doctor (via his or her computer or mobile device, right photo) in real time.

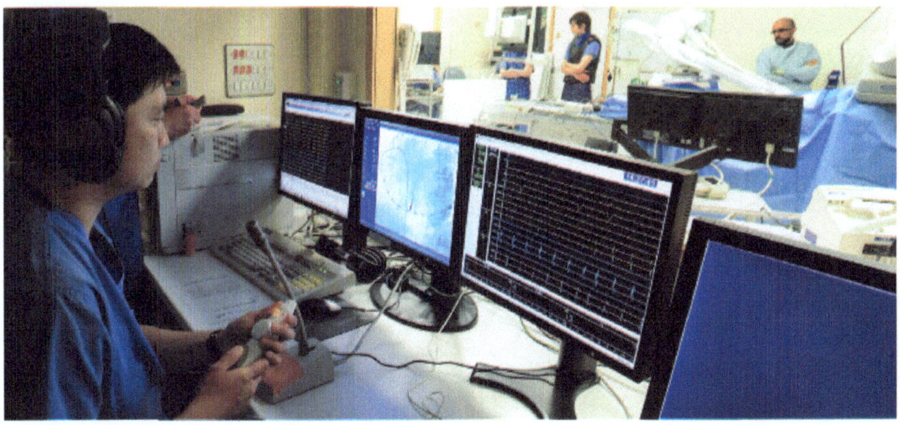

© EMPPL PA Wire/AP Photos

TELESURGERY
Using voice or computer commands, surgeons can perform operations (such as inserting a catheter during the heart surgery shown here) remotely via the Internet or a private network; a robotic system uses the surgeon's commands to physically operate on the patient.

> **Brain-to-computer interfacing (BCI).** The process of connecting the brain with a computer, such as implanting electrodes directly into the brain or using a headset that wirelessly reads and interprets brainwaves. > **Telemedicine.** The use of networking technology to provide medical information and services.

as allowing individuals living in remote areas to consult with a specialist. For instance, physicians can use videoconferencing robots to communicate remotely with other physicians or with hospitalized patients (see Figure 8-27). Physicians can also use telemedicine to perform remote diagnosis of patients (for example, healthcare workers at rural locations, childcare facilities, and other locations can use video cameras, electronic stethoscopes, and other devices to send images and vital statistics of a patient to a physician located at a medical facility).

Another example of telemedicine is **telesurgery**—a form of *robot-assisted surgery* (where a robot controlled by a physician operates on the patient) in which at least one of the surgeons performs the operation by controlling the robot remotely over the Internet or another network (refer again to Figure 8-27). Robot-assisted surgery systems typically use cameras to give the human surgeon an extremely close view of the surgical area. As a result, robot-assisted surgery is typically more precise and results in smaller incisions than those made by a human surgeon, allowing for less invasive surgery (for example, not having to crack through the rib cage to access the heart) and resulting in less pain for the patient, a faster recovery time, and fewer potential complications.

Telemedicine has enormous potential for providing quality medical care to individuals who live in rural or underdeveloped areas and who do not have access to sufficient medical care. Telemedicine will also be necessary for future long-term space explorations—such as a trip to Mars and back that may take two years or more—because astronauts will undoubtedly need medical care while on the journey. In fact, NASA astronauts and physicians have performed telesurgery experiments in the Aquarius Undersea Laboratory 50 feet below the ocean surface to help in the development of a robotic unit that will eventually allow physicians to perform surgery remotely on patients who are in outer space. Some individuals envision the eventual use of portable robot-assisted telesurgery units in space, war zones, and other environments where access to surgeons is extremely limited.

TECHNOLOGICAL ADVANCES IN THE MILITARY

The U.S. military works on a continual basis with technological and research organizations to improve military equipment, such as weapons, protective gear for soldiers, and surveillance tools. The military is also involved in researching many of the other emerging technologies already discussed, such as nanotechnology and artificial intelligence. Two specific areas of research related to the military—*battlefield robots* and *exoskeleton systems*—are discussed next.

Battlefield Robots

Robots are used extensively by the U.S. military. For instance, **battlefield robots** are used in areas of conflict to investigate caves, buildings, trails, and other locations before soldiers enter them to make sure the locations are safe (see Figure 8-28), and to help soldiers locate and dispose of bombs, landmines, and other explosive devices. In addition to land-based robots, there are also military robots designed for underwater use, such as to detect mines or perform underwater surveillance and reconnaissance, as well as *Unmanned Aerial Vehicles* (*UAVs*) or *drones* (unmanned planes) used to take surveillance photos. Currently, military

>**Telesurgery.** A form of robot-assisted surgery in which the doctor's physical location is different from the patient's and robot's physical location; the doctor controls the robot remotely over the Internet or another network. >**Battlefield robot.** A robot used by the military to ensure that locations are safe prior to sending in soldiers.

robots are controlled remotely by soldiers, though researchers are working on more *autonomous robots* that can navigate on their own, perceiving obstacles and determining their course without continuous directions from a human operator, to accompany soldiers into combat. According to national security expert John Pike, autonomous armed robotic soldiers may become a reality as soon as 2020.

Courtesy of iRobot

BATTLEFIELD ROBOTS
Designed to investigate dangerous, hostile, or inaccessible areas prior to human entry.

Courtesy of Lockheed Martin

EXOSKELETON SYSTEMS
Designed to give soldiers enhanced mobility and endurance while carrying heavy loads.

FIGURE 8-28
Military robotic applications.

Exoskeleton Systems

Another military robotic application is the **exoskeleton suit**, whose name refers to a hard protective or supportive outer structure. Currently being researched and developed by several organizations under grants from the Defense Advanced Research Projects Agency (DARPA), exoskeleton suits are wearable battery-operated robotic systems designed to give an individual additional physical capabilities and protection. For instance, an exoskeleton suit can give a soldier the ability to run faster and carry heavier items than he or she could without the suit—up to 200 pounds at a top speed of 10 mph for the *Human Universal Load Carrier* (*HULC*) exoskeleton suit shown in Figure 8-28. Exoskeleton suits in the future may include additional capabilities, such as being made of bulletproof material that is able to solidify on demand to form a shield or turn into a medical cast if a soldier is injured. Other possible features of an exoskeleton suit include changing its color automatically for camouflage purposes; relaying information via sensors about a soldier's health, injuries, and location to field headquarters; and administering painkillers or applying pressure to a wound when directed by a physician. DARPA is also involved with the development of robotic prosthetic arms that feel, look, and perform like natural arms—these robotic arms will be used by military personnel who are injured in the line of duty.

TIP

It is expected that *personal exoskeleton suits* designed to enhance an individual's abilities (such as to help elderly or disabled individuals walk or lift things more easily) will become available within the next 10 to 15 years.

SOCIETAL IMPLICATIONS OF EMERGING TECHNOLOGY

A new computing technology usually provides many benefits because it normally would not become widely available for consumers if it was not designed to solve a problem or add convenience to our lives. However, not all advances are embraced by all individuals. For instance, security and privacy issues are areas of continual concern with emerging technologies. Potential dangers include trusting "intelligent" computers and robots so much that they become a personal safety hazard, allowing medical technology to enable people to be controlled by others, and spending resources on some areas of research and development that might be better spent elsewhere. Some people also worry that technology is advancing at such a rapid pace that we cannot possibly envision all the potential repercussions until it is too late. It is important to evaluate new and emerging technologies in terms of the entire picture—their benefits, as well as their possible risks and societal implications.

>**Exoskeleton suit.** A wearable robotic system designed to give an individual additional physical capabilities and protection.

SUMMARY

THE COMPUTER OF THE FUTURE

Chapter Objective 1:
Describe what the computer of the future might look like, including some examples of emerging types of hardware.

While the exact makeup of future computers is not certain, they will likely continue to get smaller, smarter, and more user-friendly. Portable computers will continue to grow more powerful and useful; home and business computers may be built into furniture, walls, desks, and other objects. Emerging input devices include gesture-based devices; input for consumer applications that may soon become the norm include **two-dimensional (2D) barcodes**, **augmented reality**, and a variety of RFID payment systems. CPU technology is continuing to evolve and it is possible that a form of **nonvolatile RAM (NVRAM)** may eventually replace the RAM we know today. Emerging output devices include *3D display screens*, *pico projectors*, *3D projectors*, *wearable personal displays*, and displays based on variations of **organic light emitting diode (OLED) display** technology. For storage, new formats of USB flash memory drives and flash memory cards are emerging and **holographic storage** is expected to be a viable storage alternative in the near future.

Chapter Objective 2:
Understand the effect that emerging computer technologies, such as nanotechnology, quantum computers, and optical computers, may have on the computer of the future.

Future computers will likely be influenced by **nanotechnology** research, which focuses on building computer components at the individual atomic and molecular levels. Both computing and noncomputing products that use **carbon nanotubes (CNTs)** are being developed. **Quantum computing** (which uses atoms or nuclei working together as quantum bits or *qubits*) and **optical computers** (which perform operations using light instead of electrical current) are in the early stages of development.

EMERGING NETWORKING TECHNOLOGIES

Chapter Objective 3:
Name some emerging wired and wireless networking technologies.

Improvements are being made on a continual basis to wired and wireless networking technologies to increase speed and connectivity options, and to support an ever-growing number of new applications. Faster versions of the *Ethernet* standard are under development, and **Power over Ethernet (PoE)**—which sends both electrical power and data over Ethernet cables—is a relatively new option. For easy home networks, the *Phoneline* or *Powerline* standards can be used; a standard for delivering Internet over existing power lines *is broadband over power lines* (*BPL*).

New versions of the **Wi-Fi (802.11)** standard for wireless networks (such as for improved speed and security) are being developed on a regular basis. **Wi-Fi Direct** enables Wi-Fi devices to be connected directly, without additional hardware. **WiMAX (802.16)** is an emerging wireless standard with a greater range than Wi-Fi; *mobile WiMAX* is a version of WiMAX designed for use with mobile phones and other mobile devices. **Bluetooth** can be used for very short-range applications (such as wirelessly connecting a keyboard to a computer), though **wireless USB** is a new option. Several new wireless standards—such as *Ultra Wideband* (*UWB*) and *wirelessHD* (*WiHD*) are designed for wirelessly delivering multimedia content between computers, TVs, digital cameras, DVD players, and other consumer devices.

ARTIFICIAL INTELLIGENCE (AI)

Chapter Objective 4:
Explain what is meant by the term *artificial intelligence* (AI) and list some AI applications.

When a computer performs in ways that would be considered intelligent if observed in people, this is referred to as **artificial intelligence (AI)**. Some of the earliest advances in AI were in the area of chess; the most common test for AI is the *Turning Test*. One AI application is the **intelligent agent**. Examples include *application assistants*, *search agents*, *shopping bots*, *entertainment bots*, and *chatterbots*. Intelligent agents typically act as *virtual assistants* and modify their behavior based on the user's actions. They are frequently built into application programs and operating systems and are beginning to be used on Web pages. Some—like many chatterbots—use a *natural language interface*.

Expert systems perform tasks that would otherwise be performed by a human expert, such as diagnosing medical conditions, making financial forecasts, and performing credit authorizations. Expert systems use a *knowledge base* (a database containing specific facts and rules about the expert area) and an *inference engine* (a software program used to apply rules to the data stored in the knowledge base to reach decisions).

Neural networks and *robotics* are two other areas of artificial intelligence. A neural network is an AI system that tries to imitate the way the human brain works and is typically used for pattern recognition, such as speech analysis, crime analysis, and biometric identification. **Robotics** is the study of **robots**—devices, controlled by a person or a computer, that can move and react to sensory input. Robots are commonly used for repetitive and dangerous tasks; they are also being used for household tasks, for entertainment purposes, and to assist with business and personal tasks.

TECHNOLOGICAL ADVANCES IN MEDICINE

Technological advances in recent years include computers that analyze test results, implanted devices that assist an organ's functioning, and digital cameras that can be ingested to record images of a person's digestive tract. **Brain-to-computer interfacing (BCI)** is the process of connecting the brain with a computer, such as implanting electrodes directly into the brain or using a headset that wirelessly reads and interprets brainwaves, and may eventually enable paralyzed individuals to control robot assistants with only their thoughts. These and similar technological advances in medicine are embraced by some but are not without controversy.

Chapter Objective 5:
List some new and upcoming technological advances in medicine.

Telemedicine is the use of communications technology to provide medical information and services and can take a variety of forms. One application is **telesurgery**—a form of *robot-assisted surgery* where a robot (controlled by a physician) operates on a patient. With telesurgery, the robot is controlled remotely, such as over the Internet. Robots can use smaller incisions in some types of surgeries, which results in less pain for the patient and a faster recovery period. Other forms of telemedicine include remote professional consultations and diagnosis, such as via a videoconferencing system.

TECHNOLOGICAL ADVANCES IN THE MILITARY

Recent and expected future technological advances in the military include newly designed weapons, protective gear, and surveillance tools. Surveillance tools in the future may include an increased use of **battlefield robots** and the use of *autonomous robots* that can navigate on their own. The uniform of the future may include an **exoskeleton suit**—a wearable robotic system that not only protects the user but also gives him or her additional physical capabilities.

Chapter Objective 6:
Name some new and upcoming technological advances in the military.

SOCIETAL IMPLICATIONS OF EMERGING TECHNOLOGY

There are many potential societal implications associated with emerging technologies, such as unexpected results, trusting "intelligent" computers and robots so much that they become a personal safety hazard, and allowing medical technology to enable people to be controlled by others. Because virtually any new technology could be used for both good and evil, we need to weigh the societal risks and benefits of emerging technologies in order to make educated and informed decisions about what we would like our lives and society to be like.

Chapter Objective 7:
Discuss potential societal implications of emerging technologies.

REVIEW ACTIVITIES

KEY TERM MATCHING

a. artificial intelligence (AI)

b. augmented reality

c. exoskeleton suit

d. expert system

e. nanotechnology

f. neural network

g. optical computer

h. robot

i. telemedicine

j. WiMAX (802.16)

Instructions: Match each key term on the left with the definition on the right that best describes it.

1. ________ A computer system that provides the type of advice that would be expected from a human expert.

2. ________ A computer that uses light, such as from laser beams or infrared beams, to perform digital computations.

3. ________ A device, controlled by a human operator or a computer, that can move and react to sensory input.

4. ________ A wireless networking standard that is faster and has a greater range than Wi-Fi.

5. ________ An expert system in which the human brain's pattern-recognition process is emulated by the computer system.

6. ________ A wearable robotic system designed to give an individual additional physical capabilities and protection.

7. ________ The science of creating tiny computers and components by working at the individual atomic and molecular levels.

8. ________ The use of networking technology to provide medical information and services.

9. ________ When a computer performs actions that are characteristic of human intelligence.

10. ________ When computer generated images are overlayed on top of real-time images, such as to overlay information over the photo or video displayed on a smartphone.

SELF-QUIZ

Instructions: Circle **T** if the statement is true, **F** if the statement is false, or write the best answer in the space provided. **Answers for the self-quiz are located in the References and Resources Guide at the end of the book.**

1. T F Two-dimensional (2D) barcodes can store more data than conventional one-dimensional barcodes.

2. T F Nonvolatile RAM (NVRAM) chips do not lose their contents when the power to the computer is turned off.

3. T F Computers that process data with light are referred to as quantum computers.

4. T F Wi-Fi Direct is a wireless version of USB designed to connect peripheral devices.

5. T F One advantage of robot-assisted surgery is faster recovery time.

6. In quantum computing, ________ (which can represent more than two possible states) are used instead of electronic bits.

7. Many products today use carbon ________, which are a by-product of nanotechnology research.

8. ________ is a wired networking standard that allows electrical power to be sent along with data over standard Ethernet cables.

9. A(n) ________ is an expert system in which the human brain's pattern-recognition process is emulated by the computer system.

10. A ________ robot is used by the military in combat, such as to ensure locations are safe prior to sending in soldiers.

EXERCISES

1. For the following list of emerging devices or technologies, write the appropriate letter (I, P, O, S, or C) in the space provided to indicate whether each device or technology is used for input (I), processing (P), output (O), storage (S), or communications (C).

   a. ________ WiGig **c.** ________ 2D barcode **e.** ________ NVRAM

   b. ________ OLED **d.** ________ PMR **f.** ________ IMOD

2. Supply the missing words to complete the following statements.

   a. ________ storage systems use multiple blue laser beams to store data in three dimensions.

   b. ________ is a form of robot-assisted surgery in which the doctor's physical location is different from the patient's and robot's physical location and the doctor controls the robot remotely over the Internet or another communications medium.

3. Write the number of the networking standard that best matches each of the following descriptions in the blank to the left of each description.

   a. ________ Used to create a wired home or business network.

   b. ________ Used to create a home network via existing telephone jacks.

   c. ________ Used to send power along with data over networking cables.

   d. ________ Used to connect peripheral devices to a mobile phone or computer.

   1. PoE
   2. Bluetooth
   3. Ethernet
   4. Phoneline

4. Would an OLED display or an LCD display use more battery power? Explain why.

5. Would Wi-Fi or WirelessHD be better for wirelessly networking two computers within a home? Explain.

DISCUSSION QUESTIONS

1. More and more everyday devices—including cars and other vehicles—are being controlled by computers. There are advantages, such as avoiding possible driver errors and the ability to change the speed of or reroute trains automatically to avoid collisions. But are there potential risks, as well? For example, Thailand's Finance Minister once had to be rescued from inside his limousine after the onboard computer malfunctioned, leaving the vehicle immobilized and the door locks, power windows, and air conditioning not functioning. Do you think the benefits of increased automation of devices that could put us in danger if they malfunction outweigh the risks? What types of safeguards should be incorporated into computer-controlled cars, subway trains, and other automated vehicles? What about medication dispensers and other automated medical devices?

2. Interference with wireless devices is happening much more often than in the past. For instance, unlicensed walkie-talkies used on TV sets have interfered with police radios, and British air traffic control transmissions have been interrupted by transmissions from nearby baby monitors. If devices that use unlicensed radio frequencies interfere with each other, whose fault is it? The individual for buying multiple products that use the same radio frequency? The manufacturers for not ensuring their products can switch channels as needed to use a free channel? The government for allowing unregulated airwaves? Is there a solution to this problem? Who, if anyone, should be responsible for fixing this problem?

PROJECTS

HOT TOPICS

1. **WiMAX vs. Wi-Fi** As discussed in the chapter, WiMAX and Wi-Fi are both wireless networking standards.

   For this project, research WiMAX and Wi-Fi to determine their current status and the differences between the two standards. Are they designed for the same or different purposes? Explain. How are they being used today? Home networks? Business networks? Hotspots? College campuses? Mobile phone calls? Do you think the standards will coexist in the future, or will one eventually replace the other? At the conclusion of your research, prepare a one-page summary of your findings and opinions and submit it to your instructor.

SHORT ANSWER/ RESEARCH

2. **Today's Robots** As discussed in the chapter, robots can be used today for a variety of activities in businesses and the military, as well as in the home.

   For this project, select one type of robotic device on the market today—for instance, a robotic toy, vacuum cleaner, or lawn mower; a security or manufacturing robot; a robot used by the military or NASA; a robot used by law enforcement agencies; or a robotic personal assistant—and research it. Find out what the product does, what it costs, how it is powered and controlled, and if it can be reprogrammed. What are the advantages of the robotics part of the product? Do you think this is a worthwhile or beneficial product? At the conclusion of your research, prepare a one- to two-page summary of your findings and opinions and submit it to your instructor.

HANDS ON

3. **Cloud Storage** There are a number of cloud storage services (such as ADrive, Microsoft SkyDrive, Google Drive, and Box) designed to allow individuals to back up files online and share specific files with others; specialty online storage services designed for digital photo sharing include Flickr, Photobucket, and SnapFish.

   For this project, visit at least one cloud storage site designed for backup and file exchange, and at least one site designed for digital photo sharing. You can try the sites listed above or use a search site to find alternative sites. Tour your selected sites to determine the features each service offers, the cost, the amount of storage space available, and the options for sending uploaded files to others. Do the sites password-protect your files, or are they available for anyone with an Internet connection to see? What are the benefits for using these types of storage services? Can you think of any drawbacks? Would you want to use any of the storage sites you visited? Why or why not? At the conclusion of this task, prepare a short summary of your findings and submit it to your instructor.

ETHICS IN ACTION

4. **Emotion Recognition Software** An emerging application is *emotion recognition software*, which uses camera input to try to read people's current emotion. The first expected application of such a system is for ATM machines because they already have cameras installed. Possibilities include changing the advertising display based on the customer's emotional response to displayed advertising, and enlarging the screen text if the customer appears to be squinting. Is it ethical for businesses using emotion recognition software to read the emotions of citizens without their consent? Proponents of the technology argue that it is no different than when human tellers or store clerks interpret customers' emotions and modify their treatment of the customer accordingly. Do you agree? Why or why not? Is this a worthy new technology or just a potential invasion of privacy? Would you object to using an ATM machine with emotion-recognition capabilities? Why or why not?

   For this project, form an opinion about the ethical ramifications of emotion recognition systems and be prepared to discuss your position (in class, via an online class discussion group, in a class chat room, or via a class blog, depending on your instructor's directions). You may also be asked to write a short paper expressing your opinion.

PRESENTATION/ DEMONSTRATION

5. **Wired Home Network** If you have two or more computers at home and want to share files, an Internet connection, or a printer, you will need to set up a home network. Although a wireless network is an option, wired networks still exist and new options for wired networks are emerging.

   For this project, suppose that you want to set up a wired home network. Create a scenario (real or fictitious) that describes the number of computers and other devices involved, where each item is located, and the tasks for which the network will be used. Select a wired networking option (such as Ethernet, Powerline, or Phoneline) and determine the steps and equipment necessary to implement that network for your scenario. Be sure to include the cost of the necessary hardware and how the network would be physically installed. Share your findings (including a diagram of your proposed network) with your class in the form of a presentation. The presentation should not exceed 10 minutes and should make use of one or more presentation aids, such as a whiteboard, handouts, or a computer-based slide presentation (your instructor may provide additional requirements). You may also be asked to submit a summary of the presentation to your instructor.

BALANCING ACT

6. **Should Unlicensed Drivers Be Allowed to Use Self-Driving Cars?** As discussed in the chapter, self-driving cars are getting closer to becoming a reality. While currently in the testing stage, consumer products could be on the market soon. In anticipation, states are beginning to determine regulations for these vehicles. One of the biggest questions is whether or not a licensed driver will be required to be in the vehicle. One could argue that a human driver isn't necessary once self-driving cars are declared safe and legal and not requiring one would create one new benefit—the ability of unlicensed drivers (such as visually-impaired individuals and underage children) to be safely and legally transported without the use of a licensed driver. But should these individuals be allowed to use self-driving cars? Will we ever be certain enough that autonomous cars are safe to eliminate the need for a human being to be available to take control of the car if needed? Is it discrimination if unlicensed individuals aren't allowed to use these cars? If a licensed driver is required, what if that individual is intoxicated or under the influence of drugs—should that be illegal even if the car is driving? Should autonomous cars be allowed to run errands alone, such as picking up a pizza or parking the car after the passengers get out? Would you feel comfortable being driven by an autonomous car? Why or why not?

   Pick a side on this issue, form an opinion and gather supporting evidence, and be prepared to discuss and defend your position in a classroom debate or in a 1–2 page paper, depending on your instructor's directions.

INDEX

D

E